ALSO BY HOWARD KURTZ

SPIN CYCLE: *Inside the Clinton Propaganda Machine*

HOT AIR: *All Talk, All the Time*

MEDIA CIRCUS: *The Trouble with America's Newspapers*

THE FORTUNE TELLERS

INSIDE WALL STREET'S
GAME OF MONEY, MEDIA,
AND MANIPULATION

HOWARD KURTZ

THE FREE PRESS
New York   London   Toronto   Sydney   Singapore

THE FREE PRESS
A Division of Simon & Schuster Inc.
1230 Avenue of the Americas
New York, NY 10020

THE FREE PRESS and colophon are trademarks
of Simon & Schuster Inc.

Designed by Leslie Phillips
Manufactured in the United States of America

10 9 8 7 6 5 4 3 2 1

LIBRARY OF CONGRESS CATALOGING-IN-PUBLICATION DATA
Kurtz, Howard, 1953–
     The fortune tellers : inside Wall Street's game of money, media, and
  manipulation / Howard Kurtz.
        p.   cm.
     1. Journalism, Commercial.   2. Television broadcasting of news.   I. Title.
     PN4784.C7 K87   2000   00-042190
     070.4'49332632—dc21
  Includes bibliographical references and index.

ISBN 0-684-86879-2

CONTENTS

To Mary

for investing in me

ACKNOWLEDGMENTS

My thanks to those who took time out of their crazed schedules to candidly discuss their lives, the intricacies of Wall Street, and the workings of the financial press. I'm indebted to Paul Golob, my friend and editor, who always sees the big picture and has provided crucial intellectual guidance on all my books. I'm grateful as well to my agent, Rafe Sagalyn, for his savvy advice and deft touch in bringing my work to a wider audience. Above all, special thanks goes to my family for their support, and to Judy and Bonnie for occasionally letting me use the computer.

INTRODUCTION

At 2:15 P.M. on Friday, March 17, 2000, a little-known reporter blew a sizable hole in the stock of a high-flying, high-tech outfit called the Xybernaut Corporation.

The company, which makes miniature computers that can be worn as accessories, had been on an incredible tear, the likes of which had somehow become breathtakingly routine in the dizzying atmosphere of Wall Street. Its stock, which had been selling for $1.31 a share the previous October, had hit nearly $30 two weeks earlier—a more than twenty-fold increase for a firm with just eighty full-time employees—before settling back to $23 a share.

But the situation changed dramatically when David Evans, a reporter in the Los Angeles bureau of the Bloomberg News service, got online to examine Xybernaut's filing that morning with the Securities and Exchange Commission. Evans found some troubling language that he quickly filed in a terse report for the Bloomberg financial wire.

"Xybernaut Corp.'s auditor warned there's 'substantial doubt' about the maker of wearable computer systems' ability to continue as a going concern, citing its continuing losses and need for more capital," the story began.

Xybernaut stock dropped precipitously until the market's 4:00 P.M. closing bell, and again in after-hours trading, to 14¹⁵⁄₁₆. In the space of a few short hours, the company, based in Fairfax, Virginia, had lost more than a third of its market value. The power of a single journalist to punc-ture the helium balloon of soaring stock prices had never been greater. But the lightning speed of modern technology also gave corporate executives the tools to fight back.

John Moynahan, Xybernaut's chief financial officer, was on vacation in Florida and had turned off his cell phone about fifteen minutes before the Bloomberg report hit. He was extremely upset when he belatedly learned of the story. The warning by the company's accounting firm was, in Moy-nahan's view, mere legal boilerplate. The company had included it in every one of its SEC statements since going public in 1996, and raising the needed cash had never been a problem. The reporter had simply put the most alarmist spin on the story, describing Xybernaut as though it were in dire financial straits. Moynahan also thought the timing of the ar-ticle, late on a Friday, was suspicious, and wondered whether investors who had shorted the stock—betting that its price would decline—had something to do with the story.

At 9:40 on Saturday morning, Moynahan opened his laptop and signed onto a message board on Yahoo!'s Website that was devoted entirely to Xybernaut. Moynahan had founded the club, which had nine hundred members and drew as many as eleven thousand "page views" a day, and served as the site's moderator. He quickly planted his flag in that stretch of cyberspace, declaring that "in my six years with Xybernaut, the future for the company and its shareholders has never been brighter than it is today."

Many club members, who actively traded the stock, were sympathetic. "The Bloomberg piece was a hit job, more or less," one person said.

"The article and the timing smelled very fishy!" said another.

Moynahan spent the rest of the day helping the company draft a press release assailing the Bloomberg piece. A company attorney had already complained to Bloomberg executives, who stood by the story. On Mon-day morning, Xybernaut said in its statement that the plunge in the stock price "was based on reaction to an article released late Friday afternoon and was not based on any fundamental change in our operations. . . . The article did not accurately nor fairly describe our current position . . . or our future opportunities."

David Evans was unperturbed by the conspiracy theories, since no one had prompted him to check the SEC filing. This was what he did for a living, digging out the fine print that companies declined to put in their press releases. Evans was accustomed to being deluged with angry e-mail from investors who blamed him when their stocks tanked, who viewed him as the evil messenger. But he was simply using government documents to tell the full story.

On Tuesday morning, March 21, company executives issued another release that would prove even more important. Xybernaut said that the company and its products would be featured that evening on CNBC, the business network that carried immense clout with investors. The mere announcement of the upcoming segment helped boost Xybernaut's stock 24 percent, to just over $21 a share, or slightly below where it had been when the Bloomberg piece hit the wires.

At 5:39 P.M., Evans moved another damaging story on the Bloomberg wire. Weeks earlier, Xybernaut had trumpeted a "buy" rating on its stock from a research firm called Access 1 Financial, which had predicted that the price would double within six months. Indeed, the price doubled within a month. What the company did not disclose, Evans had found, was that Mark Bergman, the president and founder of Access 1 Financial, was a former Xybernaut executive who still owned options to buy shares in the company.

But Evans's report was immediately overshadowed. At 6:21, CNBC anchor Bill Griffeth introduced the segment on Xybernaut by saying: "You can wear just about everything else, why not your computer? It turns out that you can. . . . A small company called Xybernaut has already made big strides in the hands-off computer sector." The story was punctuated by upbeat comments from Moynahan, and reporter Mike Hegedus posed in the studio with a computer attached to his belt and a futuristic-looking headset that enabled him to see the monitor by peering into a small mirror dangling before his right eye. Shortly after 7:00 P.M., CNBC's *Business Center* reported that Xybernaut stock had gained another dollar in after-hours trading. In the space of five days, the company's stock had been decimated and then magically revived, thanks to the media power-brokers who wielded such enormous influence on Wall Street.

❏   ❏   ❏

When journalists cover politics, their outsider role is clearly defined. No single reporter can affect White House policies or a candidate's campaign through mere analysis or commentary. True, if several news organizations pound away in unison, they can put an issue on the national agenda or throw a politician on the defensive. But such efforts can be measured only roughly, through the fleeting snapshot of opinion polls. Much of the public distrusts the press, muting the impact of a concerted editorial attack on the president or other national figures. In this realm, journalists are score-keepers and second-guessers and naysayers, and their influence is ephemeral and diffuse.

In the business arena, however, financial journalists are players. They make things happen instantaneously, and their impact is gauged not by subjective polls but by the starker standard of stock prices. A single negative story, true or not, can send a company's share price tumbling in a matter of minutes. A report about a possible takeover attempt can immediately pump up a stock, adding billions of dollars to a company's net worth. The clout of financial journalists affects not just the corporate bottom line but the hard-earned cash of millions of average investors. In business, unlike politics, the reporting of rumors is deemed fair game, since rumors, even bogus ones, move markets. And in an age of lightning-quick Internet reports, saturation cable coverage, and jittery day traders, moving the market is a remarkably easy thing to do.

Journalists, of course, don't spew out information and speculation in a vacuum. They are used every day by CEOs, by Wall Street analysts, by brokerage firms, by fund managers who own the stocks they are touting or are betting against the stocks they are trashing. These money men are as practiced in the art of spin as the most slippery office-seeker, measuring their success not in votes but in dollars, not in campaign seasons but in minute-by-minute prices.

Amid this daily deluge, there's one inescapable problem: Nobody knows anything. These are savvy folks, to be sure, but all of them—the journalists, the commentators, the brokers, the traders, the analysts—are feeling their way in a blizzard, squinting through the snow, straining amid the white noise to make out the next trend or market movement or sizzling stock. They traffic in a strange souplike mixture of facts and gossip and rumor, and while their guidance can be useful, they are just as often taken by surprise, faked out by the market's twists and turns, their piles of research and lifetime of learning suddenly rendered irrelevant. They talk to each other, milk each other, belittle each other, desperately searching for someone who knows just a little bit more about the stock that everyone will be buzzing about tomorrow. They are modern-day fortune tellers, promising untold riches as they peer into perpetually hazy crystal balls.

Still, they wield great influence. In a confused world where everyone is jockeying for advance intelligence on what to buy or sell, information is power. The ability of a single analyst to drive investors in or out of a particular stock, once his views are amplified by the media echo chamber, is nothing short of awesome. Some reporters, to be sure, manage to ferret out useful stories amid the blurry landscape. But there is no real penalty for being wrong; the journalists, the commentators, and the analysts blithely chalk up their mistakes to the market's unpredictability and quickly turn to the next day's haul of hot information. It is a mutual manipulation society that affects anyone with a direct or indirect stake in the market, which is to say nearly everyone in America.

Ever since the southern tip of Manhattan became a fledgling financial center in the 1790s, much has hinged on the speed of information. The original brokerage houses had to be near each other so that messengers could race back and forth with the latest prices. Before long, men with telescopes and flags stood on hills and buildings so they could relay information by semaphore code between New York and Philadelphia. The launch of Samuel Morse's telegraph in 1844, followed by the invention of the stock ticker twenty-three years later, proved ideal for rapidly transmitting data around the country. The New York Stock Exchange installed its first telephone in 1878. Over the next century, radio, television, fax machines, and computers each kicked the financial markets into new and ever-faster territory.

Over the past generation these changes, and the evolving culture of financial news, have been nothing short of startling. In the first weeks of

1971, Irving R. Levine, returning from two decades of overseas reporting, had lunch with NBC's Washington bureau chief to figure out what he should do next. Levine wanted to cover the State Department, but only two backwater beats—business and science—were available. He chose business news, a subject deemed so specialized that no other network had bothered to assign a full-time correspondent.

The bow-tied Levine would offer pieces to *NBC Nightly News* when the monthly figures on unemployment or inflation were released, but the producers were rarely interested. "It's not a story," they would say.

In those days, when most American households considered the stock market foreign terrain, the business world was covered largely for insiders. *The Wall Street Journal* was a single-section newspaper. *Business Week, Fortune,* and *Forbes* were generally considered trade publications. There were no computers in the office, no cable television, no programs devoted to business. It was, Levine realized, a third-tier assignment.

Things began to change on August 15, 1971, when Richard Nixon stunned the nation by imposing wage and price controls. Now the *Today* show wanted a weekly spot from Levine. The Arab oil embargo of 1973 and the federal bailout of Chrysler in 1979 also boosted the visibility of business news. Louis Rukeyser launched his PBS program *Wall Street Week,* and the birth of CNN in 1980 produced the first nightly business report on national television, Lou Dobbs's *Moneyline.* Levine began getting invitations from business groups for paid speeches. He was summoned back from Denver, where he was giving a speech, when the stock market plunged by 22 percent in October 1987. Financial news was now indelibly part of the media mainstream.

By 1989, Levine was such a recognizable figure that the network begged him to become a contributor to its new cable business channel, CNBC. There was no money in CNBC's meager budget to pay him, but Levine reluctantly agreed to do a weekly commentary. Several years later, as CNBC became more glitzy, the straight-arrow Levine found himself abruptly disinvited. Soon afterward, he retired from television.

The business world of the twenty-first century moves with a lightning quickness that would have been unimaginable when Irving R. Levine entered the fray: online investing, global trading, an increasingly volatile stock market. And the media play a vastly more important role in pumping and publicizing the money machine. In the 1980s, an entrepreneur named Michael Bloomberg made a fortune by sending out streams of complex financial data and news reports through leased computer terminals that became mandatory on trading floors and in newsrooms. Online news operations like *TheStreet.com* and *CBS Marketwatch.com,* and investor chat rooms on such Websites as Yahoo! and *Silicon Investor,* exploded in the late 1990s. In fact, the money and media cultures have reached a grand convergence in which corporate executives boost their companies by trying to steer the nonstop coverage, while news outlets move stocks with an endless cascade of predictions, analysis, and inside dope.

Nearly everyone, it seemed, was paying attention. A decade ago, those chronicling the ups and downs of Wall Street spoke to a narrow audience comprised mainly of well-heeled investors and hyperactive traders. But a communications revolution soon transformed the landscape, giving real-time television coverage and up-to-the-second Internet reports immense power to move jittery markets. This mighty media apparatus had the ability to confer instant stardom on the correspondents, the once-obscure market gurus, and the new breed of telegenic chief executives. CNBC was now as important to the financial world as CNN was to politicians and diplomats, and like Ted Turner's network, it had the power to change events even while reporting on them. This was America's new national pastime, pursued by high-powered players and coaches whose pronouncements offered the tantalizing possibility that the average fan could share in the wealth. Like the fortune tellers of old, they gazed into the future where unimaginable riches awaited those who could divine the right secrets.

❑ ❑ ❑

The fortune tellers began 1999 bursting with confidence. The bulls had been running strong for four years, the Dow improbably surging from 4,500 to over 9,000, and that doubling of investor wealth tended to obscure the mistakes of the media and market gurus. Everyone was making money and feeling good. Of course, any other business with such an erratic track record would have felt a bit humbled. The Dow's nearly 2,000-point decline the previous August and September had sent much of the media into growling bear mode. "The Crash of '98: Can the U.S. Economy Hold Up?" asked *Fortune* magazine. "Is the Boom Over?" wondered *Time*. Walter Russell Mead wrote in *Esquire* that if the world's economic ills reached the United States, "stock prices could easily fall by two-thirds—that's 6000 points on the Dow—and it could take stocks a decade or more to recover." In the same issue, writer Ken Kurson declared: "This market will crash hard and stay crashed."

Only it didn't. In an extraordinary turnaround, the Dow was back above 9,300 before Christmas. The warnings of a few weeks earlier quickly faded. Optimism was again all the rage. The commentators and the Wall Street analysts were back on the bandwagon. Yesterday's blown predictions were fish wrap. Back in the summer of 1997, *Money* had used big red letters on its cover to scream: "Sell Stocks Now!" The Dow was then at 7,700; anyone who had taken *Money*'s advice would have missed another year and a half of a spectacular bull market. All that counted in this hyperventilating atmosphere was: What's the stock market gonna do tomorrow? And how can I get in on the action?

Everyone, it seemed, was playing the market, from the New York hairstylist who kept a twelve-hundred-dollar quote machine next to his barber's chair to the day traders at the computer-equipped Wall Street Pub in Delray Beach, Florida, to the retired bureaucrat buying on his home computer through E*Trade. Some folks were becoming millionaires, others losing their student loans and second mortgages. There were 37,129 investment clubs in the country, compared to 7,085 in 1990. More than $230 billion a year was being invested in stock mutual funds, compared to less than $13 billion in 1990. Nearly half of American households had some stake in the Wall Street boom, either through 401(k) plans or fund shares or hastily acquired stocks. Some eleven million people were trading online, a phenomenon that was less than three years old.

But more than mere money was at stake. The market was now an integral part of American pop culture. All the cable news channels now displayed little boxes at the bottom of the screen showing the latest score of the Dow and the S & P 500 and the Nasdaq Composite, whether the president was being impeached or bombs were falling on Baghdad or Belgrade. In New York, the 11:00 P.M. newscast on WCBS-TV provided updates on the Hang Seng, the Hong Kong stock market, right after the murders and fires and rapes. Mobile phones on airline seat-backs flashed liquid-crystal updates on the Dow and the Nasdaq. *Vanity Fair* featured stock guru Abby Joseph Cohen in a spread on hot commodities, along with the Lexus LX 50 and thong underwear. Sam Donaldson kept CNBC on in his office. Don Rickles and Lily Tomlin did TV ads for Fidelity Investments with superstar strategist Peter Lynch. Basketball coach Phil Jackson pitched the online brokerage T. D. Waterhouse, while *Star Trek*'s William Shatner hawked the discount services of priceline.com. Barbra Streisand and the "Fonz," Henry Winkler, searched for promising Internet firms, and found that their celebrity helped them to obtain stock at an insider's price. Mike Doonesbury, the comic-strip character, launched an Internet IPO that soared and crashed. *Time* asked porn star Jenna Jameson for her stock tips. *The New York Observer* found a woman who listened to stock reports on her radio headset while making love to her husband. Howard Stern mused about buying a stock, touting it on the air, waiting for the price to surge, and flipping it for a quick profit. Wall Street was hotter than sex in the sixties, disco in the seventies, or real estate in the eighties. And that meant the market soothsayers were reaching a wider audience, a voracious audience, each day.

No matter that some of these prophets had been spectacularly wrong. Barton Biggs, a veteran sage at Morgan Stanley Dean Witter, had warned in the early days of the Clinton presidency, back in 1993: "We want to get our clients' money as far away from Bill and Hillary as we can. The president is negative for the market." The Dow had risen nearly 8,000 points since Biggs uttered those words. But he remained one of the most quoted strategists around.

Every so often, some trader whispered the truth. Ted Aronson, a Philadelphia broker who managed more than $2 billion, admitted to *Money* magazine that he invested his own family's money in Vanguard index funds because, with their automatic-pilot approach and rock-bottom costs, they almost always beat the managed funds. But few others publicly acknowledged that most mutual funds were laggards, and the media outlets peddling financial wisdom had little reason to encourage them.

The endless swirl of market advice was built upon the notion that a get-rich-quick scheme was always just around the corner. An exploding number of mutual funds—from 2,599 in 1993 to 5,183 in 1998—beckoned from every stall in the media marketplace. The magazine covers of early 1999 fervently hawked such wares. "The Best Mutual Funds," said *Business Week.* "Best Buys," said *Forbes.* "The Best and Worst Mutual Funds," said *SmartMoney.* "Secrets of the Stock Stars," said *New York* magazine. "Hot Picks from America's Best Analysts," said *Money.*

But the advice proved ephemeral. *Money* magazine had run its annual cover story on a dozen hot stocks in 1992. A year later, only one of the previous year's dozen had made the list. And by '95, not one of *Money*'s previous forty recommendations had made the cut. Each month, each week, the media needed something new to sell, and Wall Street operators were only too happy to comply.

The thriving casino in the narrow streets of lower Manhattan created a hunger for information and a growing belief that amateurs could gain access to sensitive data as quickly and as thoroughly as big-time institutional traders. The explosion of financial intelligence itself became a growth market for the media, and for professionals determined to influence the media. One result was the spectacular rise and huge cult following of CNBC, whose programming consisted mainly of middle-aged white guys in suits talking about market trends.

A network such as CNBC, or a magazine like *Fortune,* or a newspaper like *The Wall Street Journal,* needed a steady parade of experts, analysts, and wise men to fill air time or column inches and convey the appearance of authority. It needed a nonstop flow of tips, touts, picks, and pans to lure consumers with the idea that they just might get in on the Next Big Thing.

But the whole contraption resembled a house of cards, a sustained illusion that both sides had a vested interest in perpetuating. Much of the media hype surrounding the stock market was essentially an orgy of pontification and speculation that pretends it is possible to know the unknowable. A single Wall Street analyst, his voice amplified by the media megaphone, could send a stock soaring or sinking with opinions that might well turn out to be wrong. A columnist could goose a company's stock with takeover talk that often proved to be nothing but gossip. While vast sums were riding on the latest pronouncement from the fortune tellers, they often had blurry tarot cards and cloudy crystal balls.

Nearly nine out of ten fund managers failed to beat the Standard & Poor's 500 in 1998, the culmination of a five-year trend; 542 even managed to lose money. Yet they were still trotted out by the press as the purveyors of financial wisdom. A boring, buy-and-hold strategy generally yielded greater profits over the long run than trying to time an unpredictable market. But admitting that fact would hurt the industry's quest for new investors and the media's quest for new readers and viewers. So everyone played The Game.

Few paused to notice that those dishing out the advice often had a vested interest in the outcome. Outright corruption was rare; the most notorious case involved R. Foster Winans of *The Wall Street Journal,* who had been sentenced to prison in 1985 for selling advance information from the influential Heard on the Street column he helped write in exchange for his share of $30,000 in payoffs. Yet the web of incestuous relationships was in some ways just as troubling. Market gurus touted stocks in which their firms were heavily invested. Brokerage analysts were under internal pressure to be upbeat about corporations that might hire their houses for investment-banking services; a few had even been fired for their pessimism. *Fortune, Forbes, Money, SmartMoney, Business Week, Barron's,* CNBC, and CNNfn made media stars of brokers whose investment companies they courted for lucrative advertising.

"PETER LYNCH & friends uncover the BEST STOCKS to buy NOW," blared the cover of *Worth* magazine; inside was a full-page ad for Lynch and Fidelity. This was hardly surprising, since Fidelity owned the magazine.

"Mexican Stocks May Finally Look Appealing," said the *Journal*'s Heard on the Street column. Who said so? Eduardo Cepeda, managing director of J. P. Morgan in Mexico City, who declared that "it's time to buy at least a few top names in Mexico." And his firm would be happy to sell them.

In *Business Week*'s Inside Wall Street column, Gene Marcial was bullish on Inktomi, a software provider whose stock had just dropped 20 points because Microsoft was phasing out its Internet search engine service. "Is it downhill from here?" Marcial wrote. "No way, say some pros." One of the "pros" was John Leo, head of Northern Technology Fund, which, the column noted, owned Inktomi stock and was buying more.

Seth Tobias, head of Circle-T Partners, used his slot as guest host of CNBC's popular morning show *Squawk Box* to talk up AT&T and MCI WorldCom as companies that were well positioned to benefit from the Internet boom. They are, he added, "our largest holdings."

Conflicts seemed to be lurking everywhere. When mutual fund manager Garrett Van Wagoner appeared on CNBC's *Street Signs* in January 1999, he touted an online company called OnHealth Network. Its stock, which had opened at 8¼, surged as high as 21⅞ before closing at 18½. Anchor Ron Insana had prodded Van Wagoner into admitting that his company owned more than 10 percent of the shares, but that didn't seem to matter to those bidding up the stock. Insana was furious when *The Wall Street Journal* discovered weeks later that OnHealth had sold Van Wagoner Capital Management a big chunk of stock in a so-called "private placement" for just $5.50 a share, a fraction of its market price. Van Wagoner, who now owned 16 percent of the company, insisted that there was nothing wrong with telling CNBC's viewers what he liked.

The financial media, with CNBC at the forefront, seemed to specialize in stoking the flames surrounding white-hot Internet stocks, which increasingly were driving the rest of the market even higher. After all, Net companies were sexy and fascinating to journalists, compared to, say, the Exxon-Mobil merger, which was important but dull. Even the ever-cautious Alan Greenspan, chairman of the Federal Reserve Board, said he understood that buying Net stocks was like playing the lottery. And millions of people wanted to know which tickets were most likely to hit the jackpot.

"Could Yahoo! merge with CBS? How about America Online with Disney?" asked the *Journal*'s Heard on the Street column in February 1999. But the writers quickly acknowledged that "the chatter hasn't yielded much" and "it's all speculation at this point." Such speculation, of course, invariably moved the market. And the market for tech stocks was already so overheated that it was starting to resemble the Dutch tulip craze of the

1600s. Some investors even called themselves Tulipheads. The tulips, of course, wound up nearly worthless.

USA Today ran a remarkably upbeat cover story the same day on eBay, the Net auction site that was trafficking in everything from Beanie Babies to Elvis signatures, reporting that the company's "volcanic success looks unstoppable . . . nothing, it seems, can slow eBay." Recent "embarrassments"—system crashes and a consumer fraud investigation—were dismissed as minor. The fact that the stock had dropped more than 39 points the day before, to 239, was brushed off as "almost humdrum." The day the piece appeared, eBay's stock dropped another 18 points. But who cared? The dramatic swings simply made for better copy. Fifty key Web-related stocks had jumped 187 percent in 1998, and another 55 percent in the first days of 1999, before dropping by 20 percent.

This, then, was the dilemma facing the fortune tellers as the turn of the century approached. The old rules didn't seem to apply. The old valuations didn't seem to matter. Investors were tripling and quadrupling their wealth in weeks or months, despite the cautionary warnings of the more traditional experts, and the media were breathlessly trumpeting the bull market as one of history's great events. It was, in short, one heckuva roller coaster. But the ride down could be rather scary.

1

THE KING OF ALL MEDIA

IT was the worst day of Jim Cramer's life.

For fourteen long years, the flamboyant Wall Street trader had worked insane hours, getting to the office by 5:00 each morning, shouting orders, playing each hiccup in the market to make money for himself and his small coterie of investors. He had become fabulously wealthy, grabbed a bit of fame as a magazine writer and television commentator, even launched a thriving Internet news service. He had also gotten into a couple of ethical scrapes, juggling his roles as both media hotshot and market guru, but there was no question he was at the top of his hard-fought game.

And now, on the morning of October 8, 1998, Cramer was watching it all unravel. The once-soaring stock market had been in a stomach-churning decline since July, slicing nearly 2,000 points off the Dow and making fools of those who had so confidently placed their bets on the exhilarating ride up. Suddenly, inexplicably, one investor after another had been calling Cramer and demanding his cash. Before long, half the one hundred investors in the hedge fund, Cramer, Berkowitz & Company, were bailing out. There was talk that Cramer was losing his focus, that he was spread too thin with his various media ventures. Cramer's confidence was badly shaken. No one, not a single investor, had ever bolted on him before. What had he done wrong? True, he was having a bad year; the fund had earned just 2 percent since January, compared to a 30 percent rise in the Standard & Poor's 500 index. But these mass defections were

1

his worst nightmare. All of the fund's money was invested in the ailing market, yet Cramer was required to wire the cash to his disgruntled clients by 1:00 P.M. He had six hours to come up with more than $50 million.

Most of the time, Cramer was cool in a crisis. Sitting at the trading desk in his eighth-floor office at 100 Wall Street, surrounded by four computers and a Bloomberg terminal flashing the fate of stocks in green and red, he would bark directions to his staff, scan the papers, listen to CNBC on the television set behind him, write his online columns, and scroll through his e-mail, sometimes all at once. He would pick up the black phone with the open line to Max Levine, his broker, and buy "five AOL" or sell "ten Sun Micro" as easily as a couple of lottery tickets, when he was actually betting hundreds of thousands of dollars on companies with amazingly volatile stocks.

But today was different. Cramer had triggered the crisis himself, by trying to help out Eliot Spitzer, an old pal and law school classmate. Spitzer was the Democratic candidate for New York state attorney general, and he badly needed money to finance his campaign. Spitzer's cash was tied up in the hedge fund, and Cramer agreed to let him withdraw it. Under federal rules, however, hedge funds had to treat all investors equally, and so Cramer had to announce a day on which all his clients would be eligible to pull their cash. The due date fell on October 8, which happened to come during a near-panic on Wall Street. The Dow had dropped from more than 9,300 to less than 7,500 in just 10 weeks. Cramer had persuaded a few of the defectors to stand by him, but most were determined to pull the plug. He had $20 million in cash on hand, but he needed to sell enough stocks to pay out $70 million—and he had to sell them in a frenzied environment in which prices were dropping like a rock.

In the worst blow of all, one of those abandoning ship was Martin Peretz, the owner of *The New Republic* magazine and one of Cramer's closest friends. Cramer thought of himself as having been like a son to Peretz. They had been tight since his days at Harvard Law School in the early 1980s, when he took one of Peretz's classes. Even then Cramer had a feel for the market; Peretz had found himself making money from the weekly stock tips that Cramer would leave for callers on his answering machine. Peretz was so impressed that he had given the headstrong young man $500,000 to invest, and Cramer had tripled his money. The friendship blossomed—Peretz was the best man at Cramer's wedding—and in 1996 they had teamed up in launching *TheStreet.com,* a financial news Website that was attracting a loyal following. For Peretz's fiftieth birthday, Cramer had raised $50,000 for the Jerusalem Foundation, a favorite cause for the fiercely pro-Israel publisher.

But their relationship had grown increasingly strained. Cramer was tired of the mentor-student paradigm; he was forty-three now, and he wanted Peretz to regard him as an equal. And he felt that Peretz had reneged on his word by putting up less than the full share he had promised for financing *TheStreet.com,* an accusation that Peretz strongly disputed. Cramer felt he was busting his butt on the new company and that Peretz was doing little or nothing. Yet he needed Peretz because the Securities and Exchange Commission had insisted that, as a trader, Cramer had to be aligned with a legitimate publisher in a Web operation covering the very market in which Cramer was so heavily invested. Frustrated, Cramer told Peretz that their fifty-fifty split in *TheStreet.com* had to change, and demanded a million more shares in the company. Peretz balked, viewing this as a rather piggish move by his one-time pupil, but reluctantly went along.

At a *Street.com* Christmas party in 1997, Cramer gave a teary-eyed speech, praising the staff for having gotten the fledgling company off the ground. He invoked Henry Luce, the legendary founder of *Time* magazine. When it was Peretz's turn to speak, he said: "One thing's for sure. Like Luce, Cramer's a bastard." Cramer was stunned and walked out of the party. His wife, Karen, told him never to speak to Peretz again.

Now, at Cramer's most vulnerable moment, Peretz was striking back. A couple of other investors told Cramer that Peretz had urged them to pull out of the hedge fund, saying that he knew Cramer better than anyone, that Cramer didn't care about the business anymore and was spending all his time on *TheStreet.com.* Peretz would later say he had told only one person to leave the fund, but Cramer was convinced that his longtime friend was responsible for this terrifying run on his bank. It was, in Cramer's eyes, the ultimate betrayal. He had not cried since his mother's funeral, but at night he had found himself bawling over this massive vote of no confidence.

It was, for the moment, a matter of survival. If Cramer could not come up with the money in time and the market crashed, he would be personally liable for the losses suffered by his disaffected investors. The biggest potential defector was financier Max Palevsky, whom Cramer believed had bought Peretz's argument that he had lost his focus. That was nearly impossible for Cramer to refute, since Peretz was presumed to know him so well. Palevsky's stake in the fund was so large that if he bailed, Cramer would have to close his doors. It was as simple as that. After furious negotiations, Cramer worked out a settlement that persuaded Palevsky to stay.

For the first time in four years, Cramer called his wife Karen, a former trader with whom he had cofounded the hedge fund, and asked her to leave their home in Summit, New Jersey, and come to work. Get a sitter for the kids, he said, find a way to get down here. When Karen Cramer showed up, her husband's shirt was soaked through with sweat. The computer screens were all flashing red. Declining stocks outnumbered the winners nine to one. Was this a good buying opportunity—or another 1987 crash? Cramer had little time for such speculation; he had to sell if he was to raise the cash he needed. By lunchtime the Dow was down another 264 points. On CNBC's *Power Lunch* program, host Bill Griffeth was talking about how all the bulls had turned bearish. Cramer thought the stock market would definitely crash. Karen said their only hope for saving the firm was for Alan Greenspan to somehow rescue the sinking market. But Greenspan had been saying that business was doing just fine and had made no move to halt the market's fall.

Ralph Acampora, the superstar analyst at Prudential Securities, was fanning the flames, telling his sales force that the Dow, which he had thought could drop to 7,000, could now go as low as 6,735. This forecast was crucial because Acampora was one of Wall Street's greatest bulls; if he was losing confidence, then the downturn had to be for real. Abby Joseph Cohen, the fiercely bullish analyst at Goldman Sachs, stayed upbeat about the invincibility of the American economy, but even she made a downward adjustment in her 1999 projections for the S & P 500. Trading desks everywhere echoed the message: "Cohen's getting off."

From his cluttered desk, Cramer was taking his cues from Ron Insana, a veteran anchor at CNBC whom Cramer had been watching since his Harvard days. Insana had incredible contacts and always seemed to have a sixth sense about what was happening. But despite his relaxed on-air persona, Insana, too, was nervous. Days earlier, he had called his father-in-law and told him to take his money out of the bank. He was considering putting some of his own savings into gold. No one was sure how low this market could go.

Early that morning, Insana had reason to call one of his best sources, Lyle Gramley, a former Federal Reserve governor who was still plugged into monetary policy. Someone told Insana that Gramley had heard the Fed was planning some kind of conference call, a highly unusual event between scheduled meetings. The call would be to discuss a possible easing of interest rates. The Fed had already cut rates at the end of September with no response from the market, so a second rate cut would be a major surprise. Gramley hedged a bit when Insana reached him, saying only that such a call was possible. But Insana believed this was probably spin, for his source was insisting that Gramley had it solid. The Fed had to do something, Insana thought. Too many people believed that the wheels were coming off the market.

Cramer was selling stocks all morning—many of his best stocks, the ones he hated to lose—to come up with the cash he desperately needed. Karen manned the desk while he frantically tried to talk the last few defectors out of leaving him. But even as he liquidated much of his fund and wired the money he owed, he agonized over whether to seize the opportunity to buy other stocks at bargain prices. He would have to do so on margin, with borrowed money, and if the market kept sinking he could be wiped out, as so many of his friends had been during the '87 debacle. Weeks earlier, the massive hedge fund Long Term Capital Management had collapsed. Who knew where the bottom was? Cramer was scared. Traders were never supposed to admit that, but this was a truly frightening moment.

At 1:15, Ron Insana came on the air with some breaking news. Cramer, watching the set on the file cabinet behind him, thought the mere sight of Insana would cause further losses, since he had been delivering consistently bearish news in recent days. But wait! Insana was talking about his conversation with Lyle Gramley. "Shut up," Cramer shouted, hitting the volume button. Insana reported that Gramley believed that the Fed members were arranging a conference call. The Dow moved up 30, 40, 45 points as Insana delivered the news. Now the day's loss was less than 200. Cramer had just filed a bearish column for *TheStreet.com*. "What if Insana is right?" Karen asked him. "You will never live this piece down."

Still, Cramer remained reluctant to buy. That, he soon realized, was a colossal mistake. Insana had been right about the conference call, and the Fed would lower interest rates days later. Cramer felt he should have moved the minute he had an inkling of possible Fed action. Prices were moving up; the long slide was over. The Dow began what would be a steady climb back over 9,000. It was remarkable, Cramer thought, the first time a market bottom had been created by a TV reporter's scoop.

The carnage was over. Cramer had saved the company, but he had lost millions of dollars in the process. He had lost Marty Peretz, who had humiliated him and brought him low. This was an ugly way to make a living, Cramer thought, an utterly soulless business. It had made him rich, but at a breathtaking price.

❏   ❏   ❏

From his first days as a rookie trader, James J. Cramer had craved respect. He had grown up in the Philadelphia suburb of Wyndmoor, the son of a man who sold gift wrap for a living, and had attended public schools there. He had sold ice cream and sodas at Veterans Stadium during Phillies baseball games. When Cramer got to Harvard in 1973, thanks to a scholarship and financial aid, he was conscious of his modest background among the bluebloods of Cambridge, and determined to make it through sheer hard work.

Cramer was immediately drawn to journalism and began churning out dozens of stories for the *Harvard Crimson*. He even added a middle initial, though he had no middle name, because an editor at the *Crimson*, Nicholas Lemann, thought it sounded more distinguished. When he ran for president of the *Crimson* in 1975, Cramer felt very much like an outsider. He was challenging a student from a more elite background, Eric

Breindel, a Manhattan private-school graduate, and was convinced there was a stop-Cramer movement aligned against him. But he won the job by one vote and set about trying to make the paper profitable. Faced for the first time with questions about payrolls and revenues, Cramer launched a weekend magazine and used the advertising proceeds to stem the paper's losses.

When it came to his own finances, though, Cramer was something of a loser. After college, he found himself back in Wyndmoor watching Phillies games. He called his college pal Michael Kinsley, who was then editing *The New Republic*. Cramer was introduced to Marty Peretz and became a contributor to the magazine. He soon realized, though, that he couldn't support himself on $150 an article.

Cramer worked briefly for *Congressional Quarterly,* living with his aunt in Washington, and then took a reporting job at the *Tallahassee Democrat* for $155 a week. He was toiling away at the usual mix of local stories when serial killer Ted Bundy struck at a sorority house down the block from where Cramer lived. Cramer's manic work on that story brought him an offer from a bigger paper, the *Los Angeles Herald-Examiner.*

But the move west did nothing to change Cramer's irresponsible ways with money, and he ran up plenty of debts. At one point he had just one thousand dollars to his name, went to Las Vegas, and gambled away half of it. He was living in a bad neighborhood, and when his apartment was burglarized he lost everything, including his checks. Cramer spent months sleeping on a friend's floor, or in his car with a gun beside him. He came down with mononucleosis and a jaundiced liver. He had hit bottom.

Desperate for a break, Cramer got a call from Steven Brill, who was launching a magazine called *The American Lawyer* and had been given Cramer's name by a mutual friend. Cramer moved to the floor of his sister's Greenwich Village apartment, and Brill doubled his salary to a princely $25,000 a year. Back on his feet, Cramer began investing in the stock market. While in California he had made some forays to National Semiconductor and other firms in what would later be called Silicon Valley, and he put some cash into these fast-growing companies.

Brill was such a tenacious boss that when Cramer decided in 1980 to go to Harvard Law School, Brill called the dean and told him that Cramer would have to defer his acceptance for a year because he was involved in some important investigations for *The American Lawyer.*

Back at Harvard, Cramer started watching Ron Insana on the Financial News Network, studying the intricacies of the market. In 1982, as a first-year law student, Cramer crashed a Goldman Sachs cocktail party and tried to talk himself into a summer job. "I can sell anything," he told a Goldman executive. After receiving a rejection letter from the firm, he refused to give up—there must be some mistake, he insisted—and kept calling. Finally, two years later, he got into the summer program. His dad, Ken Cramer, thought he needed his head examined. Nobody was making money in the stock market in the early 1980s.

After law school, when he finally wormed his way into a permanent job at Goldman Sachs, Cramer continued to dabble in journalism. Robert Rubin, the high-ranking Goldman executive and future Treasury secretary, vetted his pieces. In 1985, Marty Peretz asked Cramer to write a *New Republic* review of a book by Peretz's pal Ivan Boesky, the most celebrated trader of the high-flying eighties. Rubin didn't trust Boesky and wouldn't let anyone at Goldman Sachs trade with him. He worked over Cramer's review, insisting that he make clear that Boesky's methods were murky. Peretz told Cramer that he wasn't happy with the review, which mildly criticized Boesky, because he considered Boesky a genius. Two years later, Boesky pleaded guilty to filing false documents and was sentenced to three years in prison.

As a newly minted stock salesman, Cramer would "cold call" investors he'd read about in the paper. Having convinced himself from his visits to Foot Locker that Reebok was the next hot sneaker, he called investor Michael Steinhardt unannounced, and told him that he was wrong to be shorting Reebok stock. Steinhardt granted him a fifteen-minute audience, then told Cramer he didn't know what he was talking about. Reebok's stock soon soared in value.

In 1987, when he was ready to leave Goldman to start his own hedge fund, Cramer called Steinhardt again. "You're the guy who could have saved me millions of dollars," Steinhardt said. He agreed to give Cramer some money to invest and some office space while he got started.

Cramer found himself sitting next to Karen Backfisch, a former secretary who was being given a chance to work as a Steinhardt trader. They soon began dating, and after Karen left for another firm and Cramer got his own office space, she proposed that they work together. But there was a catch: She had to own half the new company. Karen was making more money than Cramer at the time and agreed to put up her own capital. It was Karen who insisted that they sell many of their stocks a week before the stock market crashed in 1987. A year later they were married.

Karen tutored her new husband in the psychology of Wall Street. On Fridays, when the market would often mount a short-lived rally, she would urge Cramer to take a walk—down to the South Street Seaport or to the Staten Island Ferry to buy a hot pretzel—rather than snatch up stocks he was sure to regret. Cramer began calling her the Trading Goddess. They became millionaires, bought a house in Summit, were written up in *Fortune.* "Are These the New Warren Buffetts?" the headline asked. The Cramers were hailed as "the quintessential Eighties couple," having earned a 23 percent return on their $19-million fund. They had just celebrated their first wedding anniversary.

Cramer once again gravitated toward journalism for a simple reason: cash flow. He belatedly realized that hedge fund managers were paid only once a year. He wrote for *Manhattan Inc.,* for Peretz's *New Republic,* for Brill's *Manhattan Lawyer.*

As he juggled his duties, Cramer's addiction to the high-pressure life brought him increasingly into conflict with his wife. The couple's first daughter was born in 1991; when the second one was born three years later, Cramer got a call on his cell phone in the delivery room. The Fed had just raised interest rates, and the firm had lost $1 million within minutes. Cramer said he was busy. Ten minutes later, the cell phone rang again. The hedge fund had now dropped another couple of million. Cramer turned off his phone—and agonized over the decision when the firm's losses mounted throughout the day. It was not the last time that he would feel torn between his family and his high-stakes work.

Karen soon resented her husband for forcing her to come to Manhattan each day to help run the fund. The Trading Goddess finally decided to stay home with the kids, but she remained a major influence on her husband.

She demanded that he cut his trading in half to avoid dumb investments, and made him bring home his trading sheets to prove it.

As the bull market took off in the mid-1990s, Cramer reaped the rewards. The hedge fund now required a minimum investment of $2.5 million, and Cramer took 20 percent of the profits. There were years when he personally pocketed as much as $10 million.

But Cramer craved recognition as much as money, which is why he poured so much emotional energy into his magazine work. Cramer's double identity was at once the source of his journalistic strength and his greatest weakness. His writing had a you-are-there quality because he was in the financial trenches, risking real money, making mistakes, and learning painful lessons. But since his most fascinating subject was himself, that also meant his writing could have an impact on the stocks he was buying and selling. Cramer tried to protect himself by always disclosing his holdings, but it was a shaky tightrope act at best.

In 1995, he was writing a financial advice column for *SmartMoney* magazine, which he had helped Hearst and *The Wall Street Journal* create. In one column, Cramer praised four small, rather obscure companies, and their stock took off like a rocket. Trading in one firm, UFP Technologies, went from 800 shares in the previous four days to 703,828 shares in the following five days. And the stock price doubled, from $2 to $4 a share. All told, three of the stocks—UFP, Rexon, and Canonie Environmental Services—surged by as much as 66 percent in a couple of weeks on the strength of Cramer's upbeat words.

But Cramer had more than words at stake; he owned stock in each of the companies. The firms were sufficiently tiny that Cramer's hedge fund owned 6 to 9 percent of each one. In fact, he had picked up more than 200,000 additional shares in the weeks before the column appeared. Within days, the value of Cramer's holdings had increased by more than $2.5 million.

This embarrassing sequence of events turned into the worst crisis of Cramer's career when it was reported by *The Washington Post.* Cramer passionately insisted that he had done nothing wrong. This was what he was supposed to do, he explained—recommend stocks that he believed in. He had been buying these stocks for two years. He had not sold them after the *SmartMoney* column appeared and had made no attempt to cash in. He had disclosed his holdings at the end of the column—a disclaimer that unfortunately had been dropped by the magazine. The SEC launched a lengthy investigation and began contacting the investors in Cramer's hedge fund.

"Maybe I should call Gore," Marty Peretz told Cramer. Peretz had been close to the vice president for three decades.

"Are you fucking kidding me?" Cramer said. He didn't want to do anything that carried even a whiff of trying to influence the investigation.

Cramer had to produce boxes and boxes of records and shelled out $400,000 in legal bills. He was finally cleared, but the damage had been done. *SmartMoney* announced that it was tightening its ethics rules. No investor would be allowed to write about small, thinly traded companies whose stock was worth less than $500 million, or about any stock in which the investor owned more than 1 percent of the company. Traders would also be barred from selling any stock they wrote about for a specified period of time. Cramer was not faulted for his behavior, but he had clearly become a lightning rod for criticism by financial writers, who were not players in the market. Cramer left *SmartMoney* soon afterward.

For all his bravado, Cramer could be hypersensitive to criticism. He called up some of his detractors after the *SmartMoney* fiasco and yelled at them. When he felt himself under assault, his rapid-fire cadence turned faster, his high-pitched voice a little squeakier. Cramer had no ability to hide his constant swirl of emotions. Once, after Lisa Napoli of *The New York Times* wrote a mixed profile about his activities and potential conflicts, Cramer declared: "I wish I had been a vicious spinmeister and just beaten the shit out of her and gotten her exactly where I wanted her . . . Give me a fucking break. Come on, I'm not this huge manipulator of stocks."

By 1996, Cramer was fixated on the idea of starting a financial Website, one in which he would have a major ownership stake. He wanted to launch the venture with *SmartMoney,* and he showed the blueprint to Paul Steiger, the *Journal*'s managing editor, over lunch at the Hudson River Club. But the idea didn't fly.

Cramer envisioned an opinion-filled Internet site that would have the inside-dope equivalent of ten Heard on the Street columns each day, and message boards where subscribers could chat. It would be a cheap wire service for what Cramer saw as the coming era of the individual investor.

While on vacation in Cape Cod, he and Marty Peretz decided to plunge ahead on their own with the venture, which they christened *TheStreet.com.* Each kicked in $1.5 million of his own money. Cramer's attorney suggested that he show the plan to the SEC, which insisted that the operation have complete editorial independence from Cramer to guard against any attempt to influence his stock holdings. Now all they needed were some journalists.

During a weekend at Cramer's country house in Bucks County, Pennsylvania, they tried to get Michael Lewis, the former Salomon Brothers trainee who had written the best-selling book *Liar's Poker,* to become their star columnist. Cramer was miffed when Lewis turned down a deal that would have given him a 5 percent stake in the new venture. But Lewis, convinced that the thing would bleed red ink until it went bust, believed that 5 percent of nothing was nothing.

Dave Kansas, a *Wall Street Journal* reporter, signed on as editor, but the Website struggled from the start and was soon in danger of folding. Cramer and Peretz had to arrange a $10-million cash infusion from a group of venture capitalists. Yet Cramer couldn't really run the thing. He was so concerned that critics would view the Web operation as a conflict of interest that he had set up the reporters and editors in another lower Manhattan building and made sure that he had no control, other than the pieces he submitted, over the contents. He couldn't talk to the staff, couldn't so much as e-mail a reporter, saying "Nice piece." And Kansas allowed his writers to criticize Cramer.

"This is ludicrous," Karen said. "You gave these guys a blank check to savage you?"

With just 37,000 subscribers paying $99 a year, *TheStreet.com* lost a staggering $16 million in 1998. Finally, Cramer and his wife visited the office to check on the finances. They discovered the place had a $50,000 walnut desk in the reception area.

"You've got to shut it down," Karen said. "These people are killing us."

❏   ❏   ❏

Jim Cramer knew he was tiptoeing through a minefield by trading stocks and constantly commenting on the market. In fact, he was becoming the most controversial financial journalist in the country. Ever since the *SmartMoney* debacle, critics had been questioning whether his writing was tainted by his trading in a $300-million hedge fund. At times, though, his journalistic efforts boomeranged on his business. And he had so many entanglements it was downright difficult to keep them all straight.

In early June of 1998, Cramer was troubled by the events surrounding a Heard on the Street column in *The Wall Street Journal.* The subject of the column, America Online, was of more than passing interest to Cramer, because his fund owned millions of dollars in AOL stock. What's more, *TheStreet.com* had a distribution deal with AOL. What Cramer found strange was that the *Journal* column had been negative, raising questions about AOL's accounting methods, and yet the stock shot up after the piece appeared, beginning a steady rise that would carry it from $77 to more than $100 a share. Cramer the journalist decided to investigate what had happened to the stock of Cramer the investor. And he had a strong hunch where to start digging.

In the days before the piece appeared, plenty of brokers seemed to know what *Journal* reporter Linda Sandler was working on. They knew the details of the alleged accounting difficulties, which AOL maintained had been approved by top auditors. Hedge funds began shorting AOL stock, betting millions of dollars that it would go down when the column was published. But Cramer and his partner, Jeff Berkowitz, reached the opposite conclusion.

"We've got to buy this stock the moment the article appears," Berkowitz said.

"The heck with that," Cramer said. They had to buy the stock right now. "We already know what the article is going to say, and the *Journal* has nothing," he said.

Cramer was so sure he was right that he wrote a piece for *TheStreet.com* explaining what was about to happen. But Dave Kansas killed it, saying that Cramer appeared to be touting one of his largest holdings. Kansas was the first to conclude that Cramer had a conflict of interest.

The morning that the Heard on the Street column appeared, Maria Bartiromo, CNBC's stock market reporter, said on the air that America Online stock appeared to be headed south. Instead, the stock soon began its spectacular climb.

Cramer was determined to tell the world about this *Journal* column, because he felt that the reporter must have tipped her hand during interviews that the piece would be negative. Having been rejected by his own Website, he turned to his old friend Steve Brill, who had started a media magazine called *Brill's Content.* He liked Cramer's idea for a piece about the *Journal* incident.

But Cramer not only owned a huge batch of AOL stock, he had repeatedly butted heads with *The Wall Street Journal* and its owner, Dow Jones & Company. Some of the conflicts were trivial; the *Journal* had rejected Cramer for a reporting job back in 1977. And some were not.

After Cramer got himself in hot water over the 1995 *SmartMoney* column on the small stocks he owned, he began fighting with Dow Jones, part owner of the magazine, over who was responsible. Cramer contended that Dow Jones had put him in jeopardy by dropping the disclosure line from his article—the sort of disclosure he had been guaranteed under a contract signed by Richard Tofel, Dow Jones's communications director. But Tofel believed that both sides had forgotten about the disclaimer for months. And the magazine's initial failure to locate its copy of the contract forced Cramer to scramble while the feds unleashed their investigators. In the end, Dow Jones agreed to reimburse Cramer for most of his legal fees, although Tofel believed that Cramer was still upset that the company hadn't paid all the bills.

Then came the battle over *TheStreet.com.* In 1997, Steve Swartz, the editor of *SmartMoney,* told Cramer that the magazine would be willing to buy Cramer's money-losing Web operation, perhaps for $10 million; he considered Cramer a huge talent and wanted to work with him again. Hearst, the other partner in *SmartMoney,* wasn't the least bit interested in Swartz's proposal. Cramer, however, believed it was Dow Jones that had vetoed the idea of working with him.

That same year, Cramer bought more than a million shares of Dow Jones stock, attended a stockholders' meeting, and demanded that the company dump a money-losing financial data service called Telerate. Richard Tofel told Cramer that that would never happen, so Cramer sold his stock (for a $4 million profit) five months later—before Dow Jones finally did sell the data service.

When Tofel learned that Cramer was working on the article about the Heard on the Street column, he fired off a letter to Steve Brill, detailing what he saw as Cramer's web of conflicts:

> He is in business in direct competition with us *(TheStreet.com)*, and has attempted, unsuccessfully, to sell us this faltering business or to get us to invest in it;
>
> He has had a commercial dispute with us, in which he has asserted that we failed to pay on his behalf a substantial amount of money he believed was due;
>
> He has sought employment from us, also unsuccessfully;
>
> He has twice bought and sold a substantial number of shares in our company, and has played the role of "dissident" shareholder, calling for the ouster of management.

Cramer couldn't stand Tofel, and he believed the feeling was mutual. They had eyed each other warily ever since college, when Cramer was president of the *Harvard Crimson* and Tofel had worked on the less prestigious newspaper, the *Harvard Independent.* Cramer felt that Tofel was a petty man who was always looking to hurt him.

Tofel, for his part, believed that Cramer was relentlessly hostile toward Dow Jones, having gone so far as to call for the dismissal of CEO Peter Kann, two other top executives, and Tofel himself. Cramer made no secret of his antipathy toward the company, and that was fine, Tofel felt, but Brill shouldn't be hiring him as a journalist to write about Dow Jones. There came a point where you were so wrapped up emotionally that it was impossible to remain objective.

Cramer defended himself in his own missive to Brill. "My, Dick has a wild imagination . . . he obviously has some ax to grind," Cramer wrote. But there was an undeniable complication: Steve Swartz was now trying a second time to buy into *TheStreet.com*. This time, Cramer asked him to get Dow Jones's blessing in advance. "Don't embarrass me," he said. Swartz maintained that this would not be a problem, and the negotiations with Hearst were proceeding in secret. Brill quickly learned of the talks from Dow Jones, and took a hard line with Cramer.

"We have to disclose this," Brill said.

Cramer had painted himself into a corner. If he disclosed the negotiations in the *Brill's Content* article, Hearst would be furious that he was breaching the secrecy of their discussions. If he withdrew the piece, he would be humiliated, since plenty of people knew that it was in the works. "It will be a scandal," he told Brill. Cramer decided that he had no choice but to finish the piece and make the disclosure.

Swartz and the Hearst officials were furious at what they saw as a betrayal. A Hearst executive quickly called Cramer's investment bankers and killed the deal for *TheStreet.com*. The decision had cost Cramer $20 million. Worse, *TheStreet.com*'s investors were livid that Cramer's big mouth had sunk what could have been a major cash infusion for the struggling company. They had had enough of their loose cannon. Under pressure, Cramer resigned as cochairman of *TheStreet.com*, taking a backseat role as just another investor. The irresistible urge to take on the *Journal* had cost him big time.

❑   ❑   ❑

It is 5:45 A.M., the sky over Wall Street is jet black, and Jim Cramer is at his desk, fuming about Hewlett-Packard.

On this Wednesday morning, February 17, 1999, he has just talked to Laura Canigliaro, the ace Hewlett analyst at Goldman Sachs, and now feels sandbagged by the Hewlett folks. Days earlier, Cramer had met with the computer company's executives at a Goldman Sachs technology conference, and they had assured him that they were having a great quarter. Right. A story in that morning's *Wall Street Journal* says that Hewlett's quarterly earnings have beaten the Street's expectations, but that its revenues are up a measly 1 percent. That's the real story, Cramer believes. They can't fool him. This is no minor matter for Cramer, for he owns millions of dollars in Hewlett stock, 2 percent of his entire fund. He had dumped $350,000 of the stock last week, but he still had to take major losses. He felt sick to his stomach.

Cramer has other reasons for indigestion as well. Dell Computer stock had dropped sharply in after-hours trading before an earnings report that was expected to be disappointing, and he is sitting on plenty of Dell. Cramer loved the Internet—he felt it captured his true voice, the real-time, manic force of his personality—but thought the gyrating market in Net stocks was utterly insane. He owned his share of tech stocks—Intel, America Online, Yahoo!, Microsoft, Sun Microsystems—but stayed away from those high-flying issues by companies that barely existed. What a colossal joke it all had become. Maybe someone should just set up a bunch of dummy companies—just cool-sounding stocks with dot-com names, no corporations behind them—and let the day traders romp through them.

Just look at eBay, which the same morning edition of the *Journal* says is considering selling a stake in the firm to America Online. Cramer calculated that eBay was trading at $86 million per employee. Eighty-six million! The place has a lousy 130 workers and is valued by Wall Street at $11 billion. It was nuts. All these yo-yos out there are watching CNBC and placing their buy orders as soon as the next guest is announced to talk about his company's Net strategy. It's a factor, no question about it, and Cramer himself has gotten sucked into the game.

A few days earlier, he was watching as CNBC promoted Ron Baron as an upcoming guest. Baron, a fund manager, was talking up the online prospects for the venerable auction house Sotheby's. In his *Street.com* column, Cramer wondered why Baron was buying up a major chunk of Sotheby's stock. Baron then called and asked Cramer why he was picking on him. Cramer said that he believed fund managers should disclose their ownership in the stocks they were touting. Cramer toyed with buying some Sotheby's shares when Baron came on the air, but everyone else had the same idea. The price had already jumped 2 points.

This, Cramer feels, is another example of how CNBC had changed the world. The great unwashed now get the same real-time information as he does. What was once an elite corps of professional traders is now a huge mob, all trying to squeeze through a narrow door. Cramer regards CNBC as part of the lifeblood of the market, so important that he moved out of his old offices, at 55 Beaver Street, because the building didn't get cable. The previous Friday afternoon, when cable service went down in lower Manhattan, he called Ron Insana during a commercial and demanded that he do something about it.

But the endless chatter on CNBC could also drive Cramer up the wall. All these gloom-and-doomers peddling their negative view of the universe: Corporate earnings are flat, inflation is a renewed danger—and here inflation has been at stunningly low levels for years. What was wrong with these people? They were the usual bear suspects, doing the brokers' bidding, trying to scare people into buying cyclical stocks like steel and chemicals that others are trying to unload. Cramer has been selling his cyclicals, just to spite these hype artists.

Despite his goatee and balding visage, framed by twin peaks of unruly hair, Jim Cramer is a man of childlike intensity. Immensely likable in the way he pours out his heart, Cramer wants to do thirty-five things at once. He wants to manage millions of dollars, be on TV, dominate the Internet, and write for newspapers and magazines—not just *The New Republic* and *Brill's Content* but *Time* and *GQ*. He even dashed off a piece for *The Washington Post* not long ago on Social Security reform. He appears not just on CNBC but on *Good Morning America* and *Charlie Rose*. He has taped an ABC pilot for his own television show, *Jim Cramer's Real Money*, which featured an awkward segment in which he advised a group of Knoxville nurses, by satellite, on their investments. He even made ads for Rockport shoes. "A Zelig for the information age," a reporter once called him.

Cramer wants to watch the market like a hawk, jump in and out of trades, feel the adrenaline rush when he shorts a stock that is deflating or grabs a bargain-priced number on the rise and dumps out of it six hours later. He wants to tell everyone what he thinks at every possible hour. He files seven or eight columns a day for *TheStreet.com,* musing on the market's every burp. He is bursting with the brilliance of his ideas, the kid who couldn't keep quiet in class. If there were no TV and no Internet, he would go door to door. He is remarkably self-absorbed, one step away from setting up a Webcam in his bedroom so he could fulminate for his fans at all hours. He is, in short, the perfect embodiment of the dizzying culture of Wall Street, determined to be faster and smarter than everyone else, louder than everyone else, more famous than everyone else.

Sometimes Cramer would muse about leaving Wall Street. The burnout factor is intense; there are no fifty-five-year-old hedge-fund managers. He promised Karen that he wouldn't do it for that many more years. But something keeps driving him to try to outsmart the market, hour by hour, minute by minute.

While Cramer is off with a broker for breakfast, his jeans-clad partner, Jeff Berkowitz, is making his morning checks. His computer is programmed to bring up *CBS MarketWatch.com, Barron's, Computer Reseller News,* CNET, *The Washington Post,* the *San Jose Mercury News, Investor's Business Daily.* There is so much media and research to wade through, and the stakes are so high. Berkowitz is thirty-one and feels like fifty. He is glad that Cramer is involved in so many media ventures because it drains some of his manic energy that otherwise might be devoted to buying lousy stocks.

Cramer returns just before the 9:30 bell, and the room turns manic. On TV, Mark Haines, the host of the morning show *Squawk Box,* says Dell is already down 11¼. "Merrill Lynch raising numbers on Hewlett!" one of his staffers shouts. Cramer sips a Diet Dr Pepper and scans his computer screens.

"EBay up 14, huh?"

"I want to buy 10 AOL," meaning 10,000 shares.

"What do we do on Lucent?"

"These are head fakes," Berkowitz says.

"Ah, fuck, Intel's not coming in. Is Intel a head fake?"

"I dunno, so we do nothing," Berkowitz says.

On the set behind him, Mark Haines is expressing relief that the Dow is down just 40. "This is not as bad as we expected," Haines says.

"It's early, Mark, it's early," Cramer mutters.

Now Cramer is standing, barking orders to his staff. "I want to sell Intel! Sell 5 Intel! Sell 5 more Micro!"

He studies the computer screen. "Fucking Intel is so powerful. How could Intel be going up?" He decides it is a temporary blip. "Sell 5 more Intel! Sell another 1,000 Yahoo!"

The *Journal* has a relatively positive front-page piece on AT&T, whose bid to buy the cable giant TCI will be approved by regulators today. Cramer reasons that this will give the phone giant a bump. "Buy 35 more ATT! Bring me another 15 AOL. Buy 10 Soft," he shouts, using his nickname for Microsoft. "Sell 15 more Qwest. Sell another 5 Intel." A moment later: "I gotta buy more AOL! Yahoo's up!" The two stocks often moved in tandem. "Buy 25 WorldCom!"

Surprised that tech stocks aren't taking more of a beating with Dell's slide, Cramer starts banging out a *Street.com* column at 10:15: "We are sitting here amazed. . . . I doubted Mark Haines when he pronounced all is well at 9:45. But I should have been buying rather than snickering." Cramer looks over the column he filed at 7:32 that morning, saying that tech stocks were "not so hot."

"I look really stupid," he says. "I wrote that piece, I'm already wrong! Jesus Christ, it's so hard."

Soon the Dow is out of the red and up 5 points. The second-guessing begins. "Everything I sold was wrong, everything I bought was right," Cramer says.

He totals up his score sheet. The firm has lost $240,000 on Hewlett-Packard, $40,000 on Intel, $180,000 on Qwest Communications. It's picked up $15,000 on Lucent Technologies and Time Warner. All told, Cramer has lost close to $400,000, and the take-out sushi hasn't even arrived for lunch.

Now he's stewing over Qwest Communications. In a conference call last week, the CEO, Joe Nacchio, assured analysts that the company was doing well. But Cramer ran an SEC check through his Bloomberg terminal and discovered that Nacchio has filed to sell a couple hundred thousand shares of his own stock. By the time this hits the papers, Berkowitz said, people will say he's bailing and will freak out. So Cramer sold 30,000 shares of Qwest at 53½. Now the stock is at 55. Maybe they jumped too quick.

Cramer is on the phone again, this time trying to sell his weekend place in Bucks County. By the time he hangs up, the Dow is up 61. On CNBC,

Burton Malkiel of Princeton University is talking about a *Business Week* cover story on the merits of index funds, which passively mimic the market. "The evidence is simply overwhelming that index funds have beaten active managers year after year," Malkiel says.

"Who's this joker talking?" Cramer says. "I listen to him, I'd be living in my car."

At 2:25, the rally has faded, and the Dow is only up 16. Tech stocks are sinking. "AOL's getting wrecked, Jeff!" Cramer says.

He and Berkowitz debate whether to buy up plenty of IBM, which is expected to make a positive presentation at an upcoming meeting. "I will not risk hundreds of thousands of dollars on a good meeting," Cramer says. "I don't want the gun to my head on this. Do 30,000."

In the final 30 minutes of trading, the bottom falls out. The Dow is down 60, down 81, down 93. On CNBC, Ron Insana talks about "one savvy hedge-fund manager I know" who "sees a seesaw market with a bias to the downside." Cramer figures it is Stanley Druckenmiller, chief investment strategist for the financier George Soros. From the floor of the stock exchange, Art Cashin of PaineWebber tells Insana that the market may be going as low as 8,700.

Tech stocks have been bloodied. Dell, AOL, Yahoo!, Qwest, Sun Microsystems, Intel are all down. Cramer is still worried about Intel. "I gotta sell another 10 Tel," he shouts. At the closing bell, the Dow is down 102.

"It's chaos out there," Cramer says.

2

SQUAWKING

EVERY weekday morning, two hours before the markets officially open for business, phone lines start buzzing across lower Manhattan. The major brokerage houses are putting their stamp of approval or disapproval on hundreds of stocks, and investors around the country are hungry for an early glimpse of these crucial judgment calls. The assessments by these Wall Street analysts often send a stock rocking or reeling—the more prominent the analyst, the bigger the bang—not because they are always right but because they are embedded in the market's metabolism. In the frenzied period leading up to the opening bell, the information is worth many times its weight in gold.

For decades, these proprietary reports were available only to brokerage clients and financial insiders. Then the monopoly was broken. Ordinary folks started getting the scoop from Maria Bartiromo.

It is Monday at 8:46 A.M. and Bartiromo is furiously typing, the phone cradled to her ear, in her tiny booth overlooking "The Garage," as one of the four trading rooms of the New York Stock Exchange is called.

"Time to sit down," says her assistant, Nicole Petallides.

"Tom, can you hold on one quick second?" Bartiromo asks. She moves to the chair against a plate-glass window, jacked up two feet off the ground, sticks in her earpiece, slides a microphone under her aquamarine jacket and clips it to her lapel. Picking up a phone extension on a small shelf next to the chair, she resumes the conversation about the world's largest computer chip maker, Intel.

"Hold on, hold on," Bartiromo says. She looks into the robot camera, smiles her sweetest smile, and says: "Mark, things just got a little worse. Robertson Stephens is downgrading shares of Intel. *Squawk Box* will return in two minutes with the story."

"Sorry," she says into the phone. "Thanks, Tom."

The commercial is over and the correspondent is back on camera. "We are looking at a broad-based selloff on Wall Street, folks," she says. "Compaq is down 22 percent as we speak." She moves on to Robertson Stephens analyst Dan Niles dropping his "strong buy" recommendation on Intel, which has not yet been publicly announced. "Robertson Stephens Downgrades Intel," says the headline beneath her face.

If CNBC was in the business of pumping out real-time information, no one vacuumed it up faster, or disgorged it in a more rapid-fire cadence, than Maria Bartiromo. Morning after morning, she worked the phones in her tiny space above the exchange at 20 Broad Street, cajoling her sources, coaxing freshly issued upgrades and downgrades from high-powered Wall Street companies even before the brokers had delivered the news to their paying clients.

Bartiromo loved the scoops, the schmoozing, the gossip, the pace, the crackling feel of money being moved by the denizens of the stock exchange. A year earlier, when CNBC executives named her the coanchor of a new 7:00 P.M. program called *Business Center,* they asked her to give up her floor duties for the morning show *Squawk Box* and simply be an on-camera star.

"There's no way you can do this," Bruno Cohen, CNBC's senior vice president, told her. "You can't be beautiful and look good and be alert at seven at night if you're on the floor in the morning."

But Bartiromo refused. There was no substitute for being around traders and watching the floor action, divining the market's mood through osmosis. This is what drove her, and if it meant working 14-hour days, she was willing to pay that price.

At 31, Bartiromo was more than just the brightest star in the CNBC firmament. She was the most famous woman in financial news, the reporter whom everyone on Wall Street called by her first name. The *New York Post,* which ran her picture as often as possible, had dubbed her the "Money Honey," and the tabloid moniker had stuck.

Few feature writers could resist adoring references to Bartiromo's anatomy. *People* magazine gushed about "her Sophia Loren looks." *Money* dubbed her the "pillow-lipped" anchorwoman. *Multichannel News* raved about her "smoky gray eyes," while *National Review* cast her as "the Sharon Stone of business cable." *Fortune* called her "CNBC's pouty anchorwoman . . . best known for her Wall Street savvy, Mediter-ranean good looks, and Mary Hart–like legs."

When Roger Ailes, the former CNBC president who hired her, made Bartiromo the first television correspondent to report from the floor of the exchange, he was well aware of her sexuality. Ailes was certain that all those young, hormone-crazed stock traders would give her plenty of hot tips. What's more, nearly 85 percent of CNBC's viewers were men.

Bartiromo displayed no false modesty about all this. She was initially disheartened by all the focus on her looks, but gradually decided that she didn't mind being called beautiful. She was willing to play the role of Money Honey. She loved being recognized by her fans. Once, when she was in Washington to interview an SEC official, a cabdriver in dreadlocks, reggae music blasting from his radio, turned to her in the backseat and said: "Maria, I have one question. Do you think oil stocks are going to come back any time soon?" A waiter at a friend's wedding asked her about various market scenarios. When *People* magazine ran a piece on her en-gagement to Jonathan Steinberg—the son of financier Saul Steinberg and the editor of *Individual Investor* magazine, for which she wrote a col-umn—that was all right, too. She even posed sitting on his lap. Bartiromo felt a special connection with her viewers. They might enjoy looking at her, but they loved her for her reporting.

Some, of course, loved her for other attributes. One admirer on the *Sil-icon Investor* site called her a "financial goddess." Said another: "Our babe can put on a look that can freeze hell." A third nearly lost it: "You should have seen her Thursday morning wowww!!! She had no bra on!"

While Bartiromo reveled in appearing brash and tough, she knew that it was all an act. She felt that as a woman she had to stand her ground in the testosterone-driven world of the stock exchange. When she first began doing live shots from the floor in 1995, she learned that some traders were deliberately bumping into her during her reports. Some were just being hostile toward an interloper; others were getting off on the idea of knocking her off stride. Once she had to tell a trader: "Excuse me, we are live on TV. Can you please get out of the way for a second?" She refused to be intimidated. After her morning shift, Bartiromo often went to the gym and worked on her kick-boxing. One day, a newspaper report claimed that a trader had grabbed her rear while she was delivering a report.

"If someone had tried to grab my ass, I would have decked him, whether I was on the air or not," she told a colleague.

One reason that Bartiromo reveled in the spotlight was that she had done years of behind-the-scenes grunt work. The daughter of a Brooklyn couple who ran an Italian restaurant in the borough's Bay Ridge section, she had worked as a booker for the Barry Farber show at radio station WMCA while still at New York University. Then she had gotten an internship at CNN, covering general news. But she was studying economics and planned to be an investment banker.

After graduating in 1989, Bartiromo took a job as a production assistant for CNN's business news. She worked her way up to associate producer, writer, producer, and assignment editor. Three times she was put on the overnight shift for months at a time. Eventually she found herself working for Lou Dobbs, the anchor of *Moneyline,* the network's high-profile business newscast. Bartiromo dreamed of becoming a correspondent, but contented herself with the life of a field producer. She would go out, interview people, write the script, edit the piece—and watch one of the reporters read her words on camera.

In 1993, Dobbs promoted her to line producer, meaning that she had to sit in the control room, direct the broadcast, and whisper instructions in the anchor's ear. It meant a raise, but it also meant that she had to show up for work at 4:00 A.M., her fourth tour on the overnight shift. Even worse, the assignment took her out of the reporting game.

Bartiromo pulled her boss aside one night. "I really don't want to do this," she told Dobbs. "I appreciate the promotion, but you're taking me out of the field, and that's what I do best. I have a nose, I have sources on Wall Street."

Dobbs was patient but firm. "Maria," he said, "you cannot always be in someone else's shadow." Dobbs knew that she wanted to be on the air but felt she wasn't ready.

Bartiromo decided to put together an audition tape. She took voice lessons to ease her Brooklynese. When she went out with a cameraman and the story was done, she would ask him to film her doing a stand-up. Some of them were awful, but she salvaged enough good takes to send a tape to CNBC. After waiting for a month, she got a call from Peter Sturtevant, a CNBC vice president.

"I think you come across very well and you know what you're talking about," he told her. There was just one problem: "We have to do something with your hair." The long-haired look had to go.

Bartiromo felt confident after meeting with Ailes, even though she hadn't been offered a job. She left her Brooklyn home, went to Manhattan, and bought two suits. The next day she was hired as a general-assignment reporter.

She sent Dobbs a computer message, saying she needed to speak to him. When she explained that she was leaving, Dobbs was dismissive.

"You're not going to learn anything at CNBC," he said. "That's terrible news. I don't understand how you could even consider going there."

When Bartiromo began reporting from the floor of the stock exchange, friends at CNN told her that Dobbs thought it was a terrible shot and hard to look at. A year later, CNN began doing the same thing. Bartiromo gave her floor position to her old network, moving to what she thought was a better spot.

By ignoring Dobbs's dismal view of CNBC, Maria Bartiromo became the leading media figure at the stock exchange. And once she launched *Business Center*, with a special focus on the glitz of Hollywood and Madison Avenue, she was competing directly with Dobbs's *Moneyline.* "Lou Dobbs has an older audience, and we're trying to broaden our audience out," Bartiromo declared in a swipe at her old boss.

Her morning routine rarely varied: She would come in at 7:00 A.M. and start calling around to the investment firms, sometimes talking on two phones at once, taking calls on her cell phone in between. She had strong relationships with some firms, such as Merrill Lynch, and her sources would simply fax over the stock picks from their morning squawk-box call. Other companies were more hostile, and Bartiromo would refrain from calling them until after 8:30. The whole exercise was a fight over an hour or so, over whether investors would hear the latest picks and pans from their broker or from CNBC.

A few weeks earlier, when Bartiromo had reported that Kevin Mc-Carthy, an analyst at Donaldson, Lufkin & Jenrette, was downgrading Intel, it had caused a major fight within the firm. She had gotten the tip from an investor outside the firm, and that immediately raised a red flag: Why was he telling her this?

"Are you short it?" she asked.

"Yes," the Intel investor admitted. Everyone, Bartiromo knew, had an agenda in talking to her. She quickly called her best source at Donaldson, Lufkin & Jenrette.

"Maria, I've gotta call you back," he blurted.

"I hear you're downgrading Intel," she said.

"Maria, yes, but—" He quickly hung up.

The firm had gotten after her guy. The executives knew that they were friends; they had been seen having dinner. Even though he wasn't the original source, Bartiromo felt that she had gotten him in trouble.

Ralph Acampora, the big-name analyst at Prudential Securities, gave her a hard time as well. Although they were friends, he would often call after she reported his advice and say: "Get the camera out of my office." If she called to confirm one of his projections, he would insist on contacting his clients before talking to her. Other, less prominent brokers would also get upset with her. "Maria, you're killing me," one told her. His clients would call and say they no longer needed him, that they could get the information faster from Maria.

Bartiromo's response was firm: "I'm sorry. You either have a relationship with me or you don't. Most of the time I'm going to get it anyway."

Two weeks earlier, a source had called Bartiromo with a tip that Morgan Stanley was making negative comments about IBM. A Morgan Stanley source confirmed that the firm was predicting an IBM sales slowdown. IBM wouldn't comment, but Bartiromo knew she had a hot story. She went on the air with Morgan Stanley's analysis, and the Dow started to drop. A few minutes later, Reuters moved a bulletin reporting that Morgan Stanley had said nothing about IBM.

Bartiromo's bosses quickly called. What the hell was going on? They insisted that she come back on the air. Bartiromo returned, mentioned the Reuters report and stuck by her guns. This was no rumor, she said. Morgan Stanley analyst Tom Kramer was saying this about IBM. Five minutes later, Reuters reversed itself with another bulletin, confirming Morgan Stanley's call on IBM. Thank God. Bartiromo knew she had been on the money, but she still breathed a sigh of relief.

Bartiromo didn't worry about whether the analysts issuing their upgrades and downgrades were right about the companies involved; that was beyond her purview. Let others judge the quality of their advice. Her interest was in getting the scoop and giving viewers the inside skinny before the opening bell. The information, she felt, had become "commoditized."

She is all business on this Monday morning in the spring of 1999. She gets the Goldman Sachs morning call on her fax machine. The firm is downgrading Compaq Computer, which the previous Friday had made a "preannouncement"—a warning to investors before the official figures were released—that its earnings for the quarter would fall below the expectations of Wall Street analysts. Morgan Stanley is also downgrading Compaq. The S & P 500 futures, a speculative bet on the market's direction, were down 22. "It's going to be a really bad day," Bartiromo says.

She douses her short brown hair with Vidal Sassoon spray and makes a last call to Instinet, the after-hours trading service, to check on Compaq's price, jotting down the "teenies," or sixteenths of a point. Nicole Petallides dims the room light, and Bartiromo is on *Squawk Box*.

"Today it is all about Compaq," she tells host Mark Haines. "That is the big story on the Street today. We are looking for a broad-based market decline today."

By 8:20 Bartiromo has the morning calls of the four major firms she really cares about—Goldman Sachs, Morgan Stanley, Merrill Lynch, and Donaldson, Lufkin & Jenrette. These are the impact calls, the companies with thousands of brokers, the ones most likely to move stock prices.

Petallides brings her a cup of coffee, and at 8:32 Bartiromo is back in the chair for a "whip," a quick once-around to all the correspondents before a commercial. "Keep your hat on, it looks like a rough day on Wall Street," she warns viewers.

Soon she is back on the phone, chatting about Compaq with a Morgan

Stanley executive. "Now, are you saying this is a credibility issue? Why, you don't like a preannouncement on Friday night at five o'clock? Unbelievable!"

At 9:00 Bartiromo slips out of the booth and down a back staircase, clacking along on three-inch heels. She walks past a small barbershop, a members-only coat room, and a large pile of shoes on the floor, abandoned by the fast-moving traders in favor of sneakers. She flashes her badge, slips through a turnstile, and strides onto the trading floor. She moves through The Garage (so named for its previous incarnation) into the larger Main Room, which is adjacent to the Blue Room and the Extended Blue Room.

The place is cooking now, crowded as a rush-hour subway platform and nearly as chaotic. The cavernous room is filled with a dull roar, the floor littered with little pieces of broker paper. Three thousand traders, brokers, and specialists are in constant motion beneath a soaring, ornate ceiling. After the opening bell rings, Bartiromo peers up at a huge electronic scoreboard, flashing the latest prices in green letters, and begins scribbling: Cisco down 3⅛. Amazon down 6. Intel down 3¾.

To the left of her stand-up spot is the America Online booth, crowded with too many sellers. The stock is already down 6 points. To her right is the Morgan Stanley booth, cramped and claustrophobic like the rest. Bartiromo takes a stroll over to the Compaq booth. It's extremely crowded, the stock already down 7 and 13 teenies, to 23⅛. Bartiromo loves analyzing the clues by watching the ebb and flow of the crowd. For all the modern technology at the disposal of the 3,100 member companies, each transaction is made by a broker handing a piece of paper to a specialist who represents a single stock, or perhaps as many as ten stocks.

Bartiromo steps into the Nomura Securities booth near her stand-up position. "All right, 411, let's go," says an assistant in a green company jacket, using his nickname for Bartiromo. He lets her jot down some information from a Nomura screen. She is listening to *Squawk* in her earpiece and realizes that she's up next.

Bartiromo does her first stand-up, looking up at a faraway camera owned by the exchange. The Dow is down 72 points. Petallides hands her some new figures while she is rattling off the latest prices. The din has grown so loud that Bartiromo cannot be heard five feet away. People are passing within inches on either side of her. "Sell 25,000 15!" a nearby trader shouts. Television sets across the trading floor flicker with Bartiromo's image, her screen presence more powerful than the slight figure on the floor would suggest. One reason that CNBC began using closed captioning in its telecasts was that brokers complained they had trouble hearing the program on the floor. A few months earlier, Lou Dobbs had told the exchange that its sets shouldn't automatically carry CNBC. Now each booth with a TV set has a choice, but most are still tuned to Maria.

A few minutes later Bartiromo does her last stand-up, followed by a tease for her 5:00 P.M. show, *Market Wrap.* "Tech stocks are the story of the day," she says.

Squawk Box is wrapping up, and the Dow's loss has been cut to 54 points as 10 o'clock approaches. "It's not a bloodbath," Bartiromo says. The turnaround underscores the weakness of CNBC's breathless, minute-by-minute approach. Even from the epicenter of the New York Stock Exchange, the future is difficult to discern. No one really knows what the next few minutes will bring. For all the hand-wringing over Compaq, the downbeat analysis, the dire warnings at the opening, the stock market moves in unpredictable ways. By the end of the day, as Bartiromo is getting ready to anchor *Market Wrap,* the Dow has jumped 165 points to another record.

❏   ❏   ❏

The reason for CNBC's extraordinary influence was simple: Lots of important and wealthy people watched it, along with a growing army of stay-at-home day traders. It was on in brokerage offices and corporate suites, in restaurants and health clubs. CEOs watched it. Foreign leaders watched it. Regis Philbin watched it. Tennis star Andre Agassi, football great John Elway, and basketball hotshot Charles Barkley were among its most fervent fans. By early 1999, ratings had jumped 59 percent over the previous year. Everyone in the low-rise, nondescript office building in Fort Lee, New Jersey, felt the excitement.

The network had recently received a letter on behalf of Saudi Prince

Alwaleed bin Talal al Saud. It seems that His Royal Highness was sailing his yacht, *Kingdom 5,* into the Caribbean and wanted permission to bounce the network's signal off his private satellite transponder. "The signal will be solely used by HRH himself while on board of his yacht to stay abreast of stock market performance," the prince's adviser wrote. "HRH relies heavily on CNBC to keep track of his portfolio." Now there was a diehard fan.

All this attention had turned the network into a gold mine, a money-making machine that was pouring $200 million a year into the corporate coffers of its parent company, almost as much as the rest of NBC. High-end financial advertisers were desperate to reach the network's affluent audience, whose median household income was $981,000. And the network was becoming more like the brokerages it covered; it planned to sponsor financial conferences in Chicago and San Francisco with the big-name analysts who so frequently filled its airwaves.

The genius of CNBC was that it took the dry realm of financial statistics and turned it into a thrill-packed game. The network was consciously modeled on ESPN's *Sports Center,* as if the correspondents were a bunch of jocks sitting around talking about the World Series or the Super Bowl. They made a big deal of the opening bell at the New York Stock Exchange, treating it like the ceremonial first pitch. There was a pregame show, a color man, a starting lineup, a half-time report, and a postgame wrap-up. There was a TKO segment, or Technical Knock Out, on technical analysis. The correspondents were shown in shirtsleeves working the phones, looking things up on computers, kidding each other, discussing their eating habits, and shooting the breeze.

The breezy approach was personified by *Squawk Box,* named for the speakerphones that investment firms use for early-morning conference calls with their brokers and analysts. The anchor, Mark Haines, was a sardonic, curmudgeonly fellow who had given everyone nicknames. Joe Kernen, a wry former stockbroker with a master's degree in molecular biology, was Kahuna. Kathleen Hays was the Bond Babe. David Faber, the dogged stocks reporter, was The Brain. ("The Brain is about to plug in, and the power surge is amazing," Haines would say.) Maria Bartiromo was the exception; no one called her the Money Honey on the air.

Most of the network's cast of characters were not blow-dried Ken and Barbie dolls. Ron Insana, the host of the midday program *Street Signs,* was a short, balding guy with glasses; Haines had a middle-aged paunch. Still, they had passionate fans. A Cleveland housewife had even created a "Hunks of CNBC" chat room.

As a young cable network, CNBC had offered a second chance for a number of television retreads, and Mark Haines was a prime example. He had been a local anchorman in Providence, New York, and Philadelphia for two decades, but had burned out on the business. He quit television, went to law school at the University of Pennsylvania, and accepted a job with a snooty Philadelphia law firm. A week before he was to start, Haines told Bob Davis, an old pal who was then helping to run CNBC, of his plans.

"You don't want to do that, you want to get back into television," Davis said.

They had lunch, and Davis made him an offer. Haines agonized, had long discussions with his wife, and decided to try it. It was August 1989. CNBC had been on the air for four months.

Haines began to tutor himself about the world of Wall Street. The stuff was really dense, but he was determined to find a way to present it in a clear manner. No one on television was really doing that. He subscribed to trade journals, scanned electronic libraries. As *Squawk Box* grew more popular and Haines grew more comfortable, he would leave the newsroom as soon as the morning show was over and work out of his New Jersey home. Haines would pick up his kids at the school bus at 3:30, perhaps go to Little League practice, then log onto his computer at 5:30 and begin reading SEC documents. The staff would hand him a packet of clips when he showed up at 6:45 the next morning, but Haines loved the Internet and all the bits of data you could find there.

Over time, he created his own database, compiling a record of what Wall Street analysts said so that he could hold them accountable. It was a huge pain, but the results were stunning. In 1997, of more than 15,000 opinions uttered, less than half of 1 percent involved a recommendation to sell any stock. It was all buy, buy, buy. Of what value were such opinions? Ninety-nine and a half percent of stocks were worth buying? These analysts all had a vested interest, Haines felt, because their firms wanted the investment banking business of the corporations they were assessing.

Sometimes Haines could barely hide his disdain. When he and Joe Kernen were chatting with SG Cowen analyst Gary Kaminsky, who responded to a query by framing a question of his own, Haines snapped: "See, we don't need you to identify the questions. We need you to identify the answers. Me and Joe are very good at identifying the questions."

Another time, his guest host, Seth Tobias of Circle T Partners, was asked his view on investing in Asia. "Cautiously optimistic," Tobias said.

"Thank you for that utterly useless comment," Haines shot back.

The snide, joking tone was the only way that Haines could do the show. Over the course of the two-hour program, the fifty-three-year-old anchor would talk about sports or movies or Xena the Warrior Princess or lava lamps or his love of Wendy's hamburgers or anything else that crossed his mind, sometimes with *Star Trek* music in the background. The denizens of Wall Street, he felt, were interested in more than just stocks. If his bosses didn't like it, they would have to dump him. Haines had always been an iconoclast. He didn't have much respect for authority, didn't like sacred cows, and didn't mind taking them on.

When the SEC published an investigative report on price-rigging by top Wall Street brokers in the high-tech Nasdaq market, Haines was so outraged that he read parts of it on the air every day for a week. He felt the probe demonstrated that investors were being ripped off and stabbed in the back by some Nasdaq brokers. Shortly afterward, exchange officials canceled their advertising on the program, although they dropped the boycott a few months later. Haines felt it was the most important thing that he had ever done on the show.

What he relished most about his daily wanderings online was the search for that nugget of information that would trip up a CEO. On one program, Haines interviewed an executive who had just built a semiconductor plant in Greensboro, North Carolina. Haines had looked up Greensboro on the Net and discovered that there was water rationing in the area. Semiconductor factories, he knew, use a huge amount of water. When Haines brought this up, the startled executive had to admit that, yes, this was a potential problem.

In the fall of 1997, when Sunbeam's stock had risen 400 percent in a year, Haines went after the chief executive, the famously nicknamed "Chainsaw Al" Dunlap. Receivables and inventories were up, Haines said. Accounts payable were up, too. "What, are you stiffing your suppliers?"

No way, Dunlap said.

Standard & Poor's research, Haines noted, was telling cautious investors to steer clear of the stock because of the risks involved. Did he have a response?

"Total bullshit," Dunlap said. It was live television, and CNBC had no way of bleeping a guest's words.

Dunlap was furious, but Haines had been right. Sunbeam's stock would fall by 50 percent over the next few months, the SEC would begin investigating accounting irregularities at the company, and Dunlap himself would have to resign.

Perhaps Haines's angriest moment came in the spring of 1998. *Squawk* was broadcasting from a conference in Williamsburg, Virginia. The guest was George Fisher, the CEO of Eastman Kodak. Haines asked whether the film company was planning a price-cutting campaign against Fuji, its chief rival, as a Prudential analyst had contended. "We certainly don't intend to launch a price war," Fisher insisted. That was on a Friday. On Monday, Kodak announced a major rebate campaign aimed at Fuji. Haines told producer Matt Quayle to cue up the interview tape, and essentially accused Fisher of having lied to him. Fisher complained to senior executives at General Electric, which owned NBC, but to no avail. In any case, Haines didn't want him back on the show. What was the point, he felt, of interviewing a CEO who didn't level with you?

As Haines's program gained a devoted following, its power to move markets became legendary. Reporters began to write about the *"Squawk Box* effect." In the summer of 1998, when Xybernaut stock was trading at 3, CNBC announced that Edward Newman, the company's CEO, would appear on *Squawk* the next morning. By the end of the day, the stock was trading at 8½. By the time Newman sat down on the set the next morning, the stock had hit 12½.

What was happening was that hyperactive day traders were bidding up the stock of any company that was going to be featured on *Squawk*. As viewers began calling up to find out the next day's guests, Matt Quayle grew nervous about the program's distorting impact. The stock of one small company, Onyx Software, had more than doubled because of the *Squawk* effect. CNBC responded by posting the list of the next day's *Squawk* guests on its Website at 5:00 P.M., so that no one would have an unfair advantage. And Quayle imposed a rule that no one from a company worth less than $100 million could appear on the program. Small-company stocks were just too volatile.

Mark Haines thought that anyone who made investments based on *Squawk Box* appearances was acting stupidly and would undoubtedly lose money. Some traders blamed him for their losses, which was ridiculous. They were adults. What they were doing was gambling, pure and simple. It was like feeding coins into a slot machine. That was awfully cold, he knew. But life was cold.

❏   ❏   ❏

When Wall Street traders appeared on CNBC, there was always an unspoken tension between their considerable financial interests and their need to be entertaining. The most coveted gig on the network was a rotating slot as guest host of *Squawk Box,* and no one loved bantering with Mark Haines and the gang more than Jim Cramer.

But Cramer's shoot-from-the-lip style always threatened to get him in trouble, and on the morning of December 2, 1998, he went too far. The talk had turned once again to Net stocks, and Cramer insisted on calling many of them "Fraud-U-Net" stocks. He brought up a Phoenix company called WavePhore, whose CEO, David Deeds, was to appear on the program that morning. Cramer vowed on the air that he was going to try "to get the truth out of the guy," which was that the stock, in Cramer's view, was badly overvalued.

"I called my stock-loan department and said, 'Listen, I want to short 25,000 WavePhore because I think this thing is a big speculative bubble,' " Cramer told viewers. "My broker told me, 'Not on your life—it can't be borrowed.' " Cramer aggressively questioned Deeds later in the show. All this was like yelling fire in a crowded theater. WavePhore's stock plummeted 38 percent that day. Investors figured that if Jim Cramer was trying to dump the stock, it was time to bail. Cramer quickly realized he had made a poor choice of words. He wasn't really trying to short the stock; he had just been trying to check on whether other brokers were doing so.

Haines had been off that morning, but when he came in the next day and saw the huge amount of e-mail about the incident, he watched the tape and told CNBC management that they had a problem. WavePhore officials, meanwhile, were going ballistic. They demanded that the SEC investigate Cramer. This was a blatant conflict of interest, they said, Cramer trying to short their stock and then bad-mouthing it on television so his bet would pay off. WavePhore said that Cramer may have been lying when he denied shorting the stock. The SEC began investigating. CNBC executives, feeling the heat, felt they had no choice but to suspend Jim Cramer.

Cramer called his lawyer. Had he done anything wrong? The attorney said he had not. But Cramer felt as if a menacing cop had pulled him over for speeding. It was scary. He had Goldman Sachs, his brokerage firm, pull all the records to prove his point. He began paying the first of $50,000 in legal bills. CNBC looked into the matter, and brought Cramer on *Squawk Box* four weeks later to be grilled by Mark Haines.

The situation was clearly awkward for Haines. He liked and trusted Jim Cramer. He was absolutely confident that Cramer did not mean that he had literally shorted the stock, for Cramer would never have attempted such a crude and blatant manipulation. Besides, Cramer had told the *Squawk* staff before the show that he was going to check on whether WavePhore could be shorted. But Cramer had certainly blundered by using such ambiguous Wall Street shorthand. This, Haines felt, was the risk you took by having on guests who invested their own or other people's money. There was always the potential for traders to use the program for their own financial ends. Still, he preferred such guests because, unlike mere observers, they knew what they were talking about.

Haines had two objectives in the interview, which had been carefully spelled out in advance by CNBC's lawyers. First, he had to defuse the potential that CNBC could be sued for slander by allowing the use of the phrase "Fraud-U-Net" stocks. Second, he had to repair Cramer's credibil-ity, because he was still a valuable guest. If Cramer flunked the interview, CNBC would never invite him back. Haines got right down to business.

"Fraud is a heavy word," he said, fingering his glasses.

"That would be wrong . . . I didn't say that," said Cramer, looking visi-bly nervous.

"If you tried to short the stock because you knew the CEO of WavePhore was going to be on CNBC and you were going to be tough on him in the interview, that could be construed as stock manipulation," Haines said.

"If I were to do that, that would have been wrong. It was not my inten-tion," Cramer said.

CNBC decided to reinstate Cramer, but network executives were wor-ried about the appearance that they were being used to move the market. They decided to hand out written conflict-of-interest guidelines to the market pros who appeared on CNBC, who now had to disclose if they owned the stocks they were talking about. What's more, their private ac-tions had to be consistent with what they were saying on the air. They couldn't talk up a stock and then sell their holdings for a quick profit. Cramer had reminded them that they were all playing a dangerous game.

3

THE YOUNG TURKS

S TEVE Lipin really wanted to go skiing. Instead, he was furiously working the phones at his weekend place in the Adirondacks, chasing three possible corporate mergers for *The Wall Street Journal*. It was Sunday, the day he always worked the hardest, trying to confirm the merger deals that would be unveiled on Monday morning. Lipin's mission was to beat the official announcement by twenty-four hours, and there was no one in the media world more accomplished at navigating the twists and turns of these corporate slopes.

It was snowing harder now. Lipin wanted to drive his wife and two young daughters back to Manhattan, but he couldn't leave until he had exhausted every last avenue. The biggest story on this Sunday, March 14, 1999, was that Fleet Financial was on the verge of buying BankBoston, a $16-billion merger of two huge New England banks. *The Boston Globe* was hot on the trail of that one. Lipin felt he should have worked the story harder to get it into Friday's paper—the *Journal* didn't publish on weekends—but it was too late now. Also, DuPont was looking to buy Pioneer Hi-Bred, the nation's largest seed company, for $7 billion. And El Paso Energy, a gas pipeline operator, was about to swallow Sonat, one of its rivals, in a $6-billion deal. *The New York Times* had gotten a short story on those negotiations into the Saturday paper. The terrain was becoming more competitive all the time. Lipin had to worry about CNBC, Bloomberg News, the *Financial Times, The New York Times*. That meant more pressure to publish earlier, to pull the trigger before the deal was nailed down—pressures that Lipin often tried to resist.

Other reporters spoke of Steve Lipin with a mixture of awe and envy. He had broken the merger of Chemical Bank and Chase Manhattan, of MCI and WorldCom, of Gillette and Duracell. And there was the biggest scoop of all in May 1998—the $36-billion marriage of Chrysler and Daimler-Benz. Lipin had worked that story for five days, a nerve-racking period in which he refused to publish what he knew until it was rock solid, even as he sweated about losing the exclusive. He could always write a story saying two companies were in talks—everyone was talking to everyone, and most of the deals never reached fruition. He didn't want to look stupid by jumping on every rumor. He wasn't going to destroy the *Journal*'s credibility by reporting on a merger that didn't quite make it. And there were almost always last-minute snags, accounting problems or power struggles, that threatened to unravel an almost-done deal. Shit happened.

With Chrysler and Daimler-Benz, Lipin began to hear that the deal was on the rocks. There was a fight about the new company's name, whether Daimler would abandon the historic Benz name for a joint entity to be called Daimler-Chrysler. But that got resolved, and Lipin took the plunge after confirming that the deal was going to Chrysler's board for approval, the strongest story he could write. It was a world exclusive, and one of his colleagues, John Keller, poured champagne in his office.

Precisely how Lipin scored time after time was the subject of heated speculation. Some rivals thought that the *Journal* was simply spoon-fed these exclusives. Jim Cramer believed that corporate executives wanted a press-release story before their announcement, one that would contain no criticism or outside evaluation because Lipin could not risk losing the scoop by calling others for comment. Lipin dismissed this argument, viewing Cramer as a walking conflict-of-interest who was obviously hostile toward Dow Jones. And he didn't particularly care what his critics thought. Lipin got the stories because he was constantly working the people who did the deals. There were ten key New York firms handling the banking and legal work for these megamergers, maybe thirty key players in all, and he had been cultivating them for years. Most of them worked within strolling distance of the Dow Jones tower on Liberty Street, across the street from the World Trade Center. I'll be working Sundays, he told them, and I want your deals. Fortunately, Lipin's wife, Amy, understood the six-day weeks and the pressure-cooker atmosphere of Wall Street; she was an options trader who dealt only with Intel, the one company he could never cover.

Lipin understood that part of his clout derived from representing the country's leading financial newspaper, with a circulation of nearly 2 million and a gold-plated reputation. He often teamed up with the beat reporters who specialized in the industry involved, giving him a leg up on other reporters who didn't have the backing of the *Journal*'s stellar staff. What's more, it was important to corporate executives, their bankers, and their lawyers to get good play for their deals. On a busy day, a merger involving second-tier companies often got overshadowed. Lipin argued that giving the advance story to him usually meant better display because the *Journal,* like all papers, trumpeted its scoops. And that produced two days of coverage for the companies involved, since the rest of the media would have to chase the story on the day that the two CEOs were announcing their already publicized plans.

Still, no one understood how much work it took just to knock down bogus stories. A few months earlier, an obscure Website in Amsterdam had reported that Royal Dutch Shell planned to make a bid for Chevron. The story didn't quite make sense, but Lipin had to spend days chasing it. You never knew when one of these things would jump from the Internet to the wires to CNBC. But the report didn't amount to anything, and Lipin didn't write it. Sometimes he had to cut his losses.

A tall, serious-looking man with reddish hair and glasses, Lipin had worked his way up from the bottom rung of the financial media. He had applied for an internship at the *Journal* after college but didn't make the cut. Instead, he headed for what he called the trade rags. He toiled at the newsletters put out by *Institutional Investor* magazine, where he became friendly with another hungry young reporter, David Faber. He moved on to *Investment Dealers Digest* and *American Banker.* Luckily, Lipin's editor at *American Banker,* Fred Bleakley, became the *Journal*'s banking editor, and he hired Lipin to cover banking in 1991. Three years later, Lipin was awarded the mergers-and-acquisitions beat, the high-pressure post he had always coveted.

Lipin's dedication bordered on the fanatical. In the spring of 1998, a week after breaking the Daimler-Chrysler story, he was chasing rumors that SBC Communications was going to buy Ameritech in a blockbuster, $61-billion merger of Baby Bell companies. Lipin was unable to confirm the story on Friday, and on Saturday night he and his pregnant wife went to the home of a *Journal* colleague for dinner. The food was spicy, and suddenly Amy went into labor. Lipin put their two-year-old daughter, Anna, to bed and, since Amy was still in the early stages, sat down to write a memo on everything he knew about the Ameritech deal. He filed the memo electronically after midnight and went to the hospital at 4:00 A.M. Cell phones weren't allowed in the labor room, so at 9:30 he raced down the hall to a pay phone. He was trying to get additional confirmation of the deal when the doctor told him, "Okay, it's time." The doctor laughed when Lipin told him what he was doing.

A few hours after their second daughter was born, Lipin was back on the phone, still working the Ameritech merger. "How's your story doing?" Amy asked from her hospital bed. She understood how Steve was wedded to his work. Even at a time like this, it was hard to disengage.

Now, at thirty-six, Lipin was at the top of his game. He started taking up golf, figuring that the golf course was a good place to unwind with his banker and lawyer buddies. It was also a way to tap into the latest market rumors. After four or five hours together, you had to talk about something. Lipin bought a set of clubs for Amy as a Christmas present. He hoped to co-opt her so she wouldn't feel like a golf widow.

David Faber, who now worked the mergers beat for CNBC, remained one of Lipin's best friends, even though they went all-out to scoop each other. On the last day of 1998, he and Amy had plans to go out with Faber for New Year's Eve. That afternoon, Faber went on the air with a big one. Bell Atlantic, he reported, was in talks to acquire the wireless carrier Air-Touch Communications, a deal of global importance that would be valued at about $45 billion. AirTouch shares jumped 3 points, to 72, on Faber's report. Lipin immediately called his friend.

"What were you thinking?" Lipin said. "Did you want to ruin my weekend?" But beneath the bluster, he was happy for Faber.

Lipin dutifully chased the story for the *Journal,* crediting CNBC, but five days later, he struck back. He reported that a British telecommunications company called Vodafone was preparing a higher bid for AirTouch that would muscle Bell Atlantic out of the deal. This time it was Faber's turn to call.

"Damnit," Faber said. "Can't I just have one for myself?"

Lipin did more than mergers. In early March he broke the story that Hewlett-Packard, the computer giant, was splitting itself into two companies. The news had come completely out of the blue. Lipin had learned that Hewlett planned to make the announcement at 6:00 the next morning. There was no way he would leave work until he could get the story confirmed. Finally, at 10:30 that night, Lipin had enough to write an article for the *Journal*'s later editions. His piece on the company's restructuring used the same vague attribution he always employed: "people familiar with the matter."

The next morning, Lipin was at the CNBC studio in Fort Lee to talk about his story. Lipin wasn't wild about being on television—he couldn't help but laugh when Faber was stopped on the street—but CNBC had a partnership with the *Journal* and he tried to help out when he could. He particularly liked to be on at 6:30 A.M. because a CNBC car would pick him up on the Upper West Side, take him across the George Washington Bridge, and bring him back before his girls woke up.

"We're talking about Hewlett and Packard divorcing," Lipin said. "This is obviously a reaction to the faltering stock price. . . . This is a radical move."

It had been a crazy month. Now, as the snowstorm gathered strength, Lipin finally drove his family back from the Adirondacks after finishing his merger reporting for the day. The stories on Fleet and BankBoston, on DuPont and Pioneer, and on El Paso and Sonat would all appear in the next morning's paper. There were times when Lipin grew tired of the daily grind. He had been pounding this turf for five years, and now he had two toddlers at home. But there was a reason he could not give it up, could not resist chasing the big mergers and winning the bragging rights by getting there first.

It was addictive.

❑   ❑   ❑

That same Monday morning, across the Hudson River, David Faber was kicking himself for not going with the BankBoston story.

One of his best sources, someone he had known for years, had told him the previous Thursday about the bank's impending takeover by Fleet. There was no way the man should have known of the merger—it was insider information, illegal to trade upon—and he wasn't directly involved in the deal. Still, Faber was convinced that the story was true. He could have done a rumor story, kicked up a fuss, moved the stock, and gotten credit for disclosing the deal—if it actually happened. After all, he had reported the Exxon-Mobil courtship as a rumor. But he liked to avoid such stories if he didn't have the facts nailed down. Putting the rumor in play through the power of CNBC simply wasn't the same as breaking the story. Besides, he would have to spend two days chasing it down, blow off his daily Faber Report segment, and risk coming up dry.

Faber knew that he would never get the kind of leaks that Steve Lipin got, the kind designed to guarantee good play in the *Journal*. Lipin was an animal, an incredible reporter, and corporate officials still viewed the *Journal* as the most prestigious forum in which to announce their mergers. So Faber had to work the outside players—the investment bankers and the lawyers who did the deals. He had known the financial and legal heavyweights involved in these megamergers for years. Sometimes they would play ball with him; sometimes they owed him. But Faber could also play hardball when necessary. If a source screwed him, he would say: "I'm going to make sure you're not mentioned on our air." It was a bluff, of course; he didn't control what others said on CNBC. But it sure got their attention.

The Brain, as Mark Haines called him, had grown up in Forest Hills, Queens, a baby-faced man with thick brown hair and an infectious smile who slipped on his glasses only to read the TelePrompTer. When he started at CNBC in 1993 after seven years at *Institutional Investor,* he was struck by the passive atmosphere at the cable network. He didn't see anyone making calls or doing enterprise reporting. That was what he knew how to do, so he kept poking around Wall Street. Soon he told a producer that he had dug up some interesting news involving Paramount Pictures.

"What do you mean?" the producer said. "It's not on the wires." That was the mentality.

Over time, as Faber continued to cultivate corporate executives and investment bankers, the producers would stick him on the air occasionally. Then he started doing a twice-weekly afternoon report called *Street Talk*. Eventually he developed a mergers beat and became a regular on *Squawk Box*. The Brain thing started when he was on vacation and Haines wanted to put something on his chair to commemorate his absence, like the mechanical gorilla that filled in for his deskmate, Joe Kernen. Haines had found a small cactus, which he felt symbolized Faber's dry personality, but one of the studio crew stuck a rubber brain on top of it. Now even the waiters and the doormen seemed to recognize him. Once, when he was strolling by a fruit stand at 53rd Street and Second Avenue, the driver of a fruit truck rolled down the window and shouted: "David? David Faber? I watch you every day!" A beautiful woman interrupted his dinner at a Columbus Avenue restaurant, handed him her card, and asked if he could get her on the air. Everyone was more conscious of the stock market these days, which meant more people were watching CNBC, which meant they followed The Brain.

At thirty-five, Faber now had the kind of access he'd always dreamed about. In the last few weeks he had had lunch with Douglas Warner, the CEO of J. P. Morgan, and Richard Fuld, the CEO of Lehman Brothers. The Warner lunch proved useful when a false rumor began to spread that J. P. Morgan was about to be taken over; it was helpful to know how these men thought to gauge the likelihood of such rumors. Faber regularly went down to Wall Street to have drinks or dinner with brokerage officials, corporate executives, hedge-fund guys. These were people he had known for years; he didn't accept calls from folks he didn't know. He knew that his sources often had a vested interest in pushing this or that deal, but that was fine as long as he understood their motives. And sometimes he just lucked out. He had been able to confirm the AirTouch story because a Bell Atlantic executive happened to answer his own phone when Faber called; otherwise, he might never have gotten ahold of the man. Faber was annoyed, however, when *The New York Times* refused to credit him in its next-day story, referring instead to "rumors of an acquisition" that "began to circulate on trading floors."

Occasionally, Faber realized that his clout only went so far. Once, while having lunch with James Cullen, the president of Bell Atlantic, he mentioned that he had just moved to a new West Side apartment but was unable to get a coveted 212 number, and that the company was sticking him with a new area code. Faber figured Cullen would try to curry favor with him by promising to take care of it. To Faber's dismay, the executive said nothing.

Faber's biggest scoop involved the collapse of Long Term Capital Management, the giant hedge fund. He had been working the story for months at a time when few people grasped the magnitude of the fund's problems. Faber reported that the fund's executives had met to fashion a bailout plan and that the Federal Reserve was involved. After the story broke, Paul Steiger, the *Journal*'s managing editor, even called to congratulate him.

At other times, Faber would not pull the trigger, and sometimes he regretted it. When Travelers was preparing to buy Salomon Brothers, he got the word from a terrific source—someone inside Smith Barney, a Travelers subsidiary, who wasn't directly involved in the deal. The law firm of Cravath, Swaine & Moore was said to be handling the merger, but Faber's sources there didn't know anything about it. He later learned that Sam Butler, Cravath's managing partner, hadn't told his associates about the deal to preserve its secrecy. When Salomon Brothers stock started to move, Faber went on the air and spit out everything he knew, warning viewers that this was still speculation. The merger was announced the next day.

Faber went back and forth on whether to report market rumors. He tried to avoid the practice, but when the insiders were buzzing and the stock was jumping, Faber felt a responsibility to share with viewers what much of Wall Street was hearing, true or not. Of course, he had to be especially careful about inadvertently spreading rumors himself. If he made thirty calls trying to find out if ABC Corporation was merging with XYZ Inc., that got the rumor mill going, and sometimes he'd hear the story repeated and realize that he had put it in play. That was the problem with Wall Street; it was like a giant echo chamber.

There was another complication in David Faber's life, and that was the bookings for *Squawk Box*. Matt Quayle, the program's twenty-eight-year-old producer, often had to decide whether to let Faber pursue a merger rumor—and possibly come up empty—or whether to cut a deal with the company to make sure that the CEO would come on the program the morning that the deal was announced.

The El Paso story was a perfect example. Faber had gotten a tip on Friday that El Paso was about to buy Sonat. He passed it on to Quayle, who began a delicate dance with the PR woman for El Paso. He needed enough details to know that the deal was for real and of sufficient magnitude to warrant booking the CEO. On her end, the El Paso woman was nervous, trying to get a commitment without revealing the crucial details.

"I can't guarantee you can come on unless you tell me what it is," Quayle said. He had learned to play rough with these people. He simply didn't trust them. Quayle often insisted that the company fax him the proposed press release after the markets closed. The woman claimed that this was a $10-billion deal, but Quayle concluded that it was really worth less than $6 billion. He was tired of the old public-relations trick in which a spokesman would inflate the value of the takeover to get CNBC to bite; the company had to cough up the exact prices.

The El Paso woman insisted she could not tell him. She would be blamed for any premature leak. But, she said, "it'll be in the *Journal* Monday." In other words, they were willing to cut an advance deal with *The Wall Street Journal* but not with CNBC.

Here was the dilemma: Quayle wanted top-notch guests, Faber wanted to break big stories. If Quayle agreed to book William Wise, El Paso's CEO, for Monday morning, he had to agree to embargo the news, thereby taking Faber out of the game. If El Paso wouldn't strike a deal, he would kick the story back to Faber for further reporting. Quayle tried to be scrupulous about this, sometimes hiding the papers on his desk if Faber walked by so he wouldn't spot any notes on a merger that *Squawk Box* had promised to sit on. In this case, the lure of television proved too great and El Paso agreed to provide the details so its leader could get some face time on CNBC.

Faber hated the way that Quayle sometimes took the ball out of his hands. Few things pissed him off more, for once Quayle had made the commitment there was nothing that Faber could do. He had first stumbled onto the practice a year earlier, when he saw the stock symbol of a technology company on Quayle's computer, a company whose merger he had been hotly pursuing. Faber was enraged by the discovery. He felt he had been naive in not realizing that *Squawk* was making these deals with CEOs. Worse, the practice deprived him of a crucial lever, the implied threat that unless company executives cooperated with him they might not get to tout their deal on CNBC once it was announced. The practice, in his mind, was the equivalent of the *Journal* implicitly offering to play exclusive deals on page A-3, with the unspoken threat that if Faber got the news first, the story would be buried on B-14.

Despite such setbacks, Faber loved his job. He loved chasing merger deals, loved talking on the air about the intricacies of taxes and depreciation and amortization. He enjoyed being recognized on the street. There was, however, one frustration. He was now part of the high-roller world of Wall Street. He was hardly underpaid by cable television standards— most CNBC stars made between $180,000 and $225,000 a year, with a handful of top anchors earning $500,000 to $600,000—but he was constantly dealing with brokers and portfolio managers who made ten or fifteen or twenty times as much as he did. Faber knew much more about the market than these movers and shakers. He would find himself chatting with some upstart twenty-seven-year-old who was making $3 million a year and wondering if he had set his own sights too low. Occasionally he thought about making the leap, about chasing his own fortune in the big casino. It was, for now, just a fantasy. The Brain was not quite ready to give up the television spotlight.

❏   ❏   ❏

The modern-day CNBC barely resembled the Consumer News and Business Channel that NBC President Robert Wright had created in 1989 to compete with the better-established Financial News Network. In those bare-bones days, some staffers had to use card tables for desks. There were reports on dinner recipes, on the pain of arthritis, on how to deal with children's temper tantrums. There were consumer programs such as *America's Vital Signs* and *Steals and Deals*. Segments would lurch from a discussion about bonds to a husband-and-wife team debating the merits of plastic versus paper grocery bags.

And there were gaffes galore. "Is somebody rolling PrompTer here?" a confused anchor once asked on the air. The phone would ring in the middle of a segment. Mark Haines once referred to securities traded through brokers' pink slips as "pink shit stocks." Reporter Bob Pisani did a piece about sex on the Internet in a room with a model clad in a pink bikini, and trading on the New York Stock Exchange came to a virtual halt. Some less than successful shows—*Your Portfolio, The Money Club, Bull Session*—came and went.

CNBC executives wanted to be more colorful than FNN, which they viewed as a collection of boring, green-eyeshade types. And the derision was mutual. Ron Insana, then at FNN, thought it was ludicrous for CNBC to keep going to the lettuce desk to check produce prices during a market meltdown.

At first, the new network reached just 13 million homes and was hardly a critical success. A "pale imitation of CNN" with a "drier-than-dry style," sniffed *USA Today*. CNN founder Ted Turner was more blunt. "Boy, that thing sucks, doesn't it?" he declared. "What a piece of garbage."

There was nowhere to go but up. When FNN was forced into bankruptcy in 1991, a financial network brought low amid charges of fraud and securities violations by top executives, CNBC topped an earlier bid by Dow Jones and Westinghouse to buy it. For $155 million, CNBC immediately added access to another 26 million homes. The network also absorbed some of FNN's top anchors, including Insana and Bill Griffeth, into the tight-knit CNBC family. Gradually, the amateurish network began to develop a personality.

CNBC went through several presidents; one of the most successful was Roger Ailes, the hard-charging Republican strategist who had worked for Richard Nixon, Ronald Reagan, and George Bush. After leaving politics in 1993, Ailes created such programs as *Squawk Box* and *Power Lunch* to give the network a sharper identity. Management had put Mark Haines on a hit list of people to be fired, but as a fellow fat guy, Ailes felt he deserved another chance. He thought *Squawk* would be a good platform for Haines's quick wit and cutting sarcasm.

Ailes more than tripled the profits at CNBC. But he quit during a power struggle over NBC's second cable outlet, which became a joint venture with Microsoft called MSNBC, and Bill Bolster took his place.

A big, garrulous man who had spent most of his career in local news and had become the general manager of NBC's New York station, WNBC, Bolster was contemplating retirement in 1996 when he was shipped from 30 Rockefeller Plaza to Fort Lee. He was surprised to find a virtual explosion in the demand for real-time financial information that would give his new network an unprecedented degree of influence. He saw CNBC as engaged in a struggle for information supremacy against the entrenched financial interests across the river.

All this had a very personal resonance for Bolster. He liked to reminisce about his childhood in Waterloo, Iowa, where his father was a businessman who dabbled in the stock market. His dad's only source of stock information was *The Wall Street Journal,* which arrived by mail two days late. It was hard to understand how the old man didn't get taken to the cleaners. The time lag gave a huge advantage to the people who worked in an eight-block stretch of Manhattan, the sort of advantage that CNBC was helping to eliminate.

No wonder the traders felt threatened by this upstart network. They had owned their lucrative little playground for decades and made all the rules. There were thousands of "market makers," the specialists who still transacted each stock sale by hand, providing the market with liquidity—making sure sellers could find buyers—but skimming off a bit of the financial cream. Even one-sixteenth of a dollar on each share could add up to millions. Maybe that was why these middlemen all seemed to have homes in France, Bolster thought. It was the good old white boys of Wall Street screwing around with everyone's money. Bolster could never get them to talk about this shadowy system, which was threatened by the rise of electronic trading and the Internet and the searing spotlight of cable coverage.

From the start, Bolster devised a romantic formulation for what CNBC did. It was about dreams: buying a home, affording a college education. The challenge, he believed, was to turn data delivery into watchable television. And so he hired not financial experts but veterans who were versed in the visual language of television: Kevin Magee from *Good Morning America.* David Friend from *Extra.* Mark Hoffman from Time Warner and

ABC. Bruno Cohen, the news director at his old station, New York's WNBC. The same was true for the line producers. Andy Hoffman, the producer who ran *Street Signs,* came from Court TV, where he had produced the O. J. Simpson trial. Bolster strongly believed that the network should talk down to the average investor. You couldn't completely dumb it down, because that would alienate the experts, but you couldn't get lost in the jargon, either. He sometimes reminded Ron Insana to stop talking up to the pros and make his analysis understandable to the little guy.

Now Bolster wanted CNBC to aim even higher, to own the big-name Wall Street analysts as well. Why not go after Ralph Acampora or Abby Joseph Cohen and pay them a Tom Brokaw salary of $6 million or $7 million a year? What, after all, was more important than dispensing financial wisdom on television?

For all the cable channel's growth, Bolster saw the audience doubling again within three years. He was working on plans to upgrade the network's Website. He was thinking about twenty-four-hour coverage now that the major exchanges were considering all-day trading, although in truth the network already covered round-the-clock trading on Instinet, the electronic operation owned by Reuters, and in Europe and Asia, where CNBC was also on the air. Bolster saw a grand convergence with the Internet in which the network would report and fact-check the babble in the market chat rooms that, accurate or not, often moved stocks.

He was also quietly plotting to create a virtual stock market of his own. The New York Stock Exchange was furious about the idea, but Bolster saw it as inevitable. He was trying to launch CNBC-2, a digital network that would essentially enable any individual to trade stocks directly with another, without a middleman, and to do so at any hour of the day or night. By working with online brokerages, Bolster wanted to create a whole new ticker of real-time prices. If you wanted to buy General Electric at 21 and saw that price on the screen, you would execute the trade online and instantly own the stock at 21—no delays, no calling your broker, no frustrating rise in the price.

But Bolster was facing plenty of competition. Small online firms— some of them backed by the likes of Bear Stearns, PaineWebber, Merrill Lynch, and Morgan Stanley—were already facilitating all-hours trading on the Internet. The Nasdaq was considering tripling its hours, from 5:00 A.M. to midnight, to accommodate the growing demand. Bolster was having trouble putting together the deal, but he had no doubt that CNBC-2 would become a reality.

Even as Bolster was planning for the future, he felt compelled to shore up the past. He came to realize that CNBC had no history, not a scrap of paper on anything that had happened before its 1989 launch. That was one reason he had struck an alliance with *The Wall Street Journal,* which was costing the network big bucks. Not only did the deal enable him to bring on reporters for the *Journal* and its sister publication, *Barron's,* and get the first word on their scoops, but it also gave the network access to the newspaper's vast archives. And if some of the Dow Jones prestige rubbed off, that could only help establish CNBC as a brand name in the global marketplace.

Bolster and his staff were also enamored of CNBC's status as a pop culture icon. When the network was mentioned in the HBO series *The Sopranos,* Ron Insana was so thrilled that he showed a clip on the air. The blue-and-white stock ticker that CNBC ran along the bottom of the screen, even during commercials, was becoming instantly recognizable. One Saturday, Bruno Cohen, CNBC's senior vice president, called a colleague at home. "You're not going to believe the cover of *The New York Times Magazine,*" he said. There was a picture of the blue-and-white ticker, a cause for celebration, even though the article had nothing to do with CNBC.

For all its flash and dash, the network still had to deliver the financial nuts and bolts. Traders would call and complain if CNBC didn't regularly run charts showing the price of futures for soybeans, orange juice, and pork bellies. And the network was trying to cash in on a no-nonsense advertising slogan: "Profit from it."

Sometimes the CNBC gang joined in the speculative sweepstakes. Maria Bartiromo informed viewers from the stock exchange one morning that her sources were talking up a firm called LSI Logic, which was being featured at a Goldman Sachs technology conference: "They believe LSI Logic will give a real bullish presentation . . . and we'll see people bidding up the stock." But LSI finished the day down $^{11}/_{16}$.

CNBC also served as an electronic billboard for reports by other news outlets. The stock of Novell, a computer software firm, jumped 15 percent after Bartiromo touted a forthcoming article in *Barron's* in which an analyst said that the stock could quadruple in five years. And sometimes a stock would pop on the mere expectation that a company would engage in some positive spinning. Dell Computer rose 6 percent after Bartiromo reported that an analysts' meeting was being held in two days and that Dell was expected to make an "upbeat presentation."

Government officials and corporate leaders alike were acutely aware of the network's impact. Gene Sperling, the White House economic adviser, and Alexis Herman, the Labor secretary, frequently did live shots on CNBC. And anyone connected to the business world saw it as a great vehicle—one that, if you were putting together a megadeal, simply could not be avoided. When Goodyear struck an alliance with Japan's Sumitomo Rubber Industries in February 1999, the news was broken on CNBC's prime-time newscast, *Business Center,* by a *Wall Street Journal* reporter. The next morning, on CNBC's *Market Watch,* Goodyear Chairman Sam Gibara was there to talk up the deal.

One week later, the *Journal* and *USA Today* broke the news that Lycos, a fast-growing Internet portal site, was merging with USA Networks, owner of the Home Shopping Network. Barry Diller, the high-profile chairman of USA Networks, and Robert Davis, the head of Lycos, showed up on CNBC's *Power Lunch* to tout the deal. "We can put the pieces together in a way that frankly competitors can only dream about," Diller said. Host Bill Griffeth called him a "visionary." When Griffeth asked why Lycos's stock was dropping, Davis said it would take time for investors to understand the complicated deal. Unfortunately for Davis, the stock sank by 27 percent over the next week.

The network injected a sense of drama into seemingly mundane events. At precisely 8:30 A.M. on the morning of February 5, 1999, correspondent Rob Reynolds broke into regular programming from outside the Labor Department to announce that the unemployment rate was unchanged at 4.3 percent. In other words, nothing much had happened. But with music blaring in the background, CNBC started hopscotching from one correspondent to another, as if it were covering the Persian Gulf War. "The broader stock market is reacting negatively to the latest unemployment numbers," shouted Maria Bartiromo from the floor of the stock exchange, though how she could be so certain seconds after the announcement was unclear. Within two hours, the Dow was up 33.

CNBC had a laser-like focus. When the Senate was debating the articles of impeachment against President Clinton, Ron Insana asked Art Cashin, a gruff PaineWebber trader on the floor of the New York Stock Exchange, about the likely impact on the market. "The market's kind of shrugged this off," Cashin replied. Traders were more worried about Alan Greenspan testifying about banking reform the next day, and "we're going to be biting our nails on that one."

Whatever its foibles, CNBC had become an indispensable means of communication, as much a part of Wall Street's circulatory system as the telephone. For Faber, Haines, Bolster, and the rest, this power was daunting at times, for there was no playbook on what they were doing. No one had ever run a network whose every sniffle could give the market chills while the Dow was dropping 2,000 points. They had to make it up as they went along.

❏   ❏   ❏

Of all the network's anchors and reporters, Ron Insana usually looked the most worried. That may have been because he knew more than anyone else. Insana was a walking business encyclopedia who could explain market movements by crisply surveying the global scene, from Argentine currency devaluation to the price of gold to China's ongoing bid to join the World Trade Organization.

And yet Insana, thirty-seven, was largely self-taught. He had gotten his start in 1984 at the Financial News Network, which hired him for fifty dollars a day out of California State University at Northridge. At the time, he knew almost nothing about finance. The FNN anchors, Bill Griffeth and Sue Herera, would ring a bell for him to bring their scripts.

Insana lost his job soon afterward when FNN laid off 85 percent of its staff, but returned four months later as a producer. The skeleton staff worked insane hours, and when both Griffeth and Herera called in sick one day, Insana was put on the air. Three months later, he had his own show. He would spin out convoluted sentences, sometimes stopping himself abruptly when he realized he didn't know what he was talking about. Fortunately, almost no one was watching.

Insana became managing editor as the network was mired in bankruptcy. On the same day that he hired a stockbroker named Joe Kernen as an on-air correspondent, he was told that he had to rescind the offer for financial reasons. Insana refused because Kernen had already quit his job. The collapse of FNN was depressing, but Insana felt he had to soldier on till the end. In 1991, when CNBC bought the network and picked up Insana (along with Kernen and Griffeth; Herera had jumped earlier), there was some resentment among his new colleagues that he was suddenly anchoring three hours a day. Insana later started a show called *Inside Opinion* and frequently visited Washington to talk to movers and shakers. He and the rest of the network were crushed by the O. J. Simpson trial, when few cable viewers seemed interested in watching business news. But the bull market started taking off just as Insana launched his signature program, *Street Signs*. The show covered the last two hours of Wall Street trading, which Insana likened to the fourth quarter of a Knicks basketball game.

Despite his sober, understated style, Insana was always working the phones, even on the set during commercials, and had developed an incredible network of sources. He talked to big-time traders like Stanley Druckenmiller, George Soros's right-hand man, and Julian Robertson, head honcho at the huge hedge fund Tiger Management. He visited secretly with such senior government officials as Treasury Secretary Robert Rubin. He was hardly a glamorous figure, but he spoke with such authority that CNBC's viewers didn't care.

Insana's ability to vacuum up inside intelligence in New York and Washington sometimes presented him with tricky decisions. One morning in February 1999, he was sitting at his cramped corner desk at the far end of the Fort Lee newsroom when the phone rang. It was a trader, a plugged-in fellow who had been one of Insana's best sources for years. And he had a red-hot tip.

The man was convinced that Chase Manhattan was angling to buy Morgan Stanley Dean Witter, the New York megabank eyeing one of the bluest of Wall Street's blue-chip investment firms. And that tantalizing tidbit presented Insana with an all-too-familiar dilemma.

Insana knew that his trader pal was almost always on the money. The way that inside information flowed through these hedge-fund firms was phenomenal. They knew everything, made reporters look like goddamn amateurs. They were desperately hungry for information, since they were gambling with millions, even billions of dollars. The stakes were enormous. Insana would never forget how oil prices shot up in 1990 before anyone knew that Saddam Hussein was sending troops into Kuwait. The traders always knew.

At the same time, Insana realized that CNBC had become a huge megaphone with immense power to move the markets. And that power, in Insana's view, called for considerable caution. The merest mention that Morgan Stanley was a possible takeover target would boost the stock within seconds. If the tip wasn't true, then it would be irresponsible for the network to air it. And even the best traders sometimes found themselves trafficking in false information. They bobbed along on a swirling sea of rumors and speculation that sometimes swept them in the wrong direction. Insana called an official at Morgan Stanley, who denied off-the-record that any merger was brewing.

Insana was certain that company executives would not deliberately lie to him or steer him off a valid story. If it were true, they would simply say no comment. Insana didn't want to be responsible for spreading the rumor and moving the stock. Instead, he passed the information to David Faber for further checking.

But the rumor was clearly out there. Within hours, Morgan's stock had jumped four points. Everything turned on perception in this business. Now that the stock was moving, Insana felt that the network had an obligation to acknowledge the rumor and try to knock it down. He told viewers of the buzz about Chase and Morgan Stanley and said that both companies had denied any merger talks. The market reacted to a million such blips a day. Sometimes you couldn't swim against the rumor tide.

4

1 0K RUN

THE holy grail of financial journalism, the obsession that drove the coverage and infused virtually every story, was predicting the direction of the Dow.

Whatever the topic—interest rates, unemployment, housing starts, producer prices, corporate profits—the subtext was the impact on the market. Would the latest news, congealed wisdom, or stray rumor bump stocks up or knock them down? No one really knew, of course, but every purchase or sale of a stock or bond was in some sense a bet on where the market was headed. And while the Dow Jones Industrial Average was an unrepresentative basket of thirty old-line stocks, it had become the preeminent symbol of Wall Street itself.

On the morning of March 5, 1999, *Squawk Box* was touting a big day on the Street. The Dow had jumped 191 points the day before, and the premarket indicators, such as futures contracts that gambled on the direction of the S & P 500, were headed way up.

"It will be like a moon shot at the open," Mark Haines said on *Squawk*. "It will literally take off like a rocket."

He was right. The Dow soared 200 points in less than half an hour. Brokers everywhere tried to cope with the surge. Jim Cramer wanted to put some chips on the table on such a big day, but not at these dramatically higher prices. He bought some aluminum and drug stocks, but that was about it. "Find me something that isn't up!" he yelled at his staff.

The momentum never slowed. The Dow closed up 268 points, carrying the average to a new record of 9,736. Joe Kernen cackled that the bears who had been calling for a further downturn "are going to squirm, are going to weasel their way out of it."

"Are you cranky?" anchor Sue Herera asked him. "Maybe you need a spa day."

The following Monday, Mark Haines slipped on his glasses and read the Friday assessment of one Wall Street analyst who had been calling for a 5 to 10 percent drop in the Dow, the latter figure euphemistically known among the pros as a "correction." While Haines read the quotes, Joe Kernen moved his mouth from side to side, mimicking someone talking out of both sides.

" 'Before the stock market is able to mount a sustainable advance, it must unwind the excesses created during the October–February advance,' " Haines said in his most condescending voice. " 'To date we believe the sentiment is still too optimistic and the breadth too negative. . . . Hopefully this process will unfold with the least amount of damage possible.' "

Haines paused a beat. "I would say up 268 is the least damage possible," he said. He did not name the analyst he was quoting. It was Ralph Acampora, the usually bullish Prudential analyst.

Haines was determined not to mention Acampora's name on *Squawk*. The man had been wrong at every major turning point in the market, he felt. The previous summer, Haines had replayed some of Acampora's predictions, complete with bull and bear sounds. Acampora was so upset at this treatment that he met with CNBC's vice president, Bruno Cohen, to complain. Haines felt that Acampora had pushed the panic button in October 1998, predicting that the Dow could drop as low as 6,500. He was convinced that Acampora's record stunk, but his criticism would remain veiled, discernible only to other market professionals.

"What baffles me is why anyone pays attention to these gurus," Haines told his viewers. Of course, CNBC had helped make them famous by constantly putting them on the air.

Acampora soon softened his stance. "We honestly did not expect a gain of 460 points between Thursday and Friday, but so be it," he wrote investors. "We will NEVER fight the tape."

On March 11, the unemployment rate rose slightly, from 4.3 to 4.4 percent. Wall Street perversely viewed this as good news, since more people out of work meant less chance of resurgent inflation, which could lead to higher interest rates, which could hurt the market. The Dow shot up again, to a record 9,897.

As if someone had thrown a switch, the media were suddenly seized by "Dow 10,000" fever. Everyone wanted to be a part of this historic moment for the Big Board. The top CNBC anchors were suddenly in demand by those who needed instant experts, even on the nighttime portion of CNBC's schedule, which was usually devoted to White House scandals and political argument. Maria Bartiromo popped up on Geraldo Rivera's evening program.

Would the Dow reach the magic mark the next day? "It really is anybody's guess," Bartiromo said. "Most of the experts I've spoken with really do believe we'll see Dow 10,000 very soon."

Everyone seemed to be a market authority. Rivera said he'd been talking to an investment banker friend, and "he tells me that this is a bubble and the bubble's going to pop."

Bartiromo was unfazed. "If I don't put my money in the stock market, where do I put it? In 3 percent CDs? That's just not very convincing."

The next morning, Ron Insana was chewing the fat with radio host Don Imus. How many stocks, Imus wondered, were listed on the New York Stock Exchange? Three thousand? Insana said it was around forty-five hundred.

"Do you know specifically, big business guru from CNBC?" Imus demanded.

Five minutes later Insana was on the *Today* show, where reporter Ann Curry pressed him for a prediction—as if anyone could predict the market.

"Is the Dow going to break 10,000?" she asked.

"Well, it has a shot," Insana said, ducking.

Curry was insistent: "You think it's going to happen?"

"I think it's indeed a possibility."

A few minutes later Insana was back on *Imus,* belatedly reporting that 3,150 companies were listed on the exchange. Imus said it was "humiliating" that a "nitwit radio host" knew the answer and Insana didn't. Insana began to explain. "You're trying to weasel out of a bogus answer," Imus barked.

The media seemed to assume that mere adrenaline would power the market into five-digit territory. But journalists tended to forget that at bottom the Dow Jones Industrial Average is an amalgamation of millions of individual financial decisions. As it turned out, several big companies had bad days on March 12, and the Dow dropped 27 points.

At 8:00 A.M. the next Tuesday, March 16, a colleague passed Ron Insana in the hall. "You think it's today, Ron?" he asked.

"In the morning," Insana said. CNBC was once again on Dow 10,000 alert. Insana was ready to do a live network cut-in for NBC if the magic moment arrived. He knew that this was mainly psychological, that in fact the recent market rally had been led by relatively few stocks. But the Dow had been created 103 years earlier, when it was launched at 41 points, and had bottomed out at 774 as recently as 1982. Ten thousand would be a piece of history.

"I certainly hope it happens soon, because I'm getting real tired of all this talk about it," Haines said on *Squawk Box.*

The Dow opened at 9:30 at 9,958. Forty-two points to go. Andy Hoffman, the producer of *Street Signs,* Insana's afternoon program, knew that the first real indication would come when Union Carbide, a Dow stock that had been buoyed by good news, began to rise. Each dollar increase in one of the thirty Dow stocks moved the average up four points.

At 9:40 the Dow was up 12. Five minutes later, up 20. Union Carbide opened—up 2½. In the control room, Matt Quayle killed the next set of commercials—an expensive decision—and sent word to newscaster Mary Civiello, who was already miked up, that he was axing the news update. On the floor of the New York Stock Exchange, Maria Bartiromo was laughing, seemingly giddy. The Dow was at 9,990. Mark Haines noted that the Dow had broken 8,000 and 9,000 on *Squawk Box;* the show had only minutes to go.

Andy Hoffman was the first to shout that the milestone had been reached. He saw 10,001 on his Bridge stock-tracking computer half a minute before CNBC's on-screen graphics caught up.

"Dow Crosses 10,000 First Time Ever" was plastered across the screen. The traders were cheering. Just down the hall, Insana was live on NBC. "The Dow made it into the record books on this Tuesday morning," he declared.

By the time Insana finished his report, the Dow had fallen back into four-digit range. The euphoria had lasted less than a minute, as if to underscore the market's fragility and the arbitrary nature of the event.

Mark Haines had left the set to tape a promo for the next morning's show. "That was such an obvious piece of manipulation it was ridiculous," Haines told the cameraman. "They got that sucker a point over 10,000. The big boys paid fifty cents more for a few shares."

Haines looked into the camera: "The question becomes, can we stay over 10,000 and how far above it. We'll talk that over with Jim Cramer, our guest host."

Two seconds too long. "Can we stay over 10,000? Jim Cramer will be our guest host."

Still too long. Haines nailed it on the fourth try, then slipped on a Fila jacket and headed for the elevator.

"I have to inhale some nicotine," he said.

An hour later, Ralph Acampora, whom Haines so openly disdained, was back on CNBC, having already praised the record at CNNfn. Shedding his recent pessimism, Acampora said that the Dow would go "a lot higher. I've been thinking about 10,000 for a year and a half now."

"He's backtracking already," said Matt Quayle. Acampora, he felt, had created his own monster. He loved making bold predictions but didn't like the heat when they turned sour.

The grind was just beginning for Ellen Egeth, CNBC's chief booker. This was her worst possible nightmare. The network was planning a 3½-hour special at 4:00 P.M., but only if the Dow closed above 10,000. That meant every producer had to book two separate shows, depending on how the market did in the next few hours.

Egeth had lined up Acampora and Mary Farrell of PaineWebber. Abby Joseph Cohen, the super-bullish analyst from Goldman Sachs, was late in confirming, as usual. Laszlo Biryini of Deutsche Bank had been willing to do the special last week, but now he was skiing in Vermont. Egeth had been going through this for four days, checking in with fund managers and analysts who had busy schedules and plenty of clients. She had reserved studio time in places like Boca Raton for top analysts who were on vacation. She had even arranged for reporter Garrett Glaser to drive to Chicopee, Massachusetts, so that he could show the big 10,000 headline in *The Wall Street Journal* as it came rolling off the presses. But since the drive took several hours, they kept having to bring Glaser back after he'd left as the blue-chip index fell short.

The analysts and money managers, meanwhile, were swamped with media requests. When the Dow broke 8,000, only CNBC had done a special, but dozens of news organizations were swarming around the 10,000 story. The Dow had become huge and television had turned the analysts into celebrities. Egeth was stuck in a perpetual *Groundhog Day,* repeating the exercise until there was a record close. It felt like her own personal hell. But today, mercifully, could be the day.

No such luck. For all the advance hype, the Big Board closed down 28, at 9,930. The morning's celebration was a mirage. Ellen Egeth would have to go through the same drill tomorrow. And the next day. And the day after that.

That Thursday, March 18, sure looked like the day. At 3:50 P.M., the Dow hit 10,000, then dropped below 9,985, then made a final surge in the last five minutes of trading. Peter Kann, the chairman of Dow Jones, which created and still owned the index, was on hand for the big moment. Mark Haines, filling in on *Street Signs,* was again calling the play-by-play.

"Here comes the closing thirty seconds," he announced. At the 4:00 P.M. bell, the Dow had just gotten back over the magic hurdle. But as traders cheered and handed out 10,000 hats, Haines knew they were in overtime. "I don't want to be a party pooper here, but this is not over," he said.

Even as Bill Griffeth, ready to host *Market Wrap,* held two scripts in his hand—one for the regular show, a thicker one for the big special—the Dow teetered back and forth as stock exchange computers registered the final trades of the last few minutes. The tension was palpable as the number on the big board, like an odometer in reverse, slipped back to 9,997.

Ellen Egeth's special was canceled again. She wanted it to happen so badly, just wanted the 10K watch to be over. The absurdity of the entire enterprise—a major media blowout hinging on three lousy points on the Dow—was suddenly clear. What's more, everyone knew that the Dow was hardly an accurate reflection of the market. The thirty Dow stocks, heavily weighted with industrial companies, were a throwback to an earlier America. There was no Microsoft or Amazon; the high-tech revolution had largely bypassed the venerable Dow. Hundreds of funds had been set up to mimic the S & P 500, which represented more than three-quarters of the market's valuation and was the benchmark by which money managers were measured. But the Dow was a brand name, the one market index known around the world, and the media loved symbolic moments. CNBC would have to wait for another chance to celebrate.

❑   ❑   ❑

Ralph Acampora didn't want to move markets. He had never quite grown accustomed to the relentless media attention, to the way his every utterance seemed to send the Dow in motion. He saw himself as just a little guy, the son of a Bronx truck driver—although one who had mastered the art of technical analysis during a thirty-three-year Wall Street career.

The problem was that most journalists, most of the people who interviewed him on television, didn't have a clue about technical analysis. From his small office at Prudential Securities, in a tower overlooking the Staten Island Ferry Terminal, Acampora buried himself with reports and research, diagnosing the statistical guts of the market. His stature had soared back in 1995, when he produced a detailed report called "Dow 7000"—a prediction that was so far off the charts, with the Dow bouncing around 4,500, that his very reputation, and that of Prudential, were squarely on the line. But the market proceeded to climb to breathtaking heights, to 7,000, 8,000, 9,000, and Acampora became known as Wall Street's raging bull, the guy who kept setting new targets that would soon be shattered.

Still, he was only human. He had grimaced on CNBC when Ron Insana called him a guru. The danger, he felt, was that the media put gurus up on a pedestal, built them up as larger-than-life figures, and invariably tried to tear them down. Journalists often turned the investment business into a circus. This was serious stuff, this was people's retirement money. Acampora wasn't telling average folks what to buy, he was just providing useful information that they should discuss with their financial advisers. But that often got lost amid the screaming headlines.

Now that he was a big Wall Street name, Acampora, fifty-seven, saw himself as media meat. What he said was often misinterpreted, misquoted, or subjected to someone else's spin. On the morning of February 8, he had gotten on the weekly conference call with 6,000 Prudential brokers and told them that he was looking for a 5 to 10 percent correction in the Dow from its high the previous month. He knew that they would all tell their clients, and that it would quickly leak to the press. Sometimes he felt like the place was bugged. What Acampora did not anticipate was that it would be erroneously reported that he was looking for as much as a 15 percent correction. Even Ron Insana had missed the important point that his call was based on the year's high, not the current Dow Jones average. "Ralph Acampora confirmed to me this morning that he was looking for a 5 to 10 percent correction in the stock market," Insana told viewers on CNBC. With the market down 45 points by early afternoon, Insana said, "It looks like Ralph Acampora had an effect on the Dow."

A couple of weeks earlier, one of the financial wires had reported that Acampora had said the Dow would break 12,000 in 1999. Completely, totally false.

"You know what you did to me?" Acampora asked the reporter, who claimed that he had gotten the information from another Prudential executive.

"You don't understand the pressure we're under to get the story," the reporter explained. The journalists just seemed to hover over him, searching for a scrap of news. Now Acampora knew how Alan Greenspan felt.

More than a year earlier, Acampora had had breakfast with Hardwick Simmons, the Prudential chairman. Wick, I'm becoming too visible, Acampora said. It's a little scary. If I make a negative call, it could hurt the firm's revenues.

That's my problem, not yours, Simmons replied. You're here to make the right call for our clients.

Acampora was a market timer. That was what he was paid to do. It was all too easy for some reporter to pick out this or that prediction from the past and say it didn't pan out. Acampora had to adjust his forecasts to rapidly swirling conditions so that Prudential's clients would not miss a big run-up in the market and could get out before things turned sour.

There were benefits to the media exposure, of course. Acampora's booming voice was now regularly heard on *Wall Street Week,* on CNBC, on CNNfn. He had been on the *Today* show and was often quoted in *The Wall Street Journal, Barron's, Business Week.* He was featured in TV commercials for Prudential funds. Acampora urged all his colleagues to get on television if they could. He used the media as much as they used him.

But what the television commentators sometimes failed to grasp is that technical analysis took time. Acampora had to gauge the market's history, its support and resistance levels. He relied in part on *Investors Intelligence,* a newsletter published by a man in suburban New Rochelle who reported the leanings of analysts from 150 other newsletters. When Acampora was writing the "Dow 7000" report, he had spent six weeks in the public library, poring over four years of copies of *The Wall Street Journal.* He had cofounded the Market Technicians Association three decades earlier, and taught technical analysis each Monday night at the New York Institute of Finance. And soon Acampora was reaping the benefits. He began driving a red sports car with a Dow 7000 license plate. And he spent considerable time on the road, drawing overflow crowds for his flashy presentations.

"Buy more—that's my whole premise. Up is good, folks," he told a Long Island audience in 1997.

During the same period, a crowd in Woodland Hills, California, gasped as Acampora used an overhead projector to flash the year 2006—followed by foot-high yellow letters calling for a Dow 18,500. "I'm glad you're a little excited," he deadpanned.

Occasionally Acampora worried about how to step off the up escalator without wrecking the gears. He asked Maria Bartiromo for advice over drinks in her Manhattan apartment. He was afraid that for him to make a bearish declaration would be construed as a major event.

"I think this is much worse than people know," Acampora told her. "I have to baby-step my way into being bearish." Bartiromo agreed that it wouldn't be a bad idea to float little trial balloons, to gradually signal his intentions. Acampora was pleased when she told viewers that he was turning negative on the market.

The press often paired Acampora with Abby Joseph Cohen, the high-profile, auburn-haired Goldman Sachs analyst who, as every profile dutifully noted, still took the bus to her office from her home in Queens. Cohen was not a technical analyst, but she had developed a "Supertanker America" thesis, one that saw the country's economy as so mighty that it could sail through all kinds of obstacles and steer the market ever higher. In 1996, the mere rumor that Cohen was about to issue a bearish report sparked a sharp selloff, prompting her to quickly arrange a conference call to deny the rumor, which sent the Dow back into positive territory.

"Ralphy and Abby," the papers sometimes called them. They worked in the same building, but they had never met. As the bull market aged, Acampora saw trouble on the horizon. Stocks couldn't go up forever. One of them had to blink first. He didn't want it to be him.

Finally, Acampora felt that he had no choice. On the morning of August 4, 1998, he turned bearish. He declared that the Dow could drop 20 percent, to as low as 7,400. Cohen wasn't budging from her bullish prediction for a 9,300 Dow by year's end. He was all alone. It was the hardest thing he had had to do since putting his beloved dog to sleep when he was twelve. When Acampora was forecasting a higher and higher Dow, everybody loved him. Everybody wanted to get rich. But no one wanted to hear bad news. Within half an hour, the Dow had dropped more than 90 points. By day's end it was down 299. Things were about to get ugly.

Acampora had been on *Street Signs* the day before and had given no hint of his dramatic call. Now Insana called and pressed him to come back, which he did.

"It isn't just one day, Ron," Acampora explained. "I think we're in the beginning of something that's bigger than I thought."

"Ralph, to be fair to our viewers who have called and contributed their thoughts, they're a little miffed," Insana said. "They felt you waffled on the market call."

"I've been a raging bull for three and a half years," Acampora replied.

"I have to say this is the worst combination I've seen in the last three and a half years. When I put it all together you're talking about a three-and-a-half-year-old bull market that's very tired. . . . Now, it's a very difficult call for me to make because I know everybody is watching me and everybody wants to be bullish. No one wants to be bullish more than I do, but when the facts come to the fore and we see that deterioration, I have to call it as I see it."

Acampora couldn't sleep that night. He didn't get on the Prudential conference call the next morning. For six weeks, he didn't talk to the press. *Fortune* ran a piece wondering whether he had been gagged. The truth was that he didn't want to hurt the market further. He needed to stay out of the limelight.

No matter; the limelight found him. As the market sank, *Time* magazine declared him one of its weekly winners, saying: "Prudential's bear looks good now, as pressure mounts on Goldman's Abby ('Bull') Cohen."

Hardwick Simmons phoned from the West Coast. "Great call," he said.

Acampora felt he had nailed it on the head. Over the next two months, the Dow declined to under 7,500, precisely the correction he had envisioned. On October 8, as the market hit bottom, he remained bearish, saying the Dow could now drop as low as 6,500. That was a mistake. But he reversed course a few days later as the Fed cut interest rates, and the slump was over.

Of course, Acampora had also predicted that the Dow could recover by the end of 1998 to just over 8,000, failing to see that it would roar back past the 9,000 level. He left out that part of the prediction when he boasted about calling the 20 percent slump. In similar fashion, at the beginning of 1998 he had predicted a year-end close of 7,300; then upped the ante to a year-end target of 10,000; that, too, was rendered inoperative by subsequent forecasts. *The Wall Street Journal* drily noted that Acampora had "modified his views often enough to make it hard to say exactly how correct his forecasts have been."

Being a rampaging bull, he was learning, was fun, exhilarating; being a growling bear often brought you abuse, as if you were rooting for the market to tank. After his February 1999 call for a 5 to 10 percent correction, Acampora felt an enormous amount of pressure. Suddenly, without warning, he got a huge wave of angry e-mail messages. He tried to answer each one, to explain his position, but it was downright disheartening.

Only later did Acampora learn that Jim Cramer had been whipping up sentiment against him in his *TheStreet.com* column. "Now we have to begin an Acampora watch. . . . How-many-days-till-Acampora-gets-back-on-the-bull," Cramer had written. Then he had the gall to make this appeal: "When it happens, you know what you ought to do? Send him a nasty e-mail."

Acampora was stunned. It was one thing to criticize him professionally, another to rally investors against him. This was a tough, tough business. It had taken him a long time to build up his credibility. It was amazing how quickly others on Wall Street could turn on someone.

The day after the latest run at Dow 10,000, Acampora was starting to feel the heat from his recent change of heart. Already, *TheStreet.com* was calling him Ralph "Make Me Poorer" and describing him as having "engaged in some Clintonesque waffling." The problem was that the Dow had jumped 700 points since he called for a 5 to 10 percent correction, and he had never quite explained the contradiction. Acampora had long been a regular on *Wall Street Week with Louis Rukeyser,* the venerable public television show that had been treating analysts with great politeness for a quarter-century. Acampora was one of Rukeyser's "elves," the little cartoon figures who received pluses and minuses depending on their record. But even the gentle Rukeyser felt compelled to ask Acampora "why you did so much jumping around in your predictions this past year—winding up, as it happens, with the fewest halos, only four, of all our elves."

Acampora calmly explained that he had made three market calls in the past six months—the big bear call the previous August, the call for a rebound in October and the prediction of a short-term correction in February. Left unspoken was that he had initially foreseen a possible slide to Dow 6,500 in October, and that his January call for a correction had essentially been wrong.

Rukeyser let him slide. "You are bullish again," he said.

"I have been since October," Acampora replied.

❏   ❏   ❏

Far from the high-rise towers and high-profile names of Wall Street, Ashok Kumar was one of an army of anonymous analysts, the hard-working grunts whose technical research provided a crucial check on the big corporate publicity machines. He was hardly a blue-chip member of a blue-chip firm. He lived in Minneapolis, not New York. He worked not for Goldman Sachs or Prudential or Morgan Stanley but for Piper Jaffray, a respected but second-tier brokerage that specialized more in research than investment banking. He was originally from India and spoke with a distinct accent.

But Kumar understood the guts of the computer business as well as anyone. Indeed, when he first came to the United States from the Indian Institute of Technology, he had worked as an engineer for Intel. He also had an MBA from Wharton, ran marathons, and worked twelve-hour days. But the thirty-four-year-old analyst had one other thing going for him: He was brutally honest. And that would land him in a heap of trouble.

Kumar did the unglamorous work of poring over public records, checking inventories, tracking shipments, and monitoring sales of personal computers. He began to develop a web of contacts in the companies he examined and throughout the industry. Thirty or forty analysts would track a major company such as Dell Computer and, within the tightly knit financial community, their views mattered. If they upgraded a stock, urging clients to buy it, or downgraded their rating to a "hold," that got noticed on Wall Street. What's more, the analysts were a vital resource for business journalists, who tapped them as quotable experts and used their work to appear more informed. The analysts' recommendations were delivered only to their clients, but in the information-starved environment of lower Manhattan, these were quickly leaked to CNBC or Bloomberg News or the Dow Jones wire.

There was a built-in tension in the relationship between financial analysts and the big corporations they covered. On the surface, the companies catered to the analysts, giving them regular access to senior executives and briefing them in conference calls with the CEO after each quarterly earnings report. The calls involved the usual spin, but they were also a measure of respect. Billions of dollars were riding on positive recommendations, and the corporate pressure on analysts to see things in the rosiest light was never far from the surface. Nearly everyone in the business re-membered how Janney Montgomery Scott had fired an analyst named Marvin Roffman after he told *The Wall Street Journal* he was pessimistic about Donald Trump's Taj Mahal casino—and Trump had threatened to sue the firm unless Roffman apologized or was dismissed. The brokerage house said that Roffman was axed for flouting company rules against unauthorized comments to news organizations, but analysts saw an un-mistakable message. Few wanted to get on a corporation's bad side and end up like Marvin Roffman.

In the summer of 1998, Kumar began to detect signs that the spectacu-lar growth of the computer industry was slowing down. He downgraded Gateway, the number four computer maker, from a "strong buy" to a "buy." Kumar notified his clients that "the long-term growth rate implicit in the current level of the stock price may be unrealistic." He concluded that Gateway's third-quarter earnings would fall short of expectations. When Kumar and an analyst at another firm issued their downgrades, Gateway's stock promptly dropped by 10 percent. Soon Kumar was feel-ing the pressure. During the next Gateway conference call, he found, management tightly controlled the situation so that he couldn't ask any questions. A couple of major portfolio managers called Kumar's boss, the research director at Piper Jaffray. If this guy doesn't stop pissing on the stock, they said, we'll yank our business. These were seasoned executives using every curse word in the book. Kumar stuck to his guns—indeed, Gateway's earnings came in even lower than he had predicted—but the danger of candid commentary was becoming clear.

That was just a prelude to what would unfold when he took on Dell. The Texas computer company was one of the darlings of Wall Street. For traders, Dell was more than just a stock; it was a religion. Dell had led the S & P 500 for three straight years, registering a staggering 4,600 percent gain. It was up by 220 percent in the past year. Dell was the stock that had bailed out plenty of struggling fund managers. But no company can sus-tain such phenomenal growth rates forever, and Kumar believed that most analysts' reports on such companies were castrated. Those who worked for investment houses could not be oblivious to the fact that their bosses needed the business provided by the very companies they were paid to assess. Even for him, it was difficult to go against the grain. Sometimes Kumar was forced to doubt his own conclusions. What did he know that forty other analysts didn't?

Still, he had to believe in his numbers, and it was clear to him that Dell was not going to meet its fourth-quarter revenue projection of $5.3 billion. In fact, he told his clients that the company would fall at least $200 million short. He intended this as a yellow warning light, not a red flag. It was Dell's fault for jacking up expectations so high. His job was to provide Piper Jaffray's customers with balanced assessments.

Kumar had always enjoyed a warm relationship with Dell, but now it quickly went sour. He was bounced from a conference call with analysts and had to get a friend to quietly patch him in. Company founder Michael Dell denied this strong-arm tactic in an interview on CNBC, but it was clear that Kumar had fallen out of favor. He felt pained, even hurt, at being frozen out. There were clients who refused to talk to him because he had dared to take on Dell, the golden goose of the stock market. He was dismissed as a naysayer, a troublemaker. He produced tables filled with numbers to back up his projections, but nobody wanted to listen. These Dell investors were like flat-earthers. Kumar couldn't understand the hostility. What was the point of his job if he simply parroted the management line?

In early February 1999, Dell went public with its fourth-quarter results. Its $5.1 billion in revenue was indeed about $200 million below projections, just as Kumar had predicted. To be sure, Dell had had the sort of fabulous quarter about which most companies could only fantasize. Its fourth-quarter revenue was up 49 percent, its earnings up 38 percent. But in the pretzel logic of Wall Street, none of that mattered. Everything revolved around expectations; the good news was already built into the stock price. Analysts always set the next target, and there was intense pressure to "make the number," regardless of how high the bar had been raised. If the company fell short, the Street devalued the stock. Dell's stock dropped more than 7 points the next day, continuing a slide that had begun as the buzz about the impending news grew louder. The stock had fallen nearly 25 percent in just over two weeks, the biggest decline of any major high-tech company. Michael Dell was relentlessly upbeat on CNBC the next day, saying that "by any standard it was a great quarter, unless perhaps you were looking for a little more revenue." But his words did little to slow the decline.

Suddenly Ashok Kumar was in demand. Reporters were calling. He appeared on CNBC for the second time in two days. He was praised in *TheStreet.com.* He felt vindicated. There was a halo effect to being on CNBC; people thought you were a respected analyst. But Kumar knew he was getting the attention only because of Dell's high profile. If he were covering mid-sized companies, he could make a dozen astute calls in a row and nobody would notice. Everyone cared about Dell, and he was the man who had blown the whistle on the world's largest direct seller of personal computers.

Kumar didn't let the brief burst of media stardom go to his head. He understood the rhythm of these things. An analyst was only as good as his last call. Soon that would be old news. If he made a bad call the next time out, he was toast.

❏   ❏   ❏

The market continued its roller-coaster ride after flirting with Dow 10,000: down 218 one day, up 169 a few days later. But the overall trend was down, away from the magic number. Internet stocks, which had been leading a weak market, were slipping. Mark Haines began wearing a lucky striped shirt, as he had done during the brief fling with 10,000, but as the Dow dropped to 9,670, the superstition seemed absurd. "Mark, the striped shirt thing isn't working anymore," Matt Quayle told him.

After the Dow had been battered again, David Faber told Ron Insana during a commercial that traders were blaming CNBC for the 10,000 hype that they believed had triggered the latest downturn. "You're driving us nuts with 10,000," one told Faber. "You're creating a psychological barrier." It was amazing how much power these investors imputed to the talking heads.

One calming presence amid the choppy seas was Abby Joseph Cohen, the Goldman Sachs bull who almost never veered from her stand that the American economy—and therefore the market—was exceptionally strong. "If anything, we believe that corporate performance will be better in '99 than at the end of 1998," she said on CNN's *Moneyline*. Five days later, Cohen's reassuring visage peered out from *USA Today*. "The precondition is in place for ongoing good performance by the stock market," she said.

The next morning, Maria Bartiromo took to the airwaves with a scoop. "Abby Speaks," the screen said. Actually, it wasn't very earth-shattering. Cohen had told her sales force moments earlier that "this market has not changed, fundamentally." Bartiromo did report that Cohen had raised her market targets slightly, predicting a Dow 10,300 by year's end, up from 9,850. Such was Abby Cohen's clout that even when she was saying roughly the same thing she had said in a newspaper interview the day before, it was news.

The bombing of Yugoslavia began on Wednesday, March 24. NATO air strikes hit the country night after night, first in Kosovo, then in Belgrade itself. Hundreds of thousands of ethnic Albanian refugees poured into neighboring countries, a humanitarian tragedy commanding the world's attention.

Wall Street didn't much care. The market had finally reversed course and resumed its push toward five-digit territory. CNBC began devoting more time to live reports from the Balkans, speeches by President Clinton, updates from NBC correspondents at the White House and the Pentagon. This reflected an effort to give investors a brief glimpse of what was going on in the rest of the world; the network had even added a weatherman. Kevin Magee, who had joined CNBC from *Good Morning America,* once said that while he loved the business network, he wasn't sure it would tell him if the president had been assassinated. CNBC wanted to make sure viewers didn't surf off to other stations to find out about a war in Europe, or whether to carry a raincoat.

Five days after the bombing began, on Monday the 29th, the market was heading for a gain of more than 180 points. "It seems that Wall Street and much of the investing world has shrugged off what's been described as one of the worst attempts at genocide since World War II," Ron Insana said in amazement. Now the prize was in sight, and the cheerleading began in earnest. By 3:30 the Dow had hit 10,029, but quickly began to slip back.

"All right, the Dow is holding at 10,007 with just three minutes left," Insana said.

"10,006 and I've got my fingers crossed," said Joe Kernen.

"We'll see if we can hang onto it, Ron," said reporter Martha MacCallum from the floor of the exchange.

At 3:59, mindful of the previous photo finish, Insana declared: "Well, on the fourth try it does appear the Dow will close above 10,000. . . . It is possibly the Dow's date with destiny."

CNBC finally began its 3½-hour special, the one that Ellen Egeth had booked so many times before. Unfortunately for the network, its first few guests didn't sound terribly excited.

"It's just what thirty stocks have done," said Alan "Ace" Greenberg, the chairman of Bear Stearns. "I don't think it's that significant."

Ken Heebner of Capital Growth Management was also restrained. "I think this move through 10,000 is a cause for caution, not enthusiasm," he said.

But Ralph Acampora was not going to rain on the network's parade. Even though he was on vacation on a boat in the Caribbean, he made sure to seize the media moment. In a hastily arranged conference call with reporters, Acampora said, "I know everyone thinks the 10,000 level is just a number and a lot of people are discounting it." But, he added, "psychologically, it's an important number." No one asked him about his call for a 5 to 10 percent correction just a few weeks earlier. Within half an hour, Acampora was calling in to CNBC. "I'm so excited about this market," he declared. "I think we have a pretty good shot at a little over 11,000 by the end of the year."

The Wall Street Journal abandoned its usual format to devote the entire front page to the big, if hardly unexpected, day. "Dow Industrials Top 10,000; Longest Bull Market on Record Smashes a Historic Barrier," the banner headline said. The Heard on the Street column featured a color picture of Abby Joseph Cohen, who again praised the strength of the economy, and fresh quotes from Ralph Acampora. It was, of course, a bit of corporate boosterism for the *Journal* to go so hog wild over the index that had been invented by Charles Dow and was still owned by its parent company. But no one was unsportsmanlike enough to point that out.

5

BAD BLOOD

FOR all the billion-dollar bets, the limos lined up outside, the traders in $3,000 Italian suits barking into their cell phones, Wall Street often resembled nothing more than a snooty high school.

There were cliques, romances, whispered gossip that everyone was dying to know. And there were plenty of people who just plain didn't like each other.

Jim Cramer had a fairly long enemies list. He didn't like Ralph Acampora. He didn't like Dick Tofel of *The Wall Street Journal.* He especially didn't like Marty Peretz, who used to be one of his best friends. And he didn't like Alan Abelson, the veteran columnist and former editor of the Dow Jones magazine *Barron's.* Cramer had attacked him in perhaps thirty articles, saying that Abelson, one of the nation's biggest bears, had been wrong since the Dow was at 800 and that no one should listen to him.

"What I cannot stand," Cramer wrote in *TheStreet.com,* "is the arrogance of the man who leads off *Barron's* every week and the contempt with which he holds those of us who have been Right instead of Wrong! His scorn of those of us who have gotten it right and made money these last 15 years that he has been a bear is utterly contemptible. . . . Stop his ravings from polluting another year of financial journalism."

Cramer was pleased when his friend Sandra Ward, the mutual funds editor at *Barron's,* took on Barton Biggs, another of Wall Street's leading bears. At the end of 1998, Ward reported that Biggs was touting Morgan

Stanley's market funds in Europe, Africa, India, and Russia—but had personally bailed out of some of the funds shortly before they posted losses for the year. "Some people inside the firm say he's thinking of retiring . . . and since he's known mainly for his writing on the markets rather than for being right on them," Ward wrote, "maybe it's time."

Abelson went ballistic. Rather than backing his colleague, he rallied behind Biggs, an old friend who, as it happened, was a regular participant in the annual *Barron's* roundtable on the stock market hosted by Abelson. When Biggs showed up for the meeting, Abelson, who could not attend, had another editor, Kathryn Welling, read a letter from him apologizing to Biggs. Abelson called Ward's article "a gratuitous, unfounded smear," "witless, malevolent graffiti," and a piece of "adolescent posturing." Ward was furious, Welling soon resigned, and Cramer rushed to tell his friend Steve Brill, whose magazine ran a piece on the flap.

Abelson was tired of being skewered by Cramer. He saw Cramer as a figure of comic relief, a wacky trader whose view of stocks seemed to change second by second. Cramer was a typical product of this maniacal market on which almost everyone was way too bullish because they had no memory of stock market declines or were too lazy to read about the past. The man was a walking media bubble, and he would burst along with the market when stocks finally tanked. In his column, Abelson described Cramer the television personality as "an unfailing and formidable threat to coherence," and Cramer the writer as "a threat to objective journalism, since he's an unremitting practitioner of subjective journalism, with only one subject—himself." And as a hedge-fund manager, Cramer was "manifestly a threat to the financial well-being of his limited partners." He was, in short, "someone who never stops talking, but never says anything."

Cramer was determined to show up his critics, and he viewed *TheStreet.com* as a prime opportunity to do so. People had snickered when he started the Website and it began hemorrhaging money. But now, after three years of struggling to keep the operation afloat, Cramer felt that its moment had finally arrived. He and his team began negotiating with *The New York Times* as a potential investor while Cramer quietly plotted to take the firm public and cash in on the Internet gold rush. The situation was so sensitive that his lawyers argued over whether he could even continue to appear on *Squawk Box,* since federal regulators could construe anything he said on CNBC about *TheStreet.com* as an illegal attempt to talk up the stock before its debut. The attorneys finally agreed that it would arouse more suspicion if Cramer suddenly stayed off the show, but he was unusually subdued on the air.

Joining forces with the *Times* would bring Cramer the gloss of respectability he so fervently desired, and would reunite him with an old high school buddy, Martin Nisenholtz, who was running the paper's new-media operation. The *Times* offered to invest $15 million in *TheStreet.com,* but all in the form of free advertising. Cramer balked, convinced that the paper's executives should put up some cash to show that they were serious. The *Times* agreed to a payment of $3 million, and the deal was announced.

Mark Haines was amused to see his favorite rebel joining forces with the country's most prestigious newspaper. *"TheStreet.com* sells out to the establishment?" he cracked.

The next day, Cramer was ready to announce that *TheStreet.com* had filed papers to sell as much as $75 million in stock to the public. But the following morning, almost as a declaration of journalistic independence, the *Times* business section ran a tough piece on Cramer, noting that his hedge fund had barely turned a profit in 1998. His largest holdings, Bay View Capital and Fairchild Corporation, were down. To rub salt in the wounds, the article featured a mildly supportive quote from Marty Peretz—as if Peretz hadn't tried to bring his business crashing down in the first place!

The *Times* article did not escape Mark Haines's notice. "They give you $15 million with one hand and they smack you with the other," he said on *Squawk Box.*

Cramer was mortified. So he'd been in a slump for a few months. So he'd made mistakes. He was human. His average return over the last ten years had been 22 goddamn percent, but that had gotten lost in the fine print.

Karen said he had gotten so much good press that he was due for a few hits. "Take it like a man," she said.

Peretz, for his part, felt that Cramer was irrationally blaming him for all his woes. Though it was true that the *Times* reporter, Joseph Kahn, was the son of a journalist he knew well, Peretz was not responsible for planting the story. In fact, he had been quite cagey with the reporter. When Kahn had called to say that he was doing a story on Cramer's bad year, Peretz said that it was a mistake to compare Cramer's record to the Dow or the S & P because he invested in a much broader range of stocks.

Oh, said Kahn, so you're still a big backer of Jim?

"There were many superb hedge funds that did not have a good year last year," Peretz replied. He knew that Kahn would take that to mean that he had not pulled his money out of Cramer's hedge fund, though in fact he had, and he deliberately failed to set the record straight. That would enable him to disguise the ugly reality without telling a lie. Once the article had run, however, Peretz realized that Cramer was certain that he had leaked the damaging story to Kahn while somehow convincing him to hide the fact that Peretz had abandoned the fund.

A brilliant, irascible man with a tendency toward micromanagement—he even helped pick the summer interns at *The New Republic*—Peretz felt that it was Cramer who had wronged him. After all, he had first helped Cramer back in law school. He had given Cramer's hedge fund a sizable chunk of his and his wife's money, had talked him up to other investors, had said that he was smart and could be trusted. A number of Peretz's friends had invested with Cramer just on his say-so. Peretz got no money out of this; he was simply trying to help both Jim and his friends.

Cramer's complaint that Peretz had failed to put up his promised share when they launched *TheStreet.com* was, in Peretz's view, a complete fabrication. He had actually put up more than his share for a few months to help with the cash flow. And Cramer's belief that he had lobbied other investors to quit the hedge fund was utterly preposterous. Peretz had urged exactly one friend to bail out. The man had invested too high a percentage of his net worth, had come in entirely at Peretz's suggestion, and Peretz felt a responsibility to say that he was leaving the fund himself. He and Cramer had been having problems for a year and a half. He couldn't keep investing his money with someone to whom he no longer spoke.

Their relationship had deteriorated so badly that Cramer hadn't bothered to call Peretz before resigning as a trustee of some of the Peretz family trusts. Instead, Cramer had an assistant call one of Peretz's accountants to say that he was quitting. Cramer had claimed that he was no longer being consulted on the trusts, but what kind of move was that? He had pulled that stunt several months before Peretz quit the hedge fund. Then Peretz had gotten hold of a pair of e-mails that Cramer had sent to a colleague, disparaging Peretz and suggesting that he would soon be playing no role at all at *TheStreet.com*. That, Peretz believed, was typical of Cramer's behavior. His character dawned on you over time. He was very contemptuous of people. He did harsh things, and sometimes he would apologize and sometimes he wouldn't. This had been going on for far too long, and Peretz had had enough.

Whatever its origin, *The New York Times* piece gnawed at Cramer. He had never even had a traffic ticket, but he had been trying to live down the *SmartMoney* fiasco, and his reputation as a tout, for four years. Now he was being portrayed as a lousy trader by the very newspaper that had just become his partner. And there was a deeper problem as well. The whole premise of his financial writing was that he would bring the reader inside Wall Street and explain how the game worked. That meant he had to be candid about his setbacks as well as his triumphs. All these other financial hotshots pretended that they were never wrong, while Cramer advertised his screwups. There was a core group of fans who loved Cramer's honesty, but he was getting a ton of hostile e-mail from his critics.

The other day he had written a column about dumping his Abercrombie & Fitch stock. He loved the company, but was worried that it was due for a fall after a great run, so he had blown out of his last 20,000 shares. The stock promptly jumped 5 points. It was the kind of misjudgment that happened a million times a day. But his detractors saw it differently. "I can't believe he has the nerve to incessantly pontificate whilst doing so poorly," said one critic on the *Silicon Investor* Website. An e-mailer told him: Listen, man, I don't need you. Why should I listen to the idiot who sold Abercrombie?

The answer, Cramer felt, was simple. He wasn't trying to get anyone to buy or sell anything. He wasn't even accepting new customers for his hedge fund. He was merely trying to provide a window on the Street. If people didn't like what he had to say, they should go elsewhere.

Still, the criticism stung. Cramer had consciously muzzled himself on

Squawk Box. He was afraid of another WavePhore incident, and he had promised his wife that he wouldn't get into trouble. He told Mark Haines that he didn't want to discuss any more small stocks, didn't want to be blamed if he said something critical and they took a dive.

On the next *Squawk,* David Faber noticed Cramer's subdued demeanor and baited him on camera. "He's afraid. It's so sad," Faber said.

"You mean the fact that every major newspaper and magazine has taken a shot at me?" Cramer replied.

Faber, who had had his share of difficulties with Cramer, explained his outburst during a commercial. "I couldn't resist," he said. "I saw you just sitting there."

Cramer decided to beat a tactical retreat, to tone down his multimedia act. Maybe his detractors had a point. Maybe he had spread himself too thin. This, he believed, was what Marty Peretz had told the investors who had bailed, and it felt like an Achilles' heel. Cramer would no longer write for *Time,* for *GQ,* for *Brill's Content.* He would make no more TV appearances except for his biweekly stint on *Squawk.* That would be fine with CNBC, which was pressing him not to appear on other networks, and with Karen, who felt that all his outside commitments were cheating the family. Cramer would concentrate on running his hedge fund without all these distractions. This was a monumental concession for Jim Cramer, an anguished admission by the man who always felt that he could do it all.

But Cramer soon became indecisive and started changing his mind. Walter Isaacson, *Time*'s managing editor, urged Cramer not to give up the column. "You had a good year in '97 and you wrote twice as much," Isaacson told him. "You love writing!" Cramer agreed to remain a *Time* contributor.

He launched a full-scale review of what had gone wrong at his hedge fund in 1998. He felt misled by the executives at Hayes, the computer-modem maker, often screamed at them, and lost $10 million when the stock collapsed. Cramer lost another $18 million when Cendant stock plummeted after the company acknowledged accounting irregularities. These were terrible judgments, but they wouldn't have been any different if he had done less outside writing. Cramer was spending a considerable amount of energy justifying himself to himself.

He decided to fight back in the online magazine *Slate,* run by his longtime friend Michael Kinsley, who had been investing with Cramer (along with Brill and other selected journalists) since his days under Peretz as editor of *The New Republic*. In an article headlined "A Message to My Enemies," Cramer declared that the public would rather hear from managers with real money on the line than from journalists who were barred from investing in the stocks they wrote about. He was in the trenches, a forbidden zone for mere reporters. If trench warfare mattered, then people should want him to write. But Cramer wasn't content simply to defend his methods. He lashed out at his detractors as well. The "off-line press" was angry because he was invading their turf and wanted to see him fail. They wanted to drive a wedge between him and his partners. But he would not be silenced, not as long as the business community failed to repeal his First Amendment rights. He was not going away.

The spectacle, in the end, was embarrassing. Jim Cramer had turned bitter. His anger and defensiveness were consuming him. He stewed over the criticism even when he was playing with his kids on weekends. He started peppering his *TheStreet.com* columns with sardonic swipes at journalists, saying that most TV talking heads didn't know anything about business. He dismissed his critics as sanctimonious clowns. The wounds were still raw. When his stocks did well for a few days during the surge toward 10,000, Cramer couldn't resist telling his readers: "This keeps up, and *The New York Times* might have to write a story about me that says I am not a bum."

❑   ❑   ❑

Fifty miles from Wall Street, Christopher Byron was ensconced in the wood-paneled basement of his Westport, Connecticut, home, surrounded by four computers, one television tuned to CNBC, and a second set getting CNN. Byron openly disdained the stock market, the financial establishment, and much of the business press, and castigated them in his weekly column for *The New York Observer* (which was also carried on *TheStreet.com*) and in a weekly column for the MSNBC Website. He also appeared regularly on CNBC's *Power Lunch* and was preparing to launch a radio show with MSNBC, from the same basement, to be broadcast over the Internet.

At the moment, the financial columnist was reading a tantalizing e-mail message. "Brand new penny stock fraud alert for you to investigate," the header said.

Byron's anonymous correspondent wrote that the company in question was "secretly controlled by a Russian national . . . with strong ties to the Russian mafia." And, he said, the gentleman is under investigation by the SEC. If Byron were to dig into the matter, he would "find a much bigger and scarier story" than his last exposé.

This was how Byron got most of his leads these days, in wave upon wave of e-mail from his readers. It was the Internet that made it possible for Byron to wreak havoc on the broad array of stocks that he viewed with disfavor.

When Byron had worked as a top editor at *Forbes* in the 1980s, it would take his staff days to unearth the corporate filings at the SEC that he and his wife, Maria, could now access with three clicks of a mouse. It was the Net, and his high-speed cable modem, that enabled him to monitor the stock chat rooms, search the media archives on Nexis, exchange ideas with readers, and file his columns. He had commuted to Manhattan by train for twenty years, working for *Time, Forbes, New York,* and *Esquire,* and had hated it. Now he could shake Wall Street without leaving his sprawling house and swimming pool along the Saugatuck River, the area where he had grown up.

At fifty-four, Chris Byron sometimes looked like an aging motorcycle-gang member, driving his gray Porsche in a white T-shirt, gold necklace, and black pants, his dark hair slicked forward in a comb-over. And he relished his rebel status. Byron took on some of the biggest names in corporate America—Barry Diller, Ron Perelman, John Malone, Gerald Levin, Edgar Bronfman, Mort Zuckerman—and assailed them in unusually personal ways. He was constantly being threatened with lawsuits but had never actually been sued in his thirty-year career.

Most journalists, he believed, were intimidated by the notion of making enemies, of losing their all-important access. Byron didn't care. He really didn't give a damn if anyone returned his calls. He didn't need to be spun by the flacks. Big corporations had massive resources to shape and control their public image, and their top executives were as inaccessible as CIA agents. Byron felt that he had found a way around the propaganda machine by dusting public records for the fingerprints of these executives. He had even discovered that a Fifth Avenue stock promoter named Edward B. Williamson III was a convicted murderer who had also pleaded guilty in a stock case after an FBI sting two years earlier. Nobody had bothered to check.

You could find out almost anything by checking the financials. He had learned that from Jim Michaels, the longtime editor of *Forbes*. So what if they don't call you back, Michaels would say. These days, Byron felt, such grunt work was largely virgin territory. Most financial columnists didn't follow the paper trail. And yet the history of Wall Street disasters was replete with information that had been hidden from investors. Byron liked nothing more than to conduct a proctological exam on a company's balance sheet.

This single-minded, relentlessly negative approach had given Byron a terrible reputation on the Street. Corporate executives called him Doctor Death and often dodged his calls. A fact-checker for the *Observer* had just reported back on her conversation with an official from an Internet start-up whom Byron had interviewed. "The man is quaking," she said. These executives figured that Byron wasn't planning to write a favorable piece. He usually went for the jugular.

Byron even bit the corporate hand that fed him. Two years earlier, his *Observer* column had been syndicated to the Go2Net Network, a San Francisco Web operation that owned the *Silicon Investor* site. When the company went public, Byron criticized its stock as overpriced and said that nobody should buy it. When Go2Net officials asked whether such an attack was necessary and Byron refused to back down, his contract was canceled. (Go2Net said it was moving away from editorial content anyway.) Jim Cramer heard about the falling out and picked up Byron's column for *TheStreet.com*.

Sometimes Byron made mistakes, and he was quick to issue prominent corrections. On a story involving Lycos, he wrongly analyzed the documents on deadline. The next day, he called MSNBC in Redmond, Washington, posted a retraction on its site, and got a ton of positive e-mail. "Your effort to not only pull the article but to explain your actions (and humbly admit the flaws) was an exceptional effort," an Intel executive wrote. Admitting error, Byron felt, added to his credibility.

Byron credited some of his recent success to Arthur Carter, the owner of *The New York Observer,* whom he had known since the 1960s when Carter was running one of the first Wall Street boutique firms. During a vacation on Block Island, Carter had lured Byron from *Esquire* by asking him to start his Back of the Envelope column for the weekly newspaper. They would sit around for hours and debate the nuances of the stock market. More important, Carter always backed him up when the threatening letters arrived.

The phone rings. It is an SEC official calling Byron back to answer some questions on federal regulations. "So has this always been the rule?" Byron asks, scribbling with a pencil on a yellow pad. "It doesn't mean everyone is grandfathered in?" More scribbles. "And what's the penalty on Section J?"

Such nitty-gritty reporting enabled Byron to serve as a kind of early warning system for companies that were heading for trouble. Boston Chicken was a classic example. He had warned back in 1996 that the burgeoning fast-food chain "basically boils down to a clever new way to lose money" and would wind up in dire straits. Take out a second mortgage on your home and short Boston Chicken stock, he urged his readers. Company officials sent letters to the *Observer,* demanded a retraction, even complained that Byron had taken a cheap shot at their meat loaf by questioning just what was in it. Two years later, Boston Chicken declared bankruptcy and closed 16 percent of its restaurants.

Byron had also sounded the alarm on Planet Hollywood. Right after the glitzy restaurant chain went public and its stock hit nearly $30 a share, Byron said it was an absurd business built on hype and predicted that the stock would crash. In the first three months of 1999 it had lost nearly 90 percent of its value and was now selling for 65 cents a share.

Perhaps Byron's proudest moment came when he took on Livent, the movie-theater outfit founded with borrowed money by Canadian impresario Garth Drabinsky, who had backed such popular Broadway shows as *Ragtime* and *Showboat.* When Byron declared the company to be in trouble in February 1997, arguing that costs were growing faster than revenues, Drabinsky threatened to sue the *Observer.* But Livent declared bankruptcy in 1998, and federal prosecutors charged Drabinsky with fraud involving the alleged hiding of more than $60 million. Byron believed that he had given the feds a road map for the indictment. He felt vindicated.

In a way that sometimes sounded mean-spirited, the columnist didn't shy away from heaping invective on his favorite targets. One was Ron Perelman, dubbed the "Finagle King," or "FK" for short, who ran the Revlon cosmetics empire. "FK shuffled so much debt back and forth between Revlon and various other operations of his that it soon became impossible to figure out which of his companies were on the hook for how much to whom—save that by summer 1998 the debt load stood at more than $1.3 billion on Revlon's balance sheet alone," Byron wrote in April 1999. He predicted that Perelman would likely have to sell the company for "a huge and humiliating loss."

The cable czar whom Byron called "Dr." John Malone also came in for abuse that month for shifting $700 million from one company he controlled, Liberty Media, to another, TCI Music, so that the latter could issue stock. "TCI Music—the thing into which the Doc-ster dumped his dreck—is itself really a pathetic little operation," Byron wrote.

Of course, Byron could also be spectacularly wrong. When Yahoo! went public in 1996 at $13 a share, he insisted that the company would never fly. Three years later, Yahoo! stock, adjusted for splits, was selling for the equivalent of more than $900 a share.

That wrongheaded prediction was no accident, for Byron was down on most Internet stocks. Their prices, he believed, were crazy and reflected one of the great historic bubbles of the twentieth century. These second- and third-tier Net companies were trading on nothing but hype. A friend of his, a former provost at Boston University, had ignored Byron's warnings and quit his job to devote himself to day trading. The presence of millions of such traders had fueled the growth of the Net stocks on what Byron called "momentum investing," a phenomenon exploited by "Wall Street sharpies" and executives who deviously added a dot-com to their corporate names. Byron created what he called the "Internet Sucker's Index" to track the foolishness.

The trend was easy to see, Byron felt, although he may have become a doomsayer too early. But it was no mystery that most of these stocks were eventually going to blow up. For all the fancy talk about new forms of valuation, Byron believed, a company had to make money in the end. Yet America had seemingly become a nation of greedheads, interested only in what Maria Bartiromo or David Faber would say next on CNBC and how they could profit from it.

Byron didn't mind that people on the Street sometimes laughed at him. He was perfectly happy to climb out on a shaky limb, to predict that Amazon was so laden with debt that it was a disaster in the making, or that Yahoo! stood to lose half to three-quarters of its value.

Some critics viewed Chris Byron as a caustic crank, especially as investors made millions of dollars riding the Net escalator that Byron insisted would soon be thrown into reverse. But he felt there were now two full generations of amateur investors who didn't remember the way some stocks had plummeted in the 1960s and 1970s, let alone in the crash of 1987. In the fullness of time, Byron believed, his sky-is-falling rhetoric would be vindicated, just as he had been proven right on Boston Chicken and Planet Hollywood and Livent. The Internet had given him the powerful tools he needed and a mighty megaphone for his contrarian views, but he would not be seduced by its irrational economics. The self-appointed watchdog of Westport would keep raising a fuss from the bowels of his basement.

❑   ❑   ❑

Merger mania had taken over the market in the spring of 1999. Every major company seemed to be talking to every other company, or was rumored to be doing so. Investors could make a fortune if they guessed right and bought a firm's stock before news of the acquisition was confirmed. Deals were going down every week: BP Amoco and Arco. CBS and King World. USA Networks and Lycos. Sketchy press reports often turned out to be true. That was why so many traders read Gene Marcial's Inside Wall Street column in *Business Week*.

A mild-mannered man from Manila who spoke with a soft Filipino accent, Marcial had come to the United States in the 1960s and attended graduate school at New York University. He spent more than seven years at *The Wall Street Journal* as the junior member of a three-person team that produced the Heard on the Street and Abreast of the Market columns before joining *Business Week* in 1981.

Marcial, who was in his mid-fifties, loved being a columnist. The pay wasn't that great, but the psychological lift was enormous. He had no desire to do anything but write Inside Wall Street. As Marcial saw it, he got inside information from the big guys—mostly fund managers—and shared it with the little guys. He had no qualms writing about rumors and speculation, because that in part was what moved the market. If Marcial heard that two companies were talking, he wrote it. That didn't mean he was predicting a takeover, just reporting that he thought it was possible. He would often write that such-and-such a firm was "ripe for a buyout," or that "some pros" saw "a takeover target." His record on takeovers was pretty bad, but who could predict these things? Anything could happen. Traders made money on takeover speculation; his readers deserved the same information.

Everything depended on having a network of good sources. Without sources you were sunk, you were doomed. Marcial used his sources and they used him; that was how the game was played. It all came down to his judgment about what was newsworthy. One of Marcial's best sources in the 1980s had been Ivan Boesky, the most celebrated trader of the high-flying decade before he pleaded guilty to filing false documents and was barred from trading in American markets. Marcial believed that many traders engaged in similar conduct but that Boesky had made the mistake of getting caught. Boesky had called him when he got out of prison and they rekindled their friendship at the Peninsula Bar.

Sometimes readers who lost money by following the column wrote Marcial angry letters, accusing him of profiting from the information. In fact, he didn't own a single stock, not even a mutual fund, even though *Business Week* policy would have allowed such purchases after a column was published.

Marcial's pitch was simple. If a small- or medium-sized company was going to announce a takeover, he would ask the executives to hold the announcement. If they gave him the scoop, Marcial said, he would write it in such a way that the story didn't appear to be coming from them. If you just announce your deal, he explained, it won't make a splash. I can give you a double hit, an added visibility boost that will reach more investors. It was the same kind of pitch that Steve Lipin or David Faber often made to bigger companies, and just as effective. Corporate officials would approach Marcial before his Tuesday afternoon deadline, asking: Is this good enough to make the column?

Marcial cut such a deal in March 1999 with 7thStreet.com, an Internet service provider that was about to forge an alliance with AOL. He had known the CEO, Stephen Gott, from the days when Gott was chief operating officer of Lehman Brothers, and Gott promised him that the scoop would hold. "The company is about to announce a pact with America Online," Marcial confidently predicted.

Marcial's column was made available online Thursday nights, and trading usually jumped Fridays in the stocks he mentioned. Marcial's impact could be nothing short of dramatic. When he touted a small medical firm called Biomatrix in June 1997, the stock rose by 122 percent the next day. In December 1998, shares in another company, EarthLink Network, soared by 263 percent the day after Marcial talked it up. 7thStreet stock was no different. It had been trading around 2, jumped to 5 that Friday, and when the company confirmed the deal on Monday it was trading at 8.

Over the longer term, however, the Marcial effect often wore off. Of the 172 stocks he had mentioned in 1997, 139 had risen in value the next day, although only 104 were in the plus column after six months. In a January 1997 column, Marcial had quoted an investor as saying that a company called Graphix Zone, then trading at 3, would become one of the largest music sites on the Web. Over the next six months the stock declined by more than 88 percent and was booted out of the Nasdaq high-tech index. Things moved in the other direction for Best Buy, the consumer electronics chain. In June 1997, Marcial had quoted Bob Olstein, chairman of the Olstein Financial Alert Fund, as saying that he was shorting the stock, or betting on its decline. In a little over three months, Best Buy stock rose by 100.5 percent, crushing anyone who had followed Olstein's advice.

Marcial leaned so heavily on his sources that he was sometimes led astray. Someone he had known for many years became involved with Ultrafem, which made a feminine protective cup that it touted as an alternative to tampons and pads. Although Ultrafem's stock had slid by nearly two-thirds, Marcial's contact introduced him to the CEO, who told him a compelling story in January 1997. Marcial quoted a Jeffries & Company analyst as calling the product "the biggest advance since the tampon was introduced in 1933." The stock jumped by 28 percent in the next month—but sales soon dropped, the firm declared bankruptcy, and shareholders filed a civil suit charging fraud. Among the defendants: Jeffries & Company, which was a lead underwriter of the firm's $40-million stock offering. Marcial blamed himself for misjudging his source. The man tried several times to reach him, but Marcial would never again take his calls.

Sometimes Marcial's sources got mad at him. In March 1999, he wrote that Polaroid, whose stock had been languishing, "may be considering a merger with a deep-pocketed company that could help turn it around." He quoted a longtime source, First Albany analyst Pete Enderlin, as saying "I have heard rumblings" about a possible deal. Enderlin told Marcial he would never speak to him again because it looked as if he were the source of the item. Marcial was sympathetic because companies sometimes cut off renegade analysts, making it impossible for them to do their jobs and threatening their employers with the loss of investment banking work.

Marcial had more than his share of critics in the backbiting world of the financial press. Jim Cramer, for one, loved to beat up on Marcial.

"I check out the Gene Marcial page," Cramer wrote, "to see whether he hypes one of my stocks, which I will then use to blow out of it immediately, because this column has zero reliability. . . . There he goes pumping some corrupt small-capper again."

Like an unpopular freshman left out of the coolest fraternity, Marcial had other detractors. Steve Lipin considered Marcial a latter-day Dan Dorfman, the most prominent financial commentator of the past two decades. The comparison to Dorfman was, in sneering Wall Street lingo, shorthand for a stock tout who was used by his sources and boldly predicted lots of deals that never happened. Marcial often crawled out on a very long limb, Lipin felt. He had scored some major scoops, but he was also wrong much of the time. To Lipin, the columnist's approach amounted to throwing everything against the wall and seeing what sticks.

Dave Kansas, the editor of *TheStreet.com,* was also tough on Marcial. He too saw the column as "practically Dorfmanesque." To Kansas, it seemed that Marcial's stories made a lot of noise, had a short-term effect on stock prices, and were summarily forgotten.

Steve Brill soon joined the anti-Marcial crowd. *Brill's Content* ran a lengthy piece recounting all the Marcial items about developments that never came to pass.

Gene Marcial thought that all this was terribly unfair. His critics simply didn't understand what he did, or why his weekly column was so popular. Jim Cramer, he felt, was mired in conflicts of interest, a hedge-fund trader who pretended to be a journalist. Cramer had been attacking him for years, even though they had never met. Steve Brill, he believed, did not have even a basic conception of journalism. Marcial's column had only slightly trailed the S & P 500—the return on investment if someone had traded on all 500 stocks in the proper proportion—but Brill's reporter kept repeating that he hadn't beaten the index. What these critics ignored, Marcial felt, was that he wasn't a mutual fund manager, he was a reporter who wrote what he heard and what he knew. For the grand price of $2.50 an issue, readers could take it or leave it. There was no other column like his. The critics could stuff it.

On balance, Gene Marcial felt unappreciated. He believed that he was *Business Week*'s most undervalued asset. In 1989 he had been the first to report on the likelihood of a massive leveraged buyout at RJR-Nabisco; nine years later he had quoted fund manager Mario Gabelli as saying that Viacom would sell off Simon & Schuster months before the publishing company spun off its educational and reference divisions. He had quoted a money manager as saying that First Chicago would be a "very attractive" target for either Banc One or U.S. Bancorp, two months before Banc One made the acquisition. Yet even after eighteen years at the magazine, Marcial still had to prove himself every week. There were regular arguments over what he could publish. And he couldn't play the market. The only real money he ever made was when he had bought an apartment off Park Avenue for $35,000 in the 1970s and sold it several years later for $200,000.

Marcial tried to expand his franchise. He wrote a book about insider trading, alleging that some executives doled out sexual favors to brokers who took major positions in their companies. But the lawyers at *Business*

Week's parent company, McGraw-Hill, made him take out most of the names, and the book failed to crack the best-seller lists. Marcial also wrote two memos proposing that *Business Week* create a television show on which he would offer stock advice. But the executives weren't television people, and the idea went nowhere.

Still, there was one bottom-line measure that Marcial believed proved his worth. In 1988, eleven people, including *Business Week*'s broadcast editor, Seymour "Rudy" Ruderman, had been arrested for illegally trading on advance copies of Marcial's column; Ruderman went to prison. And in early 1999, three Long Island stockbrokers were charged with paying a magazine distributor to fax them advance copies of Inside Wall Street, a scam that earned them $140,000 until the magazine uncovered the plot. *Business Week* gave Gene Marcial a raise and a senior writer's title because the editors had reached an inescapable conclusion: His column was good enough to steal.

❏   ❏   ❏

The speculative sweepstakes continued. On April 5, 1999, Chris Nolan, a gossip columnist for the *San Jose Mercury News,* wrote a piece suggesting a possible megadeal between a surging Net company and one of the major networks. "Is America Online going to buy CBS?" she wrote, making no pretense of having hard information. "Some say yes, some say no. But a few—looking at the talks the two companies have been having and considering the high price of entering the online media business—say it's inevitable."

The next day, the Bloomberg News service picked up the *Mercury News* column with no further reporting, making it sound like a front-page scoop. "America Online Inc. and CBS Corp. have held talks over the past year about a potential combination, including a possible purchase of CBS by AOL, the *San Jose Mercury News* reported, citing an unnamed person familiar with the discussions," the Bloomberg story said.

To make matters worse, a public relations firm representing AOL had announced a news conference the next day about a major Internet development. Tricia Primrose, an AOL spokeswoman, was flooded with calls. She was accustomed to these inquiries—the rumor list was so long, and

AOL was so frequently mentioned as planning this or that acquisition—and she never deviated from saying that the company didn't comment on rumors. But this time reporters were adding two and two and getting five, so when a Reuters correspondent called, Primrose broadened her usual no-comment to say that AOL wasn't planning a press conference on this subject tomorrow.

David Faber couldn't believe what had happened. This *Mercury News* columnist didn't know anything about CBS, and yet here was the story on Bloomberg and on the wires, and CBS stock was moving up. But Faber had more important concerns at the moment. His pal Steve Lipin had scooped him again.

On the morning of April 6, Lipin disclosed in *The Wall Street Journal* that MCI WorldCom was holding preliminary talks about acquiring Nextel Communications. Lipin liked to wait until the deal was virtually done, the cake fully baked, but in this case he and his colleagues felt that they had enough to go on. Lipin didn't like to do stories on corporate discussions that went nowhere, but this deal was clearly in play. Still, he felt that the story had to be hedged up the wazoo. The piece said at the top that "the two phone companies have yet to reach agreement on key terms and a deal may never be reached," with some of those involved putting "the odds of a deal at no more than 50 percent."

Faber had been chasing this rumor for weeks. He had even talked to the investment bankers who were putting together the deal, people from Morgan Stanley and Lazard Freres and Salomon Smith Barney, and had taken two of them to dinner just a few days earlier. And yet they hadn't let on. It was a game, a dance, and Faber didn't have enough to waltz away with the scoop. Investment bankers almost never leaked these deals to him, but they would confirm the story if he had enough to press them, to say that he knew it was true. Otherwise they would give vague responses, saying only that such a deal "might make sense." And Faber wasn't sure in his gut that this merger was happening. He knew both WorldCom and Nextel pretty well, and the deal didn't seem to add up.

Faber suggested on *Squawk Box* that MCI WorldCom might have put out the story as some sort of trial balloon. Lipin called him during a commercial and started screaming.

"Nothing could be further from the truth! I demand a retraction!" he

shouted, only half-jokingly. The two men and their families had shared a
Passover seder a few nights earlier, but Lipin was really mad. He and
Faber had grumbled many times about how unfair it was when people accused Lipin of being spoon-fed just because he worked for the *Journal,* or
made the same charge against Faber when he popped one on CNBC. Now
here was Faber hurling the same insult at him.

After the break, Faber backed away from his suggestion that this had
been a WorldCom leak. Joe Kernen, sitting across the desk, was quick to
needle him. "That Lipin breaks a story every day," Kernen said. "He's a
dynamo."

Faber couldn't contain his frustration. "I've been working on this story
for weeks. . . . These guys lied to me," he said on the air.

Lipin, watching at home, was glad that Kernen was busting his friend's
balls. Faber deserved it. Besides, Lipin felt that he had performed a small
public service. Nextel stock had been surging on all this takeover chatter.
After his hedged report, the stock had dropped slightly. He had injected a
small dose of reality into the rumor-driven world of Wall Street.

Sometimes the rumors were 180 degrees wrong. Jim Cramer had heard
that *Barron's* was planning a negative article on the industrial conglomerate Tyco International; instead, the piece hailed Tyco's CEO as "the next
Jack Welch," the highly successful chairman of General Electric. And
sometimes the rumors were deliberately bogus. On April 7, someone used
the Internet to put out a fake Bloomberg story about a merger. The hoax
was so elaborate that the Web page looked exactly like Bloomberg's, the
right colors and all, with electronic links to real Bloomberg news pages.
The perpetrator had posted a message on a Yahoo! chat board—"BUYOUT
NEWS"—with the notation, "Just found it on Bloomberg." The Yahoo!
note contained a link to the phony story, which said that PairGain Technologies, a maker of communications equipment, had agreed to be acquired by an Israeli firm called ECI Telecom. In fact, rumors of such a
merger had been bouncing around for some time.

The ploy worked, and the false report boosted PairGain's stock by 32
percent in just an hour and a half. Even PairGain's chief financial officer,
Charles McBrayer, admitted that "you'd swear on your mother it was a
Bloomberg Website."

Michael Bloomberg, the founder and CEO of the news service, made sure that a staffer contacted PairGain, the SEC, and the Websites that had carried the reports in an effort to shut down the hoax, which as it turned out had been conducted by a PairGain engineer. Bloomberg was annoyed, but he figured that this was the price of becoming a successful news service. He would have been more annoyed if the hoaxer had tried to fake someone else's site.

By late morning, when Bloomberg News moved a story saying that it had put out no such report on PairGain, the stock plummeted, though it still finished the day up 10 percent.

Among the eager buyers reacting to the false report was Jim Cramer. He had snatched up 30,000 shares and wound up losing $27,000. Anyone could fall for a hoax, Cramer believed, including him.

6

NONSTOP NEWS

THE scam that had duped savvy investors in the PairGain case under-scored the lightning pace of financial information, even phony infor-mation, at the turn of the century. And in the never-ending race to relay that information to the big-money movers and shakers, Bloomberg News was hard to beat.

But even Bloomberg, which had wired every brokerage house and major newsroom with its ubiquitous terminals, was often shut out from crucial, market-moving intelligence. Such information was being whis-pered by Wall Street analysts who enjoyed an increasingly close and cozy relationship with the companies whose stocks they monitored. The prob-lem for news organizations was that some high-powered analysts, who were afforded a special degree of access to corporate management, were trafficking in what could only be described as inside information. Matthew Winkler thought that this was a scandal.

Over the decade that he had spent running Bloomberg News, Winkler had grown passionate in his view that many analysts were being given an unfair edge. As a former *Wall Street Journal* reporter, Winkler knew the permutations of this particular game. The big companies were assidu-ously courting the analysts on whose ratings they depended and stiffing everyone else who traded their stock. It was a terrible conflict of interest, Winkler believed, and yet no one in this insular world seemed to find it strange. A company's stock would mysteriously soar or plummet on information that was simply unavailable to the great mass of investors. The practice was really rotten, Winkler felt. It wasn't right. It wasn't fair. And he decided to make the issue into a signature crusade for Bloomberg News.

The usual journalistic procedure was to uncover an abuse and then ask responsible officials for comment. Winkler decided to turn that process on its head. In the fall of 1998, he went to see Arthur Levitt, chairman of the Securities and Exchange Commission, the man in charge of enforcing the rules against improper trading practices. Winkler recited the argument that corporate executives should not be tipping their hand to selected Wall Street analysts.

"You think this is all right?" he asked.

No, Levitt said, but what do you want me to do? I don't make the laws.

"You can use the bully pulpit and say it's unfair," Winkler replied. He asked Levitt to begin by granting an interview on the subject.

Days later, Bloomberg reporter Neil Roland was asking the chairman about the practice. "As far as I'm concerned, that's cheating, and it's a stain upon our market," Levitt told him. "If some individuals or organizations are getting information that others are not getting, that means our markets are no longer trustworthy and no longer credible, and that can't be tolerated."

Soon afterward, on December 1, 1998, the stock of Western Digital surged by 37 percent with no apparent explanation. Bloomberg reporters quickly discovered the reason. High-level analysts that day were at the Phoenician resort in Scottsdale, Arizona, in a room with silk-covered walls, where they heard Western Digital's CEO, Charles Haggerty, say that business was getting much better. He explained that the company had cut down its inventory of disk drives, had boosted its market share, and was preparing to ship new products sooner than expected. Many of those assembled reached for their cell phones and placed their buy orders, pushing up Western Digital stock by $4^{13}/_{16}$, to $17^{7}/_{8}$.

The invitation-only gathering was hosted by Credit Suisse First Boston, where top executives from 140 companies were served warm lobster salad, foie gras, fillet of turbot and roasted rack of lamb, played the 27-hole golf course, and laughed at the routines of comedian Dana Carvey. The Western Digital official in charge of investor relations maintained that anyone calling him that week would have gotten the same information as those at the conference. But individual investors would not have known to make the call, and in any event would not have heard the CEO's take on the matter.

Bloomberg reporters soon learned that the conference had affected other stocks as well. Scott Cook, cofounder of the financial software firm Intuit, told the guests that advance orders for his 1999 TurboTax software had already exceeded total sales of the 1998 version. While Cook was speaking, his company's stock began rising, finishing the day up 11 percent.

Matt Winkler knew about the Phoenician gathering because Bloomberg News had been invited to attend—but only if the news service agreed that the briefings were off-the-record. Winkler refused to make such a deal, as did Reuters and Dow Jones News Service. But reporters from CNBC, *Fortune, Forbes,* the *San Francisco Chronicle,* and the *San Jose Mercury News* attended after promising not to report on the presentations the same day.

Winkler was acutely aware that, according to one survey, 99 percent of companies invited money managers to join in regular conference calls, while only 14 percent allowed reporters to listen in. He was determined to force the practice out in the open. He told his staffers to get on the calls any legal way they could—get the number from a friend at a securities firm, listen in with him, or have him tape it. Taping was the best option, for Bloomberg would put a Real Audio version of the call on its electronic news service. Microsoft was furious after one such incident in late 1998, and a Microsoft executive told Winkler that the company would file suit if Bloomberg did it again. This was proprietary information, the Microsoft man said. Winkler replied that all Microsoft shareholders had a right to hear what the software giant was telling analysts.

Bloomberg's lawyer, Rick Klein, told Winkler that he was worried. Microsoft would have a strong case in claiming that broadcasting the call was a copyright infringement.

"Here's an opportunity for you to be famous," Winkler told him. "You'll be a hero." In the end, nobody sued, and Winkler believed he knew why. It would have been a public relations disaster to sue a news organization for making such information public. He had called their bluff.

Winkler, forty-four, a soft-spoken, bespectacled man who favored bow ties, had never expected to be running this kind of guerrilla outfit. But his life had changed when he coauthored a 1988 *Wall Street Journal* profile of Michael Bloomberg.

Bloomberg was a successful Salomon Brothers trader who had been shoved aside when the company went public in 1981. Armed with a $20-million departure package, he founded a company that provided real-time data on stocks and bonds to money managers. Other firms, such as Dow Jones's Telerate unit, offered a similar service, but Bloomberg did it faster and better, analyzing all the factors that could affect a bond's price. With Merrill Lynch as a partner, he pumped the information through a specially designed computer terminal, modestly dubbed the Bloomberg, that was leased to customers.

Bloomberg's insight, long before the advent of CNBC and the rise of the Internet, was that fortunes were made and lost on the speed and versatility of financial information. He took complicated data and turned them into readily available tools—numbers, graphs, charts—that traders quickly found indispensable. At the *Journal,* Winkler viewed the rapidly growing Bloomberg business as a genuine threat to Dow Jones, and he had argued against the newspaper's decision to use Bloomberg terminals as its sole supplier of daily bond prices. When Winkler was assigned to write a profile of the rising mogul, he was determined to be fair to Michael Bloomberg, although he could not hide his skepticism.

"His plan seems almost too audacious and may turn out to be just that," Winkler's story said. "A long list of communications giants is bent on clobbering his upstart company." Still, Bloomberg found the front-page story more flattering than he would have had the nerve to make it had he written the piece himself.

A year later, Bloomberg called Winkler and asked his advice: Should he move beyond number-crunching and get into the news business? They kicked it around at a Japanese restaurant across the street from Bloomberg's Park Avenue office. Winkler pressed Bloomberg on whether he would run a negative story on the chairman of his biggest customer if the firm threatened to return all its leased terminals. Bloomberg insisted that he would. He ended the sushi lunch with an offer.

"I want you to run it," Bloomberg said. "When can you start?"

Winkler never imagined that Bloomberg would be crazy enough to become a publisher with no experience, but he was excited by the new venture. A day later, he took the job. His *Journal* editors were unperturbed, since he wasn't going to a direct competitor such as *The New York Times* or *Financial Times*. "If it works out, we'll buy you in two years," Paul Steiger, the *Journal*'s deputy managing editor, told him. In 1989, Bloomberg was barely on anyone's radar screen.

The following year, Michael Bloomberg passed up a chance to bid for the failing FNN cable network, but he soon decided to expand into twenty-four-hour television. The viewership was low—USA Networks and some local stations carried an early-morning hour of Bloomberg programming—and the look, with charts and statistics cluttering the screen, was a bit amateurish. It was losing money to boot. Bloomberg understood that television, with its reliance on the visual, was far from ideal for complicated financial subjects. He called it a "sequential access" medium, meaning that the viewer had to sit through stories selected by someone else. Newspapers, by contrast, were a "random access" medium, where the reader could pick the pieces that were most interesting or relevant. But Bloomberg believed that television was magic. Business executives would see his reporters on TV and conclude that they must be important, and would be more willing to grant an interview, maybe get on the tube themselves.

Bloomberg also launched a personal finance magazine and bought a New York radio station, WNEW-AM, switching the format from Frank Sinatra and Perry Como to business news. Bloomberg couldn't even get his kids to listen to the station; they preferred a rock outlet called Z-100. But he felt it was important to get his name out there, and he started a Website as well.

Bloomberg News was clearly a niche product, but the wealth and influence of its customers gave the operation an outsized degree of clout. Treasury Secretary Robert Rubin, an old acquaintance from his Wall Street days, told Michael Bloomberg at a dinner party that he would return a call from a Bloomberg reporter before one from the major networks.

Since it was in the business of leasing terminals, Bloomberg often found itself reporting on its corporate customers. In July 1998, when the news service was about to disclose that Deutsche Bank was looking to acquire an American bank, an executive with the German company called Michael Bloomberg. The executive threatened to pull all of the bank's Bloomberg terminals unless the story, based on information surreptitiously overheard on a conference call, was stopped. After a late-night telephone conference between Bloomberg, who was in Idaho; Winkler, who was in Europe; and their lawyer in New York, they decided to publish the piece. The threat was never carried out.

What really boosted Bloomberg's visibility was that 650 newspapers around the world carried its reports, either by renting the terminals or through *The New York Times* syndicate. Bloomberg had been giving away the service for free, first to the *Times* and then to other newspapers, so his reporters could get Washington press credentials unavailable to computerized services with no print outlet. As the company grew, Winkler began arguing that they had to start charging for the service. Bloomberg argued just as strongly that newspapers would drop the service if they had to pay for it. His real source of income, after all, came from renting the Bloomberg terminals to financial companies. Finally, when a renegade saleswoman in London began successfully selling the news service to European papers, Bloomberg saw the light. At the beginning of 1999, the company began charging American newspapers as much as $25,000 a year for Bloomberg copy. Only a half dozen papers dropped the service.

The guts of the operation remained the wire service stories, carried by the terminals that companies rented for $1,200 a month. And there were plenty of stories, a staggering 3,800 dispatches each day. Many were dry-as-dust pieces specific to one company—meaning, as Bloomberg well understood, that you would care only if you worked for the company, invested in the company, or competed with the company. Some articles were robotic in nature; they were literally written by computers, plugging new statistics into previously formulated sentences.

But many were churned out by the 710 staff members who worked legendarily long hours. Bloomberg kept a brightly-lit lounge on the fifteenth floor fully stocked—with multiple varieties of fruit, cookies, crackers, pretzels, potato chips, juice, and soda, along with picturesque tanks of exotic fish—so that his troops could work through breakfast, lunch, and dinner.

The bosses worked long days as well, and not in fancy, glass-enclosed offices; they toiled in the same cluttered cubicles as their minions. On April 2, 1999, Winkler arrived at 7:00 A.M., even though the stock market was closed for Good Friday. Bloomberg, in shirtsleeves, New Balance sneakers, and a laminated ID card ("MIKE Bloomberg") around his neck, appeared with a piece of buttered matzoh for the Passover holiday.

Winkler spent the next hour and a half overseeing the coverage of the monthly release of unemployment figures. This was an important test of one of his bedrock principles, that Bloomberg needed not only to be first with the news but to provide the context and depth of a story leisurely written for the next day's newspaper. Winkler was determined to move beyond what he called "show up and throw up" stories.

Washington reporter Vince Golle had been in the "lockup," the closed-door gathering of correspondents at the Labor Department waiting to be released with the new figures at precisely 8:30 A.M. Under Winkler's system, three versions of the story had been roughed out in advance. First there was a piece that put the still-unknown jobless figure at an estimate suggested by various economists. A second story assumed that the figure was higher than that, and a third that the number was lower than the estimate. Analysts were interviewed in advance and asked to react to all three scenarios.

Thus, at precisely 8:30, Golle's story moved on the wire: "The U.S. economy added jobs in March at the slowest pace in more than three years, and the unemployment rate unexpectedly fell to 4.2 percent from 4.4 percent . . ." The figures were followed by a quote from Richard Yarmore of Argus Research Corporation, who said that "we're still operating with a fully employed labor force." There were drawbacks to this fast-forward approach; the story got a February jobless figure wrong, but that was quickly corrected.

The real issue for Bloomberg News was the impact on bonds. Under the crazy-quilt logic of the markets, a rapid decline in the number of unemployed Americans may have been good news for the country, but because it could reignite fears of inflation, such news sent bond prices lower. In this case, the modest job growth was judged to be good news. At 9:24, a second Bloomberg dispatch reported: "Bonds gained after the report showed wage gains aren't picking up . . ."

Unlike a newspaper editor, who could only guess at what was popular, Winkler knew exactly what his customers were reading. A day earlier, the most widely read Bloomberg story, with 14,051 hits, was "Yugoslavia Captures Three U.S. Soldiers." In third place, with 3,659 hits, was "Wall Street Leaders Place Bets on Presidential Race." And not everything was serious stuff, either. The number 15 story, with 2,026 hits, was "Eight Little Rules for Dating My Daughter."

❑   ❑   ❑

The hunger for 24-hour business news made it inevitable that new players would emerge to challenge the ubiquity of Bloomberg and the television dominance of CNBC. But the new kid in town, despite a famous name, was struggling to be heard. After three years, CNN Financial News was a mere blip on the Wall Street radar screen.

From their outpost across the Hudson River, CNBC staffers had grown condescending toward their fledgling rival, just as Ted Turner had once dismissed their network as a "piece of garbage." Ron Insana would watch to see which guests were being touted on the next night's *Moneyline* and then try to book them first on his CNBC show, *Street Signs.* Matt Quayle, the *Squawk Box* producer, refused to put on the air any corporate executive or government official who wouldn't give his program the first interview before CNNfn. Some newsmakers, such as Labor Secretary Alexis Herman, insisted on rotating the order of her television interviews; when it wasn't his turn to go first, Quayle would simply pass.

But Lou Dobbs, the president of CNNfn, viewed the media world through a very different prism. He generally refused to talk about CNBC in public. He saw the network as painfully narrow, almost totally focused on the manic swings of the stock market. His operation, he felt, covered the vast expanse of the financial landscape: nightly programs on the business of technology, sports, entertainment. In promotional spots for a show called *Business Unusual,* Dobbs was seen skydiving and snorkeling, as if to underscore that the network would go anywhere in search of news. His own program, *Moneyline,* had recently been expanded to an hour to cover national and world news as well as business. And he usually tripled the ratings of his onetime disciple, Maria Bartiromo, on *Business Center.*

But Dobbs, who could be arrogant and abrasive, was a controversial figure within his own network. Some staffers even made fun of the way he dyed his hair, which sometimes turned orange. And in the summer of 1997, Dobbs came within an inch of leaving CNN, the network that he had helped Turner launch by bringing business coverage to cable television for the first time.

It was an unusual moment for such a threat. As the successful anchor of the most popular business program on cable television, Dobbs was wealthy, established, highly respected on Wall Street. He liked to boast about flying around with Henry Kravis, Robert Mosbacher, and other top financiers. And he was running his own network within a network, the spin-off that Dobbs had created just a year earlier as the culmination of a lifelong dream.

But Lou Dobbs wanted more. He wanted to transform CNNfn into a twenty-four-hour operation, and his old friend Ted Turner had refused. Dobbs found the situation intolerable. CNNfn was on the air only from 7:00 A.M. to 9:00 P.M., and if the fledgling network wasn't going to expand, then it didn't need him at the helm. Anyone could run it. He not only covered business, he was a businessman. He was convinced that a tiny network now laboring in obscurity would eventually make money. Dobbs was chagrined when other CNN officials leaked word of his ultimatum to the press, but he felt that he had to take a stand. The separation papers were being negotiated.

Finally, Turner and his board agreed to Dobbs's demands. CNNfn would expand to eighteen hours a day and make a commitment for the full twenty-four. Dobbs would have his round-the-clock network. Now it was up to him to make it work. And the obstacles were rather formidable.

Despite CNBC's dominance, Dobbs and *Moneyline* were taken seriously because they were aired on the main network, reaching the same viewers who were watching CNN's coverage of war and politics or its nightly gabfests with Larry King. But CNNfn was another story. While

CNBC was in 65 million American homes, CNNfn reached just 11 million. About 20,000 to 40,000 viewers, a fraction of CNBC's audience, were tuned in at any one time, though no one knew for sure because the network was too small to be rated by Nielsen. The names of the CNNfn anchors and reporters—Rhonda Schaffler, Beverly Schuch, Terry Keenan—were far less well known than those of Ron Insana, Mark Haines, or Maria Bartiromo. Even in Manhattan, the high-powered home of financial news, CNNfn had so little clout that it was knocked off the air at 7:00 P.M. for basketball and hockey on the Madison Square Garden Network.

At fifty-three, with his perpetual tan and his fondness for crisp white shirts with gold cufflinks, Dobbs looked like the corporate executives he had gotten to know so well. A Harvard graduate with a degree in economics, Dobbs was so much a part of the business establishment that he had once made a serious ethical blunder that was obvious to everyone but him. In 1992, he admitted receiving more than $15,000 to make promotional videos for Shearson Lehman Brothers, PaineWebber, and the Philadelphia Stock Exchange. On the PaineWebber tape, *The Wall Street Journal* reported, Dobbs had praised the firm's "twin traditions of integrity and client service." Journalists and outside critics were appalled by the notion of CNN's top business-news anchor acting as a paid spokesman for firms covered by his network. With his usual stubbornness, Dobbs said it was "nonsensical to talk about this as a conflict of interest" and that he made far more money giving speeches to corporate groups, a practice that also raised ethical questions. CNN strongly reprimanded Dobbs, who told his staff in a memo that he was "deeply sorry," adding: "I was comfortable with my judgment to the point of arrogance." No one disputed him on that point.

Dobbs had been a business reporter for KING-TV in Seattle when Turner had asked him to join his proposed Cable News Network in 1980. Most of the country was not wired for cable, and few in the news business took Turner seriously. But Dobbs believed that even though Turner knew nothing about television news, he was a great idea man. And the notion of creating a nightly business newscast was irresistible.

A businessman himself, Turner knew one thing: He was tired of negative business news. The stories he saw on television always seemed to involve fraud, the collapse of some company, a fire at a chemical plant. Business, he told Dobbs, was too exciting not to be an integral part of CNN.

Dobbs asked what kind of program he wanted. That's up to you, Turner said.

While Dobbs had hoped to model his show on the *CBS Evening News,* anchored by Walter Cronkite, he quickly realized that he didn't have the resources. In fact, he had just one correspondent. And bookings were a great problem. But Dobbs was certain that people would watch. Executives at the major networks thought business news was boring, but that was because they considered the audience too stupid to be interested in it. Dobbs believed that viewers were a damn sight smarter than ABC, NBC, and CBS imagined. He did straightforward reports with no fancy graphics or video, betting on the idea that substance alone would be enough.

The new network reached just 1.7 million households, but *Moneyline,* Dobbs's nightly newscast, was being watched in New York. The reaction from Wall Street was almost immediate. That was in part because Dobbs had hired Dan Dorfman, the nation's best-known financial columnist, as a regular commentator.

The country, however, was still getting used to the concept of cable news. A few weeks after his debut, Dobbs was out with a crew in Manhattan's fashion district when a bystander stopped him. "I know you," he said, although he couldn't quite come up with Dobbs's name. "You're the guy who does the news over and over and over."

CEOs were an even tougher audience. Corporate chieftains, in Dobbs's view, were scared to death of the press. Most business people thought of television as the enemy, and they were absolutely right. Much of the business coverage in those days was nothing short of hostile. Dobbs believed that most reporters didn't understand business or markets, and that they oversimplified their stories to the point of distortion. He was determined to change that, and over time a growing number of CEOs became willing to appear on *Moneyline.*

When the first all-business channel, FNN, was launched the following year, Dobbs looked down his nose at the new network, just as the broadcast networks liked to ridicule CNN. But Dobbs was secretly jealous of FNN for having the luxury of an all-day format to cover business. He was determined to play in that league someday.

The Black Monday stock market crash of 1987 provided dramatic evidence of how far Dobbs and CNN had come. He was deluged with calls from CEOs around the globe, from China to Ireland, trying to find out what was happening to their stocks. Even a Federal Reserve governor called him. There were no cell phones, no Internet, no CNBC, and information was hard to come by. CNN was their only link. It was clear on that day that the network's Wall Street coverage had become indispensable.

A year later, Dobbs made his move. He urged Turner to buy FNN, arguing that a twenty-four-hour business network could be both important and profitable. Turner backed the idea, and the company agreed to pay more than $100 million. Dobbs flew to Atlanta for the board meeting that would officially bless the acquisition. Pacing in the hallway, he was ready to be named president of the new network. But the Turner Broadcasting board rejected the plan. Its members felt that the company already had enough cable programming on its hands. It was a huge disappointment for Dobbs.

By 1990, Dobbs was showing signs of frustration. He wanted to be president of CNN and felt that Turner had passed him over in favor of Tom Johnson of the *Los Angeles Times*. He might well leave, Dobbs told Dan Dorfman, jabbing his finger, "and you're coming with me."

But he soon fell out with Dorfman as well. Dobbs believed that Dorfman was making too many predictions, becoming repetitious, and saying things that were too opinionated on the air. Dorfman, meanwhile, was furious that after he broke the news that Time Inc. and Warner Brothers would merge, Dobbs voted to give the *Los Angeles Times* an award for its coverage of the merger and had played down Dorfman's role. Dorfman quit and defected to CNBC.

Dobbs was soon tempted to follow him. He still hadn't lost his yearning for twenty-four-hour news. When his CNN contract expired in the mid-1990s, he began negotiating with Roger Ailes, the president of CNBC, for a job that would give him both a prominent on-air role and a voice in shaping the network's coverage.

But Dobbs decided to stay put, and in the spring of 1995, Turner pulled him aside before a meeting of the company's executive committee. Don't tell anyone, Turner said, but it would be a great idea for us to launch a financial news network. Would you like to run it? Dobbs, naturally, jumped at the opportunity. Turner told him to put together a proposal.

The climate was more hospitable this time, and the following month the Turner board approved a plan for the $10-million launch, with annual losses of $10 million expected for the next five years. Dobbs promptly declared war on CNBC. His new network was seeking a jazzier look that would attract younger viewers by focusing, for example, on workplace issues, entrepreneurs, and high technology. Dobbs tried to position the network as appealing to an audience beyond Wall Street insiders. "A business network worthy of any Rockefeller, Vanderbilt, or DuPont, and perfect for every Tom, Dick, and Mary," one ad said. It was, Dobbs felt, an incredible roll of the dice.

CNN Financial News made its debut six months and twenty days after getting the green light. Dobbs held his breath as they threw the switch three days before the end of 1995. The set on Eighth Avenue, across the street from Madison Square Garden, was still being painted, and that was the least of their problems.

The major stumbling block, Dobbs knew, was limited channel capacity. He had drafted a plan to achieve profitability in five years, rather than the usual three, because he knew how hard it would be to get a foothold in major cable markets. CNNfn started out in just 6.5 million homes. Few cable systems felt compelled to provide space for a second business channel. Dow Jones was also trying to launch a financial network, although that effort quickly fizzled.

By the summer of 1997, when Dobbs was threatening to quit unless the network moved toward twenty-four hours, CNN was in the process of being taken over by Time Warner. Although Dobbs got the commitment he wanted, he soon learned that Time Warner had other cable priorities—expanding the Cartoon Network, for example, and Turner Classic Movies. Still, Dobbs knew that he would have to triple or even quadruple his audience over the next five years if CNNfn was going to survive.

He scored a couple of coups. Dobbs began hiring local New York news anchors, such as Tony Guida and Jack Cafferty, who had instant name recognition in the nation's financial capital. He struck a deal to carry real-time stock quotes from all three exchanges, as opposed to the fifteen-minute-delayed ticker that was running on CNBC. And his CNNfn Website, with 8.5 million regular users, was so popular that Time Warner was considering spinning it off into a public company. Fifteen percent of CNN's programming now came out of his division and, because the network could charge higher rates to reach the affluent audience for business news, he was providing nearly half of CNN's advertising revenue.

But Dobbs was becoming increasingly difficult. He had intimidated much of his staff. Dobbs had once demanded that a very short producer stand on a chair so he could yell at him, and when the young man refused, Dobbs crouched down to deliver the scolding. When Andy Serwer, an editor at *Fortune,* part of the Time Warner empire, wrote a favorable piece called "I Want My CNBC," Dobbs told Serwer that he was an asshole.

Despite his $1 million-plus salary and his sprawling New Jersey farm and his newly acquired private jet, Dobbs felt that he was falling far behind his wealthy corporate buddies. More important, by the spring of 1999, Dobbs was clashing with his network bosses in Atlanta over the direction of programming and battling with Time Warner officials in New York for control of the Website. Senior executives were growing tired of his tantrums. Financial journalism at the highest corporate levels was ultimately about power, about who wielded it and who did not. Lou Dobbs and his struggling network seemed to be on a collision course.

❏   ❏   ❏

The media were racing to keep up as the Internet market continued its irrational exuberance. *The Wall Street Journal* had reported on February 17 that AOL was in talks with eBay, possibly about acquiring a minority stake in the auction site; when the two companies announced an alliance five weeks later, eBay stock shot up more than 16 points, an 11 percent gain, and AOL rose more than 8 points. On March 19, *Business Week* reported on its Website that "sources say" that "Yahoo! is hot to snap up Broadcast.com," with AOL and NBC also taking a look. Maria Bartiromo quickly picked up the report on CNBC; Broadcast.com stock shot up 31 points that day, and Yahoo! swallowed the company soon afterward. Nearly everyone, it seemed, was watching CNBC for a hint of a suggestion of a potential deal; nobody wanted to miss the next big cyberspace merger.

The traditionalists could only shake their heads in wonder as these fiery Internet stocks minted new millionaires overnight. The perpetually bearish analyst Barton Biggs had declared the previous September that stocks were ready to "plunge into the abyss," but somehow the abyss had been avoided. On *Squawk Box*, Mark Haines asked him to defend his bearish stance of recent years, as the market had climbed higher and higher. Biggs responded with an amazing confession.

"Frankly, at this point, I'm befuddled," Biggs said. "This market has broken all the rules. . . . It's an environment where crazy people and crazy stocks are making a lot of money."

Barton Biggs, chief global strategist for Morgan Stanley Dean Witter—confused? The *Squawk* gang could hardly believe it. David Faber asked what he was managing to tell his clients.

"You say you're befuddled," Biggs replied. "What are you gonna do, make up something?"

It seemed like a rare moment of candor in a world in which the experts expressed complete and utter confidence in whatever view they happened to hold at the moment. Even Haines was at a loss. How can you hammer the guy when he throws himself on your mercy? But it was hard to ask him anything further. If Biggs is admitting that he's befuddled, Haines figured, of what value are his thoughts? Actually, Haines suspected that Biggs was overstating his degree of befuddlement. What he really meant was: I know this market is overvalued, I know we're headed for big trouble, but I also know that if I say so I'll be denounced because there's no denying I've been dead wrong so far.

Haines was tempted to interrupt the interview with a politically incorrect observation: "Thanks for stopping by. Call us when your head is clearer." But he held his tongue.

7

THE CULT OF THE CEO

WHEN *Time* magazine named Kim Polese one of the twenty-five most influential Americans, it seemed, on the surface, to be a rare honor for a software writer. Polese was an up-and-coming star in Silicon Valley, a place awash in wealth and hyperbole, but she was hardly a household name. *Time*'s selection in 1997 seemed to boost her to a whole new level.

But Polese was surprised at the reaction. She took a lot of crap from certain people in the Valley for being on the list. Some, she realized, simply resented her success. Media celebrity, she was learning, was a double-edged sword.

The emerging Internet economy had become the dominant story in financial journalism. Net stocks were incredibly volatile, which provided a dramatic plot line and spawned a growing legion of day traders eager to make a quick buck off their gyrations. While actual profits remained elusive for most of these companies, there was an explosion of optimism about using the Web to sell books, flowers, toys, music, drugs, medical advice, plane tickets, and, of course, stocks. Old-line companies that dealt in oil, chemicals, cars, or consumer goods suddenly seemed hopelessly stodgy. Media companies were swept up in the excitement because they were very much part of the online phenomenon, trying to peddle stories and features that were now dubbed "content." Start-ups emerged out of nowhere, producing unimaginable fortunes for fledgling entrepreneurs.

109

In this overheated environment, the press was magnetically drawn to the new breed of Internet buccaneers.

Polese, thirty-seven, was highly respected in the technology community because she was one of the creators of Java, a universal computer language that could be used on any Website. But the press fell in love with her for a very different reason. She was a strikingly beautiful redhead in a sea of middle-aged dweebs, and she knew how to play the media's game. She became, in short order, a CEO superstar.

Even when she was a young marketing manager at Sun Microsystems, Polese seemed to have a sixth sense about the press. In 1995, without the company's knowledge, she approached a reporter at the *San Jose Mercury News* to tout her Java project, which led to a front-page story. Polese was immediately swamped with media calls, and every major newspaper and magazine in the country wound up doing a piece on Java. It was a lesson in the power of publicity.

When Polese and three of her colleagues decided to leave Sun to form their own company, she told only a couple of friends, but word quickly leaked to a Website called *Suck.com*. The young satirists who ran *Suck* dubbed her venture Yet Another Java Start-Up, or YAJSU. The next day, *USA Today* ran an article on Polese's new firm on the front page of its business section. She couldn't stop laughing when she read the piece. The reporter had called the company YAJSU.

From that day forward, the marketing of Kim Polese was indistinguishable from the marketing of her company, whose real name was Marimba. A friend told *Business Week* that she was "Silicon Valley's answer to Madonna." The California business magazine *Red Herring* put a glamorous, airbrushed photo of Polese on its cover. She resented the cover-girl status, even found it insulting. The underlying stereotype, she felt, was that a woman couldn't be much good, that it had to be all hype. Marimba was about technology, not sex appeal. But she viewed the early publicity as crucial for a fledgling firm in Mountain View, California, and it helped her in approaching Fortune 500 companies.

She also did little to discourage the attention. Polese spoke at dozens of conferences, granted hundreds of interviews, posed for an Anne Klein fashion ad. She was a fixture at Bill Clinton fundraisers. Reporters wrote about her private life, about her jazz dance and ballet performances. But there were many other opportunities that she rejected. Polese refused to be interviewed by *People.* She even turned down a company that wanted to use her in an underarm deodorant ad.

The problem, Polese believed, was that the sort of software she developed—which helped Web companies deliver their information more efficiently—was not the glamorous side of the Internet. It was plumbing. Most reporters weren't interested in plumbing, but they thrived on personalities, and they were drawn to her fast-talking, California-hip persona. She had to chuckle when journalists wrote about her brilliant PR strategy. The media coverage had been like a tidal wave, and she had merely tried to stay afloat.

But the headlines had produced huge expectations, and that was more than a little scary. Polese didn't want to start believing her own press. Perhaps she had been naive, thinking that if she talked about her vision and long-term goals, that would be reflected in the articles. Not a chance. The magazines were running huge pictures of her, which they would never do for a male CEO. The Anne Klein spread was always mentioned, although no one had chided Steve Jobs, the cofounder of Apple Computer, for posing in a Gap ad. Polese complained to a couple of editors, said that this was ridiculous, and got mealy-mouthed apologies in return. She soon realized that there was no way to control what was written about her.

Bill Ryan, a Silicon Valley publicist who worked for Marimba, deemed a sexy chief executive to be a plus. "The CEO needs to get out, to embody the company, the vision," he says. "It's next to impossible to get an article in *Fortune* or *Forbes* without a good CEO. The business press isn't interested if you don't have someone who can talk. Kim understood her job as CEO was to be a spokesperson. What's the alternative? Nobody knows who you are. They don't think you're a player. It was a start-up, and they had a huge need for PR."

Indeed, Ryan's firm, Niehaus, Ryan, Wong, offered to train clients on TV presentation, to compile video and audio clips, to book them on the talk show circuit. "The importance of broadcast media to high-tech companies is just beginning to surface," says a company document. "A single major market radio or television hit impacts hundreds of thousands of people, and a syndicated show reaches millions. . . . For high technology companies targeting consumers, broadcast media coverage is the key to their success."

Yet even Ryan saw things getting out of control. "The press always wanted Kim for every interview, everything they tried to set up, ever," he says. "They wanted to create a cult of personality. We tried to tone it down, to manage it. But reporters would say, 'We're not going to do the story unless we can talk to Kim.' "

Even Lou Dobbs could not resist the Polese magnetism. He came out to Mountain View to make a deal for CNNfn. When Polese held an event at a local restaurant called Slim's, Dobbs took the stage—"Lou! Lou!" the crowd shouted—and talked about how his network was using Marimba's technology to get automated stock quotes.

For all the enormous hype, Marimba struggled. The company had tied its fate to "push" technology, the red-hot idea of automatically sending Web information to computer users rather than forcing them to search for it. Polese thought it was absurd that push was being touted as the Next Big Thing when no one, including her, knew just what it was or whether it would work.

Push quickly flamed out, and in 1998 Marimba sold just $17 million in software, creating perception problems as the company prepared to go public. Niehaus, Ryan left the account. *Fortune* soon ran a tough piece on Polese called "The Beauty Hype." Polese told friends that she was devastated by the article. Yes, she had seemed to feed the sexpot image by showing up with clothes and sunglasses for a five-hour photo shoot. But she had worn little makeup and was stunned at the sultry photos the magazine produced. The reporter, Polese believed, had come in with a preconceived theme, a fall-from-grace story, and had ignored evidence to the contrary. Magazines were about sensationalism, about creating buzz, Polese felt, and this was not the sort of buzz she wanted.

Polese's third PR adviser in as many years, Robin Lutchansky, decided that the corporate efforts would now switch from Polese to Marimba itself. "People know the CEO better than they know the products," Lutchansky says. "It's time for the products to have equal footing. We pick and choose the things that Kim participates in very carefully. She isn't the whole story anymore."

Why did the press single out Polese when she and her male colleagues formed their own company after creating Java? "You have four people leaving the company, and one of them is a gorgeous woman," Lutchansky says. "Who would you focus on?"

Polese had grown accustomed to the spotlight by now, but she was still tired of the suggestion that she was using her looks to get ahead. It was nothing short of sexist. She was planning on taking Marimba public and wanted to kick some butt in the business world. That, she hoped, would soon become the story.

❏   ❏   ❏

In an era of round-the-clock news, the chief executive officer had become a spokesman-in-chief, marketing maven, and certified media star. No one could pitch the company like the head honcho. Journalists faced with the grinding routine of reporting sales, revenue, and stock prices thirsted for the human drama and boardroom intrigue that revolved around these corporate chieftains. Perhaps inevitably, the cult of the CEO was born.

Beginning in the 1980s, the business press had begun to lionize such outsized personalities as Donald Trump, Lee Iacocca, Leona Helmsley, Rupert Murdoch, and, of course, Bill Gates. Hard-hearted corporate raiders such as Carl Icahn and T. Boone Pickens were celebrated as charming rascals. Rogue traders such as Ivan Boesky and Michael Milken were deemed great copy before they went to prison. By the mid-1990s, many of the top corporate celebrities—Steve Jobs, Marc Andreessen, Barry Diller, Lou Gerstner, "Chainsaw" Al Dunlap—had become bigger than their companies. Other CEOs quickly learned that crafting a media image with the aid of aggressive publicists was as important as fourth-quarter profits.

No less a cultural authority than *Vanity Fair* certified Steve Case, Jeff Bezos, Steve Jobs, Michael Bloomberg, Tim Koogle of Yahoo!, Scott Mc-Nealy of Sun Microsystems, and Meg Whitman of eBay as members of the New Establishment, circa 1999.

Forbes, like many magazines, celebrated the superstar capitalists. George Shaheen, the CEO of Andersen Consulting, wasn't just a data guy, he was quite possibly a "Digital Messiah." Samuel Bodman, the CEO of

Cabot Corporation, was the "Soot King." Jay Walker of priceline.com, who sold discounted merchandise on the Web, was a "New Age Edison." And when Geraldine Laybourne, the former president of Nickelodeon, launched Oxygen, a cable network for women, she posed for the cover of *Forbes* with one of her megastar partners, Oprah Winfrey.

Savvy corporate executives wanted to be seen and heard in the media, but only on their terms. They tightly controlled the degree of access that they would provide. At a 1998 business conference, Barry Diller, the chairman of USA Networks, was scheduled for a CNBC sit-down with Ron Insana.

"How long's this gonna be?" Diller asked.

"Five minutes," Insana replied.

"Three minutes," Diller informed him.

Controlling the agenda was equally important. Steve Jobs of Apple Computer grew increasingly annoyed during an interview with CNBC's Bruce Mathis, who kept pressing Jobs on who his successor would be. "I told you we weren't going to talk about this," Jobs declared as he stood up and walked out.

If there was a CEO who might be expected to leave the art of the spin to underlings, it would be the world's richest man presiding over the computer industry's dominant company. Bill Gates's image, after all, was that of a supernerd genius and hard-nosed competitor. Yet Gates was sufficiently concerned about that image to take on individual reporters.

Wendy Goldman Rohm, author of *The Microsoft Files,* says that Gates conducted a personal campaign to discredit her when she was a freelance writer reporting on the company's antitrust problems in the mid-1990s. While Rohm was preparing a cover story on Microsoft for *Wired,* the magazine told her that Gates had spoken with Louis Rossetto, *Wired*'s founder, and urged him not to publish it because Rohm was "biased." *Chicago Tribune* editors told Rohm that Gates had said the same thing to them. And when she was working on a piece for *The Boston Globe* shortly before the Justice Department sued Microsoft on antitrust charges, Rohm says, Gates had his top PR person tell the paper that Microsoft would cooperate only if the story were written by another reporter.

And yet when she and Gates found themselves at the same Las Vegas cocktail party, the Microsoft CEO briefly bantered with her before realizing who she was, Rohm says. "I'm not supposed to talk to you," Gates told her curtly before breaking off the conversation.

Microsoft had a history of playing rough. In November 1995, after *The New York Times Magazine* published a cover story that the company didn't like, its publicists called reporters at other newspapers in an effort to tarnish the author, James Gleick. They said that Gleick should have disclosed that he had sold an Internet company he founded to PSI Net, and still owned millions of dollars in PSI stock, while Microsoft owned a 15 percent interest in UUNet, an Internet service provider that competed with PSI Net. When no one bit on this convoluted argument, the publicists wrote a letter to the editor saying that readers should have been told the article "was written by a major investor in one of Microsoft's competitors."

Gleick later confronted Bill Gates at an industry conference. "How come your PR people did this whispering campaign about me?" he asked.

"There was something about you we thought people should know," Gates replied, adding that "I could show you the list" of the reporters who were contacted.

Sometimes the counterattack was less subtle. Stewart Alsop, editor of the trade magazine *InfoWorld,* says that Gates had company staffers scrutinize the magazine's testing procedures after he ran an article criticizing Microsoft software, and called him on his cell phone. "You're making us look bad," Gates told him.

Gates himself erupted during a CBS interview with Connie Chung in 1994. Apparently annoyed at questions about how he and his wife, a Microsoft marketing manager, fell in love, Gates lost it when Chung asked about a patent infringement case against the company.

"Connie, I just can't believe how fucking stupid you are," Gates said, ripping off his microphone and walking out.

Gates sometimes seemed obsessed with getting out his message. On December 1, 1998, during Microsoft's federal antitrust trial, Gates had his deputies leak an e-mail that he had written that very morning, a veritable press release defending the company's position. Two days later, he complained in a second e-mail that they had given it only to the Associated Press. "Just putting in AP doesn't have much impact I don't think. At least we should give it to MAGAZINE people also," he said.

Gates and Microsoft weren't above singling out reporters for special access. In early 1999, Deborah Caldwell of Waggener Edstrom, Microsoft's PR firm, was determined to get some good press for Gates's second book, *Business @ the Speed of Thought.* She apparently did not want the book reviewed by aggressive business reporters who had been covering the antitrust trial, so she sent a letter to John Burgess, a business editor at *The Washington Post,* offering an

> opportunity to get an early look at Bill Gates' new book. . . . If you agree to embargo the book content until March 18, I can have a copy sent to you this week to do a review. As a business writer with broad understanding of the challenges facing business in the "Internet Age," we think you are particularly well suited to be doing the review. This is an "exclusive" offer, if you will, in that I am not in a position to be sending this book to anyone else at the *Post* in advance of March 18. We assume you would work with the book editor to do this, but please confirm.

Burgess, who had not been writing for five years, told Microsoft that he could not allow the company to handpick the reviewer. No matter; the Gates tome was published by the Warner Books unit of Time Warner, and *Time* magazine devoted a cover story to the sayings of Chairman Bill. Determined to further soften his image during the antitrust trial, Gates posed in a sweater for a *Business Week* cover story on how he planned to remake Microsoft. "Visionary-in-Chief," the headline said. And he talked about his three-year-old daughter, his charities, and his softer side for a *Newsweek* cover piece that made him sound like Mr. Rogers. The headline: "Bill Just Wants to Have Fun."

Jeff Bezos, by contrast, was far more cooperative with the press. The quirky entrepreneur who had founded Amazon.com, the online bookseller, Bezos gave interviews all the time. When he was just getting the virtual company off the ground in 1996, Bezos was lucky enough to be featured in a front-page *Wall Street Journal* story. The paper described how "a whiz-kid programmer on Wall Street suddenly fell under the spell of one of the iffiest business propositions of modern times: retailing on the Internet," but nonetheless had "quietly built a fast-growing business."

That was Bezos's biggest national publicity beyond Seattle, and it had a major impact on the business. Now his chief spokesman, Bill Curry, a former newspaper reporter, tried to make Bezos available to any journalist with a significant audience. Curry believed that the media were crucial in spreading the word about Amazon's incredible growth, which in eighteen months had pushed its stock from 9 to as high as 199. You couldn't get press without having a story to tell, and Bezos was a great story, a pioneer in an exploding industry. Bezos loved retelling the tale of how he quit his Wall Street job and had his young bride drive him across the country in a Chevy Trail Blazer while he tapped out his business plan on a laptop. Defining anecdotes were important in corporate myth-making, and men like Bezos were bankable assets for companies without factories or stores.

By the first months of 1999, Bezos was everywhere. On the cover of *Business Week.* On the cover of *Wired.* On the cover of *Fortune,* which gushed that "he's relaxed, he's funny and he's disarmingly humble." His resounding horse laugh could be heard on *60 Minutes. The New York Times Magazine* called him a "political genius" and a "brilliant, charming, hyper and misleadingly goofy mastermind." Bezos thought it was weird when the article described him and his acolytes as "bovine missionaries" because they were so dedicated to customer service—wasn't customer service what they were supposed to be doing?

His main quibble was that while reporters were understandably focused on accuracy, they didn't focus on "truth" as well. Bezos believed that there was too much "he said, she said" journalism in which quoting opposing "experts" somehow added up to a balanced story, even if 99 of 100 specialists were on one side of the issue. After all, the "experts" had badly underestimated the potential of online retailing back when he was first trying to sell the concept. The press, naturally, was also less interested in online sales, at least until companies like Amazon proved the experts wrong. Now that Amazon had become one of Wall Street's darlings, Jeff Bezos was great copy.

Bezos was getting thirty interview requests a week and agreeing to many of them, making a point not to confine himself to the media elite. Even a regional newspaper reporter working on an Amazon story was likely to get some face time with him, as long as it wasn't for a piece about money or power. Bezos enjoyed talking to journalists, liked explaining how he had invented Earth's largest bookstore, and planned to expand into other forms of electronic commerce. There was one notable exception: Bezos almost never appeared on CNBC. He saw no benefit for Amazon in being peppered with questions about his short-term stock price. He was focused solely on building a lasting company, which in turn would take care of the stock. Bezos felt that he had nothing interesting to say about the company's stock, which made him a dull guest on these financial shows. He had no interest in doing interviews for Wall Street consumption. He cared about customers, and customers didn't care about the stock price.

❏   ❏   ❏

All across America, hungry publicists for small Internet start-ups were trying to get that first story on the company's founder into print. They worked the phones, invented angles, touted the technology, hyped the boss—even if the boss wasn't as sexy as Kim Polese. It was their job to convince skeptical reporters that their man was the next Jeff Bezos, or a reasonable approximation. Thus it was that on February 12, 1999, a camera crew came to Kevin O'Connor's Manhattan apartment to watch him eat breakfast with his boys.

O'Connor was the thirty-seven-year-old chief executive officer of DoubleClick, a firm that electronically delivered Internet advertising. His two sons, ages six and two, squirmed and fidgeted amid the Cheerios and orange juice while Dad talked about the volatility of his stock. And it was all staged for CNBC.

"You started off in a basement three years ago with your friend and now look at you," gushed CNBC's Liz Claman.
"If you could solidify a dream for DoubleClick, what would it be?"
"As a kid, were you always into electronics and computers?"
"I was pretty much born a geek," O'Connor replied.

O'Connor didn't much like talking about himself or showing off his kids on national television. But he understood the power of the media in helping to establish a small Internet firm like his. People wanted to do business with technology companies that were going to be around for a while, and appearing on TV was a way of firmly planting the corporate flag.

"Breakfast With a CEO" had become the vehicle of choice for softening a battle-hardened executive's image. When Vanguard Group CEO John Brennan did the segment, CNBC showed footage of him coaching a local soccer team (albeit in a suit and tie). The next day, the PR woman for T. Rowe Price called the network, asking how she could get her CEO on. David Friend, the former producer for the entertainment show *Extra* who now supervised CNBC's morning programming, felt that they were creating a new form of celebrity.

Kevin O'Connor understood the rules of engagement. A soft-spoken man with a bemused expression who liked to go tieless, he hated answering such questions as "Were you a nerd as a kid?" But that was part of his job. The breakfast segment had not only been good for his ego, it was important for recruiting. DoubleClick now had 500 employees, but he hoped to double that. At the moment, *The New York Times* was working on a piece about the culture of DoubleClick. *Forbes* was asking about his vision of the Net over the next decade. *Fortune* included him in a cover story with such other "top e-CEOs" as Bezos, Michael Dell, and Yahoo's Tim Koogle. All this helped create the requisite buzz.

O'Connor, a former high-school wrestling coach, had founded the company in 1996 in his Atlanta basement—with an Internet idea that didn't pan out—and moved to Manhattan to launch the firm. Now he surveyed the glittering skyline from a 32nd-floor office on Madison Avenue. He often had to do extra explaining to journalists because DoubleClick was both a media and technology company. It was an advertising representative for thirteen hundred Net sites around the world, from Dilbert to MTV-Europe. But it had also developed a method to "serve" advertising onto Websites in split-seconds—and to target categories of ads to the most likely consumers—that was used by *The Wall Street Journal* and 6,400 other online operations.

A huge believer in the importance of public relations, O'Connor hired a PR firm after four months, when he had just a handful of employees, and later brought in a full-time spokeswoman. He generally got a good shake from the press, but he was frustrated by negative stories. You couldn't fight the media, couldn't get a retraction. Once he invited CNBC to cover a company picnic and got peppered with tough questions. Friends kept asking: Why did they pee on your picnic? O'Connor knew that he took these things too personally, but he couldn't help it. If someone took a shot at the company, it was like saying your kid is a moron.

The press became more difficult to deal with once O'Connor took the company public in 1998, giving him a personal stake that would soon be worth $740 million. Now a whole new wave of reporters wanted to talk about the surging stock price. They rushed to write stories when the company lost close to $5 million in the third quarter of the year. And since he had to detail the company's risk factors in filings with federal regulators—factors he deemed as remote as an asteroid hitting Earth or lightning striking him down—these were also fair game for the press.

But there were also times when DoubleClick pushed the envelope too far. A 1998 press release claiming that the company had the largest audience reach on the Net after AOL and Yahoo! helped boost its stock 40 percent. When *TheStreet.com* challenged it, O'Connor's spokeswoman, Amy Shapiro, admitted that the release "was misleading because we didn't explain it clearly enough." But investors shrugged off the exaggeration.

The darkest cloud hanging over the company was that DoubleClick had no long-term deal with one of its biggest clients, Alta Vista, the popular Internet search engine. It was like Chinese water torture, O'Connor felt, with financial reporters mentioning that potential weakness in almost every story. In January 1999, when O'Connor finally was able to sign a three-year contract with Alta Vista, he decided to leak the news in advance to *The Wall Street Journal*. Reporters, he knew, thrived on exclusivity. And it worked: The *Journal* gave the deal a nice ride—"DoubleClick Inc. can breathe now," the story began—prompting other journalists to follow up the next day.

By the spring of 1999, DoubleClick was on fire, its stock having risen from 13 to 131. Matt Quayle, the *Squawk Box* producer, hesitated to book O'Connor again, since it had only been a few weeks since the televised breakfast. Then DoubleClick struck two new alliances and the stock hit 200 in April. Now everyone wanted the stock. Jim Cramer, who knew about the company firsthand (*TheStreet.com* used DoubleClick's advertising service), bought some. Quayle figured that he couldn't wait any longer and asked O'Connor to appear on the coveted "CEO Call" segment of *Squawk Box*. It didn't hurt that O'Connor was a young, hip guy; Quayle figured that young, hip day traders might enjoy watching him.

Mark Haines was well prepared. "You're signing up a lot of people, you don't make any money," he said. And what was this $200 million that DoubleClick had just raised in the debt market? Was that for new acquisitions?

"If there's one thing you learn in business, it's raise money when you don't need money," O'Connor said.

The worst aspect of O'Connor's job was the constant rumors. He was always being asked whether he was quitting, whether another company was buying DoubleClick, or whether he was buying some other outfit. On CNBC, a reporter once asked O'Connor if he was talking to another firm. He froze, feeling like a deer caught in the headlights. It was like being asked if he still beat his wife—no matter what he said he would look defensive. After a moment, O'Connor refused to comment. But his response had sparked rumors within DoubleClick: Why did Kevin hesitate like that?

Still, O'Connor felt that the time he spent romancing the media was well invested. A balanced feature story about DoubleClick was better than the most expensive advertising. It gave you the thing small companies wanted most: credibility.

❑   ❑   ❑

Not everyone was following the path blazed by O'Connor, Polese, and Bezos. For every publicity-hungry firm on the make, there was another company so successful that its CEO felt no need to court journalists. The bigger the corporation, the higher the stock price, the greater the risk that the CEO could make a mistake that would mar the firm's carefully polished image. Inquisitive reporters began to be viewed as adversaries rather than as potential allies.

For a company that had become the toast of Wall Street, America Online did surprisingly little to work the press. Reporters often had trouble getting more than bare-bones answers from the public-relations staff, and they had little access to top executives. Steve Case, the mild-mannered CEO who had built the firm into an Internet powerhouse against all odds, rarely granted interviews. He had even turned down the chance to be profiled by *60 Minutes.*

It was a paradox. Here was a company whose spectacular growth had made it part of the fabric of American culture, whose "You've Got Mail" service had hooked millions, whose marketing plan was sheer brilliance, yet it was about as beloved as the phone company. AOL seemed to lack a distinct personality; few had a sense of what went on behind the gleaming glass facades in Dulles, Virginia. This may have been a reflection of Case's bland, plain-vanilla style. There were few heartwarming stories about Case, in part because he seemed determined to market the brand, not himself. A reserved, private man, he would have been happy never to see his face on another magazine cover or do another television interview.

Yes, he had been on the cover of *Time* and *Fortune,* and yes, his stock holdings were worth more than $2.4 billion, but Case could walk through airports unmolested. Unlike Jeff Bezos or Bill Gates, Case had ensured that his image remained deliberately fuzzy. Even Bob Pittman, the hip entrepreneur who had been a creative force at MTV, assumed a relatively low profile after signing on as AOL's president.

Case, forty-one, was surprised by the extent to which the media treated Internet CEOs like rock stars. That was fine when you had a hit album and had convinced yourself you were the most creative person on the planet, but if the next album didn't sell, you got trashed. So Case deliberately tried to turn down the volume, to modulate the ups and downs. When AOL unveiled its new 5.0 software in the fall of 1999, he dutifully pitched the product on CNN and CNBC. But he refused to participate in personality profiles or lifestyles-of-the-rich-and-famous stories, the *People* magazine stuff.

Steve Case was in some ways naive about the media. In 1996, he quietly told his board that he and AOL's communications chief, Jean Villaneuva, were involved in a personal relationship. The situation was downright messy—both were splitting up with their spouses at the time—

and Case privately told several reporters, too, having persuaded himself that they would not consider it a story. It wasn't long before the romance made the gossip column of *The Washington Post.* "AOL's Love Connection," the headline said. Even *People* reported on the relationship. A month later, *Business Week* ran a cover story on Case that Kara Swisher later described in her book *AOL.com* as "the press equivalent of a big wet kiss," with AOL touted as "the most potent force in cyberspace." But Case became furious when the reporter asked about his relationship with Villanueva. He called *Business Week's* editors and threatened to withdraw permission for the magazine to use some childhood photos he had provided. The affair wound up as a single sentence buried deep in the text. (The couple eventually got married.)

In some respects, AOL's style mimicked that of a political operation, sharp-edged and defensive. After the 1996 election, AOL tried to hire Joe Lockhart, President Clinton's campaign spokesman, as its top public-relations executive. When the White House communications director, Don Baer, stepped down in 1998, AOL went after him. And when White House press secretary Mike McCurry was looking to leave during the Monica Lewinsky scandal, he was courted by AOL as well. The job went instead to Kathy Bushkin, a onetime spokeswoman for Gary Hart's presidential campaign who had also worked at *U.S. News & World Report.* And Bushkin viewed her AOL job as part of a permanent campaign, a constant battle to protect the company's image.

Bushkin dealt with the Internet press, the business press, and the consumer press, which covered AOL like a television channel. Her colleagues kept CNBC on in their offices because America Online was always being mentioned. Bushkin also maintained relationships with the Wall Street analysts who tracked the company, in part because the press followed them closely. She particularly admired Mary Meeker of Morgan Stanley, a hardworking Internet specialist who had understood AOL's story early on and who had become increasingly prominent as the technology sector boomed.

Bushkin was a bit more wary toward Jim Cramer. He had to be dealt with because he was a significant investor in the company, but he was also part of the press. Cramer had called Bob Pittman a dozen times but had never gotten a call back; instead he had to deal with "investor relations," the corporate equivalent of PR people who handled reporters, and with executives like Kathy Bushkin.

After AOL swallowed Netscape, its most significant acquisition, in late 1998, the company decided to hold a closed meeting for investors in New York. Bushkin got nervous after learning that Cramer was on the list of attendees.

"I really don't know what hat you're wearing," she told him. Reporters were barred from the meeting; she didn't want it written up in *TheStreet.com.*

Cramer told her to relax. Investing in companies like AOL, he said, "is my day job." He did not write about the meeting.

What made Bushkin's job especially challenging was that AOL was in the news virtually every day. In January 1999, when the company reported that its fourth-quarter earnings were up 340 percent from the year before, Case and Pittman conducted a conference call with the analysts with a script written by Bushkin's staff. Next came a rapid-fire series of announcements: AOL acquires a firm named MovieFone so it can sell movie tickets online. AOL strikes a deal with a credit card company. AOL teams up with Supermarkets Online to offer coupons to subscribers. When the company decided to overhaul CompuServe, the onetime rival it had recently bought out, *The Wall Street Journal* was given the exclusive so the makeover would reap two days' worth of news. "AOL Pitches Upscale Niche in Cyberspace," the *Journal* headline said.

On other stories, however, America Online simply refused to engage. Bushkin made it a policy never to comment or provide any guidance on the seemingly endless reports about AOL romancing this or that firm. The company said nothing when Gene Marcial wrote in *Business Week* in March 1999 that there were "rumors on the Street that AOL may well be the target of the likes of AT&T for a merger of near-equals." The rumor gathered steam for days until AT&T Chairman Michael Armstrong flatly denied it.

Sometimes America Online could seem downright arrogant, brushing off press inquiries even when taxpayers' money was involved. When *The Washington Post* reported that the Virginia legislature had secretly passed a bill that could save AOL $18 million or more in taxes on a new data center, AOL spokesman Andrew Weinstein, a former Newt Gingrich aide, refused to comment on the company's role in arranging the measure.

For all his misgivings, Case, a native Hawaiian who had edited his high school newspaper and once sold seeds and Christmas cards door-to-door, understood the value of positive press. When he was in college, business had been relegated to the back pages and *Fortune* was a yawn. But now that CNBC had a cult following and Internet use was exploding and day traders were becoming a force in society, he was amazed by the popularity of personality-driven business journalism.

Things had been very different for AOL in the early days. Case had spent a decade trying to get people to pay attention to the online world, to understand the nature of the Internet. In 1992, when AOL had just 200,000 subscribers compared to nearly 2 million for the much larger service Prodigy, he chatted up Walter Mossberg, *The Wall Street Journal* technology columnist. Mossberg praised the fledgling company's simple design "as the sophisticated wave of the future." That column, Case believed, gave AOL an enormous boost of credibility.

And Case understood, if only because of past failures, the value of consumer branding. At Procter & Gamble, Case had worked on a wipe-on hair conditioner called "Abound," which flopped; at PepsiCo, he had helped Pizza Hut develop a pocket pizza called Calizza, which also vanished without a trace. He was determined to position AOL as the user-friendly alternative to geek-happy technological complexity.

Most of the press, Case believed, bought into an inside-Silicon-Valley mentality that was as insular as the inside-the-Beltway culture in which he lived. The journalists were always searching for the big breakthrough, the high-tech "killer app" that would turn some kid into the next Bill Gates. Case found the approach frustrating, especially in the early years, when he was subjected to a seemingly endless stream of stories about how AOL would never make it. Even now, the press was always discovering some new trend—the 500-channel universe, cheaper Internet service providers, high-speed cable modems—that was going to leave AOL in the dust. And some Wall Street analysts were always bad-mouthing the stock. Case took perverse pleasure in proving them all wrong. And he had done it not through whiz-bang gizmos of the kind beloved by the media but by pro-viding solid, dependable service. Some journalists had privately con-fessed to him that they had badly underestimated AOL, and that was sweet vindication.

But as the company became a behemoth, Case became more cautious about the media and learned to pick his spots. He might turn down *60 Minutes,* a top-ten network show that reached 20 million homes, but he understood the value of CNBC, which had fewer than a million house-holds watching. He agreed to let a CNBC crew come out to Dulles for an interview and tour of the grounds. Case was not disappointed. The seg-ment, by reporter Jim Paymar, was remarkably upbeat.

"Remember when America Online was America On Hold?" Paymar began, recalling the bad old days a couple of years earlier when most sub-scribers were greeted by busy signals. Now, he said, "Americans are log-ging onto AOL in droves, making the company practically synonymous with the Internet itself." Steve Case had engineered "a remarkable turn-around." Some analysts "can't think of anything slowing down AOL's prospects in the future." The CEO was seen striding the corridors, survey-ing a new building, clicking his mouse. For that kind of segment, aimed at the investment community, even Case was willing to play to the cameras.

Few people knew it, but Case was a big Bruce Springsteen fan. He knew that the Jersey rocker had spent ten years playing in tiny clubs and making a couple of little-known albums before becoming a superstar. That, he felt, had given Springsteen a certain degree of humility when he hit it big. Case viewed his long struggle to build America Online the same way, but he had never lost his wariness toward the press. In an age when the media machinery was bestowing global fame on so many of his fellow CEOs, Steve Case was determined not to become a rock star.

8

IPO FEVER

T felt like doomsday. Internet stocks were crashing. The whole market was taking a beating. The TV chatter made clear that this was it. The bubble was finally bursting.

The Compaq fiasco seemed to have sparked the collapse. On Friday, April 9, the company made its "preannouncement" warning that its first-quarter earnings would not meet the Street's expectations. Days later, Eckhard Pfeiffer, the CEO, went on CNBC to promise an ongoing dialogue with Wall Street analysts. "We will fix the credibility gap," he declared in German-accented English.

It was too late. The Compaq board sacked Pfeiffer on Sunday, April 18. The next day, the Nasdaq suffered the second-biggest point decline in its history, losing 5.5 percent of its value. America Online dropped by 17 percent, Amazon 16 percent, Yahoo! 13.5 percent, Ameritrade 30 percent, DoubleClick 25 percent. The Dow, which had been up 275 points early in the day, plummeted 325 in a few short hours.

Ron Insana questioned whether the turnaround had "truly negative connotations" for the market. On days like this, he had the air of an undertaker, grim but professionally correct.

The day's carnage spawned some violent metaphors. Jon Olesky, a Morgan Stanley analyst, told *The Wall Street Journal* that this was no mere change in "leadership" from the tech sector to cyclical stocks: "The last change in leadership that was this bloody was the French Revolution."

Some believed that the selloff had been triggered by Jeremy Siegel, a Wharton Business School professor, who had written in that morning's *Journal* that Net stocks were overvalued. He said that AOL had a market value of nearly $200 billion, yet in 1998 it had finished 311th among American companies in profits, 415th in sales, and was selling for 700 times its earnings.

On *Moneyline* that night, Siegel said his piece was merely "the straw that broke the camel's back, but the back was pretty weak. . . . I don't think it's over."

"When will it be over?" Lou Dobbs asked.

"We have never seen valuations like this," Siegel said. "Valuations like this have never been justified."

This, in a nutshell, was the debate that had been raging for several years. Investors and analysts who had made their reputations weighing the intrinsic value of companies—analyzing price-earnings ratios, sales projections, revenue streams—had found that their lifetime of learning was useless in the face of upstart Net firms run by 26-year-old kids that came to be worth billions of dollars virtually overnight. This could not last, they said. This was an overheated craze, they said. But the Internet enthusiasts insisted that the old rules were now irrelevant. The Net would so profoundly alter the economy that these sky-high valuations were right on the money. Companies with few employees, little equipment, and no profits would soar in value as a growing share of economic transactions were conducted in cyberspace. Somehow tiny eBay, which had just $34 million in quarterly revenues, was worth more than K-Mart and Sears combined, at least in the estimation of Wall Street.

The media were obsessed by these arguments in part because Internet stocks had become the 800-pound gorilla of Wall Street. The sheer market clout of tech stocks now accounted for nearly a quarter of the value of the S & P 500, boosting its volatility and affecting millions whose money was in index funds or mutual funds. If Microsoft and AOL and Yahoo! had a bad week or a bad month, nearly all investors would suffer.

Each side looked for evidence that the other was out to lunch. When the stock of the online brokerage Ameritrade skyrocketed 840 percent in the first 100 days of 1999, the Net bulls snorted with satisfaction. When high-tech firms dropped like a rock, as they did on April 19, the Net bears growled that reality, as they had long predicted, was finally reasserting itself.

Alan Abelson of *Barron's* believed that the media's Internet cheerleaders didn't know any better. They had no interest in studying the past. They had come of age in the 1990s and refused to believe that this might be an unusual period. They were heavily influenced by analysts, money managers, and others with a strong professional interest in seeing stocks go up. They had lost their journalistic skepticism. Only bears like him were willing to face the hard truth.

On the other side of the spectrum, Jim Cramer wrestled with the same issue. He was tired of listening to the journalistic naysayers rail about Internet stocks, saying how absurd it was that Yahoo! had a market cap three times that of several small countries. He had shorted Net stocks dozens of times and wound up being taken to the cleaners. No more. These stratospheric stocks may have defied the forces of gravity, but they were making money, and he was paid for his performance.

The problem was that no one—not Cramer, not Insana, not Abelson, not the highly paid fortune tellers of Wall Street—knew what these or any other stocks were going to do. Over the next week, powered by strong corporate earnings and old-fashioned manufacturing stocks, the market came roaring back with a vengeance. The Nasdaq gained back all of the April 19 loss and grew another 6 percent to reach its all-time high. AOL was up 52 points, Yahoo! up 24, DoubleClick up 71. The Dow surged 285 points, to a record 10,727, and days later it crashed through the 11,000 barrier, just over a month after its much-hyped arrival in five-digit territory. So much for the doom-and-gloomers.

The only man who seemed to be enjoying the roller-coaster ride was Louis Rukeyser, the white-haired host of public television's *Wall Street Week*. He told his viewers that such volatility underscored the advantage of calmly assessing the markets on a weekly basis, as he did. The "dangers of day-to-dayness" were something that "we've been warning you against on this program for three decades," he said. Rukeyser chided *The New York Times* for its "frightening report" on that Monday's selloff. He disdained the Internet and dismissed the likes of CNBC as "the hour-by-hour cable television ticker shows." Of course, Rukeyser's avuncular advice came after the Friday close of the markets, too late for the millions of anxious investors who lived in an hour-by-hour world.

The CEOs, for their part, kept trying to sell their companies to the Street, even when reality was rude enough to intrude. On April 27, DoubleClick reported a quarterly loss of 18 cents a share, or worse than the 13-cent loss that the all-knowing analysts had predicted. And the verdict was swift: Its stock, adjusted after a recent split, tumbled 23⅛, to 148½. "DoubleClick Clunker," the *New York Post* headline said. Wall Street seemed to be saying that it was all right for a hot Internet start-up to lose money, but not more money than the wise men had decreed in advance. Kevin O'Connor took an upbeat stance with Bloomberg, saying that his company was looking to expand in Latin America and China. His stock gained back 11½ points the next day.

Even the most influential CEOs, such as AT&T's Michael Armstrong, were conscious of playing to the press. Armstrong pulled off a coup by mounting a major takeover that didn't leak in advance. Just after 5:00 P.M. on April 22, the company announced an unsolicited, $58-billion bid for MediaOne, the nation's third largest cable company, a crucial deal that would enable AT&T to deliver telephone, video, and Internet service through the same set of wires. An hour and fifty minutes later, Armstrong was in the green room at CNN, talking up the deal by phone on CNBC. Fifteen minutes after that, he was on the *Moneyline* set, making the same points.

And sometimes no one could figure out the market. It seemed like good news when America Online reported quarterly earnings of 11 cents a share, beating the official estimate of 9 cents. "We have moved into a league of our own in the Internet world," Steve Case told analysts in a conference call.

But the stock dropped 10 points the next day. The anticipated good news was somehow already built into AOL's price, which had had a spectacular run-up over the previous week. Still, it didn't seem to matter that the company had earned $117 million, nearly triple its profits a year earlier, or that it had added nearly 2 million subscribers, topping 17 million. What mattered was that AOL had failed to beat the so-called whisper number. This was the ephemeral estimate, usually higher, that analysts gossiped about but did not commit to paper, another sign of the arcane rituals of the Wall Street elite. The unspoken estimates varied, so no one was quite sure what the magic number was. There were even Websites called *Whispernumber.com* and *Earningswhispers.com.* Billions of dollars moved on whispers.

As the whispers grew louder, AOL stock dropped by 17 percent. Pundits quickly agreed that AOL had been left at the starting gate by the AT&T play for MediaOne, for the phone giant would now be able to deliver Net service over cable wires while America Online had no strategy for such "broadband" access. The press-shy company made its president, Bob Pittman, available to reporters to knock down the criticism. Pittman touted a "fabulous" alternative phone technology, called digital subscriber lines, to *The Wall Street Journal.*

Perhaps inevitably, some of the relentlessly hyped megamergers began to unravel, receding like a desert mirage. The *Journal* reported that USA Networks was backing out of its much-touted deal with Lycos because the shareholders simply didn't want to get hitched to Barry Diller's company. David Faber reported that MCI WorldCom's pursuit of Nextel was all but dead. Steve Lipin had been right to be cautious in hedging his Nextel story in early April; despite the big headlines, the talks had foundered over price. No matter; the *Journal* was already onto the next scoop, Chevron in talks to buy Texaco. That was the thing about the merger beat, there was always another deal coming down the pike.

Mergers could be especially difficult to cover when they took place close to home. At 7:30 A.M. on Monday, May 10, CNBC staffers handed Mark Haines a fact sheet about new acquisitions by NBC. The parent network had agreed to combine its Internet properties with the Websites Xoom.com and Snap.com, and to promote them on television. Xoom stock had jumped 10 percent the previous Friday on rumors of the deal. Haines's sheet said that news of the announcement was embargoed until 8:30, but when he checked the show rundown, there was no mention of it in that half-hour block. Haines and Faber were told they could not mention the story until it crossed the wires.

Haines protested vigorously, but to no avail. He understood the notion that since the news involved CNBC's parent company, it would only be fair to release it to everyone at once. But for *Squawk* to sit on an important story, waiting for a competitor to break it, made no sense. He could not resist letting viewers in on his frustration.

"We're going to have another Internet deal to talk about shortly," he said. "We have to wait for the official word."

Faber grumbled that they had to hold off "until it's carried somewhere else."

"I'm with you, David," Haines said. "I don't get it at all."

Minutes later, once the news was out, Haines's guests were lined up: NBC President Robert Wright, NBC Cable President Tom Rogers, and Xoom's CEO, Chris Kitze. Haines pressed them on how the new venture would make money. He was accustomed to NBC's special sensitivity on internal news. He often lobbied to get Jack Welch, who ran General Electric, NBC's corporate parent, to appear on *Squawk Box,* for Haines considered him the best CEO on the planet. But Welch almost never came on the show for fear that it would look like he was using the network for self-promotion.

With the Internet stock plunge vanishing as mysteriously as it had begun, there were now bulls everywhere in sight. As the market stampeded past 11,000 in early May, the media were filled with images of bulls. "Onward!" said the headline above the bull on the cover of *Barron's.* Another two-horned beast adorned the cover of *Business Week.* "A Wiser Bull?" the magazine asked. The *New York Post,* too, was in full market swoon: "Dow Wow!"

Not even the resignation of Robert Rubin, the widely respected Treasury secretary, could upset the applecart. When Cramer's onetime mentor at Goldman Sachs announced in early May that he was stepping down, the Dow plunged more than 200 points, but recovered most of the loss later in the day as traders concluded that his deputy, Lawrence Summers, was a reasonably good successor. Rubin was conscious of the importance of using the media to reassure the financial community. Once the news was official, he quickly called Alan Murray, the *Journal's* Washington bureau chief, then came out on the north lawn of the White House to talk to CNBC's Hampton Pearson and, a couple of camera positions closer to

Pennsylvania Avenue, to chat with Lou Dobbs by satellite. The message, reinforced by hundreds of news stories, was that Rubin was leaving the economy in extraordinarily strong condition and that there was nothing for investors to worry about.

Still, it was the nature of Wall Street that whenever a fragile consensus formed, events would conspire to shatter it. When Alan Greenspan gave a speech in May to the Federal Reserve Bank of Chicago about technology's importance to the economy, traders saw enough warning signs to send the market down, although it quickly recovered.

"Greenspan Drags Down Markets," complained the *New York Post,* although the Dow had finished the day only 8½ points down.

"Greenspan Credits Technology," said *The Washington Post* in a more upbeat assessment.

"Inflation Remains a Danger, Greenspan Warns," *The New York Times* said soberly.

"Party Can't Go On Forever, Greenspan Says," reported the *Los Angeles Times,* taking the longer view.

Inflation was the great bugaboo, the merest hint of which could send traders scurrying for the exits. Rising prices were likely to prompt the all-powerful Greenspan and his Fed colleagues to raise interest rates, which would make it harder for companies to raise money, which would hurt their stocks and trash the price of bonds as well. On May 14, the news that the consumer price index had risen 0.7 percent the previous month, the biggest spike in nine years, sent stocks and bonds tumbling, with the Dow dropping 193 points. Abby Joseph Cohen said reassuringly that inflation would not be a problem, but just about everyone else was in a near-panic. Some bond traders at the Chicago Board of Trade had "blowouts," meaning that they couldn't cover their losses and had to give up their exchange memberships.

Days later, the Fed announced a tightening "bias"—meaning that the board, in Fed-speak, had "adopted a directive that is tilted toward the possibility of a firming in the stance of monetary policy." In other words, the Fed was leaning toward raising interest rates at its next meeting. Stocks dropped again, but the Dow finished the day down only 16½. Everyone was nervous.

❑   ❑   ❑

Kim Polese was so excited on the morning of April 30 that she took some of her colleagues to the Morgan Stanley office in San Francisco to watch the first trade in her newly issued Marimba stock. Then she returned to Mountain View and threw a big picnic lunch for the entire company. That night she went out with friends and celebrated some more. Her initial public offering was a smashing success.

For an exhausting few weeks, Polese had conducted a "road show" to sell Wall Street on Marimba's IPO. The opening price quickly tripled, from 20 to 60¾, and despite growing weakness in the market for Internet stocks, the Street now valued the company at $1.4 billion. And Polese herself was worth a cool $70 million.

Fortune, which had dissed Polese as the "Beauty Hype" artist, now declared approvingly that "the hype has served the company well" and that Marimba was "not really a Net stock." The magazine quoted a money manager as saying: "Marimba suffers from the problem that it has an actual business with actual revenues." This, in the convoluted world of Internet economics, was deemed a disadvantage.

There were other skeptics as well. "Marimba has been cruising on dazzlingly effective PR, if not much else, for three years now," wrote Jim Seymour, a columnist for *TheStreet.com,* who knew and liked Polese. But he marveled "at the bye into the finals that Kim's high profile has brought for Marimba. Where's the beef?"

Polese was determined to show the media that there was indeed plenty of beef. She dropped her third PR firm in as many years and hired an in-house spokeswoman, Suzan Woods, who was deluged by reporters begging for access. Woods encouraged Polese to work the press. The two flew to New York for sit-downs with *Fortune, Forbes, The New York Times,* and other publications, as well as interviews on CNBC and CNNfn. *Upside* magazine put her on the cover—"How Kim Got Her Groove Back"— with no fewer than eleven photos inside.

But Polese was still bothered by her glamor-girl image. "You're really flashy," said one executive she met on her rounds, even though she was wearing no makeup, a conservative navy pantsuit, and a high-necked beige blouse. Sometimes the hype was more real than the reality.

On *Digital Jam,* the CNNfn technology show, Polese stopped smiling when host Bruce Francis introduced her as "one of the most glamorous" CEOs. He said that her company had "disappeared from public view" but was now "back" with its IPO.

"We were a little ahead of the curve," Polese said.

Francis asked about her high profile. "As one of the few women CEOs in the high-tech industry, I did get a lot of attention personally," Polese replied. "None of it matters at the end of the day if I'm not performing."

And there was the inevitable question about Marimba's stock, which had dropped sharply along with other Internet issues. "You can't really get too caught up in the volatility day to day," she said. "We're moving towards profitability."

IPOs were great for the companies that pocketed the proceeds, but they were the ultimate racket, even when compared to the usual heavy-handed finagling on Wall Street. The average investor could only dream of getting an early crack at these offerings, most of which would skyrocket in value as soon as their precious shares were snapped up by the insiders, by the big-league brokers and institutional clients who always seemed wired into the right money-making schemes. By the time the public got a chance, the quick fortunes had already been reaped.

This was no accident, for the rules of engagement were essentially rigged. Typically, a syndicate of investment banks would manage the offering, escort the CEO on the road show for major investors, and then dole out the shares to its best customers. The very scarcity of the shares would boost their value, allowing the initial investors to "flip" them, or sell them immediately, and pocket the profit. On May 4, 1999, when the investment firm Goldman Sachs went public, there was twelve times as much demand as there were available shares. Goldman designated itself as the lead underwriter and parceled out the 69 million shares to its favored clients, shutting out the other managers—including Morgan Stanley and Merrill Lynch—and even many investors with ties to Goldman. The shares jumped 33 percent in value the first day, from 53 to more than 70, as the brokerage raised a stunning $3.6 billion. Goldman Chairman Henry

Paulsen found himself with newly issued stock worth $286 million, and the company's 221 partners, including Abby Joseph Cohen, each received a multimillion-dollar windfall.

Tantalized by such major paydays, the big Wall Street houses were wrestling each other for a share of these increasingly lucrative IPOs, particularly the Net start-ups that seemed to turn vague promises into gold.

Since 1998, IPOs handled by Goldman Sachs had jumped an average of 293 percent from their offering price, with eBay multiplying 29 times in value in just seven months. But Morgan Stanley had the hot hand now, edging out even the prestigious Goldman with five Internet IPOs since the beginning of 1999 that had raised $390 million.

Morgan's secret weapon was Mary Meeker, the workaholic analyst who was an early booster of America Online and had handled its stock offerings. Meeker had been touting Net companies since before the Net was cool, and it was she who had won Kim Polese's business and accompanied her on her Wall Street tour. Meeker had also beaten out Goldman to land the $160-million IPO for priceline.com, which peddled name-your-own-price airline tickets, and whose stock had soared a remarkable 738 percent. She was the Queen of the Internet, so influential that her detractors called her "Bloody Mary." But many reporters seemed to forget these business relationships when touting Meeker's upbeat comments about the companies whose stock she was pitching, including AOL, Yahoo!, Netscape, @Home, and Amazon. It was the equivalent of political reporters quoting a major fundraiser who lauded Al Gore or George W. Bush without mentioning the financial connection. In early May, on the day that CNBC and others quoted Meeker as praising priceline.com for being in a "sweet spot," its stock jumped 17³⁄₁₆ points, to 151—putting Morgan Stanley in a sweet spot as well.

But even superstar analysts got overextended. NextCard, which provided consumer credit on the Net, dumped Meeker and Morgan Stanley as its lead underwriter just as the company was getting ready to market its IPO. NextCard officials complained that Meeker had paid little attention to them, and switched the $75-million offering to Donaldson, Lufkin & Jenrette. "Mary Meeker is covering something like sixty companies all over the Internet sector," said one person involved in the deal. "She can't do that. No one can cover sixty companies."

Meeker, though, apparently saw no conflict between her company's business interests and her public pronouncements. She had lobbied hard to win over eBay executives before their IPO, but even though the fledgling auction company chose archrival Goldman Sachs to underwrite the deal, Meeker still published a favorable report on the stock the day after eBay began trading. Most investors who heard about Meeker's recommendation had no way of knowing that she had lost this competition for the IPO. (Goldman was legally barred from touting the stock for thirty days.) Meeker continued to press eBay's CEO, Meg Whitman, for some of eBay's future business, and sure enough, Queen Mary won a share of the next stock offering from the company she had been praising to the press.

❏   ❏   ❏

Jim Cramer was on the verge of vindication. People had scoffed when he launched *TheStreet.com* and started losing millions. But he had built the Website from scratch, barreling ahead on the sheer force of his personality. And now, he believed, it was all going to pay off. He was ready to take the thing public and cash in on the Internet gold rush. He would have the last laugh on all his carping critics.

Cramer had caught a lucky break a few months earlier. Disney, which served as *TheStreet.com*'s Internet service provider, had been paid not with cash but with warrants entitling it to buy 10 percent of the company. All Disney officials had to do was sign the papers by January 1, 1999. Cramer was sure that Disney would seize this opportunity, for its share would potentially be worth tens of millions of dollars. But Disney failed to exercise the warrants, and Cramer threw a big party with his wife to celebrate. Their chunk of the company was now worth immeasurably more.

Wall Street, naturally, wanted a piece of the action. Kevin English, *TheStreet.com*'s CEO, told Cramer that Mary Meeker was aggressively pursuing the company's IPO. English said that Meeker had even enlisted his brother, a top Morgan Stanley executive, in her campaign. But Jim Cramer was determined to steer the business to Goldman Sachs. It was Goldman that had given him his first break, Goldman that had taught him the business, and it would be disloyal to go with Morgan Stanley. The decision was one of the few major turndowns for Mary Meeker. Cramer was surprised, therefore, to read in *The New Yorker* that Meeker was dissing *TheStreet.com.* An unnamed associate was quoted as saying that Meeker had passed on the IPO because she felt the news service's market was too narrow to grow rapidly. That certainly wasn't the impression Cramer had gotten.

When *TheStreet.com*'s IPO finally hit the market on May 11, 1999, it was a smashing success. The office at 100 Wall Street had been incredibly tense until CNBC announced the opening numbers. Goldman had orginally planned to price the stock around $11 a share, but the premarket buzz boosted the opening price to $19. From there it quickly soared to $71 a share, leaving Cramer, who owned 14 percent of the company, sitting on a stake worth $220 million—all this for a 100-person news service that he had begged corporate buyers to take off his hands for two years. Cramer's only loss was in the office pool—he had bet that the stock would hit 45, Jeff Berkowitz had said 52, and Cramer's office manager Jean Cullen had predicted 61, winning the $200 pot. He had taken care of the hedge fund, too, providing the 63,000 shares given to him as a Goldman client to Cramer, Berkowitz for the bargain-basement price of $19 a share. A colleague dumped a big box of confetti on him, and he paid a congratulatory visit to the *Street.com* offices.

Cramer was touched when his father, Ken, bearing a big bag of Philadelphia soft pretzels, came up to New York with his sister, Nan, boasting that *The Philadelphia Inquirer* had described him as the boy-made-good from Wyndmoor, Pennsylvania. "Mom would be very proud," Ken Cramer said.

In a rare act of self-denial, Cramer dodged the media all day. He refused to talk to *The New York Times,* the *New York Post,* or the *Daily News,* giving only a couple of quotes to a *USA Today* reporter he had known for years. He turned down invitations from CNN, from Charlie Rose, even from his pals at CNBC. "I'm not the spokesman," he said again and again, trying to shift the spotlight to Dave Kansas, the editor, or Kevin English. Cramer was worried that *TheStreet.com*'s staffers would resent him for hogging the limelight.

But it was no use. Every story used Cramer's picture, with the *USA*

Today shot making him look like a blabbering lunatic. The truth was, although he was the largest shareholder and occasionally threw his weight around, he had virtually nothing to do with the operation's management. While his visage stared out from the top right-hand corner of the yellow-tinted Website, *TheStreet.com* was merely his hobby. When the company's executives were conducting the road show for investors, he was on vacation in the Caribbean. He wasn't involved in the editing, and he didn't know that circulation had risen to 51,000, in part by giving subscriptions to people with sufficient frequent-flier miles. Somehow, that didn't matter. To the press, Cramer *was TheStreet.com.*

After a celebratory dinner with his family that night, Cramer said he had to go to bed early so he could make his usual 5:00 A.M. arrival at the office. His sister Nan thought he was crazy not to take a few days off, not to stop and smell the flowers of financial success. "At a certain point you're supposed to relax," she said. But he was hard-wired to work like a maniac, and he was always looking for a challenge. Cramer was even muttering about getting involved in the Democratic Senate campaign being mounted in New Jersey by his friend Jon Corzine, the former chairman of Goldman Sachs.

"You're nuts," his wife told him. *TheStreet.com* had put a great strain on their marriage. No one but their closest friends knew the depth of the problems he and Karen had been having. Now, amid the celebrating, she wanted part of her husband back.

For all the excitement of selling 5.5 million shares of stock and raising $104 million, Cramer and *TheStreet.com* had to decide what to do with the cash. They were already thinking about acquisitions. And despite his caution about the irrationality of the Internet market, Cramer was now one of its major beneficiaries. Wall Street had valued his company at $1.4 billion, nearly a quarter of the value of The New York Times Company, which had 150 years of history, more than a thousand editorial employees at its flagship newspaper and a circulation of 1.1 million. This was insane, of course, but not to Jim Cramer. He was already looking at his corporate baby like Amazon, believing that they could justify these sky-high numbers if they executed an aggressive game plan.

One lingering problem was Marty Peretz, whose *Street.com* shares were now worth about $200 million. In Cramer's view, Peretz had been bad-mouthing him all over the media, even after they had agreed not to speak publicly about their falling out. A few weeks earlier, a friend called to report that Peretz had given a quote to *Fortune* about their split, telling the magazine that he couldn't keep his money with someone to whom he was no longer speaking. So much for their cease-fire.

"I can't fucking believe it," Cramer said. "How much does this guy hate me that he talked?" Peretz was a master of payback, Cramer believed; he used to talk about "owning" this or that reporter when he wanted a story, and Cramer felt like his latest victim. Now Cramer was worried about an article in the works at *Vanity Fair;* he had received an e-mail from the reporter with a series of questions that had arisen from her conversations with Peretz. He could tell that Marty was still on the warpath.

Peretz, for his part, thought that Cramer's view of the media coverage was off the wall. He had talked to reporters only when they called with questions from Cramer. What possible incentive, Peretz wondered, did he have to peddle the story of their breakup? He wasn't crazy. He was, for better or worse, in business with the guy, and his financial success depended on Cramer's reputation. If the world believed that Cramer was a lousy investor, Peretz figured, what would his advice be worth, and why would people pay to read it online?

The multimillionaires still could not bury the hatchet. It was a full-fledged blood feud now, each man nursing ancient grievances and seizing on every development as further evidence of the other's mendacity.

For all the success of *TheStreet.com,* Cramer was feeling anxious. He debated whether to buy a Porsche but decided that he didn't want to live ostentatiously, to mar his self-image as a schlubby guy from Philly. The day after the stock debut, he sent an e-mail to his Harvard pal Kurt Andersen, the former editor of *New York* magazine. Cramer said that he was suffering from "post-IPO traumatic disorder."

9

POPPING THE BUBBLE

THE bears were growling on *Squawk Box*—big, brown grizzlies climbing on rocks. The footage was startling because it eclipsed the bulls that had been peering out from newspapers and magazines just four weeks earlier. Ralph Acampora was on CNBC warning that many Internet stocks were in trouble. David Faber said that it was difficult for brokerage houses to downgrade the tech stocks because of their investment banking relationships with the firms.

"Are we suggesting that this would skew the analysts' view of these companies?" Mark Haines asked sarcastically.

By late May the Dow had dropped 800 points, back below 10,500, but the real bear market was in Net stocks, and this time the decline was even more dramatic. The specter of rising interest rates particularly hurt these debt-laden companies, and the record-setting pace of Internet IPOs was flooding the once-scarce market with more shares than there were buyers. The Dow Jones Internet index had dropped 26 percent in little more than a month. And *TheStreet.com*'s stock was feeling the heat: Two weeks after it had soared to 71 on the first day of trading, it was now languishing in the low 30s.

More important than the technical factors, though, was the sense of a psychological shift, which gave rise to a well-worn metaphor. "I think the air is coming out of the bubble," said Barton Biggs, who just weeks earlier had pronounced himself befuddled by the market. "Pop! Goes the Bubble," a *New York Times* headline said.

Even the Internet bulls who had done so much to champion the charge toward Net stocks were raising red flags. David Faber reported from his sources that Mary Meeker had put out the word that the correction was not over and that these stocks could drop another 20 percent. But Meeker, who like her fellow bulls had not foreseen this turn of events, would not appear on CNBC, choosing to hide behind her written statement instead. She rarely talked to the press unless someone was writing an upbeat profile of her.

Of all the CNBC anchors and reporters, Ron Insana looked the most worried during the decline. Most of Insana's Wall Street and government sources had been telling him for months that the Internet mania would not end well. Either the market had gone through a magical restructuring, as many investors seemed to believe, or they were in the middle of the biggest speculative orgy in history. Net stocks, he figured, could turn out to be like radio stocks in the twenties or biotech stocks in the eighties, feeding off an important new technology that nonetheless produced lots of financial losers.

Insana was puzzled when viewers called him bearish; even some CNBC staffers viewed him that way. He believed that he was just reporting the facts, that his image amounted to a Rorschach test in which people worried about taking a bath would project their fears onto him. But the truth was that Insana was quite concerned about the market. This sell-off was really vicious.

Some days, he and the gang would sit around the set and declare themselves idiots for not having bought these high-flying Net stocks a couple of years earlier. He was tired of meeting men a decade younger than him who were worth $10 million. But the last few weeks showed that he was right to be skeptical, whether viewers liked it or not.

And some did not. "Once again, CNBC got out their trusty slate of doomsters," a chat room visitor complained. The CNBC crew were always more popular when they were trumpeting the market's rising fortunes. That was one reason the network had soared in popularity along with the bull market. Almost no one liked sinking stock prices, and plenty of folks blamed the messengers. And as the market headed down, Insana increasingly found himself on his own. He was now having trouble getting some of his favorite traders on the phone. Their funds were getting wrecked, and for all the hundreds of millions they had made investors, they were only as good as their last trade. Insana saw this as the Wall Street version of Hollywood, an incredibly unforgiving business that created stars and discarded them virtually overnight.

Chris Byron was watching *Street Signs* in his Connecticut basement on the afternoon of May 25, enjoying the carnage. With one eye on Ron Insana and the other on his computer, he tracked the collapse in Net stocks: Xoom down 15 percent for the day, priceline.com down 14.8 percent, DoubleClick down 11.6 percent. Four weeks earlier, DoubleClick stock had been zooming along at 171; now it was at 86. Byron believed it was worth thirty bucks. Other companies were way off their 1999 highs: Amazon from 221 to 111; Yahoo! from 244 to 126; Marimba from 74 to 21; AOL from 175 to 115. And the impact was being felt at the top: Kevin O'Connor had already sold off more than $37 million of his DoubleClick stock. The value of Jeff Bezos's Amazon stock had dropped from $13 billion to $6.5 billion. Tim Koogle's Yahoo! holdings were down from just under $1 billion to $514 million.

The CNBC arrows, Byron noticed, were all red and pointing south. At 3:50 the Dow, which had been down just a few points in early afternoon, had dropped 53 points, and the Nasdaq was down 59. This had been going on for two weeks now; in the last half-hour of trading, everyone started selling, driving prices down dramatically.

Byron began monitoring a day traders' chat room, using a password slipped to him by a friend at Merrill Lynch. A trader named Merlin was advising his pals on a stock called BRCD: "Take your $$$$ @ 46." Byron had never heard of the stock. Some quick computer research found a Reuters story describing it as Brocade Communications, an Internet firm whose shares had just doubled in value after its IPO. Byron shook his head; even as Net stocks were dropping like a rock, these day traders were still playing the IPO game. Byron was certain that Brocade would be down in three days.

At 4:02, CNBC was showing the Dow down 119, the Nasdaq down 69.

Everyone was racing for the exits. A hedge-fund manager in San Francisco called, and he agreed that the week looked like another bloodbath. Byron clicked back to the chat room, where the day traders were worried about sinking. "Better take your water-wings," one said.

Next, Byron checked on *TheStreet.com*. The stock had dropped 7.6 percent that day and was down to 30—a 58 percent plunge from its opening-day debut. Even though the Website carried his column, Byron believed that the stock was way overpriced. Cramer's IPO had succeeded not because of his credentials—he'd just come off a terrible year—but because his two years of exposure on *Squawk Box* had made him into a nationally known Wall Street figure. Fame, not fundamentals, had driven that stock sky-high, and now, just as Byron had expected, it was falling back to earth.

Jim Cramer tried not to worry about the plummeting price. The stock was new, and naturally it would bounce around for a while. Cramer had more important things on this mind. He had to get ready for the board meeting that evening.

❏   ❏   ❏

After months of fury, of stewing in his own bubbling anger, of blaming Marty Peretz for all his problems, Cramer finally had to admit that he had been wrong.

The feud between the two estranged friends had damaged both of them, had gone on too long, had become way too public. Cramer had a dangerous tendency to get swept away by his feelings, to swing wildly along the emotional pendulum from love to bitter hate. Perhaps he had precipitated the fight in ways that he was just now starting to grasp.

Admitting error was not one of Cramer's great strengths. After the success of the IPO, Mike Kinsley had urged him in an e-mail to patch things up with Peretz. Cramer said that they just couldn't find common ground. Kinsley told him that he was being ridiculous. Cramer began to feel that he was acting like his five-year-old daughter, sulking in her room because she was mad at her play date.

The first two years of *TheStreet.com* had been torture for Cramer. He had felt like he was carrying the damn thing and that Marty wasn't lifting a finger. They had been friends for so long that Cramer hadn't properly drawn up the paperwork delineating their respective roles. He felt underpaid and was convinced that he deserved more stock.

"He did put up five million dollars," Karen reminded him. "You can't tell him to take a goddamn hike."

The bottom line, Cramer confessed to himself, was that he had an unrealistic view of how much control he should have over *TheStreet.com.* In the end, he had chosen the business over their friendship. He had also been wrong to have sent those nasty e-mails, disparaging Peretz behind his back. Karen said that both he and Peretz had a great capacity for vindictiveness, and she was right. Peretz had gotten him back, had nearly sunk the hedge fund and damaged his reputation, but Cramer's hands were also unclean.

They buried the hatchet that night at La Côte Basque, a swank Manhattan restaurant where *TheStreet.com*'s board was meeting for dinner. Cramer hadn't even been sure whether he was going to say hello to his former mentor, but when Peretz said that he had been cleaning out some old stuff and found a picture of Cramer's two girls, something snapped.

"I've been out of control," Cramer told Peretz. He said they had both done a lot of harm, had thrown too much shit at each other. The two men collapsed into each other's arms. Cramer felt compelled to make a public apology. He was relieved that the war was finally over.

"I can't emphasize strongly enough that I did things wrong," he told the board. He and Peretz were soon absorbed in a three-hour strategy session about *TheStreet.com,* which continued long into the night.

Cramer's latest worry was the huge amount of press he had gotten since *TheStreet.com* had gone public. *The New York Observer* had run a front-page cartoon of his face as a giant, bulging, bug-eyed blimp. He felt that these articles made him look like a glorified hack, a showboat, rather than someone who was a stellar fund manager. But he had an even greater concern at the moment. The Nasdaq had just voted to move toward extending its trading hours, adding a second session from 5:30 P.M. until 9:00 or 10:00, and the New York Stock Exchange was weighing a similar plan. This, he was convinced, could ruin his life.

Cramer already got to work around 5:00 A.M. He didn't see his kids enough as it was. He had gotten a taste of the new world when he took his older daughter to a Mets-Phillies game at Shea Stadium and she noticed that the scoreboard was flashing the numbers for the day's most active stocks. Did this mean Daddy would have to work during the game? No, he assured her, but with night trading he might have to, even at Shea. He was already making plans to work two or three nights a week until 9:00.

This was awful. Just as business had caused Cramer to blow up his friendship with Peretz, now he'd be risking his marriage. His father had sold gift wrap six days a week, but Cramer had millions of dollars in the bank. What was his excuse for working as hard as his father? The problem was that Cramer also had a responsibility to his investors. He had something to prove after his lousy performance in 1998. If Yahoo! or AOL was dropping in evening trading, he needed to know that. To tell his investors that he had missed an important trade because he was trying to be a better father was no longer an adequate answer. Fifteen years ago he simply would have worked every night. But he was now forty-four. On Friday nights, when the limousine drove him home to New Jersey after a long week, he would be asleep in the backseat before they crossed the river. He was getting too old for all this. Something, he felt, had to give.

❑   ❑   ❑

Dan Dorfman was also feeling the ravages of time. At sixty-eight, he was recovering from a stroke. He walked with a cane and had little use of his left arm. His once-gravelly voice, which had barked his stock market scoops on television, was weak. But he was determined to resume the work he loved.

For much of the 1980s and early 1990s, Dan Dorfman had been the most influential financial commentator, hands down, in America. His vacuum-cleaner style, spewing out all manner of predictions and prognostication, left a dust cloud of controversy but invariably moved the markets. Then, at the height of his power, he had been abruptly forced into exile, the beginning of a four-year nightmare.

Nothing had ever come easy for Dorfman. He had grown up in foster homes, never went to college, and hung out in pool halls until he landed a job in 1968 with *The Wall Street Journal,* where he later wrote the Heard on the Street column. But the *Journal* asked him to resign in 1973 after learning that one of the sources he often quoted had made it possible for him to buy hot new stock issues that weren't available to the public.

Once he set out on his own, Dorfman's visibility soared. He moved his column to *New York* magazine and then to *Esquire,* to *USA Today,* and finally to *Money* magazine. He joined Lou Dobbs's *Moneyline* soon after its 1980 launch and left a decade later to join CNBC, by which time he was earning a combined $800,000 a year. He scored some huge exclusives, disclosing the SEC investigation of Ivan Boesky and the Time-Warner megamerger. He gave speeches for $25,000 a pop. And his high profile had given him immense power to affect stock prices.

A short, balding, bushy-browed man who spoke in the brogue of his native Brooklyn, Dorfman's influence was legendary. In the early 1990s, the Chicago Board of Trade delayed the automatic execution of trading in stocks that Dorfman discussed in his daily 12:35 report on CNBC. Ninety-five percent of the stocks he touted on television increased in value, usually within minutes, though the bump was often short-lived. And his negative assessments could be fatal. In November 1995, after Dorfman cited unnamed sources in reporting that the retail chain Bradlees was headed for bankruptcy, a spokesman for the firm called his comments "a major contributing factor" in the struggling company's decision to file for Chapter 11. When *The New York Times* ran a negative piece on a firm called Spectrum Information Technologies in May 1993, the stock barely moved. When Dorfman broadcast the same news three days later, the stock dropped from 12 to 5¾.

In similar fashion, Quaker Oats stock jumped 14 percent when Dorfman reported in 1995 that Coca-Cola might make a bid for the cereal company and that the legendary stock picker Warren Buffett, a major Coke shareholder, had approved it. But no takeover effort materialized. "Dan Dorfman does not have a clue," Coke insisted. Other "scoops"— that Donald Trump would buy Caesar's World, that corporate raider Irwin Jacobs would buy Greyhound—also failed to pan out. Even those sympathetic to Dorfman began saying that he was being manipulated by his Wall

Street sources. Gene Marcial said that Dorfman was getting too many bum stories. *Newsweek* columnist Allan Sloan, a longtime friend, called him "a high-grade business gossip writer" who had "gotten much too sloppy." Jim Cramer thought Dorfman distorted the market with unreliable information funneled by his friends. Matt Winkler didn't think much of Dorfman's track record, but felt that Bloomberg had no choice but to summarize his market-moving comments each day.

Dorfman, for his part, maintained that he felt more comfortable when his sources had a financial interest in the deals they were touting. "They're putting their money where their mouth is," he would say. And he was riding high until October 1995, when a *Business Week* story effectively cut short his career.

The magazine quoted unnamed sources as saying that Dorfman was "under investigation for activities including possible illegal insider trading, wire and mail fraud, and violations of securities laws." The piece said that the Justice Department was investigating Dorfman's relationship with Donald Kessler, a Long Island publicist who was said to have been paid $5,000 to $10,000 by clients for introducing them to Dorfman. After Kessler had arranged for Dorfman to have dinner with an executive from Alter Sales, for example, Dorfman mentioned the company on CNBC. The stock price rose slightly on seven times the average trading volume, and Kessler soon received 20,000 shares from Alter Sales, which he sold. One of Kessler's associates made $590,000 after Kessler leaked Dorfman some news about another client, Spectrum Information, and Kessler received $10,000.

Dorfman protested his innocence. "I love my work and I'm not about to jeopardize it by screwing around to make a fast buck on the side," he declared. Dorfman felt that the investigation was bullshit but knew that his visibility had made him a prime target. He had received no money, had not even bought a stock in five years, limiting himself to mutual funds. He refused to recognize, though, that at the very least he was guilty of poor judgment by doing favors for crooks. Dorfman liked to say that all financial journalists were used by their sources, but most shied away from shady characters.

The worst was yet to come. *Money* magazine fired Dorfman in January

1996 after he refused to disclose his sources to the editors who wanted to follow up on the *Business Week* allegations. Dorfman thought the request was outrageous since *Money* was demanding the sources for hundreds of stories, even one involving Time Warner, its parent company. A lawyer who had given Dorfman a great takeover story called to say: "Dan, I hope you'll never mention my name. If you do, you're finished with me and a lot of people who know you." How could he betray these people who had helped him so much during his career? *Money,* he figured, was just trying to get rid of him.

CNBC hired a law firm to investigate the *Business Week* charges against Dorfman. The attorneys deposed him for hours, demanded all his records and bank statements. And the *Journal,* his old paper, raised new questions in a front-page story, saying that Dorfman never disclosed that a broker he had quoted more than two dozen times—a man later acquitted on fraud charges—had once managed a brokerage account for him.

Soon afterward came the debilitating stroke, which initially left Dorfman in a wheelchair. He had absolutely no doubt that the stress caused by the *Business Week* exposé had caused the attack. The CNBC probe finally cleared him, but his voice was too strained for him to return to the air. Bill Bolster, who had recently become CNBC president, let his contract lapse and, in what Dorfman viewed as an insult, the network stopped paying his health insurance.

Donald Kessler and six other people were ultimately convicted in the various schemes swirling around Dorfman, but he was never accused of wrongdoing. In fact, prosecutors never even bothered to interview Dorfman in the investigation, although *Business Week* did not get around to reporting that. Dorfman made an audition tape for CNBC in 1998, but network officials said that his voice was still too weak. He wrote for a magazine called *Financial World* that soon folded. His career seemed over.

In the spring of 1999, however, Dorfman was ready to return. Not in the newspapers, where he had first made his name, and not on television, where his impact was unrivaled, but on the Internet, the thriving second-chance arena for the once great.

Dorfman was mounting his comeback with a little-known outfit called

JagNotes.com. The Website was essentially a computerized newsletter of stock tips and analysts' calls. There was even a Rumor Room, which the company stressed was nothing more than unconfirmed gossip that nevertheless could affect the market. The operation was, in some ways, the ideal environment for Dorfman's return.

After Dorfman announced the *JagNotes* deal, thirty of his longtime Wall Street sources threw a surprise party for him at Jimmy Chung's restaurant. "When I walked in, you applauded me," Dorfman told the gathering. "The fact is, I should applaud you." He felt that his sources had sustained his career, although a few of them, people he had trusted, had brought it crashing down.

Shortly before Dorfman's Internet debut, a CNBC official called his producer, Philip Recchia, at home on a Sunday to ask that Dorfman join the network's Website, which was being revamped. But it was too late. *JagNotes* had offered him an attractive deal, and CNBC had turned its back on him once too often. A few days before Dorfman started his new job, he got advance word of the Exxon-Mobil deal. It was the merger of his dreams, but there was nothing he could do with it.

On May 17, 1999, Dorfman began filing a daily 1:00 P.M. report for *JagNotes.com.* On the first day, he spun a tale about Michael Bloomberg eyeing an acquisition of Gannett, the media giant that owned twenty-one television stations and seventy-four newspapers, including *USA Today,* where Dorfman had once worked. The problem, he noted, was that Bloomberg would somehow have to come up with $20 billion. Bloomberg didn't bother to return Dorfman's calls.

Dorfman also reported that "a long-rumored takeover . . . of chemical biggie Union Carbide" could "finally be approaching reality. That is, if you believe the talk that's said to be coming from inside Goldman Sachs. Such talk, of course, is hardly a confirmation of anything." Despite the disclaimer, Dorfman reported that DuPont and the German chemical giant BASF were interested in acquiring Carbide in a $5.5 billion deal. BASF said it had no such interest, and DuPont wouldn't comment.

Dorfman was back, thanks to the Net, and investors were noticing. "Reports are buzzing on Wall Street that the Chase Manhattan Corp. is in exploratory talks to buy brokerage kingpin Merrill Lynch & Co.," he wrote in his distinctive style. David Faber took to the airwaves to declare the rumors untrue, just as Ron Insana had four months earlier, but no matter. The Dorfman Effect still packed a punch. Merrill's stock soared 21 percent over the next two days, especially as Dorfman named two other possible suitors: Morgan Stanley and Bank of America. "Keep in mind that these are unconfirmed reports," he warned, raising the question of why he was touting them in the first place. But Dow Jones and Reuters credited Dorfman with moving Merrill's stock. That was how he did business, as he had in the old days.

And just like the old days, Dorfman wasn't shy about helping traders tout their own stocks. He quoted money manager Bob Olstein as praising Harmon International Industries, a maker of video and audio components in which Olstein happened to own 115,000 shares. He quoted analyst Casey Stern of Starr Securities as calling the company Cash Technologies "a relatively undiscovered gem"—except that it had already been discovered by Stern, whose brokerage had taken the company public a year earlier.

Within days, Dorfman was feeling somewhat out of it. When he reported that chemical company W. R. Grace was turning itself around, a longtime source called to berate him. Things have changed since you've been away, the source said. Nobody cares about a stodgy old company like Grace. Haven't you ever heard of Sun Microsystems, Microsoft, or Dell? Another story like that and people will think you're ready to retire.

Other things had changed as well. Dorfman felt ready for the loony bin after watching the market's takeover fever and the huge gambles that people were taking. But takeover rumors had always been his métier. Usually, Dorfman would check the stock and the options to see if they were moving on the street chatter. He felt that the typical investor deserved to hear the same rumors, true or not, as the big boys. But if the stock wasn't moving, Dorfman would shy away. He got word that Honeywell and Allied Signal planned to merge, but decided against reporting it when he saw no sign of stock activity. For once he had been too cautious. The merger was announced soon afterward.

On other stories, Dorfman had trouble letting go. Weeks after the supposed Merrill-Chase merger failed to happen, he declared that "talk is recurring" that Merrill Lynch and Bank of America might get hitched, although "whether that's true is anybody's guess."

JagNotes, which a year earlier had been a faxed newsletter service, came under the skeptical eye of Chris Byron. He was amazed that by adding ".com" to its name and moving to a Website, the publicly traded company had managed to boost its stock by 3,300 percent. The Street was valuing *JagNotes* at $200 million, despite the fact that its gross revenues for 1998 appeared to have been just $1.2 million. The valuation was based on company projections that it would be able to lure 300,000 online subscribers for $9.95 a month.

Whatever his doubts, Byron was sympathetic to the *JagNotes* mission. In his view, the big Wall Street firms making their morning squawk-box calls to brokers were engaged in a "legalized manipulation of prices" by parceling out information not available to the general public. *JagNotes* upset the applecart through its network of sources and spies, just as Maria Bartiromo did each morning (she also looked at *JagNotes* but didn't find it terribly useful). And critics complained that the *JagNotes* intelligence contained plenty of errors. A Lehman Brothers official told Byron, "That *JagNotes* thing would drive us crazy. I'd come to work in the morning and find a dozen messages from callers wanting to know why we'd downgraded Coca-Cola, for example, when we'd actually upgraded it." But Byron was unequivocal on one point: He liked Dan Dorfman and felt that he'd gotten a raw deal when he had been driven out of journalism.

Was there much difference between Dorfman's reports and the *JagNotes* rumor department? The rumor page was filled with unconfirmed suggestions that Amazon would make a bid for Borders Books, that IBM would swallow a firm called NetGravity, that Campbell Soup might split up and sell off some divisions. And occasionally these rumors would pan out: A *JagNotes* brief in May 1999 that the Baby Bell firm US West might be taken over was followed days later by a surprise attempt by Global Crossing, an upstart telecommunications firm, to swallow US West.

Dorfman's reporting was more sophisticated. He relied on sources he had grown to trust over the years, called the companies involved for comment, and sometimes was right on target. Life was harder now for the disabled Dorfman, but he liked to say that he still had his mind and his mouth. Most of all, Dan Dorfman wanted his reputation back. Somehow it seemed fitting that the leading stock tipster of an earlier age had been reincarnated on the Internet at the height of the late nineties bull market.

❏   ❏   ❏

During the same period, with Internet stocks sinking, Henry Blodget felt like he'd been hit over the head with a two-by-four.

The baby-faced, thirty-three-year-old Merrill Lynch analyst had made his name with a stratospheric prediction for Amazon.com, one that reflected his fiercely bullish view of Net stocks. It was that daringly upbeat approach, in fact, that had gotten Blodget his blue-chip job at Merrill. But now he had a problem. Amazon and other prominent Net stocks were crashing, an outcome that Blodget had most definitely not predicted. And the critics were calling for his head.

For months, the visibility, the television stardom, had been great. He was being touted as the "ax," Wall Street lingo for someone steel-plated enough to wreck a company. He had found all the attention amusing. Blodget, after all, had once been a lowly production assistant at CNN business news, where he always wore a suit and tie for his pedestrian tasks. He had left for a business trainee program because he found TV news a bit shallow, his career was going nowhere, and he was tempted by the markets he watched each day on the tube. Now that he was making $4 million a year, the chance to return to the CNN bureau on Eighth Avenue as a featured *Moneyline* analyst was unmistakable evidence that he had arrived. But with his beloved Internet stocks tanking, Blodget's outsized profile was proving a fat target for the media.

The article in the June issue of *Money* had hurt the most. The writer, Joseph Nocera, a respected editor-at-large for *Money*'s sister publication *Fortune,* had seemed like such a nice guy. Blodget had taken time to chat with him on a busy day when he could have been making more money. But the article was so personal, he felt, even making fun of his looks. "God, he's young," it began. "With his wavy blond hair, athletic frame and intense blue eyes, he looks like a West Coast frat boy who just got out of school." More important, Nocera said that Blodget was a "cheerleader" and that he was full of hot air: "When you listen closely, what you hear from Blodget is that the main reason you should be buying Internet stocks is because other people buy them. Which is to say, his analysis is itself part of the bubble."

That was unfair, Blodget felt; outsiders had no idea how much research he did. Still, he wasn't particularly proud of being a stock picker and didn't view himself in those terms. The pressure he felt in the glare of the spotlight was huge. He had to weigh every word, for any utterance could move the market and so much money was at stake. He was on call twenty-four hours a day, had to do more digging into more subjects than ever before. He felt like he was on a bridge, running in front of a freight train.

There were 2,427 analysts covering publicly-traded companies, and while even the most junior among them made around $350,000 a year, most were anonymous. In 1998, when he was working for the Wall Street firm CIBC Oppenheimer, few people had heard of Henry Blodget. But that December, he essentially gambled his career on a single call. Blodget raised his price target for Amazon, then selling at $243, to a staggering $400 a share. That prediction, quickly trumpeted by Maria Bartiromo on CNBC, drove Amazon stock up 19 percent the next day. In less than a month, the stock soared 128 percent and smashed the $400 target. Merrill Lynch, determined to compete for more Internet IPOs, quickly offered Blodget a job. The man he replaced, Jonathan Cohen, was far more bearish, having insisted that Amazon was worth less than $50 a share. Blodget was obviously more likely to speak the language of high-flying Silicon Valley firms.

Blodget was stunned by the tidal wave of media attention. He landed on *Moneyline* the night of his prediction, and later debated Jonathan Cohen on Bartiromo's *Business Center.*

To many observers, though, Blodget's Amazon call seemed like a leap of faith, a neat bit of financial voodoo. "Amazon's valuation is clearly more art than science," Blodget had written, adding that the online bookseller couldn't be judged by normal market standards. No matter. When Blodget got to Merrill and started making upbeat predictions for AOL, Yahoo!, and other Internet firms, his calls were routinely touted by CNBC and other media outlets. "Blodget's Bullish on priceline," said a headline in *TheStreet.com.* "Merrill's Blodget Speaks," said a Bloomberg headline.

One money manager had a friend at Merrill hold up the phone so he could hear Blodget's morning calls. Blodget found himself spending more time on the road, pitching companies for their investment banking business. Merrill Lynch had clearly bought itself a ticket to the Net sweepstakes, and that ticket was Henry Blodget.

Chris Byron couldn't stand him. What kind of a whore was this guy? Whenever he checked his computer screen, every Blodget recommendation was buy, buy, buy. Why didn't someone call him to account? Byron unloaded on Blodget in his online MSNBC column. He accused Merrill Lynch of a "craven flip-flop" by first telling clients that Amazon stock was worth under $50 and then hiring an analyst who argued that it was worth eight times as much. Merrill, he noted, had underwritten Boston Chicken's stock, then watched it plunge from $40 to about $4 before telling its clients to bail out. By bringing in Blodget and pumping Amazon, Byron said, Merrill had revealed itself as "an investment firm looking to suck up to a company" with plenty of underwriting business.

But then the Net escalator got stuck in reverse. *Barron's* ran a cover story in May called "Amazon.bomb," saying that the firm faced fierce competition in peddling books and music and that its stock was way overvalued. The stock dropped $12^{15}/_{16}$ the next day, to 105. David Faber accused *Barron's* of "piling on," saying that there wasn't much new in the piece. Alan Abelson, the *Barron's* columnist, had been trashing Amazon's absurd valuation for two years, even as the price of the stock had increased eightfold.

Blodget rose to the company's defense. He said that *Barron's* had raised "logical concerns" but had failed to note that plenty of other Net stocks were down. Amazon "is investing money, not losing it, so near-term profitability is not a good measure of future worth," Blodget said. He was seen in some quarters as trying to prop up the stock on whose rise he had piggybacked his career. But he also had to distance himself from the growing disaster in Net stocks. He said that the Internet sector had been "very weak lately" and that "near-term volatility is high." The market, he argued, had been diluted by a torrent of new Internet IPOs. But he wasn't abandoning his bullish stance, just covering his rear during the springtime plunge. He still had a "buy" rating on Amazon and other key Net stocks.

Blodget was driving Jim Cramer crazy. Here he was trashing Internet stocks, helping to prolong the slide, and yet sticking with his "buy" rec-ommendations. Cramer believed that Blodget was playing a dangerous game. On three occasions, Wall Street insiders told Cramer, Blodget had warned Merrill's sales force that he expected Amazon stock to drop an-other 10 percent, and that while he loved the Net, he wouldn't push the stocks until prices came down further. His own private actions, Cramer felt, were contradicting his public support for Amazon. Cramer believed that Net stocks would keep dropping until analysts like Blodget removed their "buy" ratings and let the market reach a natural bottom.

Even the day traders began to resent his sudden influence. "How did this little amateur come from nowhere to where he's at?" one said on the *Silicon Investor* site. "This guy reminds me of an umpire that called one strike right, and now he's another prophet."

"One good Amazon call, and now he's replacing Mary?" said another, referring to Morgan's Mary Meeker.

From the outside, Blodget knew, the conflicts that analysts faced seemed to involve a huge lack of integrity. But the press failed to under-stand the differing constraints faced by sell-side analysts like him, who worked for brokerages, and buy-side people like fund managers. The money men usually owned the stock they were pushing, so of course they would say that they loved Buyit.com, hoping that everyone would rush to grab the stock and it would go through the roof.

For an analyst like him, though, the most crucial element was maintain-ing open lines of communication with the likes of Amazon, AOL, and Yahoo!. Without their help, you couldn't get the information you needed, simply couldn't do your job. So Blodget felt that he had to walk a tightrope. Sure, there was pressure on him to maintain these buy ratings. If he turned negative on a stock, he had to be subtle in what he said pub-licly. He couldn't just change his ratings every few days when the winds shifted, for that would roil the markets even further. Anything he said could damage his relationships with the companies he was covering or the investors who relied on his guidance. If he suddenly switched to a nega-tive rating, it would kill the stock and Merrill's clients would get hosed. So he had to tiptoe through the bad news.

And so, on the morning of June 1, Blodget put out a research note saying that "we are somewhat concerned with AOL's ability to excessively beat analysts' earnings estimates as they have done in previous quarters." Wall Street read the signal. After the market closed, Ron Insana said that Blodget's comments had pushed America Online stock down nearly 4 points, to $102^{13}/_{16}$, a far cry from its springtime high of 175. *Moneyline* also attributed the decline to Henry Blodget. He was slowly realizing that the critics would savage him no matter what he did. He would have to shrug off the attacks. It was time for the frat boy to be a grownup.

10

STAR WARS

J EFF Gralnick, the executive vice president of *Moneyline,* is addressing his troops around a long conference table in a 21st-floor office with a panoramic view of Manhattan's West Side, from midtown to the World Trade Center.

"We're not hurrying," he tells the fifteen assembled staffers, some of whom are sitting on the floor. "We're going to try all kinds of combinations. The numbers, thankfully, continue to be rock solid. Rock solid. For all the onslaught CNBC was going to mount, they're sitting at a point-one at seven o'clock."

It is June 15, 1999, Gralnick's first day in the office after Lou Dobbs stunned the television world by resigning as president of CNNfn. Dobbs had clashed with his Atlanta bosses one time too many, particularly after he announced on the air two months earlier that CNN President Rick Kaplan was ordering him to cut away from *Moneyline* and return to a speech that President Clinton was giving in Littleton, Colorado, after the school massacre there. But the real issue was that Dobbs was determined to launch a Website called *Space.com,* dealing with all manner of space exploration, and blast off with enough IPO millions to put him in the same galaxy as his corporate pals. CNN executives insisted that this would be a clear conflict of interest for a network executive, but Dobbs faxed over an ultimatum with a 5:00 P.M. deadline. When Ted Turner, calling from his Montana ranch, failed to talk him out of the plan, Dobbs quit. After 19 years, he felt, it was time to move on. Gralnick is particularly embarrassed that CNBC got the scoop, reporting Dobbs's resignation six hours before CNN got around to telling its viewers.

The staff is still shell-shocked. Could *Moneyline* succeed without Lou Dobbs? Would CNNfn survive without Lou Dobbs?

Gralnick, a wisecracking man with a thick shock of gray hair, has been at CNN for just three months, having spent his career at the three major networks—covering Vietnam and the Persian Gulf War, presidential campaigns and conventions, running *NBC Nightly News* and the ABC Website. On his wall, beyond the nine television sets, are framed photos of him with Tom Brokaw, Peter Jennings, Walter Cronkite. In February, shortly after ABC axed Gralnick in a round of budget cutting, Bruno Cohen, CNBC's senior vice president, met with him in a coffee shop and made him a lucrative offer. Next Gralnick saw Lou Dobbs, who made an even more attractive offer. On the way home, Gralnick, who didn't really want to join CNBC, called Cohen to say he was taking the *Moneyline* job.

There was one small problem: Gralnick knew next to nothing about business. For the past three months he had been slowly learning the language, and he didn't mind asking dumb questions; if he couldn't understand something about Wall Street, maybe viewers would be confused as well. Gralnick often e-mailed his daughter, a 25-year-old rookie trader at a Connecticut hedge fund, for guidance. Now, suddenly, he and David Bohrmann, CNNfn's executive vice president, are running the place.

A larger problem, Gralnick had discovered, was that CNNfn's financial losses were far larger than Dobbs had let on, and the network was in a deeper hole than anyone had realized. Gralnick feels like the accidental father of an infant. He would feed and nurture the baby, but privately he wasn't so sure about the long-term burdens of parenthood.

Having reassured the staff, Gralnick starts focusing on tonight's program. *Moneyline* staffers in Washington, Chicago, Los Angeles, and London join the meeting by speakerphone. They kick around news stories for the program's first half-hour, which features more general news—the lead will probably be the cost of rebuilding Kosovo after the war—and debate possible business topics for the second half, which begins at 7:00.

Fred Katayama in Los Angeles suggests a piece on corporations suing to uncover the identity of critics who assail them on Websites. Gralnick loves the idea.

"When could you turn it by?" he asks.

"I don't know," Katayama says.

There is talk of Bill Gates buying a photo news agency—the story was in that morning's *New York Times*—and of a new computer "worm" virus. Another reporter is finishing a piece on struggling cities trying to get into the housing bond market. There may be a story on a national drywall shortage. And there is a questionable report about the owners of a Website called *sex.com* ostensibly making a $3.6 billion bid for Caesar's World hotels. "We've been on the fence about go/don't go," staffer Alan Wastler says, noting that the alleged bid has been reported in *The Wall Street Journal.*

"If everybody's up with it, we should be up with it," Gralnick says. "Let's also be careful we're not driving traffic to that site. We should put the word 'doubt' very high and hard." The meeting is over. "Let's all go downstairs and look at that site," Gralnick jokes.

Gralnick now has to face his number-one problem: finding the right *Moneyline* anchor to replace Dobbs on the air. Gralnick may have taken over some of Lou Dobbs's managerial duties, but Dobbs had been instantly recognizable as CNN's top business anchor, and that void needed to be filled as quickly as possible. For all his bravado, Gralnick is more concerned about this than he lets on, for it could be a turning point in the battle for business supremacy. Gralnick needs a big name, and has already made an approach to Ron Insana. While Insana was tempted by the prospect of a much bigger salary, there was no way he would leave CNBC, which had him under long-term contract. He had spent eight years building the place, almost from the ground up. All his friends were there, particularly Sue Herera and Bill Griffeth, who had also gone to Cal State Northridge and had started out with him at FNN. Next Gralnick had made an unsuccessful run at Neil Cavuto, anchor of the daily business show at Fox News Channel. Now Gralnick is considering some inside candidates and wondering whether to split the program between a news anchor and a business anchor.

While Gralnick mulls the big decisions, *Moneyline* is run day-to-day by Jenny Harris, a dark-haired, 29-year-old bundle of nervous energy. She also happens to be David Faber's girlfriend—they met, appropriately enough, at a National Association of Financial Writers ball—and that gives her an unusual window on the competition. She's still amazed at how people call out to The Brain when they're walking down the street. Harris advises Faber on his on-air manner, telling him to keep his voice down when recording a story and not to let the joking with his *Squawk Box* colleagues drag on too long. But their relationship includes a barrier—a "Chinese wall," she calls it—against discussing the breaking stories on which their networks compete.

At a meeting in Gralnick's office, Harris says: "I was thinking we could have a debate on Internet stocks between someone who says these are bargains at these levels and someone else who says they're still overvalued."

"Someone said to me the other day we should be pairing bulls and bears on a nightly basis," Gralnick says, apparently unaware that CNBC already has such a feature on its *Market Wrap* program. Gralnick likes branded segments because they can be sold to specific advertisers.

"The logical choices are Jonathan Cohen and Henry Blodget," says Terry Keenan, who will anchor the business half of tonight's show.

"Unfortunately, we had Henry Blodget on Friday night," Harris says.

Amazon stock, Keenan notes, "is below the $400 that Henry Blodget made his career on."

"Are we picking the feistiest ones?" Gralnick asks. "If we're going to have fun, let's have fun."

"Jonathan Cohen would be feisty because he was let go by Merrill Lynch for being too bearish, and he's now basically been proven right," Keenan says. (Actually, Cohen had quit to join a new firm, Wit Capital.) As for the other guest, says Keenan, "let's get one of the well-known bulls. Maybe Ralph?"

"Abby?" says staffer Paul Sloan.

"Either one of them," Keenan says.

Jonathan Cohen is soon booked, but Jenny Harris is not wild about a debate segment. "I'm tempted to just do him alone and maybe get Abby separately," she says. "The Wall Street people usually don't take each other on that much. It's not like a political debate. You don't get the same kind of passion as on *Crossfire*. It's all very polite." She is acutely aware that CNBC, which is muted at her desk next to a set tuned to CNN, can easily book such guests all day long, while CNNfn, with its limited distribution, is struggling. And now she's lost her ace in the hole, the ability to tell potential guests that Lou Dobbs wants to talk to them.

Everything seems different without Dobbs, but the official period of mourning is apparently over. In the universe of twenty-four-hour news, one day is an eternity. A group of CNNfn staffers gathered around a computer screen is laughing at a wire story on Ted Turner's latest comment from a cable television convention. "The world got along without John F. Kennedy and Jesus Christ," Turner said. "We'll get along without Lou Dobbs."

By lunchtime, the whole place is buzzing over a three-page CNBC press release that Gralnick has managed to obtain. Suddenly, Maria Bartiromo is out as coanchor of *Business Center,* the 7:00 P.M. show that competes with *Moneyline.* CNBC is trying to seize the void left by Dobbs's departure by ginning up a new version of *Business Center,* expanded from 6:30 to 7:30—*Moneyline's* exact time slot—and hosted by Ron Insana and Sue Herera. The release puts an upbeat spin on the switch, saying that CNBC has signed Bartiromo to a new contract and that she will take over the first hour of Insana's afternoon program, *Street Signs.* There is no comment from Bartiromo, who, at the moment, is on her honeymoon.

On the press release, Gralnick has written: "I particularly like the word 'popular' to describe *Business Center.*" He sees his rivals waving the white flag. "The Bartiromo era is over, and it was a disaster," he declares.

Soon it's time to spin the press. Gralnick gets a call from David Bauder, the Associated Press's television writer, and pours on the charm. *Moneyline,* he says, "is not just all chat," but specializes in real reporting. *"Moneyline* is a brand that resonates."

Who will replace Dobbs? Bauder asks. "On the record, there's no short list," says Gralnick. "We have the luxury of time here. Now we're off-the-record." Gralnick and Bauder run through some names. Forrest Sawyer, who has just left ABC, is mentioned. "Forrest is an old friend, but we haven't talked about this," Gralnick says. What about Willow Bay, who had recently joined CNN from ABC, and who is married to ABC president Bob Iger? "Willow's a player," Gralnick says. "Willow has a lot of strengths." They run through some other names.

Now Gralnick shifts gears. "Off-the-record, I'll tell you some things about CNBC. The thing they had on the air didn't work. They spent more than three million bucks launching Maria and that program. I could retire on that launch money. Our numbers last Tuesday, Wednesday, Thursday, and Friday were rock solid. Maria did her traditional point-one." *Money-line,* by contrast, often draws a respectable .5 or .6 rating.

But the early wire stories seem to reflect CNBC's spin, not Gralnick's. Jenny Harris looks in amazement at a computer printout, reading from an AP summary: "CNBC, which already dominates the lucrative market for financial news, plans to expand its nightly business show and has signed its most marketable personality, Maria Bartiromo, to a new contract." A Reuters report says the move "will boost star anchor Maria Bartiromo's exposure." Harris can't believe what she's reading.

"Why does she get all this Money Honey press when her ratings suck?" Harris asks. "We don't get any credit for that being a failure."

Harris's more immediate problem, with four hours until airtime, is a painfully slow news day. The markets are flat; a rally in Net stocks is fizzling. There's no major corporate story. Fred Katayama's piece on companies suing online critics won't be ready for tonight. Harris has killed the drywall shortage story because she couldn't get a camera crew. As for the report on cities and housing bonds, her colleague Paul Sloan pronounces the script "as dull as could be." Harris deep-sixes it.

Walking into the makeup room, where a woman is applying blue eye shadow beneath the blonde locks of Terry Keenan, Harris wants to talk to her anchor about the Internet debate. Ralph Acampora has said he's busy. Abby Joseph Cohen, whom Harris regards as a boring guest anyway, has said no. Barton Biggs has passed. They need someone to challenge Jonathan Cohen's bearish views.

"As you know, there's nothing happening today," Harris says. "To make the interview segment longer, maybe we should get an Internet bull, and I don't know who a good person would be."

They kick around a couple of names. Harris asks about Andrew Barrett of Salomon Smith Barney. "I mean, he's good on television," she says. "We can put him on and give him a hard time." They're still not sure.

"How long do you think you can talk to Jonathan?" Harris asks.

"Not any longer than three to four minutes," Keenan says. They agree to pre-interview another analyst named David Alger, sounding him out over the phone to see if his views are sufficiently different from Cohen's.

Carrying her water bottle back to her desk, Harris resumes the debate about the *sex.com* story, which has ebbed and flowed all day. Staffer Victoria Belser says that Caesar's World hotels claims to have gotten no bid from the porn entrepreneurs. "There didn't seem to be any meat there," Belser says. "We can't even use the Website. It is so raunchy and disgusting." The story is dead.

The Internet debate is not working out. David Alger couldn't do it, and Harris has given up on the idea of pairing Jonathan Cohen with another analyst. Instead, her staff books Marc Klee, a technology fund manager. The Nasdaq finished the day up a healthy 16 points, so they can debate whether Net stocks are mounting a comeback.

It is 4:15, just over two hours to air. Suddenly, Harris is startled to see Ralph Acampora being interviewed on CNBC about the fate of the Dow. "My last known target is 11,500, and I see no reason to change that," Acampora says. She is disappointed that he's doing the competition after blowing off *Moneyline*.

On CNNfn, Terry Keenan is interviewing Mark Breier, the CEO of beyond.com, who's already been on CNBC that morning, looking quite naked. "This beyond.com guy did *Squawk Box* today with his shirt off," Harris says. "What was the deal with that?" CNNfn staffers had demanded that he ditch the topless routine if he wanted to be on their air.

Gralnick emerges from his office, handing Harris last night's ratings. The program began with a .4 and finished with a .7—about 400,000 households, a pittance by network standards but the sort of affluent viewers much coveted by advertisers. Gralnick has had a conference call with CNN Chairman Tom Johnson about planning a *Moneyline* promotional campaign without a *Moneyline* anchor.

At 5:01, CNN goes live to an earthquake in Mexico City. Gralnick asks whether *Moneyline* should do a full report. He is told that there are no reports of casualties yet.

"We need pictures if there's death and destruction," Gralnick says. "Make sure, A, we have pictures, and B, we can get our guy on the phone."

Five minutes later, CNNfn is showing a Caesar's World hotel. Anchor

Jan Hopkins reads a report on the alleged *sex.com* bid. After all the anguished debate, the disputed story has gotten on the air anyway, if not on *Moneyline* itself. Such is life at a twenty-four-hour network.

An hour before *Moneyline* starts, Gralnick tells Harris he is not happy with the tease for the Internet stocks debate. A tease—a few words at the top of the show about a segment to come—is important because it can persuade viewers not to reach for the remote. "Is the strongest thing we can say that the debate is captivating Wall Street?" he asks. "There's not enough guts in the words. It needs to be a little longer and a little bit edgier."

Linda Keenan, seated on Harris's right, tries typing a new tease: "After falling so far so fast, is the worst over for Internet stocks? We'll hear from the analyst who warned that Net stocks were overpriced months ago—with his bet on where they go from here." Harris suggests a line about "painful losses" for investors.

"I can't tease Internet stocks one more time. I'm going to lose my mind," Keenan complains. "We've written this at least 60 million times."

Tony Guida, who is anchoring the show's first half, complains that "we can't answer that question: Is the worst over?"

It is now after 6:00, and they are still debating what will be a fleeting couple of sentences at the top of the program. Gralnick returns with a new idea: "Is now the time to buy? We'll ask two leading Web watchers."

With a touch of exasperation, Harris takes over the task of tease writing: "Tonight on *Moneyline*—Internet stocks show signs of life. Is it a buying opportunity, or a sucker's rally?" She doesn't like the phrase "Web watchers." Someone reminds her that it was Gralnick's idea.

"I think it's boring," Harris says.

"Make it unboring," Gralnick says.

When Cohen and Klee begin their on-air debate—after the headline "Dud.com"—it turns out they don't really disagree on Net stocks. Klee says that his John Hancock Global Technology Fund is "actually starting to look at them as buying opportunities." Cohen says that "we think there's some great opportunities there."

Terry Keenan asks for their top picks. Klee says AOL. Cohen says AOL.

What about Amazon, which Cohen had strongly opposed before Blodget succeeded him at Merrill? "We're not recommending Amazon at these levels," he says.

"I share Jonathan's opinion on Amazon," Klee says.

The "debate" that *Moneyline* has spent all day booking and packaging turns out to be a recitation of conventional wisdom. But Keenan isn't surprised at the tepid discussion. She likes having bears on—most of them have gone into hibernation or are no longer considered credible because of the long bull market—but realized after suggesting Jonathan Cohen that his situation had changed. He now worked for an online brokerage, Wit Capital, that wanted to attract more Internet IPOs, and that was likely to make him more positive about Net stocks. Still, no one dwells on such things in television. Tomorrow is always another day.

❑　　❑　　❑

Just across the river in New Jersey, Bill Bolster didn't wait long to arrange a secret meeting with Lou Dobbs. The CNBC president knew a brand name when he saw one. Dobbs was anxious for the sit-down as well. He said he appreciated the straightforward way that Bolster's network had handled his departure from CNNfn. Both men shared a certain blustery style.

Dobbs said he had heard that Bolster was tough. "You don't sound too tough to me," he said.

"I don't think I'm too tough," Bolster said. "My grandchildren don't think I'm too tough. My wife probably considers me a wuss."

Bolster wasn't ready to put Dobbs on the air, and in any event Dobbs's CNN contract barred him from competing on another cable network for nearly three years. But he figured Dobbs needed to be associated with a business network, to keep his name in the public eye as he hit the speaking circuit and launched his Website. Dobbs needed to be a big dog to continue his relationship with the major CEOs. Bolster felt that Dobbs needed him as much as he needed a link to the pioneer of televised business journalism. In the same vein, Bolster was trying to land Robert Rubin as he was winding up his term as Treasury secretary. He envisioned Rubin as an ideal commentator and Washington door-opener, someone whose sterling reputation would meld nicely with the CNBC brand.

When Bolster first heard from a *New York Times* reporter that Lou Dobbs was quitting, he saw an opening big enough to drive a truck through. Fortunately, he had already hatched a secret plan. In preparing for the expected start of evening trading hours, Bolster had decided to launch a 9:00 P.M. market wrap-up program, modeled (like much of CNBC) on ESPN's *Sports Center,* with two of his biggest stars. Ron Insana was the most authoritative voice on the staff, if a bit on the serious side, and Sue Herera, a big-haired blonde, was the best communicator that CNBC had. They had already agreed to the idea. Now, with *Moneyline* looking vulnerable, Bolster simply moved the show up to 6:30, uncorked some advertising money, and set the launch for June 21, just thirteen days after Dobbs's announcement.

The problem was that Maria Bartiromo had just gone off to get married. The timing was truly awkward. Bartiromo had gradually come around to the notion that she couldn't be at the stock exchange in the early morning and work so late into the evening, especially if the program would be moving to 9:00 P.M. But her discomfort was greater than that. *Business Center* just wasn't her. It didn't play to her strengths. She had wanted to do a program heavy on market news and filled with major guests. The network was trying to appeal to a different group of viewers by emphasizing glitz, entertainment, and the Internet. She and CNBC remained at odds. But Dobbs's resignation provided the perfect exit, a graceful way for her to leave the show.

Still, she felt, CNBC's handling of the situation had been so weird. There was a flurry of calls between the network executives, Bartiromo, and her agent in the two days before the wedding and the day after. CNBC was determined to announce that Bartiromo had signed a five-year contract, but the details hadn't been hammered out. This was the next five years of her life, she felt. She was entitled to play a little hardball.

What CNBC executives didn't know was that Bartiromo's agent was quietly testing the waters. He called Roger Ailes, who had originally hired her at CNBC and was now running Fox News Channel. Ailes had offered Bartiromo $275,000 to defect to Fox when he launched the channel two and a half years earlier. But Ailes was no longer interested and didn't take the agent's call.

Next came the squeeze play. CNBC put Bartiromo in a tough situation by announcing to the press that she had actually signed the new contract. That was flat-out untrue. She would probably sign soon, but the company was asking her to play along with a fake cover story. Bartimoro knew what was going on. CNBC didn't want the other networks to know that she was still available. Her bosses wanted to give the appearance that they had her locked up. But Bartiromo's camp struck back, floating word that she was being considered as Bryant Gumbel's coanchor for CBS's new *Early Show.*

While Bartiromo was happy to be moving to *Street Signs,* which aired from 2:00 to 4:00 while the markets were still open, the *New York Post* took a hostile tack. "Newlywed Bartiromo Pulled As Anchor," its headline screamed. Bartiromo thought that negative approach was terribly unfair. Bolster found it downright rude. He figured that Roger Ailes and his gang were responsible for the story's slant. After all, Fox, like the *Post,* was owned by Rupert Murdoch.

The rest of the CNBC team tried not to be distracted by the Maria media circus. Ron Insana started working the phones for the new program. He called Robert Rubin and booked him for a farewell interview from the White House lawn. He got the first interview with Lawrence Summers as Treasury secretary. He called Al Gore's office and got the vice president to come on. "Good luck with your new show," Gore said on the air. His partner Sue Herera landed Abby Joseph Cohen, whom Insana introduced on the program in melodramatic fashion: "When Abby Joseph Cohen speaks, the markets listen." Insana even scored an interview with President Clinton, thanks to a former CNBC colleague who now handled television requests for the White House, and tagged along on the president's tour of an impoverished stretch of Mississippi.

When the overnight ratings came in after the new *Business Center* debuted, Insana was ecstatic about his first showdown with *Moneyline.* "We beat them straight up, point-five to point-four," he declared.

Now it was Jeff Gralnick's turn to make his countermove. *Moneyline*'s ratings had dropped 22 percent in the first week of head-to-head competition, while *Business Center* was up 14 percent. But *Moneyline* could still sell each thirty-second ad for as much as $13,000, thanks to its affluent audience, while *Business Center* was charging about $8,000. To revamp the show, Gralnick wanted to hire Stuart Varney, one of CNN's original business anchors, who had left the network a year earlier for the lucrative lecture circuit. Gralnick was particularly concerned because CNBC was aggressively trying to sign Varney. Ron Insana believed that landing Varney would be a blow to the pancreas for CNN. Some CNN executives thought Varney's thick British accent might be a problem, but Gralnick knew that his network wasn't playing to Peoria, and in the business community the accent might even be a plus.

Once Varney agreed to a seven-figure deal, Gralnick wanted to pair him with Willow Bay, a tall former Estee Lauder model who had hosted *Good Morning America Sunday* for ABC, and whose blonde beauty was augmented by a master's degree in business. That created internal problems at the network, because the brass in Atlanta wanted Bay to continue as the host of CNN's evening magazine shows, which were produced with *Fortune* and *Entertainment Weekly*. But a deal was cut over a frantic weekend, and Gralnick had to tell the other contenders—Terry Keenan, Tony Guida, Jan Hopkins—that they had been passed over. The staff applauded when the news was announced on June 29, a mere eight days after Insana and Herera had launched the hourlong *Business Center*. Now all they needed was some chemistry. Unlike their new rivals, Stuart Varney and Willow Bay had never met.

When the revamped *Moneyline* made its debut on July 19, Ron Insana was watching on a monitor while he was on the air with *Business Center*. He saw that his rivals were touting what Bay called "an exclusive interview" with Larry Summers and a sit-down with Barry Diller. He had to chuckle. Both of them had been on *Business Center* a couple of weeks earlier. Insana wondered what had changed since then to justify calling the interviews exclusive.

The booking wars grew even more intense. When CNBC learned that Scott McNealy of Sun Microsystems was booked on CNNfn one afternoon, he was told that he'd be bumped from *Business Center* if he did the competition first. McNealy canceled his CNNfn appearance. And when *Moneyline* booked Tom Jermoluk, the CEO of Excite@Home, a staffer noticed a CNBC promo for him and made clear that *Moneyline* would dump him if he kept the appointment. Jermoluk stuck with *Moneyline*.

Both shows were clearly trying to market their access to top executives and policymakers. And the new *Moneyline* was almost all business, dropping the hybrid approach of including general news. Gralnick felt that that formula had never worked, that it was just Lou Dobbs trying to be Walter Cronkite. The debut program intentionally led off with Hewlett-Packard naming Carly Fiorina as its CEO, rather than the tragic death of John F. Kennedy Jr., which had dominated the news for the past two days. But the overhaul didn't end there.

CNNfn had finally figured out a way around its limited-distribution dilemma. If relatively few people were watching the financial channel, the executives figured, they would simply switch to a bigger megaphone. CNNfn created three new business shows that would air simultaneously on the main CNN network, like *Moneyline* itself, at 5:00 A.M., 11:00 A.M., and 4:00 P.M., replacing coverage of government and politics with daily discussions of Wall Street and all its permutations. Business news, once a mere sideline when Lou Dobbs had joined CNN nineteen years earlier, was increasingly taking center stage.

❏　　❏　　❏

Jim Cramer loved his biweekly gig as cohost of *Squawk Box,* so much so that he was ready to give up his Wall Street business for it. Months earlier, before the IPO, he had quietly offered to abandon the hedge fund if CNBC would make him Mark Haines's permanent cohost. He wanted to be like John Madden, the former football coach who now diagrammed the plays as a sportscaster. To others it might seem incredible that a man would walk away from managing $300 million to yap on an early-morning cable show, but Cramer figured he had two, maybe three years left as a trader. He felt like an aging athlete who had been through too many games, too many seasons. Here he was, on the traditionally slow Friday before the July fourth weekend, at the office at 5:00 A.M. so he could react to the latest unemployment figures, as he had so many times before. Life as a talking head would surely be easier. Karen, too, had been urging him to quit since the near-meltdown of October 1998.

When Cramer failed to win a full-time spot on *Squawk Box,* he tried a different strategy. In late 1998, with *TheStreet.com* losing a fortune and his war with Marty Peretz dragging on, Cramer went to see Bill Bolster to beg CNBC to invest in the operation. In return for a $2.5 million stake, Cramer said, he would agree to come on CNBC more often and would launch a weekend business show. Bolster refused. He said he had not checked it out himself but that others had told him that *TheStreet.com* "is a piece of shit." Cramer thought Bolster lacked the Net savvy to know what was good.

When Cramer was arranging a second round of financing from venture capitalists, he visited Bolster again. The CNBC president said he still didn't like the site. "Don't try to get me involved in this shit," Bolster said.

As *TheStreet.com* was making plans to go public, Cramer made a third pilgrimage across the George Washington Bridge. "There's an IPO down the road," he told Bolster. "Everyone's going to get rich."

Bolster shot back that CNBC was beefing up its own admittedly weak Website. They were in competition. We will bury you, Bolster said. Cramer half-expected him to take off his shoe and start pounding it on the table.

Cramer still wouldn't give up. He feared that if his stock offering was a success, Jack Welch, GE's chief executive, would complain that he had refused to let the network in on it. *TheStreet.com*'s CEO, Kevin English, told Bolster that if CNBC wouldn't play ball they would have to go to Fox because they needed a television outlet.

Bolster's view of the impasse was much different. He didn't think *TheStreet.com* was a good investment, and he didn't like being told that he had to televise Cramer's show as part of the package. There was no way that Bolster was going to air a program over which he didn't have complete editorial control. If Cramer and his pals did something stupid on the show, Bolster would be responsible as the president of the network. He liked Jim Cramer but saw him as a loose cannon, and had grown more uncomfortable after the WavePhore incident. At the same time, he made clear that Cramer could no longer appear on *Squawk Box* if he cut a deal with Fox. That was the way television worked. It was strictly business. The negotiations, such as they were, were over.

Feeling frustrated, Cramer had also tried to strike a deal with Lou

Dobbs, but Dobbs refused to meet with him. The CNNfn president was not only determined to protect his own lucrative Website, he wouldn't let *TheStreet.com* advertise on the network. (He took the same position with *The Wall Street Journal,* which had a successful Internet site.) Dobbs even barred Cramer from appearing on *Moneyline,* convinced that such airtime would help drive traffic to *TheStreet.com,* and perhaps away from *CNN.com.*

But in the spring of 1999, as the IPO for *TheStreet.com* was suddenly looking hot and *The New York Times* had climbed on board, Rupert Murdoch came in at the last minute with a $15-million investment, hoping to buy a piece of Jim Cramer before he went public. Part of the deal was that *TheStreet.com* would develop a weekly business show for Murdoch's Fox News Channel. Cramer wasn't wild about appearing on the new show; he wanted to remain on *Squawk Box.* But his board was pressuring him to be on the program. He was, after all, the star. Kevin English said that it was his fiduciary responsibility to help publicize the company.

Cramer went to see Roger Ailes, whose Fox News office was just down Sixth Avenue from NBC's Rockefeller Center tower. Ailes had hated his old network ever since he quit CNBC three years earlier during a power struggle, and he loved to drive NBC crazy. Ailes had not only invented *Squawk Box,* he felt he had created the star system in business news— treating such anchors as Mark Haines and Maria Bartiromo like his night-time celebrity, Geraldo Rivera—and Jim Cramer was clearly a star. He was a natural on television, full of manic energy and speaking directly to the little guy. Ailes told Cramer that *Squawk Box* had screwed him. "I don't know what fucking GE did to you," Ailes said. "You made that show. Why didn't they give you a contract?" "I've been trying to do a deal with them for two years," Cramer said. "They laughed at me."

But Cramer had misgivings about Fox. He insisted that his contract allow him to make occasional appearances on CNBC. And he did not want to commit to being a weekly panelist on *TheStreet.com* show. The next time Ailes tried to reach him, Cramer didn't call back. An assistant passed on the message that Cramer uses e-mail. "You tell him to go fuck himself. I don't!" Ailes said. What's more, he warned, Cramer had better play ball unless he wanted the new show to run against pro football.

Cramer felt that he was in an impossible bind. He was being forced to choose between his loyalty to CNBC and his loyalty to *TheStreet.com.* What's more, the move would shatter Cramer's vow of a few weeks earlier to do no television other than *Squawk Box* and to concentrate on his business. But he felt that he couldn't let the company down. He agreed to lend his celebrity to Fox News Channel.

Cramer had known for weeks that he was headed for trouble with CNBC. On the day that *TheStreet.com* went public, as Cramer was celebrating in the office with his father and sister, he got a call from Bruno Cohen at CNBC. Cohen was upset about Fox being a partner in what had become a red-hot stock offering. He said he was firing Herb Greenberg, a *Street.com* columnist who appeared regularly on CNBC, as of that morning. And Cramer's *Squawk Box* appearances would be cut back to once a month. The only reason he wasn't totally dropped, Cramer figured, was that he was good for ratings.

Cramer tried to explain how many times he had tried to get CNBC involved in the Website. Cohen didn't want to hear it and quickly hung up.

Tom Rogers, the president of NBC Cable, summoned Cramer to his office at 30 Rockefeller Plaza soon afterward. "You son of a bitch," he told Cramer. "I can't believe the way you fucked us over." CNBC had made Cramer, Rogers insisted. He was nothing before *Squawk Box* gave him national exposure. Cramer found the corporate fury ridiculous. He had been on his hands and knees, begging Bill Bolster to invest in the venture from which NBC executives now railed about being excluded. The reasoning of these executives was so absurd that he didn't know whether to laugh or cry. They were getting even for something he didn't do. This, apparently, was the price of Internet success.

These secret machinations reflected the emerging links between television and the Internet and the fierce competition to use one to promote the other. Cramer wanted to be on CNBC not just because it was fun and a boost to his considerable ego, but because he needed to market himself on the air as a way of selling *TheStreet.com.* Television was a powerful sales tool, which is why advertisers paid hundreds of thousands of dollars for a thirty-second prime-time spot. Now the very presence of a money manager on the mass medium could be turned into a perpetual advertisement for what remained a narrowcasting medium. And, in the callow tradition of Wall Street as high school, the headstrong men who straddled both worlds were constantly turning old friends into new enemies as the competitive landscape shifted.

The feuding also helped forge new alliances. As soon as Lou Dobbs quit CNN, *Moneyline* began calling Cramer repeatedly, trying to get him on the show. We were never allowed to invite you before, the booker explained. Cramer agreed to go on, for he needed to win new viewers, especially now that he was in CNBC's doghouse. But maybe this was all for the best. The last time Cramer had appeared on *Squawk Box,* he had checked the minute-by-minute hits on *TheStreet.com* and found that there was no uptick in traffic. Everyone who watched *Squawk* already knew about Cramer and his Website. Perhaps CNBC's morning audience was tapped out.

The evening audience, though, was virgin territory. He needed badly to get on the new *Business Center.* Cramer spoke to Ron Insana, who loved the idea.

"Would you come on the show if I can get you on?" Insana asked.

"I'd be there in a heartbeat," Cramer said. But they both knew that Insana might get in trouble with Bruno Cohen if Cramer showed up.

For now, Cramer was concentrating on developing *TheStreet.com*'s new program for Fox News Channel, which would air on Saturday morning and be repeated Sunday afternoon. The debut was two weeks away. They had done a series of rehearsals, and Cramer had offered to appear every week. He was convinced that the show would move stocks, the surest sign of media clout. The weekend cable audience was tiny, he knew, but if the show clicked he would push to move it to Friday night and go head-to-head against Louis Rukeyser's *Wall Street Week.*

In mid-July, Cramer made his monthly appearance on *Squawk.* Mark Haines, David Faber, and Joe Kernen had all been lobbying their bosses on Cramer's behalf. Kernen told Cramer that John Elway, the Denver Broncos quarterback and a regular CNBC viewer, had complained about his absence.

Cramer and the *Squawk Box* cast had a fine time fencing on the show, with Haines calling Cramer a "weasel" for refusing to take a firmly bullish or bearish stance on the market's prospects. "God, that was great TV," Haines said afterward. "I just loved that."

The laughing stopped, though, when Bruno Cohen asked Cramer to step into his office. That very morning, with no advance warning, Fox had taken out a full-page ad in *The New York Times* touting his future role at the rival network.

"You gave me your word you weren't going to help Fox," Cohen said.

"I never said that," Cramer shot back. "You drove me into the arms of Fox." As for his *Squawk Box* appearances, he said, "I haven't even been allowed to mention the name of *Street.com.* It doesn't do anything for me except for my ego, and frankly, my ego's had it."

"You're a liar," Cohen said.

"I would never have helped Fox if you had offered me the contract I wanted and hadn't totally dissed my Website," Cramer said. Things were really bitter now. Cramer abruptly got up and walked out. "Sayonara," he said. Cramer figured he would be kicked off the show for good.

For all his bluster, Cramer recognized that Cohen had a right to be upset. He had told Cohen that he had no contract with the new Fox show, which was true at the time, and that perhaps he would be an occasional guest. Bruno undoubtedly thought that he was operating as some kind of double agent. What no one at CNBC understood was that he didn't control *TheStreet.com,* hadn't supported the Fox deal, and had been pressured into joining the show. Still, he had made a statement to Cohen that he couldn't live up to. He should have been a man and called Cohen with the news.

Cramer brooded about the estranged relationship like a jilted suitor. He loved doing *Squawk,* loving sparring with the gang. His dad watched, his sister watched, his neighbors watched. Every other Wednesday he would get himself up for game day. He kept e-mailing Mark Haines, angling to get invited back, but he knew that it was beyond Haines's control.

One Saturday night, Karen broke her wrist while Rollerblading, and they rushed to an emergency room in Flemington, New Jersey. "Oh my God, it's Cramer," the father of another patient said upon recognizing him. "How much fun is that show? What's Haines like? When are you going to be on again?"

Cramer said he didn't know. "You're hitting him where it hurts," Karen said.

Feeling spurned, Cramer threw himself into the launch of *TheStreet.com* show on Fox. The *New York Post,* which was predictably sympathetic to Fox ventures, pumped it up in an advertisement disguised as a news story: "James Cramer wants to be the first man to conquer TV and the Web at the same time. . . . Cramer hopes to make the show big enough that he and his on-air colleagues get stopped while they're walking down Wall Street."

He couldn't wait for his Fox show to take off so he could thumb his nose at those corporate assholes at CNBC. One way or another, Cramer was going to make himself a television star, win the Web showdown, and abandon the thing that had originally brought him fame—making money on Wall Street.

11

SECRETS AND LIES

K EVIN O'Connor loved the idea of leaking his first billion-dollar acquisition to *The Wall Street Journal.*

The DoubleClick chairman had just signed off on a plan by his spokeswoman, Amy Shapiro, to get the maximum media bounce for the deal, in which DoubleClick was buying the retail advertising firm Abacus. O'Connor felt that the *Journal* was the best way to reach investors, period. But his strategy was more ambitious than that. His staff knew that it was time to pull an all-nighter.

On a Sunday evening in June, Shapiro called her favorite *Journal* reporter, Andrea Petersen, with advance word of the takeover. O'Connor also spoke to Petersen, saying that the combined company was ready "to deliver the right message to the right consumer at the right time." Steve Lipin, Petersen's colleague, nailed down a second confirmation. If all went according to plan, the *Journal* story would serve as a press release for the rest of the media.

That was just the first step. Shapiro waited until midnight to call the three television outlets that mattered most to DoubleClick: CNBC, CNNfn, and Bloomberg TV. From her Madison Avenue office, she left messages for the key morning producers and provided her home phone number. Then she went home for a short rest, and the callbacks started coming after 3:00 A.M. Shapiro booked her boss on all three networks.

When she called O'Connor at 6:00, he was groggy. He was not a morning person, and Monday mornings were worst of all. "Do I need to get up now?" O'Connor asked. Shapiro picked him up at his Manhattan apartment with a hired car and they headed out to Fort Lee. CNBC, they knew, had to be the first stop on the television tour or the network would refuse to play.

O'Connor was pumped after the CNBC session. He felt lucky to be making his pitch on these networks. "How do you think I did?" he asked Shapiro. "Did they understand what I was saying?"

They rode back to Manhattan's West Side and the CNN bureau, then to the Bloomberg offices on Park Avenue. Bloomberg TV wasn't that important, they felt, but a reporter always sat in on the interview and filed a story for the wire. By the time that Shapiro got back to the office, there was a stack of messages from other newspapers and trade publications, all reacting to the *Journal* story.

Still, even the most skillful media manipulation could not change the fact that Wall Street didn't like the deal. DoubleClick's stock promptly dropped 20 percent, from 88 to 70, as experts questioned whether the combination with Abacus was a good fit.

Within days, though, Wall Street was buzzing with rumors of another major DoubleClick acquisition. Shapiro was flooded with press calls when Gene Marcial reported in *Business Week* that "some pros" believed that O'Connor's chief advertising competitor, 24/7 Media, "is bound to be acquired by DoubleClick." She stuck to her usual script, saying that the company did not comment on rumors.

Marcial's report was right that DoubleClick was on the prowl, but wrong about the identity of the target firm. Shapiro and DoubleClick President Kevin Ryan soon flew to the Sheraton Gateway hotel at the San Francisco airport as Ryan plunged into five days of intensive negotiations with NetGravity, another online advertising firm. The secret talks were dubbed Operation Ice Cream Scoop. Shapiro never left the Sheraton and got sick of constantly eating the hotel pasta.

The *Journal* connection had worked so well with the Abacus deal that Shapiro decided to try it again with NetGravity. She called Andrea Petersen on the morning of July 12. "Listen," Shapiro began, "I have some big news for you but I can't talk about it right now. I can't even tell you where I am." Shapiro knew that Petersen would quickly surmise that there was a deal involving NetGravity, which was based in San Francisco.

"Can I call you about 4?" Shapiro asked. "You'll need about two hours to pull it together. Trust me, you're going to want it."

But Petersen was juggling other stories that day and said that they'd have to talk before then. Shapiro's problem was that the DoubleClick and NetGravity boards hadn't yet approved the acquisition, and there was always the chance of a last-minute snag. So Shapiro offered Petersen a deal: She would spill the details if the reporter agreed not to write anything about the negotiations if they were delayed or fell through completely. Shapiro felt comfortable with the arrangement. Petersen would destroy their relationship if she reported the talks prematurely, Shapiro knew, and DoubleClick had been really good to her.

The boards cleared the acquisition that afternoon, and Andrea Petersen got her Ice Cream scoop. "DoubleClick Inc. is expected to announce it is acquiring rival NetGravity Inc. in a stock deal valued at about $555.4 million, or $26.32 a share," her story said. "The move is DoubleClick's latest bid to dominate the fast-growing market of online advertising." O'Connor, who was in New York, served up the appropriately upbeat quote: "Our goal is to be the internal operating system for advertising on the Net."

Again, Shapiro made the midnight calls, and early the next morning her assistant, Jennifer Blum, took O'Connor on his television rounds. The first stop was *Squawk Box,* where Mark Haines was characteristically skeptical.

"I understand the spin you're going to put on it," Haines said. But since online advertising firms seemed to be consolidating, Haines observed, that suggested it was hard to make money.

"I wouldn't draw that conclusion if I was you," O'Connor said. The Internet, he declared, is "the fastest growing trend in history."

During the car ride to CNN, Blum told O'Connor that he had left out an important part of the script. DoubleClick had chosen that morning to preannounce its second-quarter revenues, which were up an impressive 49 percent, figuring that this would get widely picked up with the NetGravity story. But O'Connor had forgotten to talk about it on *Squawk Box.* He wouldn't make the same mistake twice. During the CNNfn interview, he stressed that the company had had a "phenomenal quarter."

NetGravity stock dropped 2 points on the announcement, an unusual thumbs-down for the firm being acquired; DoubleClick rose 2½. But O'Connor wasn't overly concerned about the market's next-day reaction. His job was to communicate with the company's core audiences—clients and potential customers—by explaining what DoubleClick was all about. On that score, he felt, the publicity plan had worked like a charm.

O'Connor wasn't the only high-tech CEO worried about massaging the media, for some of the biggest names in the corporate world were struggling. Jeff Bezos, who hated talking about his company's stock price, felt compelled to go on CNBC and *Moneyline* as Amazon continued to plummet in July. "We're not a company for short-term investors," Bezos told CNBC. When he was asked for the millionth time, would Amazon turn a profit? "It would be a terrible management mistake to make money now," he insisted. Soon Bezos was back on CNBC to talk about his announcement that Amazon was expanding into electronics and toys. But when Amazon reported losses in line with analysts' expectations, its stock plunged another 14 percent. "Blodget, in part, may be to blame," David Faber told viewers, noting that Henry Blodget had issued a slightly downbeat forecast about Amazon's future losses.

America Online's stock was also down in the dumps, and Steve Case decided to talk at length to *The New York Times,* boldly declaring that "AOL is the next Microsoft." The positive Sunday piece gave his stock a 5-point bump. But headlines could hurt as easily as they could help. When the *Journal* reported that Microsoft was planning to challenge America Online by providing free Internet access to customers, AOL stock dropped 10 points within hours and wound up at 83, way off its springtime high of 175. The company immediately agreed to have its president, Bob Pittman, appear on *Business Center,* but the stock slide continued. There were limits even to the power of television.

❑   ❑   ❑

When spin was not enough for the denizens of Wall Street, some resorted to misleading, obfuscating, even lying.

For months, rumors had swirled that MCI WorldCom might acquire the paging company Skytel Communications. Gene Marcial had reported the buzz in *Business Week* in April 1999 from money managers who were buying up Skytel. But when the Website *Corporate Sleuth* disclosed in early June that MCI had registered the Internet address "skytelworld-com.com," MCI officials refused to fess up. They insisted that the move was "not an indication of official company intention," and Skytel shares began falling. Three days later, MCI announced that it was indeed buying Skytel for $1.3 billion. The company said earnestly that it had not intended to mislead anyone.

Sometimes corporations didn't actively tell untruths but merely held back bad news. When Ashok Kumar predicted on June 8 that Compaq would make virtually no profit in the second quarter of 1999—just 3 cents a share, compared to the analysts' consensus of 22 cents—he didn't hear a peep from company officials, who had protested about his previously gloomy forecasts. The Piper Jaffray analyst knew from their silence that he had hit pay dirt. In fact, things were even worse than Kumar had imagined. Eight days later, Compaq preannounced that it expected to lose money, as much as 15 cents a share, for the quarter.

The next day other Wall Street analysts began downgrading the declining stock, too late to help their clients. Where had they been? How had thirty big-time analysts utterly missed Compaq's slide into the red? Maria Bartiromo did not broadcast their names or mention their blunder the next time she trumpeted one of their ratings. Chris Byron believed that many of the analysts were simply protecting the company, that they must have known of the $630-million swing in Compaq's finances but had chosen to stiff investors instead.

And sometimes companies simply remained silent as the news leaked out. For days, Qwest Communications stock was rising on rumors that it planned to acquire US West and trump an earlier agreement by the phone giant to be acquired by Global Crossing. On July 11, David Faber talked about the scuttlebutt on *Squawk Box* as an on-screen headline said "Those US West Rumors." "I plead guilty to fanning the flames of speculation," Faber said, throwing up his hands. Seven days later, Qwest announced a $55-billion bid for US West.

Jim Cramer, for one, was fed up with being misled. He had gone to Orlando, Florida, in June for a conference of the National Investor Relations Institute, the corporate officials who dealt with money managers, and took aim at the twelve hundred people in the audience. "We are sick and tired of being lied to," Cramer began. "I can tell you I have been lied to more than just about anyone in this room," he said. "Heck, people who worked for your previous speaker lied directly to my face."

Cramer had been preceded on the dais by Henry Silverman, the chairman of Cendant, a company that Cramer denounced at every opportunity. In the spring of 1998, when Cramer was about to leave for a week's vacation in Antigua, he had called Silverman's right-hand man and asked if he needed to worry about the stock while he was away, considering that the chief financial officer had just quit. Cramer's hedge fund, after all, owned close to a million shares.

After checking with Silverman, the executive said: "Henry says you can rest assured, you can have a good vacation." The next day, Cendant announced that some of its reported revenues were bogus. Jeff Berkowitz called Cramer at the St. James Club in Antigua, saying that the stock couldn't open because of the accounting irregularities. The share price quickly plunged from 42 to 7. Cramer, Berkowitz lost $16 million in the process. And Cramer, who had $20 million of his own money invested in the hedge fund, personally took a $4-million bath. More than the vacation was ruined.

In Orlando, as Silverman was stepping down after his speech, the moderator asked Cramer if he would like to meet Henry.

"No," Cramer said in a loud voice. "That man's cost me too much money." The two men exchanged cold stares.

Days earlier, Cramer told the audience, he had written a *Street.com* column about the wallboard industry facing a nationwide shortage. He had gotten the details from the *Chicago Tribune,* and all the Wall Street analysts had endorsed the story, based on information they were getting from company managements. Within twenty-four hours, Cramer said, he was deluged with e-mail from home builders, construction companies, and Home Depot managers saying that the story was bull, that there was plenty of Sheetrock around. The Internet, he explained, was a powerful new tool for exposing corporate lies.

Back in New York, Cramer mounted a new crusade against takeover rumors. It was irresponsible journalism to report such rumors, he believed, an abuse of the First Amendment. He knew people who went out and bought long calls—betting that the price of a stock would rise—before phoning a reporter and whispering that the company might soon be swallowed. The bad guys made out like bandits, and everyone else who bought the briefly juiced stock lost. It was a sucker's game, and it was downright fraudulent. Every editor, whether at the *Journal* or CNBC or even *TheStreet.com*, was familiar with the practice, Cramer felt, but no one wanted to get scooped. Of course, Cramer's outrage was selective; he himself traded on rumors, as he had on the phony Bloomberg report about PairGain Technologies. But for the press to trumpet rumors to the entire world made his job immensely more difficult.

Cramer still had it in for Gene Marcial, who reported in *Business Week's* July 19 issue that "takeover buzz is running high" for Cabletron Systems. Marcial quoted money manager Jim Marquez—who was himself buying up shares of Cabletron—as saying that the German firm Siemens was among the potential buyers. Cabletron stock jumped 5 percent the next day. But didn't Marcial know that Siemens had publicly denied this very rumor after Dan Dorfman had reported it weeks earlier? Cramer coined a new verb for this sort of journalism: "Dorfing."

He was particularly incensed at Dorfman's resurgence. Cramer had to look at *JagNotes* each day because rumors moved the market, but why was CNBC legitimizing its old commentator by repeating some of his forecasts? Every time Dorfman saw a deal coming, Cramer would dump the stock. As Cramer saw it, Dorfman's Wall Street pals played him like a fiddle. They would tell him which stock they were going to take up. They would load up on the stock and wait for Dorfman to float the rumor that the company was a takeover target. CNBC would repeat the rumor, people would race to buy the stock, pumping up its price, and Dorfman's sources would immediately sell it. Then the price would drift back down to pre-Dorfman levels, screwing those who had rushed to buy it. Dorfman, for his part, wasn't bothered by such criticism. He had publicly denounced Cramer after the *SmartMoney* stock fiasco and figured that this was simply payback.

One tantalizing Dorfman column appeared on *JagNotes* on the afternoon of June 23. "Talk is rife on Wall Street," he reported, that the Internet firm CMGI was negotiating with Compaq to buy its popular Alta Vista search engine. Cramer thought the rumor was completely bogus and immediately sold some of his Compaq stock. This time, however, Cramer was wrong. CNBC confirmed the Compaq talks hours later, crediting Dorfman; the Dow Jones News Service had the story the next morning, and CMGI quickly made the $2.3 billion purchase. That was the maddening thing about Wall Street rumors. Sometimes they turned out to be true.

What made the truth elusive for the average investor was a growing convergence between money companies and media companies. *TheStreet.com* and *CBS MarketWatch.com* reported on Internet stocks, but they were also part of the Net, had made huge money from their IPOs, and were worried about their own sagging stock prices. *The New York Times, Fortune,* and Dow Jones reported on Net stocks even as they weighed spinning off their own Web operations as separate companies. The *Times* and Fox News were now major investors in *TheStreet.com,* whose finances were handled by Goldman Sachs (which itself had recently gone public), and all of them reported on Goldman Sachs. Microsoft owned part of MSNBC, the NBC cable network, even as its sister network, CNBC, reported daily on Microsoft. CNBC and CNNfn were flogging their Websites while covering the Web world as well. And they all reported on the New York Stock Exchange and the Nasdaq, which were developing plans to go public and sell stock in themselves.

Merrill Lynch, one of the oldest of the old-line brokerages, had just launched an online trading service, joining Prudential, Charles Schwab, and Donaldson, Lufkin & Jenrette, along with such newcomers as E*Trade and Ameritrade. The investment banking firms were gauging the impact of the merger wave even as their own companies were gradually being taken over—Dean Witter by Morgan Stanley, Smith Barney by Salomon Brothers, Piper Jaffray by U.S. Bancorp, First Boston by Credit Suisse. They all worried about their stock price even while advising investors on other stocks, including those of their rivals, and while trying to grab banking business from the Internet companies whose stock they regularly upgraded or downgraded. The Internet CEOs routinely lied by insisting that they paid absolutely no attention to their stock price, even though the recent nosedive had not only cut the values of their companies in half but had slashed their personal net worth by billions. Who could see straight when everyone was dwelling in the same fog-shrouded territory?

❑   ❑   ❑

By July, the market was mounting another comeback. The interest-rate fears briefly subsided as the Fed boosted rates by a quarter point but signaled that there were no immediate plans for another hike. Traders were buoyed by the Clinton administration's estimate of an additional $1-trillion budget surplus over the next fifteen years, undaunted by the fact that the same experts had consistently been wrong in their budget projections. The Dow gained 586 points in a week and rocketed to a new record of 11,139 on July 2. Net stocks also came back, boosting the Nasdaq to record highs, along with the S & P. The bears were once again in retreat.

After the surge, Maria Bartiromo got word that Ralph Acampora was raising his target for the Dow, saying that the index would hit 12,500 to 13,000 by summer's end. "He just got off the squawk box at Prudential," she reported.

Mark Haines was less than impressed with Acampora's forecast. "That's a serious blow to the bullish case, but thank you," he said, his voice dripping with sarcasm.

Haines still didn't understand why the Prudential analyst commanded such respect. Acampora had predicted the market would go lower when it hit bottom in the fall of 1998. He had predicted a correction when the Dow was below 10,000 and the market kept climbing. A few weeks earlier, Acampora had been predicting Dow 11,500 but had said that there could be a 10 percent correction at any time. Gee, Haines thought, that was really helpful: The market's going to go up, unless it comes down. The biggest problem with the financial media, Haines felt, was that they never held anyone accountable for such mistakes. There were just too many gurus and savants offering their thoughts. Haines tried his best to keep track of experts such as Acampora, whose name he avoided uttering on the air.

Bad predictions, it seemed, were everywhere. More than a year earlier, *SmartMoney* had recommended, among other things, buying Brightpoint, a cell phone equipment maker. Since then, the stock had plunged from just over 18 to 6. "Analysts expected earnings at Brightpoint to grow at a 30 percent clip," the magazine now explained. "They were wrong. And so were we."

On *TheStreet.com* show, Robert Friedman, chief investment officer for Mutual Series Funds, recommended Bank One stock on July 24. A month later, Bank One shares plummeted 22.6 percent after the company warned that its profits would fall short of expectations—and Friedman did not return calls from *TheStreet.com* about his bum advice.

Dan Dorfman reported on *JagNotes* on July 13 that Timberland stock was dropping, according to his sources, mainly because of negative comments by an analyst for Deutsche Bank Alex. Brown. Two days later, Dorfman ran the headline "Did Canny Short Sellers Screw Alex Brown With a Bogus Timberland Story?" He reported that "some short sellers" were spreading a "bogus story" about the clothing company's weakness, when in fact its stock had just jumped 7⅞, to 71¾. "So anyone who bought the short story . . . is obviously suffering today," Dorfman said. Left unmentioned was Dorfman's role in spreading the story that he now seemed to be disavowing.

Dorfman was pleased, though, when Dow Chemical announced a $9.3-billion deal to acquire Union Carbide, sending Carbide's stock up 22 percent. He had, after all, touted a possible takeover of Union Carbide back in May. But he'd gotten only half the story right; Dorfman had said that the company might be acquired by DuPont or BASF, not Dow Chemical.

And Dorfman was equally pleased when *The Wall Street Journal* got into the Merrill Lynch rumor game. The Heard on the Street column reported that "talk again is swirling on Wall Street" that Merrill was "open to a deal of some kind," either with Chase Manhattan or with the insurance giant American International Group. It was like a bad rerun; Dorfman had dropped the Chase rumor three months earlier in favor of a possible Merrill coupling with Morgan Stanley or Bank of America. Even now, Dorfman himself wasn't sure whether there would ever be such a deal.

David Faber was openly skeptical on *Squawk Box*. "Yeah, the talk is around again," he said. "Some potential buyers—people who might want to take a shot at Merrill—are never unhappy to see a story like this. I'm waiting on my own reporting until I really know there are talks."

"Do you think the reporters at the *Journal* are being used by someone?" Joe Kernen asked.

"No, I'm not saying that," Faber replied.

Cramer denounced the rumor, but that didn't stop him from exploiting it. He sold half his Merrill stock for a tidy profit as the *Journal*'s report sent the brokerage's stock up 4⅜ to 71⅜, or 6.5 percent, and dumped the rest the next day.

Everyone, it seemed, was playing the speculation game. *Business Week* made news on August 2 when it rushed a report onto its Website, saying that Yahoo! had been in talks to acquire Excite@Home—itself the product of a recent Internet merger—for more than $17 billion. The story, attributed to "sources close to the companies" and quickly picked up by CNBC, pushed Excite stock up 7 percent the next morning. Unfortunately for *Business Week,* Yahoo! and Excite flatly denied the report that afternoon. "Excite@Home is not Yahooing," Insana deadpanned, hours after his network reported that it might be.

There were even rumors about possible news stories about companies. *JagNotes* reported on its rumor page that *Barron's* was about to publish a piece on the biotech company Aronex developing two cancer-related drugs. Aronex had gotten a boost a month earlier when Gene Marcial had touted the company in his column. But no such *Barron's* article appeared. Someone was clearly spreading misinformation in an attempt to goose the stock.

Days later, the Food and Drug Administration blocked Aronex from submitting its leukemia drug for approval, citing deficiencies in its data. Within an hour, the stock plunged by more than 40 percent.

❑   ❑   ❑

Jim Cramer winces when he hears the CNBC report on *TheStreet.com*'s earnings. "Missed by a penny," says the voice of reporter Tom Costello from the set behind Cramer's desk.

"He got the number wrong," Cramer grumbles. He's friendly with Costello and figures that the reporter was just reading from a piece of paper put in front of him. But the screwup has been driving Cramer crazy.

In its first quarterly report as a public company, *TheStreet.com* disclosed that it lost $6.8 million. Most of the press—Reuters, the *Daily News,* CNBC—reported this as a loss of 38 cents a share, or a penny worse than the all-important consensus of Wall Street analysts had predicted it would be.

Cramer is mad at the company's young staff for not making clear to reporters that *TheStreet.com* had taken a one-time charge against earnings for executive stock options, amounting to 8 cents a share. In fact, the company's own press release listed the 38-cent loss first, before explaining the special charge. This is a technicality, to be sure, but that was how operating revenue is measured. If the math were done correctly, the company has actually managed to beat the Street, losing only 30 cents a share.

The problem, Cramer knows, is simple: Journalists are busy, with dozens of companies reporting earnings each day, and few have time to read the fine print. This sort of foul-up probably happens a thousand times a year, but now it is happening to him. Jeff Berkowitz, Cramer's partner, keeps telling him to chill out. After all, Hambrecht & Quist, one of the company's bankers, has just put out a research note valuing *TheStreet.com* at $4.4 billion, when the real figure is $1 billion. Even high-powered finance people make mistakes.

Cramer turns up the sound as Kevin English, *TheStreet.com*'s CEO, pops up on CNBC. By now the network has corrected the earnings figure.

"I'm delighted with the numbers," English says. "For us it's a blowout quarter."

Interviewer Liz Claman says she often reads the Website. "I just love that Herb Greenberg," she says.

"Why'd you kick him off the air?" Cramer barks at the set. He's still bitter about the way the network has treated him and his *Street.com* colleagues in the wake of the IPO. He has taken to calling Bill Bolster and Bruno Cohen "the junta." He told Ron Insana that he won't be happy until Cohen is ousted and working in a backwater office on a linoleum floor somewhere. Cramer is always mad at somebody. He's gone through periods of barely speaking to David Faber, who believed that Cramer deliberately created feuds just for the sport of it. The truth is that Cramer needs an enemy to motivate himself, and now that he's mended fences with Marty Peretz, Bruno Cohen is his latest obsession. Cramer had blown a gasket a couple of days ago when Joe Kernen tried to call up a chart displaying the *TheStreet.com* Internet index and found that it had been electronically blocked, to prevent any on-air mention of the rival Website. Bruno again. The guy was really rubbing his face in it.

Cramer checks one of his computer screens; in the few minutes that English was on the air, *TheStreet.com* stock dropped from 30½ to 29⅝. Net stocks are having a bad morning. Some things, Cramer figures, are just beyond your control.

An e-mail from Karen pops up on another computer. Cramer has been filling his column with talk of their conversations, and the Trading Goddess doesn't like it. "I will be writing my own version of diary of a mad housewife soon," she warns.

On this sweltering July morning, a camera crew arrives to tape Cramer at work for the coming weekend's Fox show, which is more fast-paced and freewheeling than *Squawk Box*. Berkowitz isn't wild about Cramer's many media ventures; he once cursed out a *Good Morning America* producer who was tying up his line for Cramer's live shot just before the market opened. Cramer pulls Berkowitz and the program's producer, Gary Schreier, into the small office kitchen to make sure his partner feels comfortable.

"I'm usually a pain in the ass about this," Berkowitz says. "But you know what? I own a lot of shares." It's in his interest for *TheStreet.com* show to do well.

"Pretend we're not here," Schreier says.

In the real world, as opposed to the scene being staged for the cameras, Cramer, Berkowitz was coming off a bad week. A number of its Internet holdings got battered. The firm is still up 24 percent for the year, but the market seems to be turning down yet again.

"We're looking for a flat opening," reporter Bob Pisani says on CNBC.

"Looking for a flat opening," Cramer, standing, shouts to Berkowitz.

Suddenly it's decision time. "I-Beam only up one-eighth," Cramer says, referring to IBM.

"If Greenie's benign, it goes higher," Berkowitz says, alluding to Alan

Greenspan's congressional testimony that morning. On Cramer's computer screen is *TheStreet.com*'s lead headline: "Greenspan's Words Loom Over a Mixed Market."

"I think I-Beam's a winner," Cramer says, a pencil clenched between his teeth. "I'm taking Hewlett-Packard." He picks up the direct line to his broker. "Get me 15 Hewlett-Packard. Get me another 5 Time Warner."

Schreier, sitting off to the side like a Hollywood director, is calmly watching the jargon-filled chatter and wondering how to translate it into television. "I haven't gotten that moment yet," he says. He and his star retreat into Berkowitz's office. "Whaddya need?" Cramer asks.

"I need something black and white, something people can understand at home: 'I like this, I don't like this,'" Schreier says.

Cramer mentions that the firm owns 50,000 shares of York International, an air-conditioning manufacturer. He believes that the record July heat will boost the York stock, but Berkowitz wants to dump it. The company is about to hold a conference call with investors. Schreier looks excited.

"I like that, because everyone's friggin' hot," he says. "We can tease that: 'Can you make money off the weather? Jim Cramer's trying to. That's next.'"

The program has a "predictions" segment, borrowed from such political chat shows as *The McLaughlin Group*. Cramer's latest hobbyhorse is that Jeff Bezos has abandoned capitalism. The crew moves into Cramer's office—Schreier tells him to sit on his desk, with the trading floor in the background—and Cramer looks into the camera. "Amazon's decision to no longer care about profits will make it so all Net stocks will suffer," he says. "Until then, I think you can take a vacation from the Net stocks."

Schreier gets the footage he needs when Cramer is talking to York officials on the conference call. "They need to see it get hotter," Cramer shouts, putting his hands on his head in exaggerated despair. "This guy needs it to be 100 degrees out to make any money!"

Later, seated before the cameras, Cramer explains why the York stock was a bust. "It's hot, let's go buy air conditioners—that's a quaint idea. You have to have it first," he says. "We had no edge here. This was a mistaken trade. It was done because I tried to capitalize on something that had already been capitalized on."

Berkowitz says it's time "to take our losses, or try to break even. Move on."

Cramer agrees: "Let's sell the York." They dump their 50,000 shares for a $31,000 loss. After three hours of taping, Schreier has enough material for a segment that will last a minute and 50 seconds.

Greenspan's testimony that day is mild and has little immediate effect on the market. But over the next two days, as new economic figures suggest a hint of inflation, the Dow drops 316 points, to 10,655.

It has been a rough summer for the high-wire technology sector. By early August, Net stocks are in a painful, full-blown correction. The Nasdaq index has skidded more than 11 percent in less than a month, dropping day after day. Dozens of Net IPOs are declining in value as soon as they hit the market. Online brokerage stocks are getting killed, too. *TheStreet.com* is soon down a dizzying 78 percent, to 15½, from its opening-day high of 71 just two months earlier.

The plunge is gut-wrenching for Cramer, whose personal IPO windfall has shrunk from $220 million to $50 million. He has written a piece for *Time* on how it feels to lose so much money, but that barely captures the depth of his emotions. His friends are taking a bath because of him. His personal trainer, who is coming to see him at 3:30 the next morning, bought 200 shares at 60. His own father, who owns 1,000 shares, hesitated to bring up the stock slide on the phone.

"It's okay, Dad, it's the elephant in the room," Cramer told him.

Cramer doesn't care that much about his personal stake—he is already fabulously wealthy—except that he wants to make some major charitable donations that may now be impossible. He doesn't even list *TheStreet.com* stock on his mortgage application (he is buying a new house in Summit after the zoning board refused to let him turn his driveway into a yard for the kids). But he believes that the stock is being unfairly punished, that it has been caught in the Net vortex. Worse, his ambitious expansion plans are going up in smoke. He wants to use the stock to buy some other financial Websites, like *Corporate Sleuth,* and turn *TheStreet.com* into a one-stop supermarket. No way they can do that with the stock at 15.

He and Karen talk incessantly about whether he should hang it up at the hedge fund and make the Website his full-time job. After all, she argues, he and Berkowitz are having a great year.

"What a great way to go out," she says.

"And do what? Sit home and drive you nuts?"

Cramer knows that his trading job, his real job, is what makes him an interesting columnist, and what enables him to shrug off the stock's collapse. If his only professional outlet is a company whose stock price he cannot control, he will surely sink into a severe, dark depression.

"The whole dot-com world's coming down!" Cramer shouts on his Fox show. "I hate the dot-coms."

He isn't the only investor who is reeling. Newspapers and magazines are filled with stories about huge losses in day trading, particularly after an amateur trader who lost his shirt kills twelve people in Atlanta. "Stock Wealth Slipping Away," says a front-page story in *USA Today*. Alan Abelson can barely contain himself, writing in *Barron's* about "the hyperventilating claptrap," "carney-barker analysts," and "hilarious hokum and bunkum" surrounding Internet stocks, and chortling over the "bedraggled" stock of "an online financial rag," namely *TheStreet.com*. The Net naysayers, from Chris Byron to Barton Biggs, are being proved right. The overinflated bubble is starting to burst. Hibernating bears have come down from the chills to proclaim their views on television and in print.

No analyst has been more closely associated with the Net surge than Henry Blodget, and now, with the sector drenched in red ink, he has been flooded with interview requests. *The New York Times* devotes a story to his views. But Blodget has refused to abandon his cheerleading role. On *TheStreet.com* show, Blodget praises Amazon's growth—"If you're going to own one, own this one"—calls AOL "still the top brand in the industry," and says that Yahoo! is "in a great position."

A few days later, after the Nasdaq has plunged even further, Blodget again defends his stocks on *Moneyline*. He tells Stuart Varney that the Internet remains "a hugely profound trend" and that the bloodied Net stocks will bounce back in a couple of months. Blodget allows that investors should put "only a small percentage" of their money in these volatile stocks, a caution that he certainly did not emphasize at the height of the boom. He was no doubt mindful that a negative assessment could send his favorite stocks tumbling even further.

Unfortunately for Blodget, *Moneyline* flashes his top picks on the screen as he is speaking: eBay, down 67 percent. Amazon, down 60 percent. AOL, down 50 percent. Yahoo!, down 50 percent. At the moment, he seems less an analyst than an embattled spokesman for the companies that Merrill Lynch is paying him to scrutinize. No amount of spin can change the depressing numbers.

❏   ❏   ❏

Financial Websites were exploding on the Net, and they were hungry for writers with a name, a reputation, a following. They all wanted to be the next *JagNotes,* to boost their visibility overnight. They needed someone like Gene Marcial.

The soft-spoken Marcial now found himself receiving several offers from Internet companies to take his stock-picking act online. Some wanted him as an outside contributor; others dangled full-time jobs. The money was huge, far more than he was making at *Business Week.* The offers included stock options that could pay off big time. Marcial had long felt seriously underpaid at the magazine, and he couldn't help feeling tempted.

He talked over the situation with Steve Shepard, *Business Week*'s editor. Shepard offered him the chance to write a second weekly column for the magazine's Website, for which Marcial would be paid extra. Marcial decided to stick it out. He had spent nearly two decades at the magazine, and it was hard to cut the cord. Ironically, *Business Week* promoted Marcial's online presence by saying his column was so important that Jim Cramer regularly critiqued it, leaving unsaid that Cramer usually ridiculed whatever he wrote.

Marcial was less than happy when *Business Week* published its annual scorecard on his column. He had wanted to do it himself, as he had the previous year, but there had been complaints about the questionable appearance of a columnist judging his own performance. Shepard assigned the task to another reporter.

Marcial's results, the article concluded, were "disappointing." While the stocks he had touted jumped an average of 4.9 percent the next day, after six months they had fallen 2.2 percent. Yes, investors would have pocketed a one-day gain of 140 percent had they bought Biomira after Marcial reported that the company was to begin clinical testing for a breast cancer vaccine. But Marcial had also trumpeted FPA Medical Management as being "bruited about" as a likely takeover target, according to "a New York investment manager who has been accumulating FPA shares." Six months later, when no takeover had materialized and the company had declared bankruptcy, its stock had plunged 95 percent.

Marcial had never liked the idea of being rated like a money manager, lumped in with those who actually bought and sold securities for a living. He was looking for news, reporting on companies that might be taken over or on stocks that seemed poised for success. He wasn't predicting that these things would definitely happen. Many of these stocks had gone down because the market had dropped in late 1998; many others had gone up in 1999, but they were too recent to be included in the review. Still, Marcial understood the game. People bought and sold stocks based on what he wrote, and the magazine needed some way to demonstrate that he was accountable. He would grin and bear it, to show that he was willing to take his lumps.

Marcial got hammered again when he wrote in September that a major U.S. telecommunications company was about to invest $25 million in the money-losing Internet firm Log On America. His column boosted the average daily shares traded from 129,000 to 1.8 million, and the price from 20⅞ to 25½. When no takeover took place, however, the stock dropped to 16⅝.

As *Barron's* and *TheStreet.com* were quick to point out, Marcial quoted analyst Joe Vaini as saying that the company "should be a winner" in the race to provide high-speed Internet connections. Vaini's firm, it turns out, consulted for another trading firm whose analyst, Ray Dirks, was the only one who evaluates Log On America. What's more, Dirks's wife, Jessie Dirks, ran Dirks & Company, the investment bank that had brought Log On America public four months earlier. Marcial said that the intertwined relationships didn't bother him, that the husband-wife relationship looked incestuous but that the information was solid.

Cramer took off the gloves this time, calling Marcial's column "reckless," declaring that it was "often used as a pump-and-dump enterprise" by stock manipulators, and urging *Business Week* to drop it. Marcial believed that Cramer didn't understand journalism and just had some kind of vendetta against him.

Gene Marcial wasn't the only financial writer to feel the lure of the Web's riches. A *Newsweek* cover story—"Everyone's Getting Rich But Me"—captured the nagging jealousy among those who felt that they were missing out on the great Internet gravy train. They all knew people like Kathy Bushkin, the AOL spokeswoman, who was friendly with many journalists from her days as a Capitol Hill press secretary. Bushkin had grown so fabulously rich through AOL stock options—she sold more than $11.5 million in company stock in 1999—that she started her own charitable foundation to hand out "genius" grants. Bushkin put $3 million of her fortune into the foundation, and her husband took on the full-time job of running it.

Little wonder, then, that financial reporters who hobnobbed with the Internet's nouveau riche were constantly questioning why they were slaving away for a relative pittance.

Chris Nolan, the *San Jose Mercury News* gossip columnist who had speculated about a CBS-AOL merger back in April, had decided to get in on an insider stock deal a few weeks before that column appeared. When her friend Dean DeBiase, the CEO of a new venture called Autoweb.com, offered her 500 shares of stock just before the company went public, Nolan couldn't resist. She bought the stock at the pre-IPO price of $14 a share, then flipped it the next day (some at $29, the rest at $45) for a profit of $9,000.

The Wall Street Journal got wind of the transaction in July and questioned Nolan about the propriety of a business journalist participating in a company's IPO. "I frankly needed the money," Nolan explained. "We don't take vows of poverty and chastity when we go into the newspaper business." Her rationale infuriated the newspaper's editor, David Yarnold, who called the comment "an insult" from someone who was making more than $100,000 a year. Brushing aside Nolan's insistence that she had sought prior approval from her editor, Yarnold suspended Nolan for a week over the conflict of interest, abolished her column, and shipped her to a suburban bureau. Nolan quit soon afterward.

Rebecca Eisenberg, a *San Francisco Examiner* columnist, got tired of watching her ex-boyfriends zip around in BMWs, having gotten "filthy rich" from online trading. "If I, as a columnist covering the Internet industry know so much, why am I living on columnist wages?" she asked. Her solution was to become CEO of a start-up firm called Chemis—and to continue writing her column.

Others simply abandoned the news business altogether. Darren Chervitz, a reporter for *CBS MarketWatch.com,* had quoted a hot young fund manager named Ryan Jacob some sixty-five times in his Website reports. Chervitz soon decided to join the man he had been covering, signing on as a senior analyst with the new Jacob Internet Fund. He had been making less than $40,000 at *MarketWatch.com* and hoped for a bigger payday down the road with Jacob. Everyone wanted to be the next Dave Kansas, the former *Wall Street Journal* reporter who became editor of *TheStreet.com* and, after the IPO, found himself sitting on a $9-million pile of stock. Not a bad chunk of change for an ex-newspaperman—even if, with the Net market sinking, that stock was now worth considerably less.

12

MORNING MUTINY

FINANCIAL reporting was serious business. Everyone involved was acutely aware that billions of dollars could move on each report, each analysis, each nuance in the way the story was presented. The pressure to get it right hung in the air, unspoken.

On *Squawk Box,* however, the formula was to sweeten the castor oil of stock charts, bond updates, and futures prices with some old-fashioned fooling around. The core group—Mark Haines, David Faber, and Joe Kernen—had developed a cult following by tweaking each other, shooting the breeze, and carrying on about the significance of the lava lamps that adorned the set.

In September, after the ratings had dropped by 10 percent, CNBC management decided to crack down. Bruno Cohen had one of his lieutenants begin laying down the law to producer Matt Quayle: No more extended joking. No more sound effects. No more goofy bits of videotape. When a flock of analysts rushed to downgrade a stock after the company had announced some bad news, the gang liked to show footage of penguins, waddling along in unison. This, too, was banned. To underscore their marching orders, Haines and his colleagues went even further than they had been asked and stopped using each other's nicknames.

More than five hundred e-mails came pouring in, protesting the newly serious tone. Viewers had grown to love the on-air antics that were the essence of the show's success, and many threatened to stop watching:

"Whoever's bright idea it was to ruin Mark Haines, Kahuna and The Brain, it's going to backfire."

"You guys might as well jump off the iceberg or bridge if there is no humor left."

"Bring back the penguins, The Brain and Kahuna and the Bond Babe. If I want solemn, businesslike presentations I can watch CNNfn. . . . Don't ruin it."

"Congratulations! You've made *Squawk* as dull as a Bob Dole infomercial on penile dysfunction."

Word of the complaints reached Bill Bolster, who expressed concern that maybe management had gone too far. The edict was softened a bit, but Haines and company did their best to ignore it altogether. They were reduced to making subversive little comments, like naughty students griping under their breath about a strict teacher.

"I have a lava lamp back here, Mark," Kernen said on the air one morning, fingering the blue object on a lower shelf. "One they missed when they came and burned all the books and stuff."

During a discussion of *The Partridge Family,* a producer barked in Faber's ear: "Let's get back to business!" Faber shared the order with the audience.

The *Squawk* gang was deeply offended by the effort to rein in what they viewed as their show. Cohen and his management crew, in their view, were all local TV guys. They were big on flash and dash and knew next to nothing about business journalism. They hadn't invented *Squawk Box,* didn't understand what made it tick, and yet were determined to put their stamp on it. Their vision for the show was one that hopscotched quickly from one brief segment to the next—from news headlines to a weather report to a stock update to Maria on the floor to a business digest—so that viewers would have no chance to get bored. They had added live reports from the Instinet trading floor and from the multicolored Nasdaq board, which often repeated information that Faber and Kernen had batted around or could obtain with a single phone call.

Haines felt that CNBC's ratings slide—the other programs were down even more than *Squawk*—was easily explained. The market had been stuck in an unprofitable trading range since the previous March. With the

carnage in Net stocks, the volume of online trading had dropped signifi-
cantly, and those people are—or were—*Squawk* viewers. Management
had added more commercials, and the frequent headlines and weather reports were the kind of mundane segments that people could get anywhere.
It was hard for Haines to fathom: Just four months after giving the show a
vote of confidence by expanding it from two to three hours, management
now believed that the very things that made the program different or interesting were suddenly the wrong things to do. They had yet to offer an explanation that made the slightest bit of sense. Still, Haines felt, it was their
network, and he remained under contract—that is, he reminded himself,
until November 26, 2000.

On the last Friday in September, David Faber was depressed. Not only
did he believe that the program was in danger of being ruined, but his pal
Steve Lipin had beaten him again on a major merger story, this time in the
telecommunications field that he prided himself on knowing best. Faber
had broken three of the biggest telecom mergers of the 1990s. But when
he unfolded *The Wall Street Journal* in his Upper West Side apartment at
6:00 A.M., he saw that Lipin and a colleague were reporting that MCI
WorldCom was in negotiations to buy Sprint, a potential $100-billion deal
that would combine the nation's second- and third-largest long-distance
carriers in the biggest corporate takeover ever.

The rumor had been around for months, for Sprint was always being
mentioned as a possible takeover target. Faber had heard it from the big
hedge-fund guys with whom he often swapped tips; they were incredible
sources because they held such large blocks of stock that corporate executives often gave them sensitive information earlier than anyone else. But
in this case they didn't have first-hand knowledge.

Faber had recently interviewed Sprint's CEO, he was close to all the investment bankers who would work on such a deal, and he had checked on
it again and again. Two weeks earlier, a couple of potentially key players
had stopped returning his calls. That should have been a sign. He should
have kept working the phones. This was a story he should not have
missed.

The problem with takeover rumors, Faber believed, was that you heard
them so often that at a certain point you began to discount them. That had

been his reaction when Dan Dorfman had revived the speculation that Chase Manhattan might buy Merrill Lynch. Faber didn't think that CNBC should pick up anything that Dorfman reported on *JagNotes;* the man didn't seem to talk to investment bankers anymore, just fund managers who were engaging in speculation or talking up their holdings. But Faber knew that a top executive at Chase liked to invite a reporter over for lunch and muse about buying Merrill Lynch, hoping that the journalist would write the story, give Chase's stock a bump, and put a little heat on Merrill. The man had given Faber the same spiel when he had dined in the Chase tower some months earlier. Each time a less experienced reporter had lunch with the executive, the rumor would start up again.

Faber knew all too well that people had different motivations for leaking merger stories. Maybe Bernard Ebbers, the CEO of MCI WorldCom, was floating the idea of buying Sprint just to see how the market would react, a way of testing the waters before making a final decision.

The Sprint story was only the latest blow, for David Faber and Steve Lipin had been going head-to-head all month. They had both been on red alert over Labor Day weekend. Holiday weekends, they knew, were when Wall Street heavyweights liked to do their most ambitious deals. The investment bankers loved having an extra day to hash out the troublesome details, briefly shielded from the glare of the media attention. Then they would try to unveil the newly minted merger on the Tuesday morning after the holiday.

Lipin had taken his family to Montauk, Long Island, for the long weekend, but he could smell a big one brewing. There had been hints and rumors for days that Viacom, the media conglomerate that owned MTV and Blockbuster Video, was maneuvering to buy CBS.

Over the previous week, the *Los Angeles Times* had reported that there were talks about a possible deal. *The New York Times* had said that Viacom and CBS were exploring a possible combination of their television stations. But the *New York Times* reporter, Geraldine Fabrikant, had returned to a leave of absence after reporting the story. No one else at *The New York Times* was pursuing the possible deal over the holiday weekend.

On Labor Day evening, when Lipin and his family returned home to Manhattan, the phone rang. The deal seemed to be happening. Lipin had been tracking the CBS-Viacom flirtation and knew exactly who to call. But as the *Journal*'s first-edition deadline passed, he didn't quite have the story—the biggest media merger in history—nailed down. Lipin and two colleagues worked the phones late into the evening, and by 11:00 P.M. they had confirmed the $36-billion takeover of one of America's Big Three television networks. All but 300,000 of the *Journal*'s nearly 2 million copies had already been printed, but the scoop was theirs.

Faber had been out for the day, but when he returned home at dinnertime he found that a couple of sources had left messages for him. He was quickly able to confirm the CBS-Viacom deal. The problem was, for all the immediacy of television, he had no outlet for the story. CNBC did not run live business programming on weekends, evenings, or most holidays. Never had it been clearer to him that the network's five-day-a-week format could no longer keep pace with the round-the-clock business world. Faber checked with his desk and was told that the *Journal,* the network's partner, didn't have the story. But a CNBC staffer later called back to say that the *Journal* was about to break the news.

"Aw, fuck," Faber said. He called Lipin at 11:15.

"How'd you get it?" he asked. Faber was so wired that he couldn't sleep. He had vacuumed up all this great detail for the next morning's *Squawk Box,* but had no way of getting the news out first.

For the *Journal,* the question was whether to use the Internet to trumpet the exclusive. The paper's Website generally put up the front-page stories and Heard on the Street column at 11:00, while holding back two or three exclusives until 12:30 A.M. to make it difficult for rival papers to steal the stories. This was a sensitive issue within the company; the Dow Jones news service, which operated independently of the flagship paper, sometimes sent an envoy to a newsstand in Germany to buy the *Journal*'s European edition so that the wire could run stories earlier than the paper wanted. In this case, Lipin's editors decided to slap a 4:00 A.M. Internet embargo on the piece, just to ensure that no West Coast paper could play catch-up. The Website was supposed to send out an e-mail alert to its subscribers at 4:00, but that fell through the cracks.

Faber, meanwhile, was up in the middle of the night, awakening his girlfriend Jenny Harris.

"What are you doing?" she asked.

"I'm thinking of questions," Faber said.

At 3:45 Tuesday morning, Jim Cramer signed onto the *Journal* site and saw that the lead story—about the arrest of fugitive financier Martin Frankel—was the same as in the newspaper that had been delivered to his New Jersey home. But when he got to his Wall Street office at 5:00, he checked the site again and saw Lipin's CBS-Viacom bombshell.

By the time that Viacom's CEO, Sumner Redstone, and CBS chief executive Mel Karmazin appeared before the cameras at a joint news conference that afternoon, everyone wanted a piece of the action. Wall Street loved the deal; Viacom stock jumped 4.2 percent, while CBS was up 3.6 percent.

A few days later, however, Lipin was not so fortunate. He went hard with a merger negotiation that would end up evaporating before the ink was dry on his story. It was the kind of misstep that he was extraordinarily careful to avoid, but reporting these deals was sometimes like grabbing ahold of Jello.

"H. J. Heinz Co. is in merger talks with Bestfoods," Lipin reported on September 15, citing the usual "people familiar with the matter." The combination of the company that makes Heinz ketchup and StarKist tuna with the manufacturer of Hellmann's mayonnaise and Skippy peanut butter "would be the largest U.S. food deal ever." Although Lipin's piece included a caveat that "the talks could still collapse," even he was surprised by that morning's melodrama.

David Faber reported shortly after the 7:00 A.M. start of *Squawk Box* that there had been a halt in the Heinz-Bestfoods talks but that they had been put back on track. While *Squawk* was still on the air, however, Bestfoods issued a statement saying that "no significant acquisition or combination discussions are in progress." So much for the biggest food deal in history.

The Bestfoods statement, Lipin realized, was narrow and lawyerly, sidestepping the fact that the talks had broken down during the night. Lipin felt strongly that his story was on target when he had filed it, but he couldn't control subsequent events. Still, the deal's abrupt demise was a major disappointment, and Lipin had to eat crow in his story the next morning. The takeover speculation didn't hurt Bestfoods, whose stock jumped 8.6 percent, or Heinz, whose stock rose slightly. But it wasn't a great day for the *Journal.*

CNBC, meanwhile, was itself involved in a deal that was consummated but instantly controversial. The network announced that it had bought a 12.4 percent stake in Archipelago, an electronic stock-trading outfit that was looking to become a public company and compete with the New York Stock Exchange and Nasdaq. In other words, a television network that covered financial news was now partners with a minor-league stock exchange hoping to move up to the majors.

Bill Bolster was thrilled with the move. He felt that it spoke volumes about CNBC's progress, that his network was part of the fabric of the financial world. He was proud to have been invited to sit at the Archipelago table, whose other investors included such blue-chip companies as Goldman Sachs, Merrill Lynch, J. P. Morgan, and E*Trade—all companies that CNBC covered. Bolster had thought about the conflict-of-interest question and decided that it wasn't a problem. He had faith in the integrity of his team. Besides, some of his rivals were engaged in similar alliances: Reuters owned the Instinet trading operation, and Bloomberg owned an outfit called Tradebook. These electronic networks were already providing after-hours trading, and Bolster felt that CNBC needed to be part of that movement. Archipelago executives, for their part, saw CNBC's investment as a way to boost their company's visibility. They hoped that CNBC would run their after-hours ticker tape and would station a reporter at their trading floor, as the network already did for Nasdaq and the Big Board.

Mark Haines knew nothing about the Archipelago deal until *Squawk Box* was on the air, knew nothing more than his viewers did. He was rankled to be reading some Archipelago flack's press release about what his own network was doing. Haines had no time to think about it, so he offered viewers his gut reaction.

"Doesn't this raise regulatory issues?" he asked. "A news organization owning a marketplace?"

Bolster later approached Haines to explain the business ramifications of the deal, but said nothing about his on-air remarks. Haines was pleased by that. In his decade at CNBC, no one had ever tried to influence his coverage of any issue involving NBC or its parent company, General Electric.

But Haines was troubled by the Archipelago deal. He knew that CNBC was basically an ethical place. He would scream bloody murder if he saw anything that was fishy. But he wasn't sure that this investment passed the "Caesar's wife" test for a network that had to seem pure when it came to its relationship with business. It was the appearance of impropriety that created a problem. The public already assumed that the media had a self-serving agenda, and for CNBC to team up with a stock-trading network did nothing to dispel that perception. Journalists lived in an increasingly complicated environment, Haines knew, with corporate relationships creating a bewildering array of conflicting interests. He worried that the lines were being hopelessly blurred.

CNBC's market power was never far from David Faber's mind, either. Despite his determination to stay competitive with Lipin, he knew he had to be cautious because his words often got magnified. The Dow Jones news wire carried transcripts of his reports, accompanied by a summary. Bloomberg had a staffer assigned to rewrite what he said on the air. The headlines often hardened in the process, the caveats all but lost: Faber Says XYZ Takeover Possible. He once called Dow Jones to demand that the wording be softened—not "Faber says," but "Faber reports." He was a journalist piecing together information, not a market guru.

Few people understood the degree to which luck was involved on these stories. One night three years earlier, when Faber was in a bar on a blind date, he ran into an investment banker, and bankers would tell you anything once you got them drunk. The man spilled the beans on the impending merger between Gillette and Duracell. Faber wasn't enjoying the date, so he seized the opportunity to dump the woman—"Gotta go!"—ran home, and phoned in the story. It was read on Geraldo Rivera's CNBC talk show, the best that he could do at that hour.

Lately, though, the thrill had faded. Faber began wondering whether it would be time to move on when his contract expired in two years. The *Squawk* gang could all quit, take their act to CNN, and make twice as much. More seriously, he and Steve Lipin started talking about going into business together. Lipin, a union leader at the *Journal,* was growing frustrated by the paper's insistence on slashing retirement benefits; he had led a pinstriped protest outside the *Journal*'s headquarters, and he and his colleagues were refusing to appear on CNBC to discuss their stories. Faber figured that he and Lipin could pool their sources and their reputations and launch some kind of venture on the Web. That seemed to be where the big money was these days, where Dan Dorfman and Jim Cramer were making a nice living. But Faber worried that he hadn't done a good enough job of self-promotion, hadn't established enough of a brand name to make the leap. That would have to change.

❑   ❑   ❑

Chris Byron had been wrong, dead wrong. That day back in May when he had checked out a new stock called Brocade Communications, which had gone public at 19, he had predicted it would sink within days. But the damn thing had gone straight up. Three months later, it was now at 164.

Byron had noticed this when a friend at a New York hedge fund called to ask what he knew about another such firm, Redback Networks. He had never heard of the company. Byron quickly discovered that Redback had gone public in June at 23, and was now selling for 213. The day traders, burned by the slide in Amazon and AOL and Yahoo!, were bidding up the price of a new group of so-called "B2B" stocks, of Net companies that handled online commerce between businesses.

Many of these IPO darlings, Byron learned, dealt with Internet infrastructure. They made the routers, servers, and switchers that directed traffic on the Web. The problem, he believed, was that Cisco Systems already controlled 85 percent of the business. But the new companies issued relatively little stock, which made it easier for momentum traders to push up the price. Byron laid out his findings on these "zero to hero" stocks in an online column for MSNBC. Four of the hot new companies—Brocade, Redback, Copper Mountain Networks, and Juniper Networks—had lost $66 million the previous year. They employed a grand total of 594 people. And yet the market was valuing the companies at $21 billion. It was ludicrous, another bubble waiting to pop. Byron may have been wrong about the stocks right now, but over the long term he was sure that he would be proven right.

At the moment, Byron was feeling rather confident in his judgment.

Planet Hollywood, which Byron had trashed three years earlier when it was a high-flying stock being promoted by such celebrities as Bruce Willis, Arnold Schwarzenegger, and Sylvester Stallone, had just announced that it was filing for bankruptcy.

The better-known Net stocks were still struggling, and Henry Blodget was still trying to pump them up. Faber made no secret of his disdain for analysts—a Salomon Smith Barney analyst had once booed him as he walked down the street—but he had to treat their pronouncements as news. Faber reported on August 18 that Blodget was putting a short-term "buy" rating on Amazon and Yahoo!. Joe Kernen was openly skeptical. Blodget had gotten his Merrill Lynch job, Kernen said, "because they want someone at the firm positive on Internet stocks."

Forty minutes later, Maria Bartiromo had obtained the details. Blodget, like a summer Santa Claus, was urging people to "buy the 1999 holiday basket of Internets," including AOL, eToys, and BarnesandNoble.com. And he had enough clout to give the stocks a one-day bump. Amazon finished the day up $3\frac{7}{8}$, to $113\frac{1}{8}$. And Yahoo! was up $6\frac{3}{16}$, to $145\frac{1}{16}$. *TheStreet.com* called it the "Blodget-Inspired Net Rally." But the stocks quickly slumped again.

Cramer, meanwhile, started betting on the Maria factor. He had come to view Bartiromo as an outrageous tout. She simply trumpeted whatever the analysts at the big blue-chip firms said, and wamma jamma, the stock moved. And Bartiromo, he knew, was particularly well sourced at Merrill Lynch.

As a trader, Cramer weighed the nuances of each upgrade and downgrade: Was it an important brokerage firm? How many salesmen did it have? Was the analyst the ax in that sector of the economy? But Bartiromo's soapbox was so powerful that she rendered such reasoning irrelevant.

Early one morning, Cramer's Merrill Lynch broker called him with news that the firm was upgrading Micron Technology, a company that made semiconductor and computer products.

"That's gonna be huge," Cramer said, even though the analyst was some no-name he'd never heard of.

"Why? We're not really important on Micron," the broker said.

"Yeah, but someone at your company speaks to Maria Bartiromo."

The hedge fund was sitting on 100,000 shares of Micron. Just as Cramer had anticipated, Bartiromo quickly touted the Merrill upgrade. Soon after the market opened, Micron jumped 3 points and Cramer dumped 15,000 shares, knowing that lots of buyers would be riding the Bartiromo wave. This was absurd, he thought, and investors will sort out the truth. The stock quickly crested and began falling back to earth. Cramer, who liked the company long-term, bought back the shares after Micron had dropped 3 points, back near its original price. Now Maria's hype was gone. He'd turned a quick $45,000 profit by calibrating the power of CNBC.

Cramer began taking regular potshots at Bartiromo. Everyone said you couldn't take Maria on, but he felt compelled to do so. Her 9:27 reports just before the opening bell, when she recited the morning's key analyst recommendations, were incredibly influential. She could make stocks dance. Cramer complained on *TheStreet.com* that Bartiromo never mentioned when a brokerage house that was upgrading a company's stock was also handling the company's banking business.

Some on Wall Street wondered whether Cramer's sudden criticism was fueled by his anger at being bounced from *Squawk Box*. It was clear that Bolster would never allow him to come back. Cramer had proposed to his friend Steve Brill that he write a piece for *Brill's Content* praising Mark Haines. No way, the word came back, it will look like you're just sucking up to CNBC to get back on the show. Cramer wrote about Ron Insana instead. But he had to admit that his banishment was probably coloring his attacks on CNBC.

As always with Cramer, there was a back story. He had once been good friends with Bartiromo, talking to her regularly. But two years earlier, his lawyer had warned him to break off the friendship. *The New York Times* had run a lengthy story on Bartiromo's boyfriend, Jonathan Steinberg, who had acknowledged that his hedge fund owned some of the small stocks that he was also recommending in the magazine he ran, *Individual Investor.* It's dangerous to talk to Bartiromo, Cramer's attorney said, because you're a natural target. If Steinberg came under investigation and Bartiromo was accused of touting her boyfriend's stocks on the air, the lawyer reasoned, she could say that she was pushing your stocks instead. The notion seemed rather far-fetched, but Cramer bought it. He told Bartiromo that he felt uncomfortable talking to her and the phone calls came to an end. Now Cramer was all over her for her dealings with Wall Street analysts.

Bartiromo was unfazed by such criticism. Faber and Kernen were skewering analysts all the time, but she didn't fool around like that. She liked to tell the story straight. If Merrill Lynch had 13,000 brokers pushing a stock to its big-money clients, that stock was probably going to move. If she had the news before it was widely disseminated, she wanted to get it out there. Bartiromo wished she wielded the kind of influence she was assumed to have, but that wasn't the way her world worked. These weren't her opinions. She wasn't buying or selling stocks. She was just a reporter, working the phones in her little booth at the stock exchange and passing on the judgment of others.

But while she rarely said so on the air, Bartiromo was acutely aware of the pressure on these analysts—her friends and trusted sources—from bosses determined to do business with the companies they covered. She would never forget what had happened to Tom Brown, an analyst at Donaldson, Lufkin & Jenrette. Bartiromo had a good relationship with DLJ, talked to analysts there all the time, and one of them had called her to say that Brown had been asked to quit.

"I can't believe that," Bartiromo said.

She had dinner a couple of times with Brown, and the story came tumbling out. Brown had been critical over the years of First Union bank and its CEO, Edward Crutchfield, for paying too much for acquisitions. Crutchfield had once stormed out of a meeting when Brown raised questions about his growing compensation. At another session with analysts, Crutchfield had asked whether "that little redhead" was around to make trouble.

Brown told Bartiromo that when he had worked for PaineWebber, his criticism had so upset First Union that the bank had stopped doing business with the brokerage. Now, Brown said, the same thing had happened—First Union had halted its banking business with DLJ—and this time, he had been asked to leave. She thought Brown had been courageous to stick to his guns.

When Bartiromo noticed that First Union's stock was heading south, she gave her friend a plug on *Squawk Box.* "Kudos to Tom Brown, who was exactly accurate on First Union," she said. "The stock is down 44 percent for the year."

A number of analysts had felt the sting of the companies they criticized, just as Ashok Kumar had when he tangled with Dell and Gateway. And now history seemed to be repeating itself. Sean Ryan, a thirty-year-old analyst for Bear Stearns, had been harshly critical of First Union, but he had been oddly silent for two months. *The Wall Street Journal* reported that bank officials had grown so angry that they had briefly suspended their bond business with Bear Stearns. Then Ryan's bosses had ordered him not to make any negative comments about First Union. Both companies denied the story, but many on Wall Street were skeptical.

Business Center caught up with Ryan, who said that analysts faced "the choice of telling an unpleasant truth and prostituting your own credibility." Ryan quit soon afterward. A Georgia State University study found that analysts issued earnings estimates that were 6 percent higher, and put out 25 percent more "buy" recommendations, when their firm had an investment banking relationship with the companies involved. Ron Insana, who introduced the segment, was hardly surprised. He'd had a friend who was fired as an analyst in the early 1990s for being too critical of a client. Analysts, in his view, had become promoters and marketers for their brokerage houses. When Insana had gotten into the business, analysts made three kinds of recommendations: buy, sell, or hold. These days, nobody suggested selling a stock until it was nearly worthless. If an analyst moved to a "neutral" recommendation, Insana knew, that meant dump the stock immediately. Everything was cloaked in euphemisms. You had to know the code.

❑   ❑   ❑

Television journalists could never quite forget that they lived in glass houses. There were hundreds of terrific reporters at *The Wall Street Journal, Business Week, Forbes,* and *Fortune,* and no one knew much about them. But the tube had turned financial reporters into big-name celebrities.

David Faber increasingly found himself in the spotlight. The subtext of all those on-air jokes about his anchorman hair and sex appeal was that he was one of New York's most eligible bachelors. It seemed only natural, therefore, for Faber to announce on *Squawk Box* that he had gotten engaged. That, in turn, got Jenny Harris's name in the papers. Harris's father had been hoping for several months that Faber would pop the question. Her family was so excited about the engagement that they taped the show on which he told the world.

Ron Insana was accustomed to television fame. He had gotten his share of profiles in newspapers and magazines. He had interviewed President Clinton, Vice President Gore, the prime minister of Russia. *Business Center* had just moved to the floor of the New York Stock Exchange, the first program to broadcast from the epicenter of Wall Street. But nothing had prepared him for the August afternoon when he appeared on *Street Signs* without his hairpiece.

The balding anchor had made no secret of the toupee, which he never wore outside the office but insisted on wearing on the air. *The New Yorker* had once made fun of his "pasted-down black hair," which the magazine said made him look like a cross between *Seinfeld*'s George Costanza and Count Dracula. Insana's wife, Melinda, had been urging him to give it up, but Insana was afraid that viewers might be turned off. As a journalist, though, he was tired of perpetrating a fraud. He told Bruno Cohen that he might flip his wig one day.

Soon after his new $1,600 hairpiece arrived, Insana grew tired of the whole charade. Five minutes before airtime, he made a snap decision, telling no one. As he headed for the makeup chair, a colleague asked: "Aren't you forgetting something?"

The reaction was overwhelming. Insana had never gotten this much publicity in his entire life. He got calls from *USA Today,* the *New York Post,* the *Daily News, TheStreet.com.* Within an hour he had fifty-five e-mails, and then hundreds more. "The new Ron Insana rocks!" one said. "Ron—what a gutsy move—we think you are great!" another gushed. Viewers seemed to admire him for the public unveiling. "If this keeps up," producer Kevin Magee kidded him, "you're going to have to shave your head." So much for Insana's years of dogged reporting on foreign currency crises and hedge-fund bailouts. He was now famous for being bald.

Jeff Gralnick never appeared on camera, but his role in nasty network infighting had made him an important figure in media circles over the years. After Lou Dobbs had quit CNN, Gralnick found himself in a power struggle with his former ABC colleague David Bohrman. As Gralnick was given more responsibility to develop CNNfn programming, Bohrman was abruptly ousted and, in an extra bit of humiliation, escorted from the network's Manhattan offices. The New York media depicted Gralnick as a back-stabber who had betrayed his pal. Don Imus made fun of him in a fake newscast, saying that Gralnick had tried "to stomp on his former friend's inert body to elevate himself."

Such carping bothered the hell out of Gralnick, but he felt that it would be unseemly to respond. If he was now the heavy, well, that was the least of his problems. Gralnick was pleased that he had successfully re-launched *Moneyline* with twin anchors. But he hadn't come to CNN just to produce an evening news program; he'd already done that with Tom Brokaw at NBC. He was more ambitious than that.

Gralnick had reluctantly concluded that he wouldn't stay at CNN for long. Lou Dobbs, it turned out, had essentially been selling him smoke in a bottle. Gralnick had expected that he would help orchestrate a grand convergence of business news on television and the Internet, but now other Time Warner executives were overseeing that effort.

As a newcomer to business news, Gralnick realized, he was the longest of long shots to succeed Dobbs as president of CNNfn. He knew that the network was trying desperately to recruit Paul Steiger, the *Wall Street Journal*'s managing editor, for the job. Gralnick was a big boy and saw which way the chips were falling. You lived life in the fast lane, sometimes you ended up as road kill.

❑ ❑ ❑

Now that Jim Cramer was competing with CNBC, he was determined to improve the way that stock-market news was debated on television.

Cramer badly missed the *Squawk Box* gang and the camaraderie they had enjoyed. He tried to stay in touch, having dinner with David Faber and agreeing to appear at an American Jewish Congress fundraiser arranged by Faber's mother. But one thing that he hadn't liked about being on CNBC was a certain degree of staging. When he would appear on call-in segments, the producers would insist that he be told in advance about the stocks that viewers would raise. In fact, he was told that he could request the stocks he wanted to talk about. If he was sitting on a large block of Lucent Technologies, he could easily ask for a call about Lucent. The gimmick reminded him of the old *$64,000 Question* quiz-show scandal, where contestants were surreptitiously given the answers in advance. It all seemed terribly phony.

Now that Cramer was at Fox News Channel, Roger Ailes was treating him like a prince, allowing him to promote *TheStreet.com* on a variety of network programs. At 7:00 one morning, as *Squawk Box* was coming on the air, Cramer found himself on a chat show called *Fox & Friends*.

In his new perch, Cramer insisted on having a segment that was totally unscripted. He did not want to be told about the callers' stock questions ahead of time. The first call was from Jay in Florida. He asked about a stock called ITVC. Cramer looked blank.

"I'm not going to bluff you, Jay," Cramer said. "I don't know that stock."

Suddenly he understood why producers preferred the advance warning. Now he looked like a dope. His approach had more integrity, but it was bad television.

"How stupid did I look?" Cramer asked the host, Steve Doucy, during the break.

"You looked pretty honest," Doucy replied.

But the real problem for Cramer was that he was trapped in an environment that resembled a gong show. The callers were unsophisticated, and the hosts gushed over him in gee-whiz fashion.

"That guy is so rich, and he's made so much money for so many people," Doucy announced, dispensing with subtlety. "In other words, watch our show, make money."

E. D. Donahey, the blonde cohost, called him "the very sexy financial guy," adding: "Every stock that you recommended that I purchased went up. You are the man." She proceeded to explore the notion that the market went higher when women wore shorter skirts, promising to hike her hemlines.

Later, Cramer had to field obnoxious political questions from Mancow Muller, a flamboyant Chicago disk jockey. Things got worse when Fox cut to the scene outside its Sixth Avenue studios, where a jazzercise group was performing to music. The women shouted their stock questions as they danced, and Cramer, while responding, was shrunk to a small box on the screen. His stature, at the moment, was no larger.

❏   ❏   ❏

Bill Bolster was bemused by the notion that his reporters were suddenly being courted as big-name stars.

Well before the popularity of business news exploded, Bolster had recognized the value of hanging onto his marquee players. They were not accustomed to the limelight, he felt, and were feeling heady at all the attention. First there were the rumors that Maria Bartiromo was flirting with CBS. Now here was a *New York Post* story saying that CNN was making a run at Joe Kernen, who had once been an obscure stockbroker. Bolster assumed that such stories were floated by the journalists themselves as a way of boosting their visibility and self-importance. But he wasn't worried; he had locked up Bartiromo, Ron Insana, and Sue Herera under contracts ranging from three to five years, and Kernen had two more years to go on his contract. Bolster had taken the same tack with Matt Lauer at New York's WNBC in the early 1990s. Lauer had been unemployed for eighteen months and was doing landscaping work when Bolster hired him for the 6:00 A.M. local news. Soon afterward, when Bolster glimpsed Lauer's star potential, he ripped up the newsman's modest contract and gave him a new one for nearly half a million dollars. It wasn't long before the network snapped up Lauer, who wound up as coanchor of the *Today* show.

Over at CNN, Jeff Gralnick quickly learned that Kernen was unavailable. He knew, to the exact day, when each contract expired for the major business correspondents at the other networks. It was his job to know.

Now that CNN was airing new business shows on the main network, not just CNNfn, it would be a coup if Gralnick could pick off some of CNBC's people. He had just lured a top CNBC booker with a bigger salary. Like senior analysts and traders, high-profile financial journalists were increasingly free agents.

Bolster, for his part, was not above stealing a rival star himself. His initial meeting with Lou Dobbs months earlier was finally paying off. Dobbs was now in the process of pulling off a clever deal with NBC, apparently as a way of both getting back into television and simultaneously sticking it to his former colleagues at CNN. Dobbs had been swamped with offers from media companies, and he found that he missed the daily gyrations of financial news more than he had expected. Dobbs wanted to launch a radio show and a business newsletter, and was attracted to NBC for the strength of its brand. But getting around the noncompete clause in the three-year contract he had signed at CNN shortly before quitting was tricky business.

Bolster had withdrawn from the discussions because the deal had to be made at the network level. Few people knew it, but Dobbs's CNN contract barred him from appearing only as a regular anchor or correspondent on competing cable networks, and said nothing about a broadcast network. NBC's attorneys settled on the device of having Dobbs appear periodically on NBC and CNBC, but as a guest, not as an anchor, thus finessing the restriction. The move also cleared the way for Dobbs to join CNBC when his old contract expired. CNN executives were livid, but NBC appeared to have outfoxed them.

Mark Haines was deeply troubled by the Dobbs deal. CNN had raised legitimate ethical questions when Dobbs tried to stay at the network while also launching *Space.com*. How could a CEO also work as a financial journalist? Jim Cramer skirted the edges, Haines felt, but he was a minority shareholder in *TheStreet.com* and didn't run the operation. If Lou Dobbs wanted to be an Internet executive, more power to him, but that should disqualify him from passing himself off as a journalist. Could Dobbs really be objective in covering the dot-com world, where he planned to make millions with an IPO? Could he say the whole arena was overpriced, when such an observation might cost him dearly? Could he question the business models of other Net operations similar to his? Could he interview other CEOs upon whom he might depend for advertising or venture capital? No way. A serious conflict of interest was inevitable, Haines believed. Dobbs was largely off television for now, but if and when he became a regularly scheduled CNBC anchor, things could come to a head.

Haines grew even more concerned when Dobbs hosted a Webcast for Fidelity Investments and the company acknowledged that it was talking to him about other promotional activities, such as speaking to groups of clients. The potential conflicts were rapidly multiplying. Haines understood that NBC wanted Dobbs for his star power, but how many hats could one man wear?

Even as these chess moves were playing out, the struggle over *Squawk Box* continued. One morning Johnny Bench, the former Cincinnati Reds baseball star, was making a guest appearance on the show. He was obviously a big fan. He wondered aloud why the lava lamps were missing. Then he reared back and delivered a high, hard one.

"I've got to talk to Bill Bolster," Bench told viewers. "We're too serious on this show. I feel like I'm getting ready for a funeral." Apparently sensing he had gone too far, Bench added: "I'm sorry."

"That's okay," Mark Haines replied. "Somebody has to say it."

13

RAGING BULL

WHEN the market was doing well, the cable shows were filled with endless hours of upbeat talk. The sky was the limit. Everyone seemed to be wearing bulls' horns. And no one was charging harder than Ralph Acampora.

After slipping and sliding for months, the Dow had posted a new record, hitting 11,326 on August 25. The milestone prompted CNBC to quickly flash the headline "Dow 12,000?" On *Moneyline,* the man introduced by Willow Bay as "the hyperbullish Ralph Acampora" said he still saw the Dow closing in on 12,500 to 13,000, though he admitted that he had been wrong in saying it would happen by summer's end.

"Maybe by October you'll see twelve-five," he declared.

Net stocks also clawed their way back from the grueling 11 percent correction in August. The Nasdaq hit a new record in mid-September, recovering from its second swoon of the year, on a day when the core rate for wholesale prices fell 0.1 percent, briefly easing fears of inflation.

Henry Blodget was ready to declare victory. "We do think the Internet stocks will have a strong fourth quarter," he told CNBC, although the biggest Net stocks were still trading at roughly half their springtime highs.

Even Jim Cramer announced that he was buying dot-com stocks again, a complete reversal of his impassioned declaration a few weeks earlier that he was swearing off for the year. Someone e-mailed Cramer to ask

216

whether Blodget was the real thing. Nah, said Cramer, he was a waste of time, yet very much a creature of this hyperactive Internet market. But Cramer couldn't fight the numbers that AOL and Yahoo! were putting on the board as they started to climb back from their summertime lows. Expediency—the church of whatever works—was the market's religion. The financial cardinals were getting with the program.

Still, Cramer didn't much like the overall market. He was keeping more than half his assets in cash. The hedge fund was up 26 percent for the year, and he didn't want to blow it in a market downturn, not after his disastrous record in 1998. Cramer felt that he couldn't be bullish all the time. He was sitting on his lead.

Almost no one—not the analysts, not the fund managers, not the cable commentators—had an inkling of what would happen next. In September the Dow plummeted more than 1,000 points in less than a month, down to 10,213, or barely above where it had been the previous March. There were jokes that the stock exchange would again have to hold a party and hand out Dow 10,000 hats.

Of course, the market didn't drop in a straight line. When John Berry, the veteran Fed-watcher for *The Washington Post,* reported that the Greenspan board, having raised interest rates for the second time that year in August, was unlikely to do so again in October, CNBC touted the story all day, and the Dow rose 66 points. "Mr. Berry is a little easier to understand than Mr. Greenspan," Art Cashin of PaineWebber told Ron Insana.

But the Dow dropped 205 points when Steve Ballmer, the president of Microsoft, declared that tech stocks, including Microsoft stock, had reached "absurd" valuations. The Nasdaq was hit even harder, suffering its fourth-biggest point drop in history. Ballmer's costly comments sliced $1.2 billion off his own $23-billion net worth.

That was just the prelude. On September 28, amid a deepening sense of gloom, Acampora flipped again. The man who had once called for Dow 12,500 or 13,000 by the end of the summer now said that the Big Board could drop as low as 8,900 by year's end. It was a stunning, screeching U-turn by such a prominent analyst.

Acampora hadn't quite been ready to go public with his bearish forecast, but on a recent trip to Europe he had quietly told some Prudential clients that he would soon have to adjust his Dow targets downward in the face of the market's weakness. Some of these clients, in turn, leaked word to American investors, creating considerable buzz that Acampora was about to trash the stock market. At that point, Acampora felt that his hand had been forced.

"In the last couple of days pretty much everything has broken down," he wrote on Prudential's Website, never hinting that his earlier prediction had been flat-out wrong. He urged clients to sell their worst-performing stocks. The "hyperbullish" Acampora who had sounded so confident on *Moneyline* was gone. The market dropped 200 points after his early afternoon call was trumpeted by CNBC, but bounced back later in the day. Mark Haines was stunned by the audacity of Acampora's latest reversal and began poking fun at his sudden bearishness.

Acampora was furious at the way Haines and Joe Kernen were ridiculing him. Every time he opened his mouth, these guys would laugh it up at his expense. He was always wrong, always a jerk. Haines was acting like a mad dog. Acampora didn't know what he had done to Haines to deserve this cruel treatment.

Perhaps he had been too bullish over the last few weeks, Acampora reasoned. Fair enough. But he was a technician. If it was sunny for months and then the storm clouds began to gather, he had to change his forecast. The market looked terrible, Acampora felt; bonds were weak, the dollar was weak. He owed it to his clients and to Prudential's sales force to get them the information first, not to worry about making pronouncements on television. To Acampora, the most important thing was his discipline, the dispassionate analysis to which he had devoted his life. If he had to change his market projections and some cable loudmouths didn't like it, so be it. He was a big boy. He had long since grown accustomed to life under the media microscope.

This time, though, the criticism really nagged at him. Nonstop television coverage had turned the entire process into a carnival. Stock market analysis had somehow been reduced to entertainment for the masses. Acampora couldn't understand it. Whether he was right or wrong, he was a serious guy. He didn't shoot from the hip. His judgments were based on extensive research. Yet he had become a punching bag for *Squawk Box*.

Ron Insana tried without success to get Acampora to appear on *Business Center.* But Acampora was so angry that he decided to boycott CNBC completely. Call off the dogs, he said. Acampora told Insana that his clients and his salesmen wanted to kick the crap out of him whenever he showed up on CNBC because they were tired of seeing him get slammed on *Squawk Box.*

Acampora wanted to turn the tables and ask Haines and Kernen if they even knew what technical analysis was. His job was to shift as the market zigged and zagged. That's what he was paid to do. Yet they would pillory him for changing his mind. It was so unprofessional, but maybe that was how you got ratings. Still, Acampora had to wonder: If he was right and the Dow dropped to 9,000, would they give him any credit?

Insana understood that Acampora had become camera-shy because he was being pummeled. This was somewhat unfair, Insana believed. The financial media hammered analysts who made wrong predictions and stuck with them while the market went the other way. But the media also hammered analysts for seeming to equivocate. Forecasting the market was inherently hazardous, and Insana felt that they should cut the experts a little slack. The *Squawk* guys did their thing, but he had a different style, and he hoped eventually to lure Acampora back.

Acampora was far more pleased by a CNN profile that even he had to admit was a puff piece. The footage showed Acampora in a red cap driving his 1962 red Corvette, chatting in a plaid shirt in his "luxurious apartment," giving investment advice to his two sisters, touting his forthcoming book on how the Dow would double—a stance that rang hollow in light of his latest bear call. In words that carried more resonance than he might have intended, Acampora fretted about all his publicity, saying: "I fear that one day if I really make a mistake, a lot of people will get hurt."

When it came to the market's current decline, though, Acampora was determined to remain offstage. *Moneyline* tried to book him, to no avail. Jenny Harris wondered whether Acampora and the other big-name analysts really moved the markets anymore, since stocks had bounced back just hours after Ralph had predicted a downturn. Harris believed that the market was now being driven by Net stocks, which got the shivers from any bit of news or commentary involving the direction of interest rates. She couldn't believe that a single *Washington Post* columnist, who had merely said that a Fed rate hike was unlikely, could drive up the Dow. Times had changed. Maybe the days when a Ralph Acampora really mattered were over.

In Acampora's absence, Insana began working his hedge-fund buddies. There was a hot rumor that a major fund was on the verge of being unable to cover its bills. He called his pal Julian Robertson at Tiger Management, one of the nation's largest hedge funds, which was having a tough year. The financial community was so close-knit that everyone knew what Tiger owned, such as US Airways, and other fund managers would deliberately try to wreck their rival's position to boost their own standing. Robertson denied that Tiger, whose investors had pulled $5 billion from the fund in the first nine months of the year, was in trouble. Days later, however, Tiger limited the amounts that investors could withdraw from its funds.

Insana reported that another major fund—which he believed, but could not confirm, was George Soros's operation—was wreaking havoc in the gold market by pushing up prices to punish competitors who had bet against gold. This was Wall Street at its meanest. Insana was convinced that things were going to get uglier still, especially if the market kept dropping.

Television added to the sense of impending doom. CNN and CNBC ran pieces on the history of market disasters in October. Everyone was buzzing about the sinking Dow.

"Are we indeed in a bear market?" Geraldo Rivera asked Sue Herera on his evening CNBC program.

"A lot of analysts I talk to on the Street say we may be in for a prolonged downturn," Herera replied.

In this anxious environment, journalists liked nothing better than a rhetorical shoot-out between well-known personalities. And they weren't above staging such a match, especially as it became clear that Abby Joseph Cohen was sticking with her bullish stance. Cohen maintained that the declining market was actually undervalued and was calling for the Dow to reach 11,500 by the end of 1999. Soon Insana was intoning on

Business Center: "Abby says the market will go up. Ralph says the market will go down. The tug-of-war of the titans."

Of course, the two market gurus were hardly examining the same issues. Cohen was focused on long-term factors, such as strong corporate profits, moderate inflation, and relatively low interest rates. Acampora was a market timer, tracking the growing proportion of declining stocks and technical indicators that he now felt pointed downward.

Acampora had finally met Cohen and found her to be a very nice lady.

"What do you think of all this press coverage?" he asked.

"It's amazing," Cohen replied. "We're so different."

But the media insisted on casting them as rivals. "Abby vs. Ralph," the on-screen headline said. Television had made them famous, and now it was time to dramatize their disagreement. The media had their plot line, a story that reduced the numbing complexity of market gyrations and interest rates and economic trends to an old-fashioned spitball fight.

On Friday morning, October 15, Mark Haines appeared on *Squawk Box* wearing a combat helmet. It was his way of signaling that the market was being hit by heavy artillery.

The Dow had been under siege all week, with one-day declines of 231 and 185 points. Alan Greenspan had touched off a near-panic the previous evening by warning banks to make sure they were prepared in case stock prices declined, even invoking the specter of the Dutch tulip bulb craze. When the monthly rise in wholesale prices was announced that morning at 1.1 percent, the biggest increase in nine years, Wall Street was shaken by the double whammy. The Dow plunged 222 points in the first eighteen minutes of trading, prompting the stock exchange to impose trading curbs designed to limit volatilty. For a few brief seconds, the Big Board actually dropped below 10,000 for the first time in six months, finishing the day at 10,019. The 267-point loss was the worst in a year, and the week's 6 percent drop the worst in a decade. Internet stocks also got bloodied.

"The Big Skid," said CNBC. "Market Madness," said Fox. "Stock Market Plunge," said CNN.

"Wall Street may be even weaker than today's slide suggests," Stuart Varney said on *Moneyline.*

Everyone was speculating about whether the decline resembled the

run-up to the October 1987 collapse that had wiped out 22 percent of the
market's value in a single day. CNBC, hearkening back to another October, began running brief snippets called "1929 Revisited," recalling the
culture of that ill-fated year of the crash that launched the Great Depression.

Jim Cramer, following a classic buy-on-the-dips approach, invested another $25 million in stocks during the week, leaving his fund with $100
million in cash. This was perhaps the 500th sell-off he had endured as a
trader, and despite his penchant for bargain hunting, he was not optimistic.

"I don't think it's over yet," Cramer said on Fox. "A lot of people expect
there will be more selling Monday."

But there was no Black Monday. Once again, the experts were wrong.
The Dow rose 450 points the following week, as modest inflation figures
gave investors a sigh of relief. The Big Board jumped another 261 points
the week after that, to end October at 10,732, in part because Greenspan
had talked about technology helping the economy and investors took that
as a positive sign. Tech stocks pushed the Nasdaq to yet another record.
For the moment, at least, Ralph was flat wrong and Abby was closer to
right. It had become a yo-yo stock market, stretching out when interest-
rate fears subsided and snapping back at the merest hint of higher rates.

Technology stocks were more important than ever; the *Wall Street
Journal*'s editors finally juiced up the staid Dow, adding Microsoft and
Intel, among others, to the index, while booting out the likes of Chevron,
Goodyear, and Sears. But the rise of tech stocks was making the market
more and more volatile. Indeed, the Dow had dropped by more than 100
points on a third of the year's trading days. In an effort to make sense of
these swings, investors and journalists were constantly searching for
"bellwether" companies.

When IBM warned of soft sales because of Y2K computer problems
and its stock dropped 19 percent, the market took a hit. When Intel's earnings disappointed analysts by 2 cents a share, despite a 21 percent jump in
profits, there was plenty of handwringing about the fate of computer
stocks. When AOL and Microsoft beat the Street's expectations and
prospects for the industry seemed improved, the market got a bump.

And even the hint of a shortfall could hurt: Maria Bartiromo, reporting on a decline in the stock price of Cisco Systems, blamed "possible rumors that the company may not meet analysts' expectations." Each trend seemed to last an hour and a half.

The all-knowing experts were proved wrong again when a federal judge found on November 5 that Microsoft was a monopoly that routinely tried to crush its competitors. The media were filled with warnings that Net stocks would be hammered.

"Many investors were expecting a big sell-off in the software giant," Ron Insana said on *Business Center.*

"Investors braced for a broad technology bloodbath," Stuart Varney said on *Moneyline.*

It didn't happen. Microsoft stock dropped just 1.75 percent, and the Nasdaq rose to its seventh record high in seven trading sessions. For all the round-the-clock blather, as the Big Board jumped from 10,000 to 11,000 to 10,000 and back again, even the fortune tellers were stumped.

❑   ❑   ❑

Chris Byron was in his Connecticut basement, talking about stocks as usual. But this time people around the country were listening. Byron didn't think much of Net stocks, but the Net was giving him an audience.

He was conducting his noontime Internet radio show for MSNBC on November 8, and while things didn't work perfectly—the program started late because he'd had trouble getting connected—people could hear him through the speakers on their computers. In his slow, understated style, Byron began expounding on Xybernaut, whose stock was up more than 50 percent that day.

"Yesterday this company was worth $50 million as a market capitalization," he said. "Today it's worth $75 million. I wonder why. What did they do overnight to add $25 million?"

It turned out that Xybernaut had issued a press release saying the company planned to sell "wearable" computers that could withstand freezing temperatures. Byron was unimpressed.

"Let's take a look at what their earnings are," he said. "Aw, gee whiz. There aren't any earnings, darn it."

What about revenues? Could this line be $336 million? No, it was

$336,000. And the company had $5.8 million in expenses, Byron said. And some of its top executives had recently filed papers to sell some of their holdings. Finally, Byron cut to the chase: "It's one of these bull market stocks that catch fire when people will buy anything."

Byron was fiercely proud of his work and quickly grew defensive when one of his employers challenged him. He had been particularly happy with his recent column on Martha Stewart, a rare rave review. Byron had nothing but good things to say about the new IPO by America's most famous homemaker and her rapidly growing media company. Not only did Byron admire her financial acumen, he wrote in *The New York Observer,* but "Ms. Stewart is a pretty good-looking woman . . . and I've studied her close up from behind on a Stairmaster (she works out at my gym)."

Martha Stewart found that an amusing assessment, and called to say so. "I'm glad you think I have a nice ass," she joked.

But when the column appeared on *TheStreet.com,* those words had been excised. Dave Kansas, the editor, thought Byron had crossed the line.

Byron was livid, and he grew even angrier when *TheStreet.com* refused to run another of his columns a month later without bothering to tell him. The piece on Ann Taylor stores and their customers was also written in Byron's macho-man prose:

> If she's a good-looking dame to begin with (and I'm sure you get my drift), then a nice $300 pantsuit from Ann Taylor can really finish off the presentation. I mean, who wants to steal a sideways peek at somebody galumphing into the office in sensible shoes and a pair of Gap khakis that make her butt look like a truck rig swinging onto I-95 when the same gal, tricked out from an afternoon at Ann Taylor, will look like ready money any day of the week.

This time, Byron felt, the editors had gone too far. They were sanitizing his column for political correctness, deleting whatever might be deemed offensive or inappropriate. Once you started down that road, there was no end to it. Before long, the editors might be spiking pieces they didn't agree with or cutting out passages that didn't fit their agenda. Byron called Dave Kansas and said he was yanking his column from *TheStreet.com.*

Kansas was taken aback. If money was the issue, he said, he'd be glad to pay more for the rights to the *Observer* column. No, Byron said, it was a question of editorial control.

Kansas thought that Byron's argument about heading down a slippery slope was self-serving lunacy. The Ann Taylor column was sexist and embarrassing, so he had killed it. He wasn't in the business of running pieces about how great chicks looked in certain clothes. Those were the kind of judgments that editors were paid to make. He couldn't simply run Byron's columns, or anyone else's, without scrutinizing them. On the phone, Byron had gone into a rant about how *TheStreet.com* was worried about its underwriters, and by the way, how come he had never been given any stock in the company before the IPO? That, Kansas felt, was just surreal.

Still, Byron's argument about the underwriters bothered Kansas, for he had been absolutely staunch in resisting that kind of pressure. In October, *TheStreet.com* had published a piece about the online grocer Webvan that had forced the company to delay its IPO. The story had spilled the beans on Webvan's road-show presentation to investors, which included details that were not in its official prospectus. The SEC grew concerned that Webvan might have violated the "quiet period" rules against touting a stock shortly before it goes public. The problem for Kansas was that Goldman Sachs was handling the Webvan IPO. And Goldman Sachs, Cramer's old firm, had also provided the financing for *TheStreet.com*. Kansas's publisher told him that several Goldman Sachs bankers had tried to get the story spiked. When that failed, Kansas learned, they were making noises about doing things differently on future deals. When it came to resisting corporate pressure, Kansas felt, he didn't need any lectures from Chris Byron.

Byron, though, had a stubborn sense of his own integrity that had to be protected at all costs. He quickly cut a deal to move his *Observer* column to MSNBC's Website.

❏   ❏   ❏

Everyone knew that Wall Street analysts were influential, but sometimes their raw power was nothing less than stunning.

In October, David Faber began hearing rumors of accounting problems at Tyco International, the industrial conglomerate, and saw that the company's stock was declining. He got on the phone with some fund managers and quickly learned that the negative buzz was emanating from one man—David Tice—who ran the Dallas-based Prudent Bear Fund and frequently shorted stocks for a living. Tice's firm had given clients a report questioning a drop in Tyco's cash flow and some $3.9 billion in charges related to the acquisition of other companies. At 3:10 P.M. on October 13, the New York Stock Exchange halted trading in Tyco because of a huge imbalance between panicky sellers and scarce buyers. Faber went on the air at 3:36 to attribute Tyco's problems to the work of a single analyst. Even so, the damage was immediate: Tyco shares fell more than 7 points, to 96, a decline of nearly 10 percent in three days.

The next day, Tyco's CEO, Dennis Kozlowski, mounted a furious media counterattack, flatly denying Tice's charges on CNBC and CNN and in a conference call with reporters. "There are absolutely no accounting issues at Tyco," Kozlowski declared on CNBC's *Power Lunch*. He called Tice "completely wrong" and asked his attorneys to consider legal action against anyone putting out false rumors. Major brokerage firms, from Goldman Sachs to Bear Stearns, rushed to Tyco's defense. But it didn't matter, for investors had been spooked. The stock dropped another 10 percent, to 87. All told, David Tice had sheared more than $6 billion off Tyco's market value.

A single analyst could also have an impact by being the first to obtain leaked information from the company—the "selective disclosure" issue that so troubled Matt Winkler at Bloomberg. *The Wall Street Journal* disclosed on October 14 that Todd Slater, an analyst with Lazard Frères, had been told by an official at Abercrombie & Fitch that the retailer's sales were up just 12 percent for the quarter, which was less than the "whisper" estimate of 15 to 17 percent. Lazard notified some of its clients, who quickly began dumping the stock. When Abercrombie & Fitch made the figures public five days later, other brokerage houses were furious about the leak, and investors fled in droves. Abercrombie stock plunged by 19 percent that day. Perhaps it was a coincidence, but the following week SEC Chairman Arthur Levitt addressed a group of Wall Street analysts, denouncing selective disclosures and saying that the analysts were too concerned with protecting their cozy relationships with the companies. Mark Haines liked the speech so much that he read part of it on the air.

There were other times when some analysts must have obtained inside information, though no one could prove it for sure. Cramer watched in puzzlement on October 26 when there was a huge trading surge in the drug company Amgen, pushing the stock price down 4 to $75^{15}/_{16}$. The next day, the mystery was solved. The *Journal of the American Medical Association* reported that the company's drug leptin, which had caused fat mice to lose weight, had yielded disappointing results in human tests. Such medical journals were always sent to news organizations in advance with a strict embargo on the publication date, but someone had undoubtedly let the news leak. Cramer found the whole thing galling. Wasn't this sort of trading against the law?

Chris Byron was more disgusted than ever with these lazy hacks who called themselves analysts. Where had they been on Xerox? The stock had dropped by nearly a third after the company announced that it was having a dismal third quarter and that earnings could sink as low as 47 cents a share, even though analysts had been predicting 58 cents. One major brokerage house after another rushed to downgrade the stock once the damage had been done.

Byron called Xerox officials in Stamford, Connecticut, and asked why the analysts had been so optimistic in the first place. It seemed that the company had given them upbeat guidance at an investment conference the previous month, based on nothing more than confidence that its salesmen would meet their usual quotas. Didn't analysts call suppliers any more? Didn't they do any independent research? Byron devoted his *Observer* column to the fiasco: "How come the biggest and best known copying machine company on earth is apparently falling apart before our eyes and the analysts on Wall Street all seem to be blinking in startled amazement at the spectacle?"

These analyst forecasts, in Byron's view, had become a legalized form of price manipulation. The brokerage houses would buy up a company's stock, publish lowball estimates for the next quarterly earnings, and everyone would act pleasantly surprised when the company somehow "beat the Street" by a penny or two, looking for all the world like it was on a roll. And the media played along with the game, relentlessly reporting the artificially low estimates and then breathlessly touting the better-than-expected results. Almost no one, Byron believed, was holding these analysts accountable.

At the end of October, David Faber was in balmy Boca Raton covering a CEO conference when he learned that Henry Blodget had just downgraded Amazon, the stock he had ridden to fame. Weeks earlier, Blodget had been touting Amazon as a great buy for the holidays. But now Amazon had announced a loss of $197 million for the third quarter, nearly quadruple the red-ink level of a year earlier and part of a staggering half-billion dollars in losses over five years. Jeff Bezos, who was turning the operation from a bookseller into an online mall, acknowledged in a conference call with analysts that the company would not be profitable until 2002. Once again, the analysts moved after the fact. Four other brokerage houses downgraded the stock, and now even Blodget, the company's staunchest defender, was lowering his rating from a "buy" to a "long-term accumulate." Still, Faber thought it was a courageous move, given that Merrill Lynch had recruited Blodget to get the company a seat at the trough for more Internet banking business.

Two hours later, Blodget appeared on CNBC, tieless with a white shirt and rumpled hair, from the Merrill trading floor. He seemed determined to cushion the blow by saying only nice things about his favorite company.

"We still do like the stock long-term, it's just a less aggressive rating," he said. It was merely "taking longer than we expected" for Amazon to narrow its losses.

What should investors do? "This is going to sound contrary to our call," Blodget said, "but I think you can buy the stock now. I do think it will have a strong fourth quarter." The reassuring words didn't matter; Amazon stock dropped 6.5 percent that day. Henry Blodget had just told his clients that Amazon was no longer a "buy," yet here he was telling CNBC viewers to buy the stock anyway. No wonder people were skeptical of Wall Street analysts.

❑   ❑   ❑

A month later, the market was sizzling again, day after day of impressive gains. The bulls came charging back. Ralph Acampora broke his media silence on November 12 by appearing on his favorite show, Louis Rukeyser's *Wall Street Week,* where the questioning was always gentle.

"Well, Lou, there's one word that I think is really very important for a long-term bull market, and the word is rotation, and we've seen a lot of it," Acampora said. "And then this summer, I was a little concerned about the direction of rates, and I backed away a little bit."

A little bit? Acampora had predicted that the Dow might plummet as low as 8,900. It was the second straight year that he had forecast a plunge that never happened. Now, of course, he was back to being bullish, and so was everyone else.

Bears were seemingly becoming an endangered species. Rukeyser quite publicly booted one of them, Gail Dudack of Warburg Dillon Read, off his roster of regular panelists, saying she had been wrong "for the past 156 weeks running."

On November 16, the Fed raised interest rates a quarter-point for the third time in 1999. John Berry's *Washington Post* story had been wrong, along with perhaps half the economists on Wall Street. Even Mark Haines's joking ritual of guessing whether there would be a rate hike from the thickness of Greenspan's briefcase that day was wrong; the briefcase was thin but the board boosted rates just the same. Remarkably, the market shrugged off the increase and the Dow soared 172 points, to 10,932. The S & P 500 posted a new record. The Nasdaq hit its eleventh record in 13 days and was up 50 percent for the year. Two days later, a 153-point burst sent the Big Board hurtling past 11,000 for the first time in two months. The dizzying, thousand-point decline that the experts failed to foresee had been erased with a swiftness that left them equally perplexed.

Amid the euphoria, Ron Insana found reason to worry. He was particularly concerned by the surge in certain Chinese stocks in the wake of the U.S. agreement to bring Beijing into the World Trade Organization. Dransfield China Paper jumped in two days from 44 cents to $29 a share. China Prosperity International, fresh from its IPO, skyrocketed from 25 cents to $35. What did we really know about these outfits? Insana wondered. What if they were bullshit companies? Every time he or his colleagues mentioned one of these hot stocks on CNBC, it got even hotter. But how could you ignore them when the world was changing so fast?

Insana's concern was well-founded. The next day, Dransfield China shares dropped 25 percent, and China Prosperity plunged 40 percent.

Even Cramer was getting a bit dizzy. He wasn't sure he wanted to hold onto shares of a Net company called E.piphany, which was absurdly valued at $2 billion. But one of his young staffers explained that E.piphany had just bought a firm called RightPoint. This was wacky, Cramer thought. One unknown, overvalued company pays too much for another unknown company, and that was supposed to goose the stock? Cramer stopped snickering when E.piphany jumped 36 points. Maybe he was getting too old for this business.

With the party growing louder and all arrows pointing north, the normal human tendency to expect more of the same kicked in. "Dow 12,000 by 2000," said a CNN headline. "Markets Seem Ready to Rise to New Heights," said *USA Today*.

Maria Bartiromo, touting one of her favorite analysts, said on *Squawk Box:* "Tom Galvin over at DLJ has been very accurate on this market. He continues to see millennium melt-up," meaning that once the Y2K computer fears were eased, "everyone will want in the door and the market goes higher."

The herd mentality was back. The once-befuddled Barton Biggs issued a bearish forecast, but nobody paid much attention. Even David Faber, who openly disdained analysts, reported that Ed Kerschner of PaineWebber "sees the Dow at 12,500 by the end of 2000."

The late-summer swoon was magically forgotten, as if such a thing could not possibly recur. Christmas was coming, and the bulls were stampeding. The market was up, the ratings were up, and everyone was feeling rich again.

14

TULIP TIME

JIM Cramer was worried sick about losing his baby. He was obsessed with *TheStreet.com,* which he had labored so hard to bring into the world, and now, just six months after the euphoria surrounding its stock-market birth, the company was secretly being offered for sale.

No one outside a small circle of insiders knew what was happening. Cramer continued to write for the Website, fulminate on the Fox show, hawk the product in hard-sell television ads. But *TheStreet.com* was on the block, and he was heartbroken.

Cramer's deep-seated need for an enemy was being amply fulfilled by the CEO, Kevin English. The two men were at war. It was, in many ways, a classic struggle between a company founder and the professional manager brought in to run the firm. To Cramer, *TheStreet.com* and its growing band of 94,000 subscribers was a vibrant community bubbling with the potential to become a brand-name franchise. But English, after evaluating the business model and the mounting losses, had concluded that the stockholders might best be served if he found a buyer.

A former executive at Xerox, Lexis-Nexis, and Control Data Systems, English had frustrated some of the staff with his style; he liked to play golf and was sometimes hard to get on the phone. And Cramer, the largest stockholder, really got under his skin. While English wanted to do deals with other companies, Cramer wanted to build the business based on his grandiose vision. He and Marty Peretz, putting aside their recent bitterness, had now formed an alliance against their handpicked chief executive. Back in June, English had sent the board an e-mail saying that Cramer and Peretz were becoming intolerable. Cramer, with his histrionic style, was clearly the lightning rod. Cramer felt the die had been cast: him or me.

During the summer of 1999, English quietly explored the idea of selling *TheStreet.com* to its online rival, *CBS MarketWatch.com*. Cramer had learned of the talks from Roger Ailes, who knew people at CBS. Cramer had kicked around the idea of a partnership several times with the *MarketWatch* chairman, Larry Kramer, but they had agreed to remain gentlemen competitors. English billed the prospective deal as a merger of equals, but Cramer believed that the CBS gang would be running the show.

The deal didn't materialize, but weeks later English told his directors by e-mail that he was now negotiating to sell the site to E*Trade, the online brokerage firm. It was tragic, Cramer felt. Everyone would be fired except for him and a couple of the other columnists. There were also talks with other online business sites, from *Briefing.com* to *Quote.com*.

Cramer pleaded for a reprieve. Give us a year to improve the financial picture, he told English. But the CEO was apparently convinced that *TheStreet.com*'s paid-subscription model didn't offer much hope for a turnaround. When the third quarter results came in, net losses had doubled to $7.8 million, and the red ink had now produced a cumulative loss of more than $35 million.

Publicly, though, it was stiff-upper-lip time. "We have achieved a tremendous amount of success in a short period of time," English told reporters in a conference call.

Things came to a head on October 18, the day of a scheduled board meeting, at *TheStreet.com*'s offices on Rector Street. During a morning session without Cramer or Peretz, board members grilled English on his game plan—indeed, whether he had any plan other than selling the company—and made clear that they were dissatisfied with his leadership. Late that afternoon, Cramer and Peretz joined the other directors—Dave Kansas, a *New York Times* official, two venture capitalists, and a PR executive—for the official board meeting. The panel reviewed English's business plan, which included a note saying that since the CEO and the founders were unable to work together, perhaps the company should be sold. Though the dispute was well known to the board, Cramer was disgusted to see the impasse stated so starkly, in black and white. He had to leave early for a scheduled chat on Yahoo!, and he departed with a blast.

"You guys do whatever you want with the company," Cramer barked. "You want to sell it? Fine!"

The board went into executive session, asking English and Kansas to step outside. Without Cramer's polarizing presence adding to the tensions, Peretz pushed hard for a change at the top. After months of turmoil, the board voted to dump Kevin English, replacing him with Tom Clarke, who had joined the company just a few weeks earlier.

Worried about a public bloodletting, the directors gave English a generous financial parachute. He would continue to receive his $350,000-a-year salary until his contract expired in 2003. English had sold all 83,333 of his shares when the company went public, netting him $1.6 million, but he still owned options on another 521,316 shares. Both sides signed a nondisparagement agreement under which they would not engage in public badmouthing.

When *TheStreet.com* made the firing public on November 5, the stock got hammered. After the Website moved the story at 2:42 P.M., the stock dropped more than 11 percent, to 16⅞, below even the original offering price on the day of the IPO. Hambrecht & Quist, one of the company's own bankers, downgraded the stock.

It looked like a total fiasco, Cramer knew. Investors must have smelled something fishy when the CEO is ousted after a year. The *Street.com* team could have called reporters and whispered the real reason, but Cramer felt that they should play by the rules. The coverage, naturally, was negative. *MarketWatch.com* described its damaged rival as engaging in "gadfly financial journalism." *Business Week* dubbed the company "TheDive.com."

The irony was inescapable. Jim Cramer made his living trading and writing about stocks, and increasingly spent his time trying to make sense of the turbulent world of Net stocks. Now he was learning from the inside how hard it was to launch a dot-com company whose market wealth far exceeded its meager resources, and how frustrating it was to watch the stock price plunge after the Internet wave had carried them so high. His personal bubble had burst.

The next day, as the stock dropped to 14½, Chris Byron said on his Internet radio show that *TheStreet.com* executives were "discovering to their dismay that you really can't make any money in this business. The best day they ever had was the day it went public." Without mentioning his own recent departure from *TheStreet.com,* Byron said: "This is not a healthy situation. Their cash is running out reasonably fast."

But the company was still sitting on $136 million, and that worried Cramer even more. With the stock so low and the cash reserves so high, they were sitting ducks for a takeover attempt. A smart venture capitalist with a company needing a financial infusion could make an irresistible offer.

Cramer was convinced that the stock would rebound, even as English started selling some of his stock options. Cramer bought 60,000 shares for his hedge fund, shelling out more than half a million dollars, almost as an act of faith. Then he took his family to London for a week, trying to get unplugged, refusing even to bring his laptop.

It didn't work. Cramer was in one of his obsessive periods where he couldn't think about anything else. Even when he was coaching his daughter's soccer team, he was brooding about how to save *TheStreet.com.*

The problems didn't vanish with English's departure. Cramer was starting to feel like a pariah at the company he had cofounded. He believed there was a faction on the staff that felt he had no business writing about stocks while he was trading them. He was convinced that they hated him, just as he had once felt that half the *Harvard Crimson* was against him, just as he had felt that Peretz was out to get him. Cramer wanted more than anything to be taken seriously, to be respected, and he felt that was the case everywhere but at his own news service.

One Sunday, Cramer told Karen that he didn't like the Website's message boards.

"I hate *TheStreet.com!*" she screamed. "Just don't talk about it any more!" Karen felt that her husband was a perfectionist who was never satisfied. She had asked him a dozen times to keep the *Street.com* talk out of the house. They had plenty of money. Who the hell cared about this Website that he didn't even control?

"This is my legacy," Cramer explained.

"Your legacy is not *TheStreet.com,*" she said. "Your legacy is your children. Stop it!"

Cramer couldn't help it. He was totally stressed out. He felt so closely linked with the goddamn thing. They had created a great product, but his vision was being corrupted and he was barred from doing anything about it. And now, in the ultimate indignity, the stock was in the toilet. As Cramer knew as well as anyone, there was no room for sentimentality in the shark-infested waters of Wall Street.

❑   ❑   ❑

While *TheStreet.com* was sinking, DoubleClick was soaring. On the afternoon of Friday, November 12, the stock suddenly jumped more than 27 points, an increase of nearly 20 percent, to 167¹⁄₁₆. And Kevin O'Connor couldn't understand why.

He had just gotten off a plane in Arizona for a technology sales conference. It was an unwritten rule at the company that employees were not supposed to keep checking on the stock price, but his spokeswoman, Amy Shapiro, couldn't resist asking someone how DoubleClick was doing that day. She gave O'Connor the eye-catching news.

"What's going on?" he asked, amazed.

Shapiro soon discovered that they had been through a classic episode of media hype, but not one orchestrated by the company. While DoubleClick was still losing money, like most Internet firms, it was getting considerably more attention these days. O'Connor was ranked high on *Fortune's* list of the top fifty e-businessmen, and *The New York Times* had asked him to join a roundtable discussion on technology. The company was planning a Monday announcement of a new alliance with IBM, but it was a modest initiative at best. IBM was going to promote a DoubleClick venture called Ad Server in developing online strategies for other businesses.

One of the smaller firms involved in the announcement, Net Perception, had asked its PR outfit, Waggoner Edstrom—the same company that represented Microsoft—to quietly put out the word. The publicists were supposed to send e-mail invitations to a select group of tech reporters, alerting them to the news conference. The announcement was under embargo, meaning that it could not be reported until Monday.

The invitation was tantalizing:

WHAT: IBM, net.Genesis, Net Perceptions and DoubleClick TechSolutions will make a major joint announcement regarding Web solutions.

WHEN: Monday, November 15, 1999, 10:00 am Coffee Break.

WHERE: Pavilion Room, Personalization Summit, Fairmont Hotel, San Francisco.

Shapiro quickly realized that the PR firm had blown the event out of proportion by billing it as a "major" announcement. Somehow the invitation had leaked to the wire services. "IBM, a major software developer and the No. 2 online advertiser, along with DoubleClick, which operates an online ad network, and several partners said on Friday they planned a 'major joint announcement' on Monday," Reuters reported. CNBC quickly picked up the news.

What was driving the stock, Shapiro realized, was the implication that IBM and DoubleClick might be planning a merger. It was damage control time. Although the market had closed, she and her colleagues called as many reporters and investors as they could to tamp down the excitement. An IBM spokesman phoned Reuters to say that the media advisory had been inadvertently released. In a follow-up story, the spokesman was quoted as saying that "this is not an announcement of some merger deal."

But the foul-up didn't hurt DoubleClick at all. Its stock continued to rise over the next two weeks, buoyed by the record-setting pace of the Nasdaq market. After plunging over the summer along with AOL and Yahoo! and Amazon, DoubleClick was approaching its all-time high.

❑   ❑   ❑

Business reporters chase down rumors for a living, and for those working at CNBC, there was no escaping the recurrent rumor that their parent network was about to be sold. It was a bizarre situation for David Faber, reporting on backroom dealings involving his own company that could well affect his job. Mark Haines had felt compelled to ask NBC executives about the rumors the last time they were on *Squawk Box*.

Faber didn't dismiss the whispering out of hand. He had reported a year earlier that General Electric had been in negotiations with Viacom to sell NBC. The two CEOs, Jack Welch and Sumner Redstone, had secretly met, Faber's sources told him, but the talks had broken down over issues of control, and Viacom went on to buy CBS instead.

The *Squawk* gang realized that the story was back when they saw a copy of the *New York Post* on the morning of November 24. "GE OFFERS UP NBC," the bold headline said. "Time Warner Given $25 Bil Price Tag."

But the evidence turned out to be nothing more than some offhand comments by Rupert Murdoch, the tabloid's billionaire owner. During an interview on his own network, Fox News Channel, Murdoch had said: "I understand that the business has been offered to Time Warner for $25 billion and that one or two well-known people on their board are very much in favor of . . . buying it and the rest of them are very much opposed to it." That was it. But both companies quickly denied that such discussions were taking place. In fact, a GE spokeswoman ridiculed Murdoch's "musings" with "a flat-out denial."

Faber couldn't figure out what Murdoch was up to. Was he trying to help Fox by making trouble for NBC? Was he trying to stick it to his longtime nemesis Ted Turner, the number two executive at Time Warner? Was he just running his mouth?

Joe Kernen observed that the *Post* headline made the supposed offer sound like an undisputed fact, despite the high-level denials.

"If I'm a headline writer at the *Post* and Rupert Murdoch says GE is offering up NBC, that's going to be my headline no matter what anyone else says," Haines observed.

"My headline is, Jack Welch is the greatest CEO of all time," Faber chimed in.

Their skepticism turned out to be justified. Later that day, an executive close to Murdoch told *The New York Times* that "Rupert misspoke" and had made "a bit of a mistake" by merely repeating what he had heard. It was, in other words, just high-level gossip. NBC was safe, at least until the next round of rumors.

The media loved these pissing-match stories. When the *Squawk* gang began mocking a *New York Times Magazine* writer for his crude portrayal of the show—he had called Haines a "fatso" and figured that the Brain must be an "idiot"—reporters gobbled it up. But a more far-reaching, if complicated, tale was unfolding behind the scenes.

Bill Bolster had started making secret trips to Europe. CNBC was on the air there, though Bolster had to admit that much of its programming was pretty poor. He was quietly meeting with officials from eight foreign stock exchanges, pushing a plan for a consolidated ticker with real-time prices that would air only on CNBC. It would unite the markets of Britain, France, Germany, Belgium, and beyond, transcending the language barrier. A television version of NATO, so to speak. Eventually, Bolster hoped to turn CNBC-2, his long-planned digital channel, into the international trading network. If an investor in Des Moines wanted to trade Daimler-Chrysler stock on the European exchange, he could do so. Bolster was looking for someone to take his job, running the American network. That was old hat by now. He was ready to go global.

❏   ❏   ❏

Matt Winkler seized his opportunity when Bloomberg News threw a Christmas party in Washington. Plenty of important people were there, from Treasury Secretary Lawrence Summers to Commerce Secretary William Daley. But Winkler made a beeline for Arthur Levitt, the SEC chairman, to pursue what had become Bloomberg's single-minded crusade.

"When are we going to see something on selective disclosure?" Winkler asked.

"It's coming, it's coming," Levitt replied.

Days earlier, Winkler's staff had weighed in with another opus on the injustice of corporations releasing crucial information to the favored few. Winkler orchestrated a multimedia launch, releasing different versions of the story for the news service, Bloomberg TV, Bloomberg Radio, and the Bloomberg magazine. The piece began with the tale of fund manager Mark Trautman, who had watched helplessly one day as Clorox stock dropped 14.5 percent, a decline that cost him $1 million. What he didn't know was that Clorox Chairman Craig Sullivan had just warned investors on an invitation-only conference call that the company's profits wouldn't meet expectations for the next two quarters. If an investor was excluded from the all-important call, he was simply out of luck. The Bloomberg story cited other examples involving such companies as Apple Computer and Wal-Mart. A Morgan Stanley Dean Witter analyst, complaining of the cost of staging fancy conferences for selected investors, summed up the prevailing corporate attitude: "We don't want any Joe Blow to waltz in."

Soon after Winkler's chance meeting with Levitt, SEC officials leaked word to Bloomberg and several other news organizations that the following day they would propose a federal rule to ban selective disclosure of corporate information. Winkler was thrilled. This, he felt, was what journalism was all about, grabbing hold of an issue and forcing the authorities to do something about it. Much of Wall Street opposed the initiative, apparently concerned that analysts would be unable to justify their jobs without such inside dope. But *The Wall Street Journal,* Winkler's old paper, weighed in with an editorial hailing the SEC proposal. "When Web companies openly admit they gave their IPO business to Morgan Stanley hoping to get a favorable tout from Mary Meeker, you have to wonder who the analysts are really working for," the paper said. It was all the more curious, therefore, when Dow Jones formally opposed the rule, saying that it could hurt the *Journal's* ability to scoop its rivals.

Winkler couldn't understand why the rest of the press wasn't more excited about the issue. Perhaps too many reporters had cultivated Wall Street sources and didn't want to alienate them. These sources—analysts, brokers, corporate executives—were the ones who benefited from the chummy arrangements, and they could be invaluable in passing on tidbits to the press. The journalists didn't want to bite the hand that was so generously feeding them. Winkler was glad that his upstart operation had refused to play the game.

❏   ❏   ❏

The Christmas shopping season had boosted the dot-com frenzy into the media stratosphere. From the fat e-commerce sections in *The Wall Street Journal* and *The New York Times* to the *Vanity Fair* spread on young IPO millionaires and the Internet cover stories in *Fortune, Time,* and *Business Week,* the Web economy was cooler than cool. It was "about wealth at a level never before imagined by the human race," as *New York* magazine modestly put it. And it was often hard for readers to tell the advertising from the upbeat articles trumpeting the virtues of futuristic cell phones, Palm Pilots, robotic dogs, and the cornucopia of products now available on the Web. Online ads, such as the Ameritrade commercial featuring the gyrating, ponytailed "Stuart" helping his hapless middle-aged boss buy stocks, had moved from the business channels to the major networks. E*Trade agreed to sponsor the halftime show at the 2000 Super Bowl. In one great roaring burst of holiday hype, the Net had finally gone mainstream.

Steve Case and Jeff Bezos were no longer addressing a narrow audience on CNBC; they were hawking their cyberwares on *This Week with Sam Donaldson and Cokie Roberts.* Donaldson observed that America Online's market value of $186 billion was bigger than the gross domestic product of Sweden, Austria, or Chile.

"We think we have an opportunity to someday be the most valued company, the most respected company in the world," Case said.

Bezos was chosen as *Time*'s Man of the Year, an almost unimaginable honor for a thirty-five-year-old who had launched his company four years earlier with $300,000 of his parents' money and now boasted more than 13 million customers. Bezos had "helped build the foundation of our future," the magazine gushed. Amazon was still losing hundreds of millions of dollars, but that, in the business media culture, somehow added to Bezos's allure.

As the online shopping phenomenon gained altitude, Net stocks continued their torrid tear. When Henry Blodget appeared on *TheStreet.com* show, the session was more of a lovefest than the grilling he had endured on *Moneyline* three months earlier.

Jim Cramer was no Blodget fan, but Gary Schreier, the producer of the Fox show, told him that he should praise the Merrill Lynch analyst on the program. Since Blodget's first appearance in July, the tech stocks he had recommended had bounced back big: Yahoo!, up 85 percent. Amazon, up 73 percent. AOL, up 64 percent. The issue wasn't whether Blodget was a sufficiently savvy analyst to be useful to Cramer's hedge fund, Schreier said. The question was whether he had helped Fox viewers make money, and Blodget clearly had.

Blodget glossed over his recent cautionary note on Amazon, saying that it was a stock to buy "long-term." He compared Bezos's company to Wal-Mart. While there might be some "popping of the balloon" after Christmas, Blodget said, "they will win." He also recommended DoubleClick, much to the annoyance of Cramer, who had just sold most of his DoubleClick stock. Henry Blodget had taken a beating when dot-com stocks were down, but now he was riding high again.

Yet a strange metamorphosis was under way. The technology giants that had once fueled the market, from Microsoft to Amazon, suddenly seemed old hat. Wall Street was swooning over the onrushing wave of B2B stocks, the business-to-business Internet ventures whose rise was absolutely blinding. A company called VA Linux, which made software to compete with Microsoft's Windows, skyrocketed by 700 percent on the day of its IPO. It was followed the next day by an industrial auction site called FreeMarkets, which blasted off by nearly 500 percent at its market debut.

Companies that no one had heard of until twelve minutes ago were suddenly worth billions. In the first week of December alone, Digital Island was up 150 percent, Freeserve up 71 percent, MicroStrategy up 43 percent, i2 Technologies up 40 percent, Intertrust Techs up 39 percent, Infospace.com up 34 percent, Internap Network Services up 34 percent. The Dow jumped 247 points in a single day. For a year, two years, three years, critics had warned that the market was overvalued, and now, with the Nasdaq shattering one record after another, it was heading into another solar system. And no one, least of all the talking heads, knew quite what to make of it.

"How long can this go on?" asked Stuart Varney on *Moneyline.* "You ever see anything like this before?"

"No one has ever seen anything like this before," said Bruce Steinberg of Merrill Lynch.

"Is this as crazy a market as you have ever seen?" Ron Insana asked on *Business Center.*

"It is certainly bizarre," said Art Cashin of PaineWebber.

The stock market had not been rational for some time, David Faber believed, and now it had moved to a new level of utter absurdity. It was no longer about price-to-earnings ratios or revenue multiples or the relative merits of one business versus another, the sort of thing that he talked about every morning. It was sheer supply and demand, anxious buyers chasing stocks simply because they were going up.

Faber knew very little about these new companies like Exodus Communications. On December 8, when Exodus was trading at 144, Faber reported that Blodget had started covering the stock and set a price target of 200. Exodus, he warned viewers, was now trading at an incredible 34 times its revenues. By day's end, Exodus was at 165, an increase of 15 percent.

In a hyperactive market, Faber had cast himself in the role of grizzled skeptic. He saw that DecisionOne Holdings, an Internet firm, began to soar simply because it was mentioned as a possible contractor in a VA Linux press release. Faber was talking to traders who specialized in bankruptcy debt, and they warned him that DecisionOne was bankrupt. Anyone who bought the stock could find that it was worthless after the creditors carved up the assets. Faber reported the bankruptcy status on the air on December 10, and DecisionOne's stock dropped 23 percent in the next couple of hours.

In similar fashion, Faber helped pop the balloon of Commerce One, a firm that linked suppliers on the Internet and whose stock had skyrocketed after its IPO from just under 9 to 331. Faber reported on December 28 that the "lockup" period that prevented company insiders from selling their stock had expired, which meant that the number of available shares on the market could nearly double. Commerce One stock dropped from 331 to 250 that day, and to $209^{15}/_{16}$ the next day. Faber, who was flooded with angry messages from investors, made an on-air crack about "stupid viewer e-mails."

The result of such reporting was that Faber was getting trashed in the Internet chat rooms. "David Faber just did one of his famous hatchet jobs," one investor wrote on Yahoo! after the DecisionOne report. "He said they are bankrupt, and of course smiled [all] the time. He is a prick that gets his rocks off on tanking stocks." Said another: "David Faber is nothing but a journalistic WHORE." Faber was bemused by these attacks, wondering how he could be denounced for disclosing the inconvenient fact that a publicly traded company was bankrupt. He could save people money, if they would only listen.

Mark Haines felt that they had all been through this before. Back in

1996, it was exotic computer hardware stocks such as Iomega, which had shot up from 20 cents to $27 a share, and now it was back at 4. Next came the first generation of Internet stocks; most of them, except for a few big names such as Amazon and Yahoo!, were well below their euphoric highs. This frenzy would end the same way, Haines thought; a few winners and lots of losers. Haines found the media hype about all the new gadgetry to be embarrassingly overheated. How many people wanted to download data on the tiny screen of a tiny cell phone? Did the average consumer really need to be able to call Khartoum from Death Valley? Were there really enough obsessive-compulsives out there to support a service that allowed you to check your e-mail while at the gas pump? Of course, Haines used his cell phone only 10 minutes a month, and he had once thought that no one would go to the trouble of renting and returning movies. Maybe he was just out of it.

Gene Marcial was besieged by publicists trying to get him to mention the latest flimsy Net firm in his *Business Week* column. He felt that he had to go with the flow and show that he was in the know on these sizzling new stocks, but he knew that they could drop as quickly as they soared. You had to avoid the land mines. One day in November, Marcial got a call from David Cooley, a Cleveland money manager he had known for years and who understood what he needed for the column. Cooley was pushing a Net service provider called Internet Initiative Japan, in which he was invested. The stock had gone public in the United States four months earlier at 23; now it was at 67¼. Marcial wrote up the Japanese company, with plenty of praise from Cooley; the stock jumped 18 points the day after the column appeared. But rather than fading, as many stocks had done after being touted by Marcial, it kept going and was now at 120. This was exciting stuff, Marcial thought. Cooley had given him a real gem.

Marcial kept hearing his skeptical colleagues in the corridors of *Business Week*. Oh my God, they said, this will end. This has to end. But Marcial didn't believe that the soaring market was a speculative bubble. The tech sector, he felt, would create new Amazons, new Yahoos, new Ciscos.

The journalists, the money men, the big-time traders were all off balance. Everyone wanted to ride the tidal wave and no one really understood its dimensions or its dangers. Jim Cramer was having trouble sleeping.

Every single compass and benchmark he had used in his career was now worthless. He had a pile of research on his desk—on McDonald's, on Whirlpool, on J. C. Penney—and none of it mattered. No one cared about price anymore. If a stock was up 600 percent, investors saw it as a pit stop on the way to a 1,000-percent gain. Brokers were constantly trying to sell him on newfangled Net firms—CopyTele, Presstek, Corel, Valence—that they promised would be the next sure thing. Cramer was amazed by a *Wall Street Journal* article on day traders who were making money on Yahoo! and the Internet firm CMGI and yet had no idea who the CEOs were. This really was a brave new world where information counted less than instinct.

And yet Cramer had little choice but to play. He heard Mark Haines say on December 5 that the CEO of Vitria Technology would be on *Squawk Box* the next morning. Cramer knew almost nothing about the software firm, but he spent nearly $1 million on 5,000 shares of the stock, and it quickly jumped 9 points. Cramer told Jeff Berkowitz that he was going to sell it, having turned a $45,000 profit on the strength of a single CNBC promo. He realized the next day that he should have waited until the Vitria executive appeared on the show; the stock had jumped even higher.

Two days later, Cramer decided to sell some of his Yahoo! stock at the closing bell, even though he loved the company. Yahoo! was joining the S & P 500 that day, meaning that index-fund managers would have to wait until day's end, under their policy, and buy 20 million shares to balance their portfolios so that they properly mimicked the S & P. Yahoo! rose an astonishing 67 points that day, to 346, a 24 percent increase. The Internet portal's market value, according to Wall Street, was now twice that of General Motors. Cramer knew it was time to get out when the hapless index funds started buying at the inflated price; Yahoo! promptly tumbled to 311 the next day. This sort of manipulation was a travesty, Cramer thought, but as a trader he had to seize such opportunities.

In such a frenzied environment, Dan Dorfman was nearly as influential as he had been in his CNBC days. In his *JagNotes* column on December 6, Dorfman quoted a New Jersey money manager named Rick Eakle on his outlook for the market. Dorfman reported that "in a more speculative vain" (no one had caught the misspelling), Eakle liked a "bulletin-board stock"—meaning it was not yet listed on a major exchange—called MarketCentral.net. Eakle was quoted as praising the financial news portfolio as a "mini-Yahoo!" and predicting that the stock price would increase ten-fold over the next year. In the three hours after Dorfman's 1:00 P.M. report appeared on the Website, MarketCentral shot up 64 percent, to 4⁷⁄₁₆, on seven times its average daily volume. The Dorfman Effect was alive and well.

But *TheStreet.com* smelled something funny. Cramer's news service reported that Eakle was a paid consultant to MarketCentral, the very company that he was trumpeting. The clear implication was that Dorfman had been badly used. The stock began to decline.

Dorfman was surprised by the criticism. Eakle, he believed, hadn't told him of the arrangement. He couldn't ask every money manager he interviewed what that person was doing with the rest of his life. He had assumed that Eakle owned stock in MarketCentral. He had warned his readers that the comments were speculative. Eakle told *TheStreet.com* that he had in fact notified Dorfman of his tie to MarketCentral and that, in any event, there was little wrong with "taking advantage of the news media." Still, Dorfman didn't understand why *TheStreet.com* kept nipping at his heels. It had to be related to the fact that he and Cramer couldn't stand each other.

JagNotes insiders felt that *Street.com* executives had grown jealous of their progress. *JagNotes* had just launched its service in Europe, where *TheStreet.com* was still trying to get off the ground, and was hiring well-known analysts like Elaine Garzarelli of Garzarelli Capital. Its bulletin-board stock was languishing at 5¼, down from 21½ the previous spring, but the company believed that it was close to winning a listing on the Nasdaq. *JagNotes* executives were planning to start a digital television network, using Dorfman as a star commentator and extending their brand name beyond the Internet world. Little wonder, they felt, that *TheStreet.com* had made Dorfman such a target.

Such feuds were overshadowed by a stock market that improbably kept climbing in the final days of the century. On December 23, 1999, the Nasdaq index, which had hit 3,000 just seven weeks earlier, topped 4,000 for a few moments before slipping back to 3,995 by day's end. CNBC and CNN began running "Road to 4000" logos, trying to manufacture some drama as they had in the hoopla surrounding Dow 10,000. This time, of course, it was over a benchmark that was unfamiliar to 99 percent of the country.

The index kept flirting with the 4,000 mark. "Just Missed," a CNBC headline said on December 28.

At 7:30 the next morning, David Faber reported that a PaineWebber analyst named Walter Piecyk had just told his clients that Qualcomm, a fast-growing wireless technology firm whose stock had begun the year at 26 and was selling at 503, would hit 1,000 within a year. Faber believed that this sort of melodramatic call was grandstanding, especially since the projected price was 55 times the company's estimated revenues in 2001. This guy was clearly trying to emulate Henry Blodget and his famous call on Amazon. "If you're an analyst and you want to make a splash and you're not that well known, you put a $1,000 price target on Qualcomm, and you do it on a day when we got nothing else to talk about," Faber told *Squawk Box* viewers. What's more, he declared, "analysts don't know much of anything."

But they knew how to give a stock a mighty pop. In little more than an hour, Qualcomm had jumped to 575 in premarket trading, and later that morning Walter Piecyk found himself on CNBC and CNNfn and being interviewed by *The Wall Street Journal*. He was twenty-eight years old.

Qualcomm, meanwhile, gave the Nasdaq a strong boost. "We're still two hours away from seeing if the fourth time is a charm," Maria Bartiromo said when she opened *Street Signs* that afternoon. By the time that Ron Insana closed the show, the Nasdaq had reached 4,040. "Time for a special edition of Nasdaq 4,000," Insana said. As for Qualcomm, the stock closed at 659, an increase of 156 points, or 29 percent. At 6:43 the next morning, Jim Cramer sold some of his 10,000 Qualcomm shares in premarket trading at 746. Cramer made an extra $3 million by selling Qualcomm before the stock dropped back to 647 by day's end.

The larger story was that the Nasdaq was up a stunning 86 percent for the year, the biggest annual gain by any stock market in American history. As the all-electronic Nasdaq unveiled the world's largest video screen at its new Times Square headquarters, its index far outpaced the Dow, which had climbed more than 25 percent for the year, and the S & P 500, which had risen more than 19 percent. Net stocks were simply on fire. Even *TheStreet.com*'s down-in-the-dumps stock jumped 14 percent after the company announced a marketing alliance with America Online. Kim Polese's Marimba was up 50 percent from its springtime low. Kevin O'Connor's DoubleClick was up a breathtaking 1,000 percent for the year. Yet even that paled beside Qualcomm's yearlong gain of 2,259 percent.

Some commentators cautioned that these stellar performances masked important weaknesses in the broader market. Half the stocks in the Nasdaq lost ground during 1999, as did nearly two-thirds of those on the New York Stock Exchange. But the Net stocks were growing at such a phenomenal rate that they simply pulled the indexes along with them.

A few party-poopers spoke up against the din. Barton Biggs told *The New York Times* that the stock market was overvalued by 50 percent. Ed Yardeni, chief global economist for Deutsche Bank—or "Dr. Ed," as he called himself on his Website—said that Y2K computer problems would plunge the country into a recession. But most of the bears were heading for the hills. "Basically, our function is to piss in the wind," Alan Abelson of *Barron's* said in a remarkable confession. "But I certainly would rather have been right. In other words, I wish the Dow was at 500."

Chris Byron acknowledged on the front page of *The New York Observer* that he had been wrong about Amazon and Yahoo!. If a reader had ignored his dismissal of Amazon in 1997 as a "barking dog" and bought a share at $18, it would now be worth $1,164. His blunder on Net stocks, Byron said, was in "misjudging just how strong—and ultimately, unstoppable—the bull market of the late Clinton years has proved to be."

The bulls, not surprisingly, were bolder than ever. Ralph Acampora held a year-end conference call with reporters, raising his target for the Dow in 2000 to between 13,500 and 14,000. And "here's the big one," he said, predicting that the Nasdaq could hit 5,000. "This is an extension of the bull market I originally wrote about in late 1994," Acampora said. "I had to swallow hard when I saw the numbers for my Nasdaq projection. I said, wow." Acampora mentioned only parenthetically that less than three months earlier he "was calling for a bit of a pause, a correction."

A Canadian reporter reminded Acampora that he had trashed dot-com stocks back in August. "Maybe my timing wasn't too good on that comment, but I did get back into them," Acampora said. "We were fortunate enough to shift gears."

When the conversation lagged, Acampora seemed to worry that he hadn't made much news. "Is my number just like everybody else's number?" he asked. "Does Abby have a big number?"

Told that Abby Joseph Cohen was sticking by her 2000 forecast that the Dow would reach 12,300, Acampora said: "That's not too exciting." He quickly added that "even comparing us is silly," though he was the one who had raised the comparison.

The business magazines were caught up in the millennial excitement. *Fortune*'s Joe Nocera christened the 1990s "the Nasdaq decade." *Kiplinger's Personal Finance* magazine called for "Dow 25,000," an ambitious projection for the next decade that nevertheless lagged behind that of a controversial book published earlier in the year, *Dow 36,000*.

Abby Joseph Cohen rang the opening bell at the New York Stock Exchange on December 30, and she had lost none of her bullishness. "We think stock prices are moving yet higher from here," Cohen told CNNfn.

On the last day of the twentieth century, Steve Lipin was sitting with David Faber on the *Squawk Box* set. Lipin, whose boycott of CNBC had ended when *The Wall Street Journal* signed a new contract with his union, was there to talk about his article that morning on the history of big corporate mergers. "David told me he was doing 'Deals of the Decade,' so in my continuing effort to top him, I had to do 'Deals of the Century,' " Lipin deadpanned. Mark Haines and the gang donned party hats and blew little horns. The Dow, which had begun 1999 at 9,181, finished the year at a record 11,497.

What made all this possible—from the white-hot stocks to the feverish commentators and magazines and Websites that touted them—was money, the incredible volume of money coursing through the arteries of Wall Street. There was almost a collective gasp when the *Journal*'s Heard on the Street column reported that Mary Meeker, queen of the Internet analysts, would receive a 1999 compensation package of as much as $15 million. No analyst had ever been in that rarefied zone before, and yet, under the Street's wacky economics, it made sense. Meeker's employer, Morgan Stanley, had made as much as $100 million for the year launching Net IPOs for which she was the luminescent drawing card.

The staggering amount of available money carried the usual temptations. New York trader Alan Bond was indicted for allegedly accepting more than $6.9 million in kickbacks from brokerage houses. Bond was a fixture on television, a regular on *Wall Street Week,* and his media friends rushed to his defense. "Alan is my friend and he has served our viewers well. . . . We hope he will be completely vindicated," Louis Rukeyser said.

But there was no need to load the dice when the casino was cooking. Now that Net stocks were soaring, everyone looked like a genius. Nearly half the nation's fund managers were beating the S & P 500, the highest proportion in six years. Cramer's fund was up 63 percent for the year, more than double its margin four months earlier, because he bought up Net stocks that had skyrocketed in the final weeks. George Soros's Quantum Fund, which had been down 19 percent in July, moved heavily into tech stocks and rode the market to a 35 percent gain for the year. Morgan Stanley, Merrill Lynch, and Goldman Sachs each handled more than $1 trillion in corporate mergers for the year. The ratings for *Squawk Box,* which had been depressed when the market was stalled and management had complained that the show was too irreverent, were at an all-time high. For the first time ever, CNBC, once a fringe business channel, surged ahead of CNN, the all-news cable leader, in the daytime ratings.

The networks were making money, the day traders were making money, the fund managers were making money, the venture capitalists were making money, and the analysts such as Blodget and Meeker were making previously unimaginable amounts of money. The only ones not making money were the Internet companies themselves, whose cocky cowboys had mesmerized Wall Street into betting billions on their future profitability. That these untested B2B businessmen could take the stock market by storm while bleeding red ink was a tribute either to the revolutionary strength of the New Economy or the sheer brazenness of the fortune tellers who were cheering them on.

15

NOTHING BUT NET

THE celebration on Wall Street has come to a rather screeching halt," Ron Insana announced. That was putting it mildly.

It was Wednesday, January 5, 2000, and interest-rate fears were spooking investors once again. The Dow had plummeted 500 points in the first two trading days of the year, back below 11,000. And the Nasdaq, which had reached such euphoric heights days earlier, was being hammered even worse. The index was in the midst of a 9.8 percent plunge, back below the 4,000 mark, just shy of an official correction, as the high-flying tech stocks that had made so many people rich suddenly lost altitude. Many investors, having felt such tremors before, reacted like earthquake-fearing Californians: Was this it? Was this the Big One?

Insana was hardly surprised by the swift sell-off. On December 30, he had delivered an on-air commentary saying that the stunning surge in the Nasdaq was disturbingly similar to the run-up in the Dow shortly before it crashed in 1987. If the tech index gave up just the gains of the last two months, he said, it would drop 30 percent. In normal times, such a bearish pronouncement might have triggered a wave of angry e-mails and phone calls to CNBC. But Insana got no reaction. No one cared. He figured that people were completely inured to the idea that the market might go down. A different crowd was in charge these days. The bears were dead. Many of the bearish brokers he had known over the years were out of work. They could make intellectually credible arguments about why the market should be going down, but when the Dow shot up another 4,000 points and they kept clinging to their theories, their services were no longer required.

On the air, Insana did what he could to emphasize what positive news there was. You couldn't just sit there spewing gasoline from your hose. The downturn was painful, he felt, but hardly unprecedented. His hedge-fund buddies had warned him that they might be selling stocks in early January to delay the tax liability they would have incurred by taking profits in December. People were getting more accustomed to these wild market swings rather than heading for the window ledge.

On *Squawk Box,* Joe Kernen observed: "I see Ralph Acampora on a monitor up there."

Mark Haines jumped right in: "It was just a week or so ago that Ralph got really enthusiastic. He's going to remain bullish through the correction, then at the bottom of the correction he'll say we've got further to go."

For Net stocks, the news was all bad. Even the once-unstoppable Qualcomm dropped 21 percent, prompting the CEO, Irwin Jacobs, to defend the company on *Squawk Box.* "It would be nice if we didn't have this kind of volatility, but it's a fact of life," he said.

Amazon announced that its losses would continue to mount despite a strong jump in holiday sales, and even Henry Blodget couldn't put a good face on the company's report. Amazon's results were "not spectacular," Blodget said, "and the market is likely to be disappointed based on some very aggressive expectations." After his negative reaction, Amazon stock dropped 15 percent that day, which in turn dragged down the Nasdaq. "Blodget Comments Help to Batter Net Stocks," *TheStreet.com* reported.

Jim Cramer couldn't understand what Blodget was doing. Why didn't he just downgrade these stocks already? It was very unnerving. Blodget seemed to be trying to have it both ways—to mildly criticize the stocks, hurting them further, and yet tell Merrill Lynch's clients to keep buying them.

Cramer found the fast-moving environment a bit frightening. It was hard to know whether to jump out of Net stocks or snatch them up at these suddenly lower prices. Reuters moved a report saying that one of his favorite analysts, Jamie Kiggen of DLJ, was downgrading DoubleClick.

But it turned out that the story was wrong; the downgrade had come from another analyst, at A. G. Edwards. Cramer held onto his DoubleClick stock.

When the market closed that day, Gateway Computer warned that it was having problems getting parts and that its fourth-quarter earnings would be about 37 cents a share, not the 49 cents that Wall Street analysts were expecting. The stock began dropping in after-hours trading. Cramer wanted to go home, but this was a major blowup at a major company. He and Jeff Berkowitz began checking on Compaq, Dell, Intel—the stocks were all moving, even though most of the brokers they were calling had left for the day. Cramer was struck by the power of the do-it-yourself investors to control the action after Wall Street had gone dark. He wondered whether traditional brokers were becoming irrelevant.

On Thursday, as tech stocks were bloodied for the third straight day, rumors were swirling across Wall Street. Sue Herera reported that "there are rumors in the market, unconfirmed of course, that there will be an upcoming *Washington Post* story about the Fed's long-term concern about the effect of growing interest rates on the economy." No such story materialized.

Ron Insana said that the Nasdaq was plummeting in part because of "a rumor that Microsoft would miss its quarterly number." He said he had checked with a hedge-fund trader who regarded the rumor as "nonsense." Even so, Insana felt he had no choice but to tell viewers what was moving the stock market.

At 4:04 P.M., just after the markets closed, trading was halted in Lucent Technologies. The company announced that it expected earnings of 36 to 39 cents a share for the fourth quarter, well below analysts' expectations of 54 cents. Insana noted with suspicion that someone had sold 90,000 shares of Lucent just before the closing bell. Somebody obviously knew that the news was coming. Lucent stock began dropping like a rock.

On Friday morning, David Faber proudly announced that "the penguins are coming out." Analysts at four brokerage houses—Merrill Lynch, Salomon Smith Barney, SG Cowen, and Lehman Brothers—had downgraded Lucent, but only after the stock had plunged 30 percent in after-hours trading. Faber provided the details while *Squawk Box* aired footage of the birds waddling into the water. The show's ratings were so strong that CNBC officials had finally abandoned their attempt to crack down on the hijinks. Corporate executives, however, had never underestimated the program's importance. Lucent's CEO, Richard McGinn, appeared later that morning to vow that his company's performance would improve.

The fever broke over the next few hours. In two days, the Dow had gained back the 500 points it had lost on Tuesday and Wednesday to close above 11,500, a new record. The Nasdaq jumped 155 points, erasing some of the red ink of the past three days. The downturn ended as mysteriously as it had begun. The Big One had not yet arrived.

❑   ❑   ❑

It was 10:30 P.M. on Sunday, January 9, 2000, when the phone rang in the Pacific Palisades, California, home of Peter Gumbel.

The British-born *Wall Street Journal* reporter recognized the voice of one of his sources, a man he had been wining and dining for years. The source said that he had just been briefed on a deal of breathtaking proportions: America Online was buying Time Warner. It was already 1:30 A.M. in New York, and the East Coast papers had all finished printing their Monday editions. The biggest corporate takeover in history was, for the moment, the best-kept secret on Wall Street.

Gumbel immediately called Kara Swisher, the *Journal*'s Internet reporter in San Francisco, and started waking up other colleagues in New York. Swisher, who had just come from a rooftop dinner with Steve Case's brother Dan, the chief executive of the Hambrecht & Quist brokerage, logged onto her AOL account, where she often reached her high-tech sources. It was not yet 11 o'clock in California.

At the moment, the top executives of America Online and Time Warner were gathered in the 30th-floor offices of AOL's law firm on Manhattan's Lexington Avenue, where their respective boards had approved the corporate marriage just four hours earlier. Both Steve Case and Gerald Levin, Time Warner's CEO, had gone to extraordinary lengths to keep the deal under wraps. The investment bankers and the lawyers had not been brought in until early Saturday morning, with Mary Meeker of Morgan

Stanley bicycling her way across Central Park and showing up in a green track suit. The deal-makers, who often leaked such stories on Sundays, were held captive in the building while the kitchen staff stayed on to prepare meals.

Swisher found a number of AOL executives online, which made clear that something big was up, since it was now 2:00 A.M. in the East. Their names showed up on her personal "buddy list" of those who were logged on to AOL. Swisher knew some of the secret screen names that these executives used to avoid detection, and she sent instant messages to others who had the technological means to hide their presence online. The messages went through, meaning that the AOL honchos were indeed signed on. Most of the executives ignored Swisher, which convinced her that there must be a deal, for they usually responded quickly.

She fired off another round of instant messages with a stark declaration: "We know." Several of the AOL officials abruptly signed off, apparently spooked by her presence. Finally, Swisher got one online source to confirm that the world's largest Internet company was indeed buying the world's largest media conglomerate.

At 3:00 A.M. Eastern time, armed with three confirmations, Gumbel shrugged off his last-minute apprehension and filed a headline for the Dow Jones News Service: "Time Warner in Pact to Merge with America Online—Sources." He followed with two more headlines: "AOL's Steve Case to be Chairman of New Company" and "Time Warner's Gerald Levin to be CEO of New Company."

Gumbel felt the adrenaline pumping as he banged out a few paragraphs for *The Wall Street Journal*'s Website. It was somehow fitting that he would break the biggest business story of the new century on the Net. Gumbel felt a special moment of triumph that he had gotten a merger scoop that had even eluded Steve Lipin.

CNBC Europe, which was jointly owned by NBC and Dow Jones, quickly trumpeted the scoop. Bloomberg News followed twenty-two minutes later, crediting Dow Jones, and Reuters forty-five minutes after that. Shares of AOL and Time Warner were already surging on the London stock exchange.

Gumbel was exhausted, so while CNBC was reporting the news on its

American network at 4:30 A.M., Kara Swisher headed to the *Journal* office in San Francisco and was on the air by 5:00 to talk about the exclusive.

Just after 5:00, CNN reported the news that it was about to become part of Steve Case's cyber-empire. A top Turner Broadcasting executive had told CNN's chairman, Tom Johnson, that the company would make a major announcement early that morning, but Johnson did not know what it was until he saw the Dow Jones wire story. The network's reporters had been beaten on the story about their own company and were scrambling to catch up.

"We have Time Warner, parent of this network, and AOL, America On-line, merging," anchor Deborah Marchini said. "We don't have a price tag." She said that "AOL's Steve Case will have a role in the future of the new company, but it has not yet been announced precisely what that role is going to be." As the morning wore on, CNN kept reporting that AOL and Time Warner would "join forces" in a "merger of equals," even though Case's company would own 55 percent of the stock and clearly was buying the much larger Time Warner.

At 5:20, Jeff Gralnick was awakened by the phone in his Connecticut home. It was Shelby Coffey, the former *Los Angeles Times* editor who had recently been hired as the new president of CNNfn.

"We've got a major news story," Coffey said.

"The last time I got a phone call at five A.M., the pope had died," Gralnick said. Why, he wondered, would Gerry Levin sell the company? The benefits to AOL were clear; the company would get access to Time Warner's cable systems, enabling it to deliver its data far more quickly than over telephone wires, and would capture the much-prized content of CNN, HBO, Warner Brothers Studios, *Time, Fortune, People,* and *Sports Illustrated.* But what would Time Warner get out of it?

At 5:30, Jeff Berkowitz called Jim Cramer at the office with the news that he had just heard on the radio. "Wow," said Berkowitz. Cramer, too, was blown away. This seemed to validate all those seemingly wacko valuations for Internet firms. Was AOL now the most important media company in the world? Would CNN now be more powerful than ABC, CBS, or NBC? More important, what would this do to AOL's stock? Cramer had always liked the company, and *TheStreet.com* had its own site on America

Online. He quickly bought 10,000 shares at a price that had already jumped 10 points in premarket trading.

Just after 6:00 A.M., Tricia Primrose, an AOL spokeswoman with the management team in New York, woke up Marc Gunther, a *Fortune* reporter. Gunther had been scheduled to interview Case that day at AOL's Dulles, Virginia, headquarters for a story whose working title was "Steve Case Wants to Take Over the World." Primrose told him that the interview had been canceled. "We're buying your company," she said.

Once the boards had acted—Mary Meeker made a rousing speech to Time Warner's skeptical directors during a nine-hour meeting—Kathy Bushkin, the AOL communications chief, had gotten final approval from the lawyers for the press release she spent all night writing. Now that the release was out, Case and Bushkin, among others, were pleased that the story hadn't leaked earlier, which they feared would have complicated the final negotiations and played havoc with the stock price.

At 6:45, Coffey called Jenny Harris with the news. In her sleepy haze, Harris assumed that Time Warner had bought AOL; it didn't dawn on her that her huge, far-flung company could be swallowed by Case's upstart firm. After all, Time Warner had four times the revenue and 70,000 employees to AOL's 12,000. Yet it was America Online that was acquiring her employer for a stunning $165 billion. This, Harris thought, was the triumph of market cap, the ability of a company whose stock was highly valued by Wall Street to use that lofty price to acquire far bigger corporations. For all the stories that *Moneyline* had run on high-flying tech stocks, Harris suddenly realized just how big the Internet had become.

Fifteen minutes later, Harris's fiance, David Faber, was on the air at CNBC, telling *Squawk Box* viewers that this was "only the biggest, most staggering deal of all time." Faber had been calling around—he knew every one of the lawyers and investment bankers who had put together the deal—but there was no way they would have leaked the story unless he had confronted them with the reality that the details were dribbling out. Minutes later, Faber's phone rang. It was a publicist asking if he wanted to talk to Steve Case and Gerald Levin. With the entire world clamoring for information on the megamerger, the two CEOs had decided that their most important task at the moment was to sell the deal to the Brain. They spoke for fifteen minutes, and Faber was the first reporter to describe their high-level spin beyond the boilerplate of the press release.

At 8:30 Case and Levin catered to another key constituency, discussing the deal in a conference call with Wall Street analysts.

When the chief executives held a news conference at 11:00, Steve Case looked like a boy who had just won the lottery, grinning and high-fiving and hugging Gerry Levin. The famously casual Case was even decked out in a gray suit and yellow tie, while the older Levin appeared tieless and in loafers. Case had not been kidding when he had declared that he wanted to make AOL the most respected company in the world, and now he was closer to realizing his dream. The media had written off his fifteen-year-old firm so many times, had ridiculed the notion that AOL could play in the big leagues, but Case was convinced that he was leading a revolution that would finally unite print, cable, and the Net. The press-shy CEO seemed to sense that he had to assume a more public profile if he was to run a company with such global brand names as CNN and *Time.* Case boldly declared that this was the start of "the Internet century." He was, for the moment, the biggest rock star around.

At 12:22 P.M., Case and Levin appeared on CNN with Stuart Varney and Willow Bay, the first preferential treatment that the Time Warner network had gotten all day. The *Moneyline* duo was in the awkward position of interviewing their current and future bosses, and the questioning was fairly gentle.

"You will be chairman of a behemoth," Bay told Steve Case. "How do you envision this partnership working?"

"Would you say that this is a triumph for the New Economy?" Varney asked Case.

Varney did ask whether Ted Turner had been eclipsed by the massive deal. "Ted has always been a hero of mine," Case said.

Half an hour later, Case and Levin showed up on CNBC's *Power Lunch,* where Faber, Bill Griffeth, and Steve Frank of the *Journal* took a more aggressive approach.

"Eighty percent of the cash flow of this combined company will come from your company, and yet your shareholders will own only 45 percent," Faber told Levin. "Why were you willing to sign off on a deal like that?"

"The market cap of AOL was twice that of Time Warner," Levin replied.

In the space of a few hours, Case and Levin spoke to *The Wall Street Journal, The New York Times,* the *Los Angeles Times, The Washington Post, USA Today,* the *Financial Times, Business Week,* and *Newsweek,* then did back-to-back interviews with ABC, CBS, and NBC, saying the same things over and over.

At 2:00 P.M., an exhausted Case asked Kathy Bushkin: "When do we get out of here?" Bushkin fudged by telling him 3 o'clock, but he was actually booked for another hour beyond that. She was proud of Case for being a trooper.

When the closing bell sounded at 4 o'clock, Time Warner stock had surged nearly 40 percent, from 64¾ to 90, an extraordinary run-up reflecting its sudden admission into the wired world. But AOL stock had dropped 1⅞, to 71. Investors were concerned that a company that had always been valued by the limitless, blue-sky standards of Internet economics now might have to adjust to the slower growth of a real-world bureaucracy grappling with the production of television, movies, magazines, and books.

Jeff Gralnick was keeping one eye on the stock price. He had been given a nice batch of Time Warner stock options when he was hired less than a year earlier, and in two months he would be eligible to use a third of them. But the AOL deal had changed the rules of the game. Time Warner executives were suddenly free to exercise all their stock options at any time. The stock was important to Gralnick because he was trying to decide whether to cash in his chips and resign. He had put off the decision when his wife, Beth, was thrown from a horse and broke her hip, but the AOL takeover made it impossible not to think about just what his future was with this new corporate colossus. The day after Coffey had been hired to run CNNfn, Tom Johnson told Gralnick that he wanted him to stay but would make it easy for him if he decided to leave. Maybe he would take Johnson up on his gracious offer.

At the moment, Gralnick's more immediate concern was how *Moneyline* would cover the momentous news involving its corporate parent. The *Moneyline* staff was annoyed that Case and Levin would not return for a live interview, forcing them to rerun the earlier discussion with Varney and Bay. The greater problem was that top CNN executives were insisting that they call the deal a merger, not a takeover.

Gralnick had a series of tortured conversations with Coffey, who maintained that CNN couldn't very well report that Time Warner had been bought by AOL when management was describing it as a merger. Gralnick refused to play along with what he saw as a polite bit of corporate fiction. Let me show you the AP story, the Bloomberg story, he offered. We need to describe the deal the same way as the rest of the business press.

In a late-afternoon conference call, Coffey, Gralnick and Jenny Harris debated the question with the network's lawyers. One of the attorneys asked what difference it made if CNN characterized the deal as a merger. "It makes a huge difference," Harris said. "If an Internet company is taking over the biggest media company in the world, it's a watershed event." The call seemed to turn the tide. In a compromise of sorts, Stuart Varney opened *Moneyline* by saying that the deal was "billed as a merger of equals," but that "Wall Street treated Time Warner's stock like it was a hot acquisition."

Jenny Harris didn't care about the Time Warner stock because she didn't own any, not even in her retirement plan. She was more concerned with making it to the weekend, when she and David Faber were getting married. Throughout the afternoon, she could not find a single analyst who would come on the show and criticize the deal. Wall Street experts and financial reporters alike had a tendency to gush over any corporate combination that was new and bigger and sexier. Even so, the coverage on *Moneyline* came close to cheerleading, with such glowing headlines as "Mighty AOL" and "AOLectric." When the show broke for a commercial, a narrator said: "Tonight on *CNN NewsStand:* A global powerhouse is born."

While *Moneyline* was on the air, Lou Dobbs, who seven months earlier would have been anchoring the program, was discussing the deal in his first appearance on CNBC's *Business Center.* "It's certainly a validation of the Internet," Dobbs told Sue Herera. Perhaps it was a validation of Dobbs's decision to join the Net world as well.

Over the next few days, despite the initial enthusiasm about the mighty

AOL, the market turned thumbs-down on the deal. By Wednesday, AOL stock had dropped 19 percent, chopping $32 billion off its market value. Henry Blodget turned up on CNBC to defend the company he had long touted as an Internet powerhouse. "What the market will ultimately realize," Blodget said, "is that this is absolutely a relatively cheap stock."

But some on Wall Street were not so sure. Cramer felt that he had to eat some crow for touting the merger. He had lost more than $250,000 on his Monday morning decision to buy 10,000 shares of America Online.

❏   ❏   ❏

From the moment he had founded *TheStreet.com,* Jim Cramer had passionately argued that the only Website worth a damn was one that charged its customers. He openly disdained the notion that free sites, which included most of the Web, could make money. He was absolutely convinced that premium content, such as his column, was worth paying for.

Those who disagreed were "suicidalists," Cramer had written in the fall of 1999, who "have never run a business. They have never sold a thing. They are deceivers and fools. But they have their adherents, even within the walls of *TheStreet.com.* It makes me livid. I regard these people as betrayers and scoundrels who would take the money we have all invested in *TheStreet.com* and throw it away."

Now, publicly and painfully, he had to eat his words. *TheStreet.com* board had voted to go free.

This was another issue on which Cramer and Kevin English, the former CEO, had fervently disagreed. Cramer's position was simple: Over my dead body. But it turned out that English had been right. Even Cramer finally had to admit that the company was slitting its own throat by charging subscribers $99 a year. Advertisers, particularly those outside the financial world, just didn't buy the paid model. They wanted more eyeballs to justify their investment. Cramer's site had 2 million "page views" a day, but that was about a fifth of the traffic generated by *CBS Market-Watch.com,* which had just launched its own television show. Lycos, a popular Web portal, had repeatedly approached Cramer about providing a link to *TheStreet.com,* but only if the company stopped charging for access. The loss of revenue from the 100,000 subscribers, *Street.com* executives insisted, would be more than offset by increased advertising dollars if the site were available to all Web surfers.

The stock remained in the doldrums as the internal debate raged. Even the company's underwriter, Hambrecht & Quist, had a "hold" rating on the stock, much to Cramer's amazement. Finally, the company's new CEO, Tom Clarke, worked out a face-saving compromise for Cramer. The main site, including Cramer's many columns, would go free, but they would create a separate paid site for those who wanted to read Cramer and a couple of other columnists in real time, rather than on a delayed basis. The premium site would also offer detailed information on IPOs and other bells and whistles for financial junkies.

Now they had to sell the idea to Wall Street. Marty Peretz suggested that Cramer call some analysts with the news, but Cramer refused. He didn't think he should be browbeating brokerage houses to upgrade the stock. And he didn't want to give analysts advance information about the decision to go free, the sort of insider practice that he regularly denounced.

Cramer did make one move designed to goose the stock. He told Bloomberg News that he was giving up his $275,000 salary at the online service, which he had never really wanted in the first place, in exchange for 30,000 options to buy the company's stock within a year. He wanted to show the world that he believed the place had a strong future.

The day after the AOL–Time Warner deal, *The Street.com* announced its decision in a press release. "Going free for news is a must if we are to compete worldwide for readers," Cramer was quoted as saying. Hambrecht & Quist upgraded the stock from a hold to a buy, but it only rose ⅝, to 19⅛.

A man given to endless bouts of anguish, Cramer was still stewing in his own resentment. Cramer had gotten upset when Gregg Hymowitz of Entrust Capital appeared on *Squawk Box* and criticized Globalstar Telecomm, a stock that he acknowledged having shorted, and Globalstar had dropped several points. How was that any different than when Cramer had gotten in hot water for criticizing WavePhore, a stock that he hadn't even shorted? Yet nobody uttered a peep when other financial players talked down a stock.

On New Year's Day, while others were celebrating the new millennium,

Cramer had banged out an extraordinary rant for *TheStreet.com:* "I got screwed a few years back, and I am still angry about it. I made a mistake, but I paid for it in a way that still gets my back up, and I may never be able to forgive those who decided to do me in because I think they did it for competitive reasons and not ethics."

Cramer was bereft of enemies at the moment, given Kevin English's departure, so he was resurrecting some of his old favorites from the *SmartMoney* debacle of 1995. His critics were jackals, cowards, and opportunists, he insisted, part of a journalistic lynch mob that came after him because he was too popular. "When I speak my mind, I now expect an inquisition," Cramer declared. "Why don't others? And why is it just me?"

Cramer continued to lash out at Hymowitz. On another edition of *Squawk Box,* Hymowitz praised a small firm named Epicor Software, whose stock jumped from 7 to 12 and then fell back to 7. (Hymowitz's company never traded on these commentaries.) Cramer published an e-mail from a woman named Bonnie H. who tried to buy Epicor online at 8½ after hearing Hymowitz tout the company. The woman lost money when her order was not filled until the stock hit 11⁵⁄₁₆, and then sank to 7. "I know better than to act on impulse, jumping into a stock just because some analyst is talking about it," she wrote, admitting that she had made a "really dumb move."

Mark Haines saw Bonnie H. as a pretty weak poster child for protecting the innocent. After all, the woman admitted in the same letter that she was trading her IRA money 200 times a year. That was just plain stupid. Haines didn't want any restrictions on what stocks could be discussed on CNBC. He liked learning about small companies that could become big companies. Haines had checked the law books and confirmed that anybody could say anything about a stock as long as it was truthful and the person did not buy or sell into the turmoil he had caused. Besides, Cramer had conveniently overlooked the fact that Hymowitz had also pounded the table for an outfit called Ion Networks, whose stock not only jumped a few dollars that day but had doubled over the past month. Haines was accustomed to Cramer casting himself the star in a never-ending melodrama. Cramer's subtext, he believed, was always Jim as victim or Jim as crusader. That often detracted from what he wrote. Haines wished that his former guest host would get over his obsession with himself.

On the financial front, things were going quite well for Jim Cramer. Yet while most people reveled in good fortune, Cramer had a way of putting a negative twist even on his own success. Why, he wondered, wasn't he getting any publicity for his fabulous year at the hedge fund? Cramer was dying to write about it—Hey, I'm up 63 percent, he would say, so you'd better read my column—but had an agreement with *TheStreet.com* that he would not discuss his performance as a fund manager.

Cramer started venting to Jeff Berkowitz. He said that he felt like calling Joseph Kahn, the *New York Times* reporter who had criticized his lousy record in 1998, and challenging him to update the story. Forget it, Berkowitz said. Not a good idea. Maybe Kahn will call you.

"Are you fucking kidding me?" Cramer demanded. "It's not of interest that I did well. It's only of interest if I fail."

❑   ❑   ❑

The whiplash market was straining plenty of necks. Just when the stock market seemed to have stabilized, the Dow plunged 1,800 points in little more than a month. Interest-rate jitters returned with a vengeance. Blue-chip names were battered day after day. Just before things turned sour, *Fortune* questioned whether "this market is stark, raving overvalued and it will not last." A *Wall Street Journal* headline wondered "How a Drop in Stocks Could Slam the Economy." No one wanted to find out.

The bulls did their best to prop up the sagging stocks. On Monday, January 24, the Dow fell by 243 points, but Maria Bartiromo had some reassuring news for *Squawk Box* viewers on Tuesday morning. "I just hung up with the chief strategist at Goldman Sachs, Abby Joseph Cohen, clearly one of the best bulls around," Bartiromo said. "She made a case why stock prices should continue going higher in the year 2000."

It didn't help. The Dow promptly dropped 125 points, although it recovered to finish the day with a gain of 22. Three days later, on January 28, the Dow plummeted another 289 points, to 10,738, and the Nasdaq suffered the second-biggest point drop in its history. In fact, four of the Nasdaq's five biggest point declines had taken place in January 2000.

All sorts of big-name Net stocks were way off their previous highs: Amazon down 40 percent, despite Jeff Bezos's Man of the Year status. E*Trade, down 64 percent. Priceline, down 63 percent. eBay, down 39 percent. Qualcomm, down 45 percent. *TheStreet.com,* down 76 percent. Henry Blodget told *The Wall Street Journal* that there would be a shakeout in which some Internet firms would be unable to raise enough cash to survive. Which ones? Blodget, ever the Net booster, refused to name them.

Cramer wondered whether this was the end. Was this how the era of soaring tech stocks finally petered out, not with a headline-grabbing bang but with a whimper? He didn't know. Neither did anyone else.

Ron Insana, if not growling like a bear, was doing a pretty passable imitation. From an economic conference in Davos, Switzerland, he interviewed Vice President Al Gore, who was campaigning in the New Hampshire primary with former Treasury chief Robert Rubin.

"There are people here who are worried that the stock market could suffer a debilitating setback," Insana said. "Were the stock market to crash on your watch, how would you respond?"

Gore didn't bite. "I'm not buying into that kind of hypothetical," he said.

Less than an hour later, with the Dow having dropped below 10,700, Insana was quizzing Rubin's successor, Lawrence Summers, who was at the White House. "Some people are worried that the U.S. economy is at a dangerous inflection point," Insana said. "Are you worried?" Summers said that he was not.

Neither, apparently, were the investors pouring money into tech stocks, which were suddenly much more attractive than old-line companies. The following week the Fed raised interest rates a fourth time, by another quarter-point, but the Nasdaq gained 9 percent for the week, hitting a new record. White-knuckle dives that once depressed the market for months were now being shrugged off in a week or two. The volatility was strange, given that the United States was now in the midst of its longest economic expansion, a nine-year boom that had generated great wealth, tamed inflation, and lowered unemployment to just 4 percent.

Despite this unparalleled success, the Dow was still heading south. On

February 9, a series of coordinated attacks by computer hackers shut down some of the world's most popular Websites. Traders could not get onto E*Trade. News junkies were shut out of *CNN.com.* Book buyers lost access to Amazon. Yahoo! and eBay also went dark. Investors were clearly frightened, since the Internet, whose very openness had been touted as a revolutionary tool for business, was clearly quite vulnerable to attack. The Dow dropped 258 points that day and 218 the next, to 10,425.

"You have two economies going on," Ralph Acampora said on *Business Center,* ending his boycott of CNBC. That had become the new Wall Street shorthand. Even the most celebrated icons of the Old Economy had lost their luster. Warren Buffett, the most admired stock picker of his generation, was now being criticized in some quarters as a has-been. The stock of his company, Berkshire Hathaway, which had never been split, had dropped from $81,000 a year earlier to $50,900, in part because Buffett invested in such old standbys as Gillette and Coke and did not buy technology stocks, saying he did not understand them. "Does Warren Buffett still carry that halo effect?" David Faber asked on *Squawk Box.* An unfounded rumor that Buffett was ill soon pushed Berkshire Hathaway down even further. And when Buffett was reported to have bought a stake in Citigroup—news that once would have automatically boosted the stock—there were few ripples. Jim Cramer wondered whether Buffett even mattered in the Internet era.

Ron Insana felt that the Old Economy stocks—Alcoa, Wal-Mart, McDonald's, Home Depot, Coke—were dead in the water, while the New Economy stocks—not Microsoft or AOL but upstarts such as JDS Uniphase and Akamai Technologies and Cell Genesys and Avigen—were hitting insane levels. Biotech and telecom stocks were on fire. A new B2B company called WebMethods soared from 35 to 213 on its first day of trading. Insana believed that this was either a transforming moment in history or the greatest run of Wall Street bullshit that anyone had ever seen. The science behind these high-flying technology companies was too difficult for most journalists to grasp. Insana didn't know whether the new fiber-optic networks would revolutionize communications or not. No one could tell the difference between the promise and the reality.

"A lot of people are scared," David Faber told viewers. "They don't know what to make of it."

The dual story line kept gathering steam. "The Nasdaq, really blowing the Dow away here," Insana said on *Street Signs* as the high-tech index broke through the 4,500 mark for a new record. But the next day, February 18, both indexes plummeted on new interest-rate fears, with the Dow dropping 295 points, to 10,219. The Big Board had just staggered through a full-blown correction, having lost more than 10 percent of its value.

Perhaps it was inevitable, in this nerve-racking environment, that questions would be raised about the megadeal that the financial community had hailed just a month earlier. There was chatter that America Online was ready to drop its acquisition of Time Warner. After all, AOL stock had steadily dropped from 73 to 50, slashing the company's value and making the deal far less lucrative for Time Warner stockholders.

Dan Dorfman quickly picked up the buzz. "One sharp trader I know," he wrote on *JagNotes,* "is buying America Online on some Street talk that its merger with Time Warner will be called off."

David Faber got more than a dozen calls about the rumor, which was spreading faster than a computer virus. Apparently it was bouncing around other Websites as well. The gossip was pushing down AOL's already depressed stock, and Faber figured he should knock down the story if he could. All it took was a couple of phone calls.

"There is no truth to that rumor," Faber said in his midday report. "It evidently started on a Web-based rumor service." The wild market swings were providing fertile soil for such rumors, and seemed to enhance the power of big-name analysts as well. AOL stock jumped 17 percent on February 23, when Henry Blodget and a Merrill Lynch colleague issued a two-page report that said nothing that other analysts hadn't said before, other than that the company was well positioned after the Time Warner deal. This was, of course, an effort to pump air into a deflating tire. Even with the jump, AOL was at 58, still 20 percent off its value before Steve Case embraced Gerry Levin.

But America Online was an exception as investors continued to move billions of dollars from the Wal-Marts of the world into New Economy stocks. "Nasdaq Roars as Dow Dives," said the lead story in *USA Today.* On February 25, the Dow closed below 10,000 for the first time since April 1999. The plunge to what was now an anemic-looking 9,862 had everyone—the traders, the analysts, the commentators—shaking their heads. Minutes before the closing bell, Ron Insana announced that the Dow had now dropped nearly 16 percent from its all-time high in mid-January. The Big Board was off to its worst yearly start since 1920. The only remaining question was whether the Dow's decline and the specter of higher interest rates would eventually ground the high-flying Nasdaq as well.

Jim Cramer didn't care much about the Dow stocks anymore, about the companies that made the cars and sold the soap. If he stuck with such stocks as Maytag and Whirlpool, even Dell and Intel, he felt that he would be outmoded. All the years he had spent analyzing banking and drug stocks were now worthless. The action, Cramer believed, was in the newfangled Nasdaq stocks. Half his holdings, amazingly enough, were in companies that either didn't exist or weren't public two years earlier.

The intellectual heart of the hedge fund was now the twenty-four-year-old research director, Matt Jacobs, who was slowly educating him on the nuances of what companies such as Ariba and Broadvision did. It was, for Cramer, like learning a foreign language. He had just taken home a stack of files on Human Genome and 24/7. He worried not about the competition between Ford and General Motors but between i2 Technologies and Oracle. He and Jeff Berkowitz had to go on the road again, which they hated, to learn about these fledgling companies. And the game now had to be played at warp speed. They considered buying some Vitria Technology when it was down 15 points, but Matt Jacobs wanted to hear the company's presentation at a technology conference. By the time he got back from the meeting, Vitria was up 20 points.

Cramer began preaching his new gospel and trashing the Old Economy stocks in a speech on February 29, excerpts of which were shown on *Moneyline.* "Jim Cramer was arguing at an Internet conference that technology is the only thing worth buying," the program said.

But Karen Cramer warned her husband that his approach was short-sighted. "At what point is it arrogant to ignore that the nightly news will be focused on the Dow?" she asked. That was a real concern. If the press kept hyping the Dow plunge, Cramer figured, investors might really get worried and bail out of tech stocks as well.

As if to dramatize how surprised the financial pundits were by the

Dow's swift decline, Ralph Acampora officially abandoned his bull status. The man who just weeks earlier had called for the Dow to hit 13,500 to 14,000 by the end of 2000 surrendered his horns on *Wall Street Week,* switching to a neutral stance. "The blue chips look like they have a good bit more to go," Acampora said. "They may even go down 20 percent." Acampora worried that people wouldn't understand he was making a three-month projection—in the end you had to believe in your research— and that he was still quite high on the Nasdaq. Still, it had come to this: Even the market's biggest booster had nothing good to say about the Old Economy, the one that had powered the decade-long bull market and was now being airily dismissed as some sort of dinosaur.

16

CRASH LANDING

NO matter how far Net stocks rocketed into the financial stratosphere, the companies involved eventually faced a rather down-to-
earth problem. Their dot-com magic might have dazzled Wall Street and
fueled enough media hype to pull investors along for the ride, but they still
had to deal with the mundane business of attracting customers, generating
earnings, and paying their bills. And if the slightest hint emerged that
these enterprises might be faltering, their very altitude heightened the
danger that they would crash and burn.

During its short life as a public company, *TheStreet.com* benefited from
Jim Cramer's ability to draw enormous media attention, but his visibility
also guaranteed a harsh spotlight for its financial problems. Still, even as
the stock price steadily dropped, the internal strife remained largely hidden from public view.

But on February 17, much to Cramer's dismay, Steve Lipin told the
world that *TheStreet.com* was looking for a buyer. And Cramer, the man
who loved to talk and explain and analyze and elucidate, was gagged by
his board of directors. Worse, he felt that he had been out-Cramered by his
opposite number at *CBS MarketWatch,* Larry Kramer, in the battle for online supremacy.

For his part, Lipin didn't care much about a deal involving
TheStreet.com—its market cap was just $400 million, a mere rounding
error in the megadeals he usually pursued—but his *Wall Street Journal*

editors were hot for the story, undoubtedly because of Cramer's celebrity status. For Cramer and his company, the impact of Lipin's piece was explosive, for it revealed for the first time that *TheStreet.com* had been shopped to other Internet outfits.

Cramer felt that he was being punished, even though he had tried to do the right thing. Some months earlier, Thomas Middelhoff, the CEO of the publishing conglomerate Bertelsmann, had told Marty Peretz that he was interested in buying 20 percent of *TheStreet.com.* The offer had prompted the company to hire the investment bank of Wasserstein, Parella to explore the transaction. Middelhoff backed out, however, after doing a deal in Germany with the *Financial Times,* leaving *TheStreet.com* all dressed up and without a partner.

Not long afterward, Larry Kramer, a former editor of the *San Francisco Examiner,* invited Cramer to dinner and suggested that the two companies merge because the competition was holding down both their stocks. *MarketWatch* had more than three times the number of readers as *TheStreet.com*—3.2 million a month, compared with 908,000—but its stock had also plummeted, from 108 to the low 30s, since its IPO in early 1999. A combined company, Kramer declared, could feature the best of *MarketWatch.com* and *TheStreet.com.*

Cramer took the suggestion seriously but said that it would be difficult for him to support a sale unless Kramer's company offered a premium above the market price of *TheStreet.com* stock. Kramer said that he would have an answer soon.

While Cramer felt obligated to take the feeler to his board, he still argued that it would be better for some other big company to take a major stake in *TheStreet.com* rather than having *MarketWatch* buy it outright. Karen told him that he was being stupid. "A major company wants to buy you and you don't want to play?" she said. "What if you were long that stock? Wouldn't you be all over the CEO, screaming at him?"

She was right. If a sale was in the best interests of the stockholders, who after all had been losing big time on their investment, Cramer felt that he couldn't screw them for his own vanity. He didn't want to act like one of those corporate executives he so often castigated. And so, in the first week of February, he took Larry Kramer and Tom Clarke, *TheStreet.com*'s new

CEO, to lunch after a Robertson Stephens technology conference in New York. *MarketWatch* still wanted to merge, Kramer said, but could not pay even two dollars over the current price for *TheStreet.com* shares. Cramer knew that Peretz and the other board members would not agree to sell unless they got a premium price.

"Let's just keep duking it out, then," Cramer said.

Soon afterward, Cramer was contacted by Paul Allen, the Seattle billionaire and cofounder of Microsoft, who expressed interest in buying the company. Cramer flew to Seattle, where he met the people running Allen's latest Internet venture. Allen's deputies made it clear that they wanted Cramer to remain involved—he not only owned 14 percent of the stock, his columns accounted for 17 percent of the Website's traffic. After returning to New York, Cramer dropped out of the talks and left the matter to his board. He didn't want to be the catalyst for selling *TheStreet.com*.

When a *Wall Street Journal* reporter left a message for him at home on the evening of February 16, Cramer didn't call back. He would have returned the call if it had been Steve Lipin, a journalist he respected, but in this case he didn't recognize the reporter's name. The article by Lipin and a colleague on *TheStreet.com* appeared in the next morning's paper.

Cramer asked his board members whether they had spoken to the *Journal,* and all said that they had not. Two days later, the *Journal*'s Heard on the Street column reported the follow-up lunch that Cramer and Tom Clarke had had with Larry Kramer, identifying *MarketWatch* as a potential buyer. That column, Cramer believed, was clear evidence that the *MarketWatch* folks had leaked the story to put pressure on *TheStreet.com*.

"Jim, you've been had," Jeff Berkowitz told him. "This guy's tougher than you. He's willing to do shit you aren't willing to do." Cramer felt that Kramer had played him for a sucker.

Both partners knew how investors would react to the news that *TheStreet.com* was putting itself on the block. "Hey, the stock goes to 10," Berkowitz said. He was close. Within days, the company's stock dropped from 18 to 12, well below the original offering price of 19 the previous spring.

Cramer had had enough. After zipping his lip for days, he decided to punch back. He told *Business Week* that *"CBS MarketWatch* tried to drive our stock down as low as possible and buy us. If that's their game plan, you can forget about it." The magazine dubbed him "The Streetfighter.com." Let the board sue him for sounding off, Cramer felt. He knew that Dave Kansas and the other journalists at *TheStreet.com* were glad that he had spoken out.

Larry Kramer was in London when he got a spate of calls from British reporters about Jim Cramer's broadside against *MarketWatch*. "What are you smoking?" he asked one. When he heard the story, Kramer was outraged at the notion that he had leaked word of the talks. He hadn't even known that *TheStreet.com* had hired Wasserstein until a friend read him the *Journal* piece over the phone. And he certainly hadn't talked to the *Journal* about his lunch with Cramer. Besides, it was hardly a clandestine meeting; lots of people had seen them leave the technology conference for a restaurant a block away.

Why, Kramer wondered, would Cramer suspect that he was engaged in a Machiavellian plot to disclose the tentative talks? Such stories almost always had the effect of knocking down the stock of the would-be buyer and boosting the stock of the takeover target. Jim, he knew, was an emotional guy. He was clearly looking for someone to blame for his stock tanking.

When he finally talked to Cramer again, he tried to be conciliatory. "You know, there are people in my office who knew we had lunch," Kramer said. "If that got out because I talked to anyone about the lunch, I apologize."

"This kind of shit happens all the time," Cramer allowed.

Still, Kramer felt that he had been unfairly ambushed. The *San Francisco Chronicle* was even making the ludicrous assertion that he might have violated SEC rules by trying to manipulate *TheStreet.com*'s stock. People were buying the spin that he was the leaker. Kramer was sorry that he had ever talked to these guys.

❑   ❑   ❑

By the spring of 2000, nearly everyone had heard of DoubleClick. Kevin O'Connor's picture was in all sorts of newspapers and magazines, but this was hardly cause for celebration. No longer was O'Connor the rising young CEO who was building a digital-age powerhouse. He was now, as

U.S. News & World Report put it, "the Internet's busybody." *The Washington Post* was calling DoubleClick "one of the most vilified companies in the online world." O'Connor was being accused of no less a transgression than invading the privacy of untold millions.

As the political storm gathered force, O'Connor felt enormously frustrated. Everyone loves an underdog firm, he believed, but at some point you become a big, established corporation and the coverage gets rougher. The press loves to build people up and then tear them down. O'Connor was convinced that the media were blowing this privacy issue way out of proportion, and that only one side—the side that painted him as a bad guy—was being told.

The opening salvo had been fired in January, when *USA Today* accused DoubleClick of having amassed 100 million files on individuals' online behavior—usually anonymous, but generally without the Web surfers' knowledge. The problem, the newspaper said, was that DoubleClick was combining this database with the archives of the direct-marketing firm Abacus, which O'Connor had acquired for $1 billion in 1999. And the Abacus files included the phone numbers and purchasing habits of retail buyers, which meant that DoubleClick could now match the online preferences to specific individuals—and sell that information to other firms. This was precisely what the company had once said it would not do. A DoubleClick executive was quoted as saying that the company gave Web users the right to opt out of such online data collection, but *USA Today* noted that Internet sites often buried this disclaimer in their fine print.

As *Business Week* and other publications jumped on the story, O'Connor continued to defend DoubleClick's behavior, insisting that his company was not engaged in cyber-stalking. He took out full-page newspaper ads promising an online campaign to educate consumers about their options. Yet he felt uncertain: Was he dealing with a few critical stories, a troubling trend, or a full-blown disaster? He recalled having read in George Stephanopoulos's book about the Clinton White House that one could rarely tell in advance when a negative story was about to take off.

O'Connor tried to make the complicated argument that the success of the Internet itself was at stake in preserving access to such personal data. Most Websites could not remain free of charge unless they used sophisticated tracking methods to make money for advertisers by serving up banner ads on which people would actually click. If the advertising dried up, DoubleClick executives insisted, Websites would be forced to charge fees to stay in business. This argument, he learned, was a decidedly tough sell.

Finally, O'Connor grew concerned enough to hire a crisis-management firm, but by then the media brushfire was burning out of control. On February 17, DoubleClick confirmed that the Federal Trade Commission had launched an investigation of its practices, and attorneys general in New York and Michigan were threatening lawsuits. The company's stock dropped 15 percent that day, falling from 106½ to 90¾. O'Connor didn't like to obsess on his stock price, but it was hard to ignore a body blow that had cost the company a billion dollars of its market value.

He gamely insisted that the privacy-invasion story wasn't much of a story at all. "There was no new information here," O'Connor said. "We've been telling folks our plans all along." But his image, and that of the company he had worked so hard to build, had clearly been tarnished. *USA Today* declared that DoubleClick had "become the media's poster boy for bad behavior on the Web."

O'Connor and his deputies finally decided that they had no choice but to surrender, to drop their effort to match individuals' online behavior with their retail purchasing. A debate broke out over how the public retreat should be worded. Company executives, saying that they should act as a team, drafted a release in which the corporate "we" explained the decision, but O'Connor overruled them. He felt that as the CEO he should take personal responsibility. On March 2, DoubleClick put out a press release announcing the about-face. "I made a mistake," Kevin O'Connor was quoted as saying.

DoubleClick had never really faced adversity before, O'Connor told his staff. Everything had always been great. But adversity, he said, was what tested a great company. This was his test. He was certain that there would be more to come.

❏   ❏   ❏

From the heart of Silicon Valley, Kim Polese started speaking out against greed. It was an unusual message, to say the least, from someone who had sold $4.6 million worth of stock when she took Marimba public the previous spring. Yet Polese had become increasingly concerned that there was too much money sloshing around the Valley, too many IPOs, too many shaky companies, too much wretched excess. And unlike those who merely did their grousing over white wine at fancy Mountain View restaurants, she voiced her doubts to *The Wall Street Journal.*

"It is in many ways obscene wealth. It is extreme," Polese told the newspaper. "There definitely is a Gold Rush mentality." Polese didn't stop there: "I worry about this because I feel more and more the greed factor and these absurd expectations that you should be worth $50 million by the time you are 30, or you have failed in some way. I think we really are in a period of irrational exuberance, as Greenspan would say. Or just pure insanity."

Polese was speaking from personal experience. When she needed to hire a senior executive, a headhunter told her that applicants would expect to make $20 million to $40 million in the next four years. All she could do was laugh. Polese didn't exempt herself from those who were creating the problem. Marimba had to pay competitive salaries, and she had given stock options to each of her 200 employees, right down to the clerical staff. Everyone got caught up in the race.

This was all driven by Wall Street, Polese felt. The relentless focus on overvalued companies had fostered a climate in which everyone wanted to grab his share while things were going wild. Day traders were buying or selling Marimba stock based on rumors in Internet chat rooms. The days when institutional investors made intelligent assessments of a company's worth were over. She hated this intense focus on raw wealth.

Not surprisingly, Kim Polese's broadside created some resentment on the Street. But a number of colleagues in the industry told her it was about time that someone took a stand. Polese was concerned about the insidious attitude of entitlement and expectation, the way in which money had become the overriding goal, the only goal, for the younger generation of computer nerds. Too much dumb money was being thrown at bad companies, she felt. People had to understand that there was a difference between substance and hype. It was too easy to jimmy open the Wall Street cash register and go public. Many of these new companies would fail, and that, Polese felt, would be a good thing, an overdue lesson in financial reality.

❏   ❏   ❏

If ever there was a safe, sound, and not terribly exciting stock for cautious investors, it was Procter & Gamble, the maker of Tide, Pampers, and Crest, well-known consumer products that people needed in good times and bad.

But on March 7, Procter & Gamble warned that its earnings would drop 10 to 11 percent for the quarter, although Wall Street had been expecting an increase of as much as 9 percent. Company executives blamed rising prices for raw materials such as oil and wood pulp. No matter. Procter & Gamble stock plummeted 27¹⁄₁₆ points, to 60⅜, axing $36 billion from the company's net worth.

"They essentially dropped a bomb on the Street," Ron Insana said on the *Imus* show. "Wall Street hates that. Analysts are very angry." Suddenly, it seemed, even established blue-chip stocks were bouncing around like volatile Nasdaq companies. "Isn't any investment safe anymore?" *The Wall Street Journal* wondered. The P & G fiasco helped push the Dow down 374 points, its fourth-biggest point decline ever, to 9,796. "It's starting to feel like the wheels are coming off the Dow," Insana said on *Street Signs*.

But March madness had barely begun. The Nasdaq crashed through that 5,000 barrier on March 9, just three months after breaking 4,000 and four months after topping 3,000. Ralph Acampora, who had predicted that the index would hit 5,000 by the end of 2000, promptly appeared on CNBC and upped the ante, declaring that the Nasdaq would reach 6,000 within twelve to eighteen months.

Unfortunately for Acampora, the technology winds suddenly shifted with a vengeance. By March 15, the Nasdaq had plunged 9 percent in just three days. Mark Haines began joking that the index had reversed course just as Acampora began talking it up. Acampora was steamed. He couldn't believe the way the man kept crucifying him. Haines had conveniently overlooked the fact that his Nasdaq 6,000 call was a long-term projection.

That same morning, *Journal* reporter Steve Frank appeared on *Squawk Box* in the uncomfortable position of downplaying his own exclusive. Frank had reported on *Business Center* the night before that eBay and Yahoo! were holding secret talks about a partnership and, possibly, a merger. He had cautioned, however, that he was relying on an anonymous source who had put the odds of a partnership at no greater than fifty-fifty and the chance of a merger as more remote. But eBay had soared in after-hours trading, from 211 to 235, with Yahoo! moving up slightly.

Now the *Financial Times* was reporting that the talks had broken down the previous week, and Frank was playing defense. "These two companies talk all the time," he said on *Squawk Box*. "All these companies talk all the time." A deal might emerge in a few weeks or, Frank conceded, "something might never happen." Investors could practically hear the air coming out of the balloon. By day's end, eBay had plunged 21¼ points, and Yahoo! had dropped 10¼ points.

For all the high-decibel blather about the demise of Old Economy stocks amid the growing dominance of technology companies, the market still marched to its own peculiar rhythms. On March 16, for no apparent reason, the Dow soared 499 points, its biggest point gain in history, completing a surge of more than 800 points in just two days.

Acampora, who had relinquished his bulls' horns, told his troops that he was surprised. God bless the market, Acampora said. I didn't see it coming. But Ron Insana remained cautious, warning that "the jury is out on whether this is a real turnaround for the Dow."

The jury wasn't out much longer, for the Dow was rebounding strongly. On March 21, the Fed raised interest rates for the fifth time in less than a year, by a quarter-point. Rate hikes were generally seen as bad for stock prices, as investors feared that companies might be caught in a credit squeeze. Instead, the Dow gained 221 points, to 10,907, completing a two-week rise of 1,100 points that surprised the know-it-all crowd as completely as the early March swoon. The Nasdaq gained 102 points, and the S & P 500 hit a new record. The market seemed to be thumbing its nose at Alan Greenspan's increasingly blatant effort to cool off stock prices.

"Confused? Who wouldn't be?" the *Journal* said in its lead story. A *Fortune* headline put it more colorfully: "What the Hell Is Going On?"

Stuart Varney had been covering the American markets for twenty-five years and had never seen anything remotely resembling these sky-high technology prices. He began hectoring his guests when they pitched new-wave tech stocks. He was particularly struck by a fiber-optics manufacturer called JDS Uniphase, whose stock had risen over the past year from less than 15 to just under 140, and was selling for 300 times the company's projected earnings. Everyone needed a reality check. Varney did the math: JDS Uniphase was valued by Wall Street at more than $100 billion. That was greater than the market cap of General Motors and Ford combined. On March 21, when Brian Finnerty, an analyst with C. E. Unterberg, said on *Moneyline* that he was recommending JDS Uniphase, Varney lectured him on the numbers.

"How do you sleep at night recommending a stock like that?" Varney asked. Finnerty said that it was not very difficult.

❏   ❏   ❏

It had to be the most ridiculous idea that David Faber had ever heard.

When a hedge-fund manager suggested to him that Rupert Murdoch's News Corporation might be angling to buy General Motors, Faber dismissed the idea as complete bullshit. When a second hedge-fund trader passed on the tip, Faber again blew it off. But when a third hedge-fund man told him of the possible maneuver, Faber decided to do some digging.

After talking to several financial people involved in the planning, Faber began to see the unusual logic behind the move. Murdoch was interested not in building Chevys and Oldsmobiles but in acquiring GM's DirecTV satellite unit, which would boost his global television empire. If Murdoch and John Malone's Liberty Media made a hostile bid for GM, according to this plan, they would sell off the automaking division and keep the satellite firm. Faber pondered whether to report the story, since he knew that such a takeover was unlikely. He figured that his sources were feeding him the information to revive a plan that had stalled, in the hope of cashing in on it. But the machinations provided a revealing window on Murdoch's media strategy and his view that GM stock was relatively cheap.

On the morning of March 23, Faber called Gary Ginsberg, the spokesman for News Corporation, and told him that he planned to go with the story. Ginsberg did not try to dissuade him.

Shortly after noon, Faber delivered his report. "As crazy as it may seem," he told viewers, News Corporation "has been working for months on a strategy by which it could make an unsolicited bid for General Motors." While such a deal was not likely to happen, Faber said, Murdoch and "a handful of investment bankers" were involved in a "serious effort."

Minutes later, while Ginsberg was in a meeting with twenty staffers, two colleagues came rushing in. "CNBC just reported we're in talks with GM," one said. "Our stock's down 3. GM stock's up 7."

Ginsberg rushed out a denial. "News Corp. Says CNBC Report on GM Bid is 'Entirely False,' " a Bloomberg headline said. Faber was enraged. He immediately called Ginsberg.

"What the fuck is this?" he demanded.

"We're denying we've had talks with GM," Ginsberg said.

"I never said you had talks with GM," Faber shot back.

Ginsberg said nothing.

"Did you see the story?" Faber asked. Ginsberg admitted that he had not.

"If you're going to deny you're considering it, then I'm going to go on the air and call you a liar," Faber warned.

CNBC management was concerned. Bruno Cohen asked Faber for an explanation and said that Jack Welch, the GE chairman, would want to know if the story was solid. Faber was furious at Murdoch's people. He knew for a fact that everything he had reported was absolutely accurate. He went back on the air to announce that "News Corp. is denying they are in talks. I never said they were in talks." Still, GM stock jumped 5¼, to 87, on triple its average trading volume, and satellite company stocks took off in the wake of Faber's report.

But Ginsberg's denial had deflated the story. The next morning, Murdoch's *New York Post* dismissed the report as nothing but a "rumor." *The Wall Street Journal* seemed to make fun of the story, citing Faber by name for the first time ever. "Plenty of investors decided this was a story that should be true, whether or not it was," the *Journal* scoffed. Faber was annoyed that the paper was taking a slap at him. That night, Faber had dinner with Steve Lipin, and the two old friends fell into a discussion about the differences between television and print. Faber concluded that his story might have worked better as a Heard on the Street column, for a newspaper reader could go back and check the wording and the nuances. Maybe he had written it with too hard an edge. He had included all the caveats, but no one wanted to listen. Perhaps it was the inherently high volume of television, where every report, no matter how artfully hedged, sounded like a screaming headline.

Lipin was going head-to-head with Faber less often these days, for he was easing himself out of breaking news. After five years as the *Journal*'s mergers and acquisitions reporter, he was feeling burned out. He was writing more analysis pieces and contributing to a new column about Wall Street dealmakers. He was spending more Sundays with his family rather than chasing the latest merger buzz. Lipin was torn over his new role, wasn't ready to completely abandon the scoop business. But it had been a long, hard road, and it was time to move on.

Faber was feeling no such impulses. He kept up the torrid pace, and on March 29 he was on the verge of another major exclusive. He had spent a week running down rumors that Tiger Management, the giant hedge fund whose holdings had dwindled in two years from $21 billion to $7 billion, was preparing to shut down. Even second-tier schlubs at investment banks were calling him with the rumor. Faber knew that Ron Insana was friendly with Julian Robertson, Tiger's founder, but this was the sort of story you couldn't get from the top guy. Faber spoke to Tiger staffers, former employees, and people who were negotiating with Robertson to take on some of his investors.

At 12:55 P.M., a few minutes before his scheduled Faber Report, he got a call confirming that Tiger was closing Jaguar, the largest of its six funds. Faber didn't want to ad lib on such an important story, so he decided to wait for the 2 o'clock opening of *Street Signs* as a better venue to break the news. But after getting word that CNBC would be carrying President Clinton's news conference at 2:00, shutting him out for at least an hour, Faber rushed on the air ten minutes before the president started speaking.

"Sources close to Tiger," Faber said, "tell me it is their expectation that Tiger is closing down Jaguar, a fund that was down roughly 13 percent for the year. . . . It has had very sizable losses over the last eighteen months. . . . It is unclear whether Tiger and its sixty-seven-year-old leader will be shutting the doors of the company as well."

In lower Manhattan, Jim Cramer was listening intently. Knowing that Tiger had a large stake in Intel, Cramer watched Intel drop six points on Faber's report and quickly bought 100,000 shares in the computer chip-maker, on top of the 50,000 shares that his firm already owned. Faber's scoop reverberated across Wall Street because Julian Robertson had built his firm by investing in old-fashioned value stocks and had been battered by refusing to shift to red-hot tech stocks. Faber's story, Cramer believed, was the most important news of the week.

By 3:25, Faber was back on the air to report that Tiger Management it-self was shutting down. Then he drove home to the Upper West Side be-fore stopping by the CNBC bureau in the Carnegie Hall Tower to do a 6:30 update for *Business Center.* Faber had gone home to lie down be-cause his back was hurting. He had developed a ruptured disc that had grown quite painful. The high-pressure life of a stock market reporter was taking its toll.

❑   ❑   ❑

Jenny Harris's husband is driving her crazy.

She is making calls at her desk in the *Moneyline* newsroom on Eighth Avenue, chasing another one of his scoops. It is late on the afternoon of March 30, and CNN, like dozens of other news organizations, has been scrambling to get an interview with Julian Robertson. But David Faber and Ron Insana got there first—Robertson had his press person call In-sana with the offer—and sat down with the retiring investor at 10 that morning. Two excerpts have already aired, which Harris watched on the small set on her desk, the one she always keeps tuned to CNBC.

At 4:15, the phone rings. It's David. "Is the next part of your interview going to air?" she asks. "Jesus Christ!" The tape is being held for *Business Center,* meaning that it will be up against *Moneyline* itself.

Harris finds herself in a strange position. Personally, she is happy that David is scoring these exclusives. Professionally, as a CNN executive, it burns her up. A few weeks earlier, her staff had chased Faber's scoop that the German firm Deutsche Telekom was trying to upset the merger of US West and Qwest Communications by offering to buy both companies. They had matched part of his story the previous week about Murdoch and General Motors. They had chased the Tiger news yesterday. CNN would never report a Faber story unless its reporters could confirm the news independently, for the network did not want to credit its arch rival, CNBC.

To make matters worse, Robertson refused to grant an interview to Harris's reporter, Greg Clarkin, even after talking to Faber and Insana. Clarkin finally told Robertson that he was coming to the lobby with a camera crew and would not leave until the trader came down. Now Clarkin has called to say that he got some on-the-run comments from Robertson. It is a huge relief to Jenny Harris. She doesn't like to be touting David's stories at CNN, but on news of this magnitude she has no choice but to play catch-up.

Harris isn't happy with the tease about the "tiger roar" that her colleague Linda Keenan has written, so she starts fiddling with it.

"A famed investor bails out—Julian Robertson explains why he's closing Tiger," Harris types.

"Robertson talks?" Keenan suggests.

"His exit warning," Harris says. "No, his farewell warning."

Scanning a wire story, Harris sees that Robertson has called the stock market "a Ponzi pyramid destined for collapse." She calls Clarkin.

"Are you going to use the quote 'Ponzi pyramid'? Good." She feels sorry for Robertson, but only briefly. "He's got a billion dollars—what do I care?"

The week's big story is a major slide in the Nasdaq, which dropped another 187 points today, part of a three-day plunge that has left the tech index 12 percent below its record high of 5,048 on March 10. Two days earlier, the Nasdaq had dropped 125 points after Maria Bartiromo reported that Abby Joseph Cohen was recommending that investors reduce their stock holdings from 70 to 65 percent of their portfolios. Several prominent Net companies, including Drkoop.com, founded by former surgeon general C. Everett Koop, are in financial trouble. MicroStrategy plunged 62 percent in one day soon after a *Forbes* magazine story on its questionable accounting practices prompted the company to slash its inflated earnings for 1999. VA Linux, which zoomed 700 percent on its first day of trading, has dropped from 320 to 50 in four months. Qualcomm is 45 percent below the target price that young Walter Piecyk loudly projected and continues to defend. Harris wonders whether investors have grown so accustomed to this crazy volatility that they will simply yawn and buy more Net stocks.

Willow Bay emerges from her office. She briefs Harris on her pre-show interview with Paul Meeks, a Merrill Lynch analyst who will be their leadoff guest. "He thinks there's more downside," Bay says. "He wants to wait until things flatten out, at which point he's buying these guys," she says, pointing to a scribbled list that includes eBay and Inktomi.

"One thing you want to ask him is what is the mood going into tomorrow," Harris says.

There are always a hundred possible angles to chase. Harris is checking a CNBC report that a large crowd has gathered outside the Nasdaq's Times Square headquarters. But it turns out that the throngs are for the teen heartthrob band 'N Sync, who are visiting the MTV studios across the street.

❑ ❑ ❑

At 6:50 on the morning of March 31, Mark Haines loads his plate with slabs of sausage and bacon.

The catered breakfast buffet on the sixth floor of the Fort Lee headquarters is the most obvious sign that CNBC is in a festive mood. The network has just beaten CNN in daytime ratings for an entire quarter, the first time that this has ever happened, and *Business Center* has even bested *Moneyline,* whose ratings have been dropping since Lou Dobbs's departure.

Haines, too, is feeling pretty good. The *Squawk Box* ratings are at an all-time high, a 48 percent increase over a year earlier. He has put behind him the deep disgruntlement he felt when management tried to tone down the show's hijinks. He has even signed a new contract.

Everyone is unusually loose as David Faber saunters in just as the show starts and slips into his chair across the desk from Joe Kernen. "It's Friday," Kernen says on the air. "He's wearing jeans. He was swinging his rear around when he came in. It's disgusting."

"Why are you watching his rear?" Haines asks.

During a break, Faber starts reading a *Wall Street Journal* story about CNBC topping CNN in the Nielsens. "CNN has their head so far up their ass," he says. "When is Gerry Levin going to fire these bozos?"

When Faber gets up and heads toward his newsroom desk, Kernen tells him to get a new pair of pants. "I think you're sexually aroused," Faber shoots back.

Faber calls a source to check on rumors that AT&T may be buying a controlling stake in Net2Phone, an Internet telephone service. He had reported a month earlier that America Online was trying to buy Net2Phone. He got the AT&T tip late yesterday but didn't have the energy to run it down. After leaving a voice-mail message, he checks the wires: too late. Dow Jones reported last night that AT&T is in talks with Net2Phone but that no deal appears imminent.

The buzz at CNBC this morning is all about Maria Bartiromo, who had been touted on the front page of the previous day's *New York Post*. "Money Honey: I Want to Be Kathie Lee," the headline said. The tabloid had picked up a *People* magazine interview in which Bartiromo declared that she would love to be the new sidekick on Regis Philbin's morning show, where she would soon be having a tryout.

At 7:30, while *Squawk* is in progress, Bartiromo is on the *Today* set in Manhattan with Katie Couric. She's being interviewed because her new Friday night show, *Market Week*—the one she was promised when she was dropped from *Business Center*—premieres tonight. Her colleagues have been tittering at the constant CNBC promos in which Bartiromo looks downright sultry as the camera zooms in on her face and lips.

Bartiromo, who despite her trial balloon is under long-term contract to CNBC, tries to dampen the speculation that she might team up with the hugely popular star of *Who Wants to Be a Millionaire?* Joe Kernen is listening intently.

"She said Regis tries to help people become millionaires, but I help people become billionaires," he announces to the staff.

Kernen, who is getting plenty of publicity himself—he was named one of Playboy's best-dressed men—is jazzed up about Bartiromo's moment in the sun. He remembers when he was a frustrated stockbroker making cold calls, and when CNBC hired him as a $30,000-a-year writer. Now he wants to "go mainstream"—television talk for advancing beyond the cable world—and thinks Bartiromo's new prominence may help.

"We're all going to be rich!" Kernen shouts to no one in particular. "Maria's breaking out!"

At 7:45, Faber sees a press release about the AT&T investment. "Mark, this Net2Phone deal is a done deal," he announces on the air. Two hours later, not long after the opening bell, Tom Costello says from the Nasdaq that Net2Phone is up 9⅝, to 65.

The show is over, and Haines is taping a *Squawk* promo that will be introduced later in the day by Sue Herera. "You think I can get away with calling her Big Hair? Thanks, Big Hair?"

Retreating to an elevated parking lot to smoke a cigarette, looking out on the driveways of Fort Lee, Haines grouses about the inanities of television. When Bartiromo reported Abby Joseph Cohen's pullback Tuesday, the control room kept telling him in his ear to go back to Maria every few minutes for a recap. That repetition, Haines feels, makes modest reports sound far more alarming than they really are. He finally started joking about their all-Abby-all-the-time approach.

Still, Haines now expects to finish his career at CNBC. Other networks have offered him more money, but that would have meant commuting into Manhattan, and he likes working in New Jersey and getting home early enough to pick up his kids. Haines feels far more fulfilled than when he was a local anchor rattling off a bunch of meaningless murders, fires, and car wrecks. During his mother-in-law's seventy-fifth birthday party at Tavern on the Green, a ten-year-old boy handed Haines a note, obviously penned by a grown-up, asking whether he should buy a certain stock. People are constantly coming up to him, even when he's picking up lumber at Home Depot, and saying that they make a lot of money watching his show. It was hard to put a price on that kind of feedback.

❏   ❏   ❏

Slumping in the chair of his new 24th-floor office next to the Fulton Fish Market, a spectacular view of the Brooklyn Bridge to his left, Jim Cramer looked like a defeated man.

He sounded terrible, his voice reduced to a hoarse whisper. His natural ebullience was gone. Swigging a bottle of Poland Spring water, dressed in a gray polo shirt that matched his mood, Cramer ran through his list of options yet again. There were no good options, and he knew it. He could either sacrifice his career or watch *TheStreet.com* die a slow, painful death.

Roger Ailes had beaten him.

In recent months, Cramer had become convinced that the only way to save the company was for him to leave Fox and strike a deal with another network. *TheStreet.com*'s stock price, which had jumped from 19 to 71 on that wonderful opening day, was now down to 11. The market, Cramer felt, was sending a clear message. Stocks didn't lie.

TheStreet.com desperately needed a way to grow, a plan to convince Wall Street that its prospects were bright. Without a higher television profile, CEO Tom Clarke told Cramer, they would have to spend $25 million a year on promotion just to keep *TheStreet.com* afloat. There was no escaping the fact that Fox News Channel reached only 47 million homes, compared to 72 million for CNBC and 76 million for CNN. *TheStreet.com* also needed a corporate partner with the financial muscle to help the company expand in Europe and Asia. Faced with a dire situation, Cramer asked Ailes to talk to Rupert Murdoch about a broader partnership between News Corporation and *TheStreet.com*.

Clarke and his deputies prepared a memo asking that Fox buy 20 percent of *TheStreet.com* and help market the service in European and Asian markets. But James Murdoch, the media mogul's son, who ran the company's worldwide Internet unit, turned them down. They met again, to no avail. In a final sit-down with James Murdoch, he told them that this was not going to happen and that they had to stop bothering him. Clarke said that *TheStreet.com* might have to find another partner.

By early March, Cramer had come to view Fox as a giant obstacle to his efforts to use his journalistic profile to promote the Website. As long as he was doing the Fox show, Bill Bolster would never let him back on *Squawk Box*. Even guest appearances on other networks were difficult; Ailes had called him months earlier after he did an interview with CNN's Terry Keenan.

"I never want to see you again on CNN, and Rupert doesn't either," Ailes said.

Karen had thought from the start that the Fox deal was the dumbest thing her husband had ever done, and he was no longer in a position to argue. He had gone from a cult figure on *Squawk Box* to a panelist on an obscure program that reached perhaps 100,000 viewers on the weekends. His father and his wife could not see the show. People didn't respect the network. They might as well put his picture on milk cartons. His star was clearly fading. Fox had made him small.

Angry and frustrated, Cramer started boycotting his own show. Determined to send a message, he missed three straight Friday tapings. Ailes quickly realized what was happening. Typical Cramer, he thought, holding his breath until he's blue in the face when he doesn't get what he wants the instant he wants it.

By the third week in March, Ailes had had enough of Cramer's little tantrum and summoned him to Fox's Sixth Avenue offices. Ailes made clear that he would not sit by passively if Cramer flouted his contract or tried to quit the program that Fox had created for him. He felt that Cramer was blaming him for the fact that his stock had crashed, was frustrated that Murdoch wouldn't provide any more money, and had persuaded himself that the company's fortunes would soar if he could just get back on *Squawk Box*. Ailes liked Cramer but was coming to believe that he had the personality of a rattlesnake, that he wound up stinging most of those with whom he did business.

"If you want to play rough, we'll play rough," Ailes said. Cramer's battle with Marty Peretz, he warned, would be child's play by comparison. The dispute could wind up in court. "Do what you have to do, Jim, but we'll do what we have to do," Ailes said.

Cramer felt that Ailes was threatening him, and he was worried. He decided to show up for the March 24 taping.

Financially, at least, Cramer was in good shape. In late February, worried about the market, he and Jeff Berkowitz had taken $160 million of their $360-million fund off the table, shifting the money from stocks to cash. Cramer had even put his own money into New Jersey municipal bonds. For two weeks, while everyone else had been racking up profits on the market, he felt like shit. But then came the late March dive in tech stocks, and they had avoided a bloodbath. Earlier that morning, with the Nasdaq seemingly poised to rally, they had continued to hold back. Now the index was down another 100 points. Their one big bet of the day had been buying Veritas Software, which Cramer had thought would get a bump by being added to the S & P 500. But the ploy backfired when the S & P gave the stock less weighting in the index than had been expected. Cramer, Berkowitz lost half a million dollars on the trade.

Cramer had also been exploring other avenues to boost *TheStreet.com.* He arranged to move his column from *Time* to *New York* magazine, where he had done some of his best writing until his buddy Kurt Andersen was fired as editor in 1996 and he quit in protest. Now the magazine had been taken over by the publishing firm Primedia, which, as it happened, was headed by Tom Rogers, the former NBC Cable chief. Soon after Rogers cursed him out for defecting from CNBC to Fox, Cramer had sent word through Steve Brill, a mutual friend, that he had not misled Rogers, that the Fox deal had been negotiated by Kevin English without his participation. When Rogers became CEO of Primedia, Cramer had called to wish him good luck. Rogers was friendly, saying that Brill had explained that Cramer hadn't been double-crossing him. Now the two men cut a deal for Cramer's column, a down payment on a strategic plan that Cramer expected to produce other ventures between *TheStreet.com* and Primedia.

Even so, Cramer figured that the new alliance might not be enough, especially if Ailes continued to hold *TheStreet.com* show hostage. Cramer was so frustrated by Fox's limited distribution of the program that when David Faber reported that Murdoch wanted control of DirecTV, Cramer praised the idea in his online column—and went on to detail how the satellite capability would help Fox and, not coincidentally, him:

> I know I have thought about this idea a lot since the previous management of *TheStreet.com* decided to make a deal with Fox News to run our TV show. The sheer fact that we are not carried in so many important jurisdictions . . . makes it impossible for us to do any national promotion for the show. It also keeps the show from

helping *TheStreet.com* gain the requisite readers we need to grow because the lack of distribution makes the show too obscure. . . . The channel can't reach key areas we need to penetrate. . . . I love the show and think it is terrific, but, in my opinion, it is just not seen by enough people to really help, if not hurt, our company. As the co-founder and largest shareholder, of course I have to do what is right for the company.

The column caused an internal flap at *TheStreet.com*. Jonathan Krim, who had been brought in by Dave Kansas as executive editor, told Cramer that he was cutting those paragraphs because they sounded too self-serving.

"But that's the uncensored me," Cramer said.

"We don't censor you on the stock market," Krim said. "This is not about the stock market. This is about *TheStreet.com.*"

Saving *TheStreet.com* had become Cramer's never-ending obsession. He checked his computer again. In the last hour, the stock had dropped another dollar, to 10¼.

While Ailes had never said what he would do if Cramer quit, Cramer had convinced himself that the former Republican strategist would try to ruin his reputation. This, he recalled, was the man who had pummeled Michael Dukakis while helping George Bush win the presidency in 1988. All Ailes had to do, Cramer figured, was to float some trumped-up charge about him trying to benefit financially from a stock that he had touted on the show. That would trigger another SEC investigation, and no one would give Cramer the benefit of the doubt. The bogus charges of the past had made him vulnerable. He had been investigated over the handful of stocks he had promoted in *SmartMoney*. He had been investigated over the WavePhore incident on CNBC. Three strikes and he would be out.

In the stark, highly charged, us-versus-them terms through which Cramer viewed the world, he had to choose between his company and his good name. If he stayed at Fox, *TheStreet.com* would probably fail and he would have to ride the stock down to zero. Cramer could afford it. His shares in the company were now worth $40 million, but he had also made tens of millions of dollars as a trader. Others, however, would not be so lucky. People who had bought the stock, including his friends and relatives, would see their investment wiped out. And they would blame him, even though Cramer did not run the company.

He saw no way out. Cramer was terrified that if he went to war with Fox in an effort to save the company, his reputation would wind up in tatters. He had to think about his wife and daughters. He didn't want them to feel like Ivan Boesky's family. He had to save his day job, his Wall Street job, and if the price of self-preservation was losing *TheStreet.com,* Cramer felt that he had no choice but to pay it.

The match was over. He had lost. Ailes had won. Checkmate.

❏   ❏   ❏

On Monday morning, April 3, reality hit Wall Street in the face. The Nasdaq plunged a stunning 349 points, the biggest single point drop in its history. Sparked by the news that Microsoft had failed to reach a settlement in its federal antitrust lawsuit, the high-tech index was now down to 4,223, or 16 percent lower than its record high on March 10. (The Dow, the repository of those much-derided Old Economy stocks, jumped 300 points the same day as investors moved their money into blue chips.) Nasdaq 5,000, which had instantly triggered predictions of Nasdaq 6,000, was already a distant memory. Even Ralph Acampora turned negative on the Nasdaq. One of the few happy people in the financial world was Bruno Cohen, who watched CNBC score its biggest one-day rating ever as people tuned in to watch the carnage.

After the closing bell, with his microphone off, Ron Insana turned to David Faber. "This is how you crash tomorrow," he said. "This is a lot like the day before in '87." The day's trading volume was not that high, and Insana believed that there were more sellers waiting in the wings.

On Tuesday morning, the Nasdaq started to fall at 10:30, and fell, and fell, and fell. Three hundred points, four hundred points. At 11:30, a hedge-fund trader called Insana. "You realize we're crashing, don't you?" Insana said.

CNBC staffers were nervous about inflaming an already bad situation, and so Bruno Cohen convened a meeting with Insana, Matt Quayle, Ellen Egeth, and others to talk about the day's coverage. The word crash, they decided, could not be uttered on the air. Meltdown would be preferable, at least until things got worse.

The Nasdaq was in free fall. The Dow, which had been up 196 points earlier in the day, got pulled along in the downdraft as investors sold anything for which they could find a buyer. This was clearly it. The doomsayers had been right.

"They're heading for the exits on Wall Street," Bill Griffeth said at 1:00 P.M. on *Power Lunch*. "The panic selling has kicked in," reporter Charles Molineaux said on CNNfn, which had preempted the regular programming on CNN.

"Nasdaq, Dow Getting Massacred," said a headline on *TheStreet.com*. "Tech Bubble Pops," said *Marketwatch.com*.

At 1:18, the Nasdaq was down 574 points, the Dow down 504 points. Investors had lost a breathtaking $1.2 trillion of their wealth. On the air, everyone looked tense. The Nasdaq had dropped 13 percent in the space of three hours, a bigger decline in percentage terms than during the crash of 1987. Combined with Monday's losses, the Nasdaq, which had made so many people so much money over the past year, was in a full-fledged bear market. Even Henry Blodget, who was traveling and following the action on a handheld Internet device, was so stunned that he had no advice to offer. The momentum players who had chased these stocks on the way up, often with "margin" loans from brokerages, were now chasing them even harder on the heart-stopping ride down. EToys had fallen nearly 90 percent since Blodget had put the stock in his "holiday basket" recommendations. As companies such as Amazon and Yahoo! and JDS Uniphase lost billions of dollars in value, Insana tried to provide some perspective. "Internet stocks collapsed, biotech stocks collapsed, B2B stocks collapsed, all before Nasdaq fell as sharply as today," he told viewers.

Maria Bartiromo first used the term "market meltdown" when *Street Signs* began at 2:00. "I've always warned people that the Internet stocks in particular are highly volatile, including Amazon.com," Jeff Bezos said on the air.

But just as suddenly, the market started bouncing back from its terrifying lows. At 1:43, the Nasdaq was down 332 points; by 2:33, it was down just 148. One of the greatest collapses in market history was being followed by one of the greatest comebacks—all in the same session. Each day's gut-wrenching volatility seemed to overshadow the drama of the day before. It was as though all of Wall Street was operating on warp speed.

"If you tuned in a few minutes ago, you missed one of the wildest days of the last thirteen years," Insana said as *Street Signs* was winding up at 4:00 P.M. The Nasdaq finished the day down 75 points, meaning that it had gained back 500 points in 2½ hours. The Dow, after staggering through a 700-point swing, the most volatile day in its history, finished down just 57. CNBC smashed its ratings record of the previous day. Had the market simply bottomed out, Insana figured, people would have turned off the set in disgust, but the turnaround had kept viewers addicted.

During the height of the craziness, Jeff Gralnick was having lunch with Shelby Coffey, the new CNNfn president, and they kept getting interrupted by calls about the market plunge. But Gralnick, who had just returned from a vacation in Barbados, would not be distracted. He announced that he would be leaving CNN by early summer.

"What can I do to change your mind?" Coffey asked.

"This is not a negotiation," Gralnick said. "I want to leave."

Gralnick was disgusted with CNN. Coffey had announced that he was expanding CNNfn to twenty-four hours, which he viewed as a way to position the network for the digital future, but Gralnick thought that the idea was ludicrous. There was no way the brass would spend enough money to get the struggling network on enough cable systems to matter. Once AOL took over, Steve Case would probably care more about beefing up the Web side of the operation anyway. They were creating these new cable shows and using brilliant young kids who were working their tails off on programs that would be seen by no one. Gralnick just didn't get it. If it were up to him, he would either spend a fortune to save CNNfn or, more likely, shut the thing down.

The reason for *Moneyline*'s ratings decline, Gralnick felt, had nothing to do with Stuart Varney and Willow Bay or the quality of the program, which he fervently believed was far better than that of *Business Center.* The problem was that CNBC had established itself in the public mind as the place to turn for business news. The fact that CNBC was beating CNN during the day was a huge watershed. Even his favorite blue-collar bar near his home in Connecticut had one set tuned to ESPN and the other to CNBC. When CNN aired stock market news during the day, Gralnick believed, it seemed like an alien presence, serving mainly to remind viewers that they should be watching CNBC. With a smaller lead-in audience, there was no way that *Moneyline* could thrive. The night before, CNN had run an expanded show dealing with the Microsoft verdict and got a .3 share; CNBC had more than tripled that. *Moneyline*'s audience was down 7 percent since Lou Dobbs's departure, often performing better than the network itself, but Business Center was up 47 percent. They were getting killed day after day, Gralnick felt, because they had failed to recognize that CNBC had become the dominant brand in financial news.

Gralnick had celebrated his birthday the day before, and this, he felt, was no way for a sixty-one-year-old man to live. He had come to CNN to help build a business and that was not happening. He didn't agree with what the network was doing and had no authority to change its direction. Gralnick was getting no psychic or professional satisfaction from running *Moneyline*. It wasn't fun anymore. Having no job would be better than this. And so, he made clear before lunch was finished, he was out of there.

❏   ❏   ❏

The Big One arrived on Friday, April 14, 2000, a full-blown, white-knuckle, breathtaking market collapse. It struck with devastating force, causing carnage in the Dow, the Nasdaq, and the S & P. Triggered by the ever-present fear of inflation—a report that consumer prices had jumped 0.7 percent the previous month—the financial quake had an almost apocalyptic feel, as if it were a cosmic punishment for all the wild-eyed investors who had been swept away by the euphoria of 1999.

By 10:00 A.M., Jim Cramer was worried about what he called the Friday Crash Theory. The Nasdaq, after all, had dropped every day that week, by 258, 132, 286, and 93 points. At 12:30, after Alan Greenspan had given an empty speech, Cramer was threatening to shoot the next person who asked where the market's bottom was. That was the problem. No one had a clue. Cramer started selling stocks. Everyone was selling. It was a tsunami of selling.

Chris Byron seemed bemused by the wreckage. "These stocks were driven along by momentum investing, and they are coming back to earth," he said on his noontime Internet show. "The Nasdaq is the roach motel of Wall Street. You can check in, folks, but you can't check out. When everyone wants to sell, there ain't no money to buy."

At 1:10, the Nasdaq was down 152 points, the Dow more than 300. It was then that the plunge began in earnest. Jeff Berkowitz argued that they should pick up some stocks at bargain prices, and so by 2:30 he and Cramer were buying Intel, Procter & Gamble, Merck, American Home Products, and Mellon Bank. And yet prices kept sinking. They bought more Intel; it dropped again. They bought still more Intel, and again the price headed south. They had lost money so fast that they could hardly believe it. This was the worst that Cramer had ever seen the market. Where was the goddamn bottom? It was like being in a murky pit where no one could quite feel the edges. His head was ringing. The atmosphere out there was one of fear, gripping fear. Cramer's own investors started calling, the first time that some of them had phoned since the October 1998 plunge that had nearly wiped him out. They wanted to be reassured that he would be on top of the situation. The problem was, Cramer was scheduled to leave Monday on a Mexican vacation with his family that they had been planning for a year.

At 3:30 the phone rang. It was Karen. She had already canceled his tickets. Cramer said he might still be able to make the trip.

"Jim, we're the largest shareholders in the company," Karen said. "It would be moronic for you to go." She was obviously right. If he bailed out at a moment like this, maybe it was time to retire. As stock prices rebounded slightly, Cramer found himself mediating a debate between Berkowitz and their head trader over whether to buy stocks in the hope that the market would rebound on Monday. They decided to commit $40 million, and quickly lost $6 million on the trades. It was one pressure-packed roll of the dice.

"The Nasdaq, along with the Dow, now suffering its worst point decline in history," Ron Insana said on *Street Signs*. He was losing his voice, so it sounded as though he were reporting from a funeral. Insana knew that this was a crash—indeed, he had all but predicted a 30 percent Nasdaq drop back on December 30—and was pleased when a bond manager he was interviewing used the word. Insana didn't think things had reached the level of panic—ordinary folks weren't bailing out of their mutual funds yet—but it was ugly.

"This is an unbelievable drop," Tom Costello said from the Nasdaq's multicolored studio. "This is shaking the belief that technology will rule the world for the next fifty years," Joe Kernen said. He even acknowledged that some people were using "the C-word."

It was, for the moment, the only story. "Historic carnage on Wall Street," said Rhonda Schaffler on CNN.

"Running for Cover," said a headline on *TheStreet.com.*

"Bloody Friday," *MarketWatch.com* said in huge letters.

And bloody it was. The Dow had fallen a stunning 618 points, to 10,306, the worst point drop in its history. But the tech wreck was even worse. The Nasdaq had plummeted a record 355 points, to 3,321, completing a 25 percent drop for the week and a 34 percent decline from its high just a month earlier. A third of its value had simply vanished into the ether. In five trading days, investors in both exchanges had lost an unimaginable $2 trillion. The week's damage was worse than in 1929, worse than in 1987, worse than anyone had any right to expect.

The individual casualties were just as hard to grasp. In one day, Cisco had lost nearly $7 billion in value, Intel and Microsoft $5 billion, Qualcomm $3.5 billion. JDS Uniphase had given up half its value in a month; Brian Finnerty, the analyst who had pushed the stock on *Moneyline,* was back on CNN, calling the day's trading "almost irrational." In just four weeks, DoubleClick had dropped from 120 to 60⅞. Marimba was down from 66 to 22⅜. *TheStreet.com* had plummeted from 14 to 5½. The stock had fallen more than 90 percent from its opening-day high, making the company look increasingly ripe for a takeover.

The talking heads tried to calm the public, pointing out that the Nasdaq had merely slipped to the level of five months earlier. "It's really not the end of the world," Louis Rukeyser said that night on *Wall Street Week.*

But the disastrous day did more than hand the grizzliest of the bears a rhetorical victory by vindicating their lonely warnings that the sky-high prices could not last. It was an unmistakable declaration that the endlessly hyped New Economy was not immune to the laws of physics. Millions of investors had made impressive amounts of money during the long bull market, but the party could not go on forever. Serious people were now worried that the slumping market could cause an economic downturn. The fear of risk was no longer an abstract discussion. In offices and bars and supermarkets, even those who held stocks only in a retirement plan were commiserating about the depressing turn of events. Bloody Friday was a sharp kick to the country's solar plexus.

After a nail-biting weekend, stocks bounced back Monday as the Nasdaq set a one-day record with a gain of 218 points. Cramer's bet had paid off, giving him a $14 million profit on the stocks he had bought before the bell. On Tuesday, the Nasdaq shattered the previous day's record, soaring 254 points. Like an earthquake film in reverse, sealing the ground that was torn asunder, the index more than recouped the losses of the Friday crash. The Dow was right behind with a two-day leap of 462 points. The bulls were ready to exhale.

Wall Street had become the hottest soap opera around, dominating the front pages, the network newscasts, and the talk shows. Jim Cramer on the *CBS Evening News*. Ron Insana on *NBC Nightly News*. Jim Cramer on *Crossfire*. Maria Bartiromo on *Hardball*. "Is the Bull Market Really Over?" *Newsweek*'s cover asked. The new national pastime—the pursuit of market wealth—was bigger and more nerve-racking than ever.

On the *Today* show, Matt Lauer asked Cramer whether the plunge in *TheStreet.com* stock meant that investors were telling him "the bubble has burst."

"Yes," Cramer said. "And I can tell you that it's a sobering and humbling experience. I went from being top of the game to being pretty humiliated."

What about the rest of the dot-com world? "It's over," Cramer declared. "The gold rush is over."

Was he right? Was the rebound a temporary phenomenon? Was the get-rich-quick mentality a thing of the past? Would there be another crash, a bigger crash, next week or next month? Who knew?

This was, after all, the stock market, a strange and confusing land where, in the end, nobody knows anything.

❏   ❏   ❏

The continuing struggle at *Moneyline* was no minor matter to the founder of the first all-news cable network. Ted Turner was determined to do something about it. And his attempt to boost the network's signature business program produced the most dramatic showdown in the twenty-year history of CNN.

Turner was ticked off at Stuart Varney after the anchor had asked him on *Moneyline* whether John Rocker, the controversial relief pitcher for Turner's team, the Atlanta Braves, should be fired. Turner gamely defended his player, who was under fire for having made a series of racial and ethnic slurs in a *Sports Illustrated* interview. While that may have been a minor irritant, the incident apparently confirmed Turner's growing conviction that what CNN business news needed most was the man he had first hired to create the operation. For Lou Dobbs to return to the *Moneyline* anchor chair would, in Turner's view, instantly restore the program to preeminence.

Turner discussed the idea with his old friend, who was clearly interested. In a tacit admission that he missed the television spotlight, Dobbs was willing to return to *Moneyline,* a remarkable turnaround since he had left the network in a huff just ten months earlier. But many of Dobbs's former colleagues, who regarded him as a divisive figure, hated the idea. CNN Chairman Tom Johnson and Rick Kaplan, the network's president, were distraught when they learned of Turner's plan. Turner told Johnson during two calls that Dobbs was a great talent and that Varney was not getting the job done. But Johnson argued that Dobbs was an incredibly difficult man who treated people terribly. Kaplan called from Illinois, where he was teaching a college course, and caught Turner as he was about to board a plane. "What you're going to do is suicidal and will destroy CNN," Kaplan said. "I don't know how I'll be able to stay with you." He would not walk out abruptly, Kaplan said. He would stay through the presidential campaign, but after that he would probably have to leave. Turner tried to brush the objections aside and asked for Kaplan's support. The tensions continued to mount. CNN executives wondered how they could hire Dobbs when he was still running *Space.com* and had a contract with NBC for a radio show and a newsletter.

On Thursday, April 21, Turner summoned Johnson and Kaplan to his fourteenth-floor office at CNN Center in Atlanta for a final discussion. Johnson walked into the room ready to quit. He had his resignation letter in his pocket, along with a statement that he planned to release to the press. The effort to rehire Dobbs was about to cost Turner the man who had run his network for the past decade. Turner preempted the move by making a personal appeal to Johnson. "I need you to be there for me," he said in his gravelly voice. "I've been there for you. We need to make this work. I know I can only ask you this once." Johnson replied that he had been ready to hand in his resignation, but that he could not turn down an appeal based on their long friendship. Still, Johnson and Kaplan argued vehemently that the Dobbs move would be a disaster, that his return would tear the network apart. Turner stressed that Dobbs would not be returning as part of management. Installing Dobbs as president of CNNfn had been a mistake, he conceded. This time Dobbs would just be an anchor. "I don't understand how you're going to sell anybody on the concept that the CEO of a dot-com can be the anchor of *Moneyline*," Kaplan said. "That will destroy the network." But Turner was undeterred. Dobbs would do his *Space.com* work in the morning and come in to anchor in the afternoons, he said. Turner did not see a problem. Kaplan, who made no secret of the mutual disdain between him and Dobbs, pressed his case with Richard Parsons, Time Warner's president. How, he asked, would they explain to *The Wall Street Journal* or *The New York Times* that a business executive was anchoring *Moneyline?* Time Warner executives soon opposed the move as well.

Still, the return of Lou Dobbs seemed all but assured, especially when word of the talks appeared in the *Journal* and the New York tabloids, a leak that CNN executives were convinced had emanated from Dobbs's side. But in the final negotiations with Time Warner officials on Monday, April 25, with the *Space.com* issue still looming large, the deal fell apart. Turner talked to Dobbs one last time, then called Johnson and told him that the plan was dead. Dobbs now said publicly that he was happy at *Space.com* and would not be returning to CNN.

Jeff Gralnick was furious over the damage caused by the high-level showdown. It was classic Lou Dobbs, Gralnick felt; he got a burst of publicity, appeared to be loved, and, in the process, made Stuart Varney and Willow Bay look like a backup crew ready to be cast overboard at a moment's notice. It was all that Gralnick could do to cope with the bruised feelings.

An equally emotional clash soon unfolded at Fox News Channel. Roger Ailes put out the word that he was unhappy with Cramer for declaring on the air, on the day of the crash, that *TheStreet.com*'s depressed stock was a good buy—particularly after telling the producer to fuck off when he asked what Cramer's weekly prediction would be. Cramer seemed to sense that he had gone too far; he apologized in his column to those who thought he had been "shameless," even while insisting that many of his fans owned the stock and deserved to hear his thoughts. But he had handed his critics a sharpened sword. Ailes had the network's lawyer send Cramer a "cease and desist" letter, scolding him for violating his contract by having appeared on CNN and NBC without advance permission. And Ailes slapped Cramer in the press, having his spokesman tell the *Daily News* that "we do not approve of the touting of stock on the air for personal gain."

That was like jabbing an exposed nerve. Cramer was so upset that he boycotted the next four shows. He was afraid to go on the program. Ailes's spokesman, in Cramer's view, had just laid out a new policy that would prevent him from talking about any stock he owned on *TheStreet.com* show. Sure, he was looking for a way to extricate himself from the clutches of Fox, but this was serious business. If he went on the air and talked about his holdings—which was the whole point of his being on television—then the SEC could come after him. The commission could accuse him of pumping and dumping stocks, saying that Fox had a new policy—there it was in the newspaper—and he had flouted it. That was what had happened during the *SmartMoney* investigation, when SEC officials had questioned whether he had violated the magazine's disclosure policy. It had been a searing experience, had nearly ruined his reputation. Now the issue of Cramer both owning and talking about stocks was haunting him once again. Three times he asked Fox to clarify the policy, to no avail. He refused to step into the trap. Cramer knew that if he missed one more program, Ailes could sue him for breaking his contract. So be it. He would rather be sued by a big media conglomerate than by the federal government.

Ailes saw this as nothing but a diversionary tactic. Cramer's own editor, Dave Kansas, had criticized him for touting the company's stock. There was no new policy on discussing stocks; Cramer, Ailes felt, was just looking for an excuse to bail out. Ailes had invested Fox's time and money in developing *TheStreet.com* show, and he wasn't about to let Cramer violate his contract and go to a competing network. Ailes began making plans to sue Jim Cramer. Cramer told his CEO of the impending lawsuit. "These guys are just incredible," Tom Clarke said. "They're willing to disparage us publicly."

Someone had to blink. On Wednesday, May 17, *TheStreet.com* announced on its Website that it was canceling the Fox show. Clarke had decided to launch a preemptive strike before Fox could sue his biggest stockholder. *TheStreet.com* made the rather flimsy argument that it was Ailes who had breached the two-year contract by castigating Cramer. But Clarke's statement also acknowledged the larger reason behind the dispute, that his company was disappointed at the failure to strike a broader deal with Rupert Murdoch. The war was finally out in the open. Kansas and his colleagues showed up for a final Friday taping, but Cramer went home and hit the sack.

On Monday, May 22, Fox sued Cramer and *TheStreet.com* for breach of contract. Cramer, who wasn't paid for his appearances, felt that Fox didn't have much of a case but could probably keep him off the other networks until the contract expired in May 2001. Now that they had vaporized their own television show, such obscurity would not be good for him or *TheStreet.com*. He was still free, under the contract, to make occasional appearances on *Squawk Box,* but CNBC seemed to want no part of him. This was the ultimate frustration, and the battle was just beginning. Cramer was still worried about Roger Ailes ruining his reputation. After his fierce battles with Marty Peretz, Bruno Cohen, and Kevin English, he felt badly about the wreckage of yet another business relationship. But that was life. He still had a high-pressure hedge fund to run, a struggling Internet company to save, a personal reputation to protect, and a strained marriage to preserve. He would keep charging forward, fists up, pummeling his critics, as he had always done before. It was the only way he knew how to play.

❑   ❑   ❑

The Dow broke through 11,000 again, fell 600 points, and continued to bounce around. The Fed raised interest rates a sixth time in May—this time by a half-point—and the Nasdaq kept sinking, below the level of the crash, before surging into June by a record 19 percent in a single week. Stanley Druckenmiller became the latest hedge-fund trader to resign, bowing out of George Soros's Quantum Fund after betting too heavily on tech stocks and watching the fund drop 22 percent. United Airlines agreed to buy US Airways and leaked the story to *The Wall Street Journal, The New York Times* and *The Washington Post* on condition that the newspapers not call anyone for comment. Fox announced a new prime-time drama called *The $treet.* Ron Insana started writing a column for *Money* magazine. *Fortune* ran a story on Maria Bartiromo called "The 'Money Honey': How Sweet She Is." David Faber was offered several million dollars, or ten times his CNBC salary, by Morgan Stanley Dean Witter, but despite the temptation found it difficult to abandon his life in the cable spotlight.

Beyond the head-spinning action, what was clear was that the intense volatility would continue and that the manic-depressive market would keep driving investors insane. Amid the market swings, there was only one constant: the reporters, the commentators, the analysts, and the fund managers serving up their insights, their predictions, and their often conflicting advice. Buy, sell, go long, go short, grab tech, dump tech, sit on your hands. It was guru gridlock out there.

For all their supposed glamor, what the fortune tellers did week in and week out was numbingly repetitious. Cramer and Faber and Acampora and Bartiromo and Lipin and Insana and Byron and Blodget would frantically search for new information or rumors about all manner of stocks and companies, spewing out reports and opinions designed to give their readers, viewers, and clients some sort of edge. Then they would do it again, and again, and again. What infused their daily labors with drama and excitement were the enormous amounts of money at stake, the fierce rivalries they faced, and the palpable pressure to deliver for their audience.

They were like drivers in a demolition derby, forced to compete at faster and faster speeds. Everything was a blur: the upgrades and downgrades trumpeted on cable, the Internet bulletins flashing across the screen, the chatter on the message boards, the analysts making ever bolder projections, the stocks ricocheting in ever wilder swings. Suddenly racing around the track at 200 miles per hour was no longer good enough; the drivers had to hit 500 just to keep up. A few months later, the once-unimaginable 500 seemed like a leisurely cruise, for everyone was now circling the track at a thousand miles per hour. To slow down was to fall behind, to lose traction, to crack up.

The Dow would rise and fall, the Nasdaq would surge and plummet, AOL and Amazon and Dell and Microsoft and Qualcomm would zig and zag, often in stubbornly unpredictable ways, and the conventional wisdom would shift a dozen times a week. The fortune tellers could not afford to dwell on yesterday's mistake or miscalculation because they had to perform again today and tomorrow. They were well paid and sought after and increasingly famous, but they were also captives of the mercurial culture of Wall Street and the inexorable illogic of gyrating stock prices. They were crucial cogs in the financial hype machine and victims of its relentless expectations. It was, they knew, a world that was at once warmly seductive and chillingly cold-blooded. They would keep on going, keep on churning until they too faltered, and fresher, younger faces were brought in to take their place.

AFTERWORD

On October 19, 1987, as the market was plunging 508 points, I sat next to a Wall Street trader in a flannel shirt who seemed icy cool amid the sweaty chaos. His name was John Mulheren, and although he had lost nearly $20 million of his own money, he calmly ordered associates in his $300-million arbitrage outfit to buy up stock that was plummeting in price, telling himself that he would be just fine "if this is not 1929."

Four months later, Mulheren was arrested near his New Jersey home carrying an Israeli-made assault rifle and muttering about using it to kill trader Ivan Boesky. A manic-depressive, Mulheren believed that Boesky had given his name to authorities investigating insider trading. Indeed, Mulheren was later found guilty of helping Boesky manipulate stock prices in exchange for inside tips and was sentenced to a year in prison, although the conviction was overturned on appeal.

Wall Street, I concluded, was a crazy place.

On March 29, 1990, I was in the federal courthouse in lower Manhattan when a grand jury indicted Michael Milken on 98 counts of fraud, racketeering, insider trading, stock manipulation, and other charges. The indictment described the junk-bond king as "the leader of the conspiracy" to defraud the clients of his firm, Drexel Burnham Lambert, and would eventually lead to the company's demise and Milken's imprisonment. But the most eye-catching figure in the indict`ment, which nearly leaped off the

303

page, was that in 1987, the height of the go-go era, Milken had been paid $550 million for his labors.

Wall Street, I concluded, was a greedy place.

On February 10, 1995, I published the story about Jim Cramer owning four small stocks whose value had soared after he touted them in his *SmartMoney* column. Cramer had insisted, in his rapid-fire, high-pitched way, that he was simply explaining how the game worked and had no intention of pocketing the profits, and I believed him. But I also believed that it was wrong for a money manager to be trumpeting stocks that he owned without the magazine letting readers in on the secret.

Wall Street, I concluded, was a morally ambiguous place.

Over the course of researching and writing this book, the seductive dance between the media mavens and the money men, between those who predict and those who gamble huge sums, was downright mesmerizing. The challenge was to unravel the way billions of dollars moved on the rumors and the leaks and the nods and the winks and the head fakes and the hoaxes. In the political world, elections are won and lost, poll ratings rise and fall, based on each passing spin cycle. But the world of Wall Street spin is more like a dozen simultaneous games of three-dimensional chess, a daily, dizzying match in which stock prices, corporate earnings, and millions of individual investments are riding on the outcome. In this overheated environment, the degree to which basic facts can be massaged, manipulated, and hyped is truly troubling.

And that raises the fundamental question: Amid the endless noise, whom do you trust?

A single analyst has way too much power to send a stock soaring or sinking. This is largely because the media mindlessly trumpet each prediction as if it were chiseled on stone tablets. And if the analyst's assessment turns out to be utterly, spectacularly wrong—well, by then it's old news. Zero accountability.

Conflicts of interest are hidden in broad daylight. Analysts bang the drum for a company's stock while lobbying to win the firm's investment banking business, and almost no one raises a fuss or bothers to point out the connection. Money managers blanket the airwaves to tout stocks in which they are "long," or feed positive items on these stocks to financial columnists, and almost no one dismisses this as blatant self-interest. The media's willingness to play along with this insider game is nothing short of appalling. It's as if a presidential candidate's chief fundraiser put out a report predicting a great future for his man, and this caused a spike in the politician's approval rating. As a matter of minimal ethics, not to mention common sense, television anchors and reporters should routinely force every guest yakking about a stock to disclose whether he owns it, is selling it, or is doing business with the company. (The wisdom of these guests, of course, knows no bounds. At the beginning of 2000, Byron Wien of Morgan Stanley confidently declared on CNBC that in the fall Bill Bradley would defeat John McCain to win the White House.)

Journalism serves as a vast echo chamber for rumors—some true, some unfounded, some off the wall—that have an electric impact, jolting some stocks and short-circuiting others. Normal news standards melt in this high-energy environment, powered by reporters determined to scoop each other on the latest wisp of a possibility. Money managers, bankers, and brokers provide a steady stream of self-serving tips about mergers, alliances, and deals that often fail to materialize. No matter. On Wall Street, rumors rule.

The expectations game, as practiced by analysts and media folks alike, is an eye-opening racket. What matters is not how a stock performs but how it performs according to some artificial benchmark decreed by two dozen or so financial wise men. Making huge profits is no longer enough; the overarching imperative is beating the Street. Companies juice their books to deliver an "upside surprise" and avoid falling short of the all-important conventional wisdom. Power shifts from the corporate players themselves to the self-appointed referees who blow whistles during the game and the news outlets that carry the action.

Chief executive officers goose their stock by serving as glorified salesmen, packaging their announcements, fiddling with their numbers, providing overly optimistic guidance to analysts and, when all else fails, leaking major developments to a favored news outlet and then booking themselves on television to provide the predictably optimistic spin.

All this unfolds in a backbiting atmosphere of high school–style feuds that shape much of the commentary. Jim Cramer fights with Alan Abelson, with Gene Marcial, with Dan Dorfman, and these critics denounce him just as fervently. Mark Haines openly disdains Ralph Acampora. Chris Byron rips Barry Diller, John Malone, Ron Perelman, and Henry Blodget. CNBC battles with CNNfn for ratings and guests, with Bloomberg for breaking news, with its partner *The Wall Street Journal* for merger scoops. Rumors bounce around cyberspace, from Dorfman's on-line column to other financial Websites, make their way onto television, and move stocks with the speed of a mouse click. Amid the sound and fury, readers and viewers are left to sort things out.

The fact is, America is drowning in financial information. Anyone with a hankering to play the market can instantly command an extraordinary array of data, statistics, analysis, projection, and pontification from around the globe. The problem is that much of this information and advice is in direct conflict. Some experts are always cheering on the raging bull, others warning of a major collapse just around the corner. Buy and hold, or hit the day-trading levers as fast and furiously as one would operate a Sony Play Station? Try to be Ralph Acampora or Warren Buffett? Hire a seasoned broker or do it yourself online? Worry about earnings or place your bet on future growth? Fly high with the tech stocks or slowly grind it out with the cyclicals?

In a nation with an MTV attention span, it's no surprise that financial advice explodes in brief, laser-like bursts, turning winners into losers and back again in the blink of an eye. It's as though half the population is tuning in for a daily showing of "Who Wants to Be a Zillionaire?" What's frustrating is the arrogance and the stubbornness of the fortune tellers, who reap fame and wealth with the implicit promise of riches around the rainbow and rarely admit their mistakes. From the hotshot analysts to the big-time brokers to the corporate chieftains to the media hordes who eagerly merchandise it all, the Wall Street establishment rarely loses, even when the masses come up empty.

Let's say you want to invest in Schlock.com. You study the company's business plan, gauge its future, look at where the stock price is and where it was last month and last year. Then you take the plunge and buy 100 shares at $50 a share. Two weeks later, Maria Bartiromo comes on the air and reports that some Morgan Stanley analyst you've never heard of is downgrading the stock; it drops five points. A week later, Gene Marcial discloses in *Business Week* that Schlock.com is a potential takeover target for Supersoft Industries; the stock jumps 10 points, but slumps by 15 when no merger takes place. Then there is talk in an Internet chat room that *Barron's* may be coming out with a negative piece on Schlock.com; it drops another 3 points, even though the article turns out to be mildly favorable. Two months later, Schlock reports $100 million in earnings, twice as much as a year ago, but Wall Street analysts moan because the per-share earning is two cents less than they, in their wisdom, had expected. The stock drops 12 points, and Jim Cramer writes a *Street.com* piece about how he hates the CEO and has sold all his holdings. Whenever the company is discussed on CNBC, they flash a yellow chart with the lines heading south. You finally dump it for a $2,500 loss. The next week, the *Journal*'s Heard on the Street column says the company is bringing out a new generation of schlock and the stock jumps 14 points while you gnash your teeth.

That's the maddening reality of a market where a gust of rhetorical wind can buffet your stock like a sailboat in a hurricane. Over time, of course, good companies perform well and justify their stockholders' investment. But in a wired world where everyone is looking for a short-term edge, it's all too easy to get upended by a small group of experts whose self-interest is not always apparent.

Beyond the brokers and the analysts, online columnists and advocates have all sorts of motivations and questionable sources, and hardly anyone to hold them accountable. Journalists fan the rumor flames in search of a hot story, and rarely bother to follow up on the analysts' ratings that they repeat like the day's mantra, even when the calls turn out to be flat wrong. The media act as a great seducer ("The Best Mutual Funds!" "Secrets of the Stock Stars!"), luring people to tune in or log on or open their checkbooks on the promise of major paydays to come. And yet these are the shaky reeds on which millions of investment decisions rest.

On one level, of course, the avalanche of available information is a godsend. The typical investor can now get more real-time data from more sources than ever before in history, a far cry from when Bill Bolster's father checked the mailbox for his two-day-old *Wall Street Journal*. Investors can hear directly from CEOs on television, study the performance charts online, and reach their own judgments, rather than blindly following the advice of an overcompensated broker. But making sense of these onrushing streams of data is easier said than done.

Just as people who never thought twice about Ma Bell now must choose their own telephone carrier and wireless company and payment plan, the new era of financial overload puts the responsibility squarely on the investor's shoulders. If he or she chooses to place market bets on the advice of Abby Joseph Cohen or the inside-dope predictions of Gene Marcial or the reporting of Maria Bartiromo, or on the tantalizing funds constantly touted by *Forbes* or *Money* or *SmartMoney,* there's no right of redress if the cash evaporates. The get-rich-quick impulse that draws people into the grand Wall Street casino carries with it the very real possibility that they will lose their chips. It's a grown-up game without a safety net.

One inevitable byproduct of the information explosion is that the venerable Wall Street establishment is being squeezed as never before. At the start of the twenty-first century, the average Joe can now download the latest data without an investment adviser, buy stock online without a broker, and follow its minute-by-minute progress on cable television or on the Net—all of which eliminates or reduces the need for the highly paid middlemen who greased and controlled the system in the last century. The information for which an investor once would have willingly paid Merrill Lynch or Goldman Sachs is now routinely spread by CNBC and CNNfn, by Bloomberg and *TheStreet.com* and dozens of rival Net services. This, too, is a welcome development, but it is a daunting one as well, not only for the Street professionals who may become obsolete but for the investor going it alone in this brave new world.

There are, without question, plenty of honest, hardworking journalists digging up good information from the far corners of the business world. And there are plenty of investors who have smartly used such information to make lots of money in the long-running bull market. But it would be a significant improvement if more media outlets resisted the temptation to engage in hype and rumor-mongering in an attempt to stand out from the crowd. The broader problem may be the self-promotional drumbeat sounded by so many of these outfits, the notion that only they can give you the greatest mutual funds, the best deals, the hottest tips, the shortest route to tomorrow's big payoff. Yes, they provide solid information, and yes, some of it is valuable, but they are also acting as carnival barkers, trying to drag consumers inside the tent with promises of death-defying stunts. They have hitched their fortunes to the Wall Street game of enticing the consumer, whispering of virtually "inside" information, peddling the elusive promise of wealth. The painful crash of April 2000 served mainly to dramatize how spectacularly wrong the Wall Street wizards can be.

The bottom line, to use the phrase so favored by business executives, is that it's up to ordinary investors to resist the blandishments that seem to shout from every newsstand, television set, and computer screen. It's up to us to cut through the endless static. Buying and holding quality stocks generally remains the best long-term strategy for the average investor, and those who are determined to dart in and out of volatile high-tech securities must understand that they can lose a pile of dough as quickly as they might make it. Today's sizzling stock is tomorrow's washout, and the corporate executives, analysts, fund managers, and journalists who turn out to be wrong will simply move on to the next mouth-watering trend, leaving the suckers behind. The fortune tellers, in short, will always be with us. Those who blindly follow them have no one to blame but themselves.

SOURCES

All conversations quoted were either witnessed by the author or based on interviews with one or more of the participants, except as noted here.

INTRODUCTION

xvii The original brokerage houses: John Steele Gordon, *Forbes ASAP,* Aug. 23, 1999

xx "The Crash of '98": *Fortune,* Sept. 28, 1998

xx "Is the Boom Over?": *Time,* Sept. 14, 1998

xx "stock prices could easily fall": Walter Russell Mead, *Esquire,* Oct. 1998

xxi "We want to get our clients' money": *Forbes,* July 1993

xxiv "Is it downhill from here?": Gene G. Marcial, *Business Week,* Feb. 8, 1999

xxiv "Could Yahoo! merge with CBS?": Paul M. Sherer and Kara Swisher, *The Wall Street Journal,* Feb. 5, 1999

xxv "volcanic success looks unstoppable": Kevin Maney, *USA Today,* Feb. 5, 1999

1. *THE KING OF ALL MEDIA*

11 "I wish I had been a vicious": Kathleen Doler, *Upside, Nov. 1998*

2. *SQUAWKING*

24 "her Sophia Loren looks": *People,* Dec. 15, 1997

24 "pillow-lipped": Pablo Galarza, *Money,* July 1998

24 "smoky gray eyes": Jim Forkan, *Multichannel News*, Feb. 2, 1998

24 "the Sharon Stone": David Lieberman, *USA Today,* Oct. 14, 1997

24 "CNBC's pouty anchorwoman": Henry Goldblatt, *Fortune,* Oct. 26, 1998

26 "Lou Dobbs has an older": David Lieberman, *USA Today,* Oct. 14, 1997

3. *THE YOUNG TURKS*

44 "rumors of an acquisition": Laura M. Hobson and David J. Morrow, *The New York Times,* Jan. 1, 1999

48 "pale imitation of CNN": Monica Collins, *USA Today,* Apr. 18, 1989

48 "Boy, that thing sucks": Tom Shales, *The Washington Post,* Jan. 9, 1990

4. *10K RUN*

66 "Prudential's bear looks good": *Time,* Sept. 14, 1998

66 "modified his views": Greg Ip, *The Wall Street Journal,* Aug. 10, 1998

72 "The precondition is in place": David Rynecki, *USA Today,* Mar. 23, 1999

5. *BAD BLOOD*

74 "What I cannot stand": James J. Cramer, *TheStreet.com,* Jan. 5, 1998

75 "Some people inside the firm": Sandra Ward, *Barron's,* Dec. 28, 1998

75 "an unfailing and formidable threat": Alan Abelson, *Barron's,* Mar. 15, 1999

77 "There were many superb hedge funds": Joseph Kahn, *The New York Times,* Feb. 25, 1999

80 "This keeps up": James J. Cramer, *TheStreet.com,* Mar. 10, 1999

84 "FK shuffled so much debt": Christopher Byron, *The New York Observer,* Apr. 5, 1999

84 "TCI Music": Christopher Byron, *The New York Observer,* Apr. 19, 1999

87 "The company is about to announce": Gene G. Marcial, *Business Week,* Mar. 15, 1999

88 "the biggest advance since": Gene G. Marcial, *Business Week,* Jan. 27, 1997

88 "may be considering a merger": Gene G. Marcial, *Business Week,* Mar. 1, 1999

88 "I check out the Gene Marcial page": James J. Cramer, *TheStreet.com,* Apr. 15, 1998

90 "Is America Online going to buy": Chris Nolan, *San Jose Mercury News,* Apr. 5, 1999

90 "America Online Inc. and CBS Corp.": *Bloomberg News,* Apr. 6, 1999

91 "the two phone companies have yet": Steven Lipin, Nicole Harris, Rebecca Blumenstein, *The Wall Street Journal,* Apr. 6, 1999

92 "you'd swear on your mother": Mark Maremont, *The Wall Street Journal,* Apr. 8, 1999

6. *NONSTOP NEWS*

95 "As far as I'm concerned": Neil Roland, *Bloomberg News,* Nov. 19, 1998

97 "His plan seems almost too audacious": Michael W. Miller and Matthew Winkler, *The Wall Street Journal,* Sept. 22, 1988

98 "I want you to run it": Michael Bloomberg, *Bloomberg on Bloomberg,* Wiley, 1997

107 "Yahoo! is hot to": Linda Himelstein, *Business Week Online,* Mar. 19, 1999

7. *THE CULT OF THE CEO*

110 "Silicon Valley's answer to Madonna": Steve Hamm, *Business Week,* Sept. 1, 1997

115 "How come your PR people": David Diamond, *Wired,* Aug. 1999

115 "You're making us look bad": Elizabeth Lesly Stevens, *Brill's Content,* Sept. 1998

115 "Connie, I just can't believe": Wendy Goldman Rohm, *The Microsoft Files,* Time Business, 1998

116 "a whiz-kid programmer": G. Bruce Knecht, *The Wall Street Journal,* May 16, 1996

117 "he's relaxed": Katrina Brooker, *Fortune,* Nov. 8, 1999

117 "political genius": Peter de Jonge, *The New York Times Magazine,* Mar. 14, 1999

120 "was misleading because": Suzanne Galant, *TheStreet.com,* July 29, 1998

120 "DoubleClick Inc. can breathe": Andrea Petersen, *The Wall Street Journal,* Jan. 29, 1999

123 "the press equivalent of a big wet kiss": Kara Swisher, *AOL.com,* Times Business, 1998

124 "rumors on the Street": Gene G. Marcial, *Business Week,* Mar. 8, 1999

125 "as the sophisticated wave": Kara Swisher, *AOL.com,* Times Business, 1998

8. *IPO FEVER*

127 "The last change in leadership": E. S. Browning, *The Wall Street Journal,* Apr. 20, 1999

134 "the hype has served": Melanie Warner, *Fortune,* June 21, 1999

134 "Marimba has been cruising": Jim Seymour, *TheStreet.com,* May 3, 1999

136 "Mary Meeker is covering": Gregg Wirth, *TheStreet.com,* Apr. 30, 1999

137 She had lobbied hard: Laura M. Halson, *The New York Times*, June 6, 1999

9. *POPPING THE BUBBLE*

141 "I think the air": Susan Pulliam and Terzah Ewing, *The Wall Street Journal*, May 25, 1999

147 "a major contributing factor": Anthony Ramirez, *Palm Beach Post*, Nov. 5, 1995

148 "a high-grade business": Allan Sloan, *The Washington Post*, Oct. 31, 1995

148 "under investigation for activities": Michael Schroder, *Business Week*, Nov. 2, 1999

150 "a long-rumored takeover": Dan Dorfman, *JagNotes.com*, May 20, 1999

150 "Reports are buzzing": Dan Dorfman, *JagNotes.com*, May 26, 1999

151 "Keep in mind": Dan Dorfman, *JagNotes.com*, May 28, 1999

151 "a relatively undiscovered gem": Dan Dorfman, *JagNotes.com*, June 9, 1999

151 "talk is recurring": Dan Dorfman, *JagNotes.com*, June 16, 1999

152 "legalized manipulation of prices": Christopher Byron, *The New York Observer*, Apr. 12, 1999

153 "God, he's young": Joseph Nocera, *Money*, June 1999

155 "craven flip-flop": Christopher Byron, *MSNBC.com*, Mar. 16, 1999

155 "very weak lately": Amy Feldman, *Daily News*, May 27, 1999

10. *STAR WARS*

176 "James Cramer wants to be": Lisa Brownlee, *New York Post*, July 16, 1999

11. *SECRETS AND LIES*

177 "to deliver the right message": Andrea Petersen, *The Wall Street Journal*, June 13, 1999

178 "is bound to be acquired by DoubleClick": Gene G. Marcial, *Business Week*, July 19, 1999

179 "DoubleClick Inc. is expected to announce": Andrea Petersen and Steven Lipin, *The Wall Street Journal*, July 13, 1999

180 "AOL is the next Microsoft": Saul Hansell, *The New York Times*, July 4, 1999

183 "takeover buzz is running high": Gene G. Marcial, *Business Week*, July 19, 1999

184 "Talk is rife": Dan Dorfman, *JagNotes.com*, June 22, 1999

186 "Analysts expected earnings at Brightpoint": Gerri Willis, *SmartMoney*, Aug. 1999

186 Robert Friedman, chief investment officer: Aaron L. Task, *TheStreet.com,* Aug. 30, 1999

186 "Did Canny Short Sellers": Dan Dorfman, *JagNotes.com,* July 15, 1999

186 "talk again is swirling": Charles Gasparino, *The Wall Street Journal,* Aug. 12, 1999

187 "sources close to the companies": Linda Himelstein and Peter Elstrom, *Business Week Online,* Aug. 2, 1999

187 ˙Days later, the Food and Drug: Dan Colarusso, *TheStreet.com,* Aug. 5, 1989

192 "the hyperventilating claptrap": Alan Abelson, *Barron's,* Aug. 9, 1999

193 "disappointing": Jeffrey M. Laderman, *Business Week,* Aug. 9, 1999

194 "bruited about": Gene G. Marcial, *Business Week,* Jan. 26, 1998

194 "often used as a pump-and-dump": James J. Cramer, *TheStreet.com,* Sept. 17, 1999

195 "I frankly needed the money": *The Wall Street Journal,* July 15, 1999

196 "If I, as a columnist": Rebecca Eisenberg, *San Francisco Examiner,* June 13, 1999

196 Chervitz soon decided: Cory Johnson, *TheStreet.com,* July 19, 1999

12. *MORNING MUTINY*

210 "The new Ron Insana": Phyllis Furman, *Daily News,* Aug. 20, 1999

13. *RAGING BULL*

224 "Ms. Stewart is a pretty good-looking": Christopher Byron, *The New York Observer,* Aug. 26, 1999

224 "If she's a good-looking dame": Christopher Byron, *The New York Observer,* Sept. 27, 1999

227 "How come the biggest": Christopher Byron, *The New York Observer,* Oct. 25, 1999

14. *TULIP TIME*

236 "IBM, a major software": Monica Summers, Reuters, Nov. 12, 1999

237 "I understand that the business": Lisa Brownlee, *New York Post,* Nov. 24, 1999

237 "Rupert misspoke": Bill Carter, *The New York Times,* Nov. 25, 1999

239 "When Web companies openly": *The Wall Street Journal,* Dec. 17, 1999

239 "about wealth at a level": Michael Wolff, *New York,* Dec. 6, 1999

240 "helped build the foundation": Joshua Cooper Ramo, *Time,* Dec. 27, 1999

245 "taking advantage of the news media": Gregg Wirth, *TheStreet.com,* Dec. 9, 1999

247 "Basically, our function is": Nick Paumgarten, *The New York Observer,* Dec. 27, 1999

247 "misjudging just how strong": Christopher Byron, *The New York Observer,* Dec. 27, 1999

15. *NOTHING BUT NET*

260 "suicidalists": James J. Cramer, *TheStreet.com,* Sept. 25, 1999

261 "I got screwed": James J. Cramer, *TheStreet.com,* Jan. 2, 2000

262 "I know better": James J. Cramer, *TheStreet.com,* Feb. 4, 2000

263 "this market is stark": Shawn Tully, *Fortune,* Jan. 24, 2000

16. *CRASH LANDING*

271 *"CBS Marketwatch* tried": Marcia Vickers, *Business Week,* Mar. 6, 2000

273 "the Internet's busybody": Fred Vogelstein, *U.S. News & World Report,* March 6, 2000.

273 "one of the most vilified": John Schwartz, *The Washington Post,* Feb. 18, 2000

274 "There was no new information": Gregg Farrell, *USA Today,* Feb. 25, 2000

274 "the media's poster boy": Greg Farrell, *USA Today,* Feb. 25, 2000

275 "It is in many ways obscene": Thomas Petzinger Jr., *The Wall Street Journal,* Dec. 31, 1999

276 "Isn't any investment safe": Karen Hube and Ruth Simon, *The Wall Street Journal,* Mar. 8, 2000

277 "Confused?": Jacob M. Schlesinger, *The Wall Street Journal,* Mar. 22, 2000

279 "Plenty of investors decided": Joseph B. White and Gregory L. White, *The Wall Street Journal,* Mar. 24, 2000

299 "We do not approve": Phyllis Furman, *New York Daily News,* April 26, 2000

INDEX